PROBATION
AND AFTER-CARE

PROBATION
AND AFTER-CARE

ITS DEVELOPMENT IN
ENGLAND AND WALES

DOROTHY BOCHEL

1976

SCOTTISH ACADEMIC PRESS
EDINBURGH AND LONDON

Published by
SCOTTISH ACADEMIC PRESS LTD
33 Montgomery Street, Edinburgh EH7 5JX

Distributed by
Chatto & Windus Ltd
40 William IV Street, London W.C.2

© Dorothy Bochel 1976

First published 1976

SBN 7011 2179 3

Printed in Great Britain at
the Alden Press, Oxford

CONTENTS

Acknowledgments   vii

1. The Search for Alternatives to Prison   1
2. Early Days and First Assessment   33
3. A Permissive Service   58
4. The Case for Central Control   79
5. A Period of Expansion   101
6. A Major Review   123
7. The End of 'Dual Control'   150
8. Social Casework for the Courts   166
9. Social Work in the Penal System   205

Bibliography   241
References   249
Subject Index   278
Index of Names   287

ACKNOWLEDGMENTS

This study would not have been possible without the co-operation of the Home Office, the Church of England Temperance Society and National Police Court Mission (now the Church of England Council for Social Aid), the London Police Court Mission (now The Rainer Foundation) and the National Association of Probation Officers. I am greatly indebted to them for permission to peruse and make use of unpublished material, for the accuracy and interpretation of which I am wholly responsible. I am grateful for assistance of various kinds to Miss W. M. Goode, the late Mr. Frank Dawtry, Mr. David Haxby, Mr. Donald Bell, the late Mr. G. T. Morley Jacob, Mr. Ronald Howell, Mr. G. E. Holden and the Rev. J. B. Harrison, all officials of one or other of the above bodies during or part of the time during which I was engaged on the work.

I began the research whilst in receipt of a Graduate Research Scholarship from the University of Manchester. The topic was suggested by Mr. Brian Rodgers, then of the University's Department of Social Administration, to whom I owe much for this and for subsequent advice and criticism. My thanks are also due to Professor Nigel Walker, then Reader in Criminology in the University of Oxford, who was helpful particularly in suggesting sources of finance; and to the Marc Fitch Fund for the provision of some financial support. Permission to quote from Crown copyright material was given by the Director of Publications at Her Majesty's Stationery Office.

The typing has been patiently and accurately dealt with by Mrs. Alice Robertson and Mrs. Moira Bell, and to Mrs. Bell I am also grateful for valuable assistance with the final preparation of the manuscript.

To my father, the Rev. J. Harry Smith, who has assisted in a variety of ways, to my children Hugh, Janet and Margaret, who have shown considerable forbearance, and to my husband John, who has been throughout a source of advice and encouragement, I am especially grateful.

'There can be no doubt whatever that
this Bill will prevent crime, and to a
large extent empty our jails.'

THE EARL OF MEATH
in the debate on the Probation of
Offenders (No. 2) Bill, 1907.

CHAPTER ONE

THE SEARCH FOR ALTERNATIVES TO PRISON

The introduction of the probation system in England and Wales in 1907 was a relatively late development arising out of a century-old movement to reduce the number of imprisonments by providing alternative ways of dealing with offenders.

Imprisonment had assumed importance in the penal system only in the late eighteenth and early nineteenth centuries when, as a consequence of criminal law reform influenced by the liberal penal philosophy which emerged during the 'enlightenment', as well as of the unwillingness of colonial communities to accept transported convicts, it replaced capital punishment and transportation as the penalty for many crimes.

The prison system, administered by a variety of authorities and not centralised until 1877, had to adapt to the increased pressure. During the course of the century it was subject to considerable public scrutiny. There was concern about conditions, cost and administration, and argument about the purpose of imprisonment and the methods required to achieve the desired objectives.

Towards the end of the century discussion of the purpose and methods to be employed in the penal system was influenced not only by changing social attitudes but also by the emergence of new theories about the causes of crime, and in particular those of the positivist school of criminology which explained crime by reference to the biological characteristics of individuals. Deterministic theories of this nature undermined the assumption, on which the criminal legislation and penal system of the century were based, that men commit crimes of their own free will. They had the effect of calling into question the purpose of punishment, and of focusing attention on the individual criminal and on the need to take positive action to bring about his reform.

Against this background doubt was cast on the deterrent value of imprisonment and the appeal of rehabilitation of the offender as a penal objective grew.

Some questioned the effectiveness of imprisonment whatever its

1

objective. In an address to the New York Prison Association in 1895, William Tallack, Secretary of the Howard Association, one of the many reforming societies born of the humanitarian movement, stated that the past fifty years had brought an increasing conviction that reformation was not solely, or even mainly, achieved by imprisonment.[1] In particular there was criticism of the imprisonment of children and of first and minor offenders, on the ground that they would be contaminated by association with members of the 'criminal class'. In his book published in 1873, *The Gaol Cradle, Who Rocks It?*, Benjamin Waugh, later known for his concern with the prevention of cruelty to children, went so far as to wonder whether the time had not perhaps arrived when juvenile imprisonment should be abandoned altogether.[2]

One solution was to separate children from adults whilst continuing to deprive them of liberty, and the use of reformatory schools as alternatives to prison was sanctioned by Parliament in the Reformatory Schools (Youthful Offenders) Act, 1854. In the case of children, the Victorians, influenced by humanitarian considerations characteristic of the period, were able to waive, in the interest of possible reformation, strongly held precepts about individual responsibility.

Although the number of reformatory schools increased quite rapidly during the following ten years,[3] the imprisonment of children, and dissatisfaction with existing alternatives, continued. The schools were not seen as a useful alternative to prison in all cases. Committal was for a period of at least two years, an unnecessary and overlong arrangement for some types of offender. It was feared that minor offenders would be contaminated by association. Also considerable public expense was involved in spite of the introduction of the principle of parental contributions. Moreover, those who considered that punishment should increase in severity with each consecutive crime, or that it should be proportionate to the seriousness of the offence, saw the reformatory school as too severe a penalty for relatively minor or first offences.

As well as contamination, the stigmatising effect of a prison sentence was frequently cited as an argument against the imprisonment of the young. A memorandum to the Home Secretary from the Howard Association in 1872, prompted by its discovery of 'some peculiarly painful instances of this evil', drew attention to the recent imprisonment of children as young as seven or eight years, 'the victims of privation and parental neglect'. The Association wished to point out that 'this practice, while at first greatly tending to terrify a young child, soon leads to a familiarity with prison life,

2

and to corruptions and evil communications, and brands him, perhaps permanently, with a cruel and ruinous stigma.'[4]

Even Edward Cox, Recorder of Portsmouth, who attacked what he called 'the Sentimentalists' for their assumption that reform and not deterrence is the main purpose of punishment,[5] felt, in common, he said, with many magistrates and judges 'the very strongest aversion to sending young people to prison—especially for offences that are not the product of positive and unmistakable wickedness'. A prison was 'the worst school that could be devised for youth'.[6] Those of this persuasion were however 'met by the difficulty the law has made for us. What is to be done with the young offender?'[7] The only alternatives, wrote Cox, were the fine, which punished all the family and not the culprit (and was, no doubt, beyond the means of most offenders' families at this time, resulting only in imprisonment for non-payment); dismissal with a reprimand which seemed insufficient to impress the offender; and a recognizance to come up for judgment when called upon, together with a threat of severe punishment for any further offence.[8]

A few years later in 1880 official concern at the imprisonment of children was expressed by Sir William Vernon Harcourt, Home Secretary in the new Liberal government, who urged the wider use of alternatives such as committal to industrial and reformatory schools and the powers recently given to magistrates' courts by the Summary Jurisdiction Act, 1879.[9] This Act provided that a person convicted of a trivial offence could be discharged conditionally without any punishment, on giving security to appear for sentence if called upon, or to be of good behaviour.[10]

It was one of a series of measures[11] designed, in the course of reform, to expedite justice by extending the jurisdiction of summary courts, and to prevent the full force of mechanistic laws from falling upon young or petty offenders. The Summary Jurisdiction Act of 1879 provided a further alternative to imprisonment for those courts anxious to avoid, or willing to forgo, the removal of the offender from the community—the arrangement widely employed by the age for dealing with social deviance. Its provisions had their roots in common law practices such as the power to use recognizance—an undertaking by the person before the court, with or without sureties, to reappear when called upon, and to observe conditions set by the court. There is evidence that this ancient practice was deliberately used in the early nineteenth century in England and in some States of America by courts seeking alternatives to imprisonment. Recourse was also had to the device of bail—the taking of sureties without recognizance—which, whilst originally intended to ensure the return of the accused to the court for trial or judgment, was extended by some to provide an opportunity for the provisional suspension of punishment. These practices are widely accepted as the legal origins of the probation system.[12]

A variety of expedients of this nature were resorted to during the nineteenth century as the legal basis for isolated experiments with supervision in the community, which might be said to foreshadow the probation system. A well-known early example is the method of disposal used by the Warwickshire county magistrates Sir Eardley Wilmot, Sir Grey Skipworth, Mr. Wriothesley Digby and others, and recounted by the distinguished lawyer and reformer, Matthew Davenport Hill, who had practised in their court in the 1820s. Considering imprisonment distasteful and ineffective, and reprimands insufficient to make a lasting impression, upon coming across a willing and apparently suitable employer, they would commit the youth to his care.[13] Some accounts, but not Hill's, assert, without indicating the source of their information, that the magistrates passed a token sentence of one day's imprisonment upon the offenders dealt with by this method.[14] They do not appear to have made use of recognizances or bail in these cases, and there was no sanction such as the possibility of recall or the forfeiting of sureties.

As a young man with 'leisure to reflect upon the consequences which flowed from the administration of criminal justice', Matthew Davenport Hill watched this practice with great interest.[15] He noted also its deficiencies. In Warwick, where cases arising in most of Warwickshire including Birmingham were then heard, the employer was not always present or easily summoned for consultation and appraisal by the court. So in many cases the arrangement could not be considered at all. Also, apart from seeing in their own court some who were reconvicted, the Warwickshire magistrates had no means of checking the efficacy of the method.[16]

When later Hill found himself, as Recorder of Birmingham, with the opportunity to make such decisions, he also handed over young offenders to suitable 'guardians'.[17] Hill does not explain what legal device was used by him or by the Warwickshire magistrates for this. William Tallack suggests that he used a system of 'magistrate's bail' to suspend sentence and release the offender,[18] but the United Nations *Probation and Related Measures* assumes[19] that he gave a nominal punishment as is said to have been the case in Warwick, subsequent supervision being therefore in addition to, and not a substitute during the suspension of, sentence. If so, Hill and the Warwickshire magistrates had no legal sanctions at their disposal

4

should the offender betray their trust. Hill dealt with this problem by treating very severely any 'probationer' convicted later of a further offence.[20] He appears to have entrusted parents and 'friends' as well as employers with the supervision of offenders.[21] In a biography, his daughters recount that he gave a number of receptions to people who had helped in this way,[22] such as 'the artisan, the small employer, the little shop-keeper.'[23]

Whilst following the example of the Warwickshire magistrates, Hill tried also to improve upon their system by keeping a register of those released and by arranging, with the help of the Chief Superintendent of Police, for 'a confidential officer' to visit the guardian, inquire about the conduct of the offender, and record his findings.[24] Hill thus had some check on the outcome of his decisions.

The other deficiency of the Warwickshire system noted by Hill was not of such moment in Birmingham. Employers and parents were more easily contacted when it was necessary to assess their suitability or obtain their co-operation as supervisors. In this respect, Hill wrote, he was trying 'the experiment' under more favourable circumstances than obtained in Warwick.[25]

Hill was obviously pleased with the success of the method and at his ability to demonstrate it quantitatively as a result of his enquiry and record-keeping system. He was, however, a man of his period in considering that leaving the offender in the community, exposed to much the same pressures and temptations as before, was the method's 'one enormous defect'. To balance against this there was 'one redeeming feature, which is worthy of the most attentive consideration—the young offender is received into the bosom of a family'.[26]

In their memoir of Hill, his daughters report that 'aided by leading organs of the press' (he himself had made many sorties into journalism whilst studying for the bar) he attracted the interest of others to the method. 'The plan was soon adopted in several places', they wrote,

> and an attempt was made by the magistrates of the Middlesex Sessions to introduce it in the part of London under their jurisdiction. But here it failed from the appalling fact that scarcely one among the juvenile delinquents of the metropolis possessed either employer, parents, or friends.[27]

This is no doubt a reference to its use by Edward Cox, Recorder of Portsmouth and simultaneously Chairman of the Second Court of Middlesex Sessions,[28] who as well as calling upon parents or friends to enter into recognizances to bring a person up for judgment, with sureties, as an alternative to imprisonment,[29] is said[30] to have experimented with supervision during the period of suspension by appointing a special 'inquiry officer' to supervise the behaviour of probationers in Middlesex. It has been pointed out that Cox's method of employing recognizances to come up for judgment, with sureties, and a special officer for the supervision of offenders, represented a considerable advance towards to-day's essential elements of probation, compared with Hill's token punishment, rudimentary supervision and follow-up enquiries.[31]

A further usage of supervision, more closely related to the later development of a probation service but not to the introduction of the system in the country, was made possible by the appearance in the courts, from 1875 onwards, of police court missionaries employed by the Church of England Temperance Society, one of the many Victorian organisations which arose in response to the problems created by the heavy and widespread drinking of the period. There is evidence that, in discharging offenders under the Summary Jurisdiction and other Acts, magistrates would sometimes call upon a police court missionary to exercise informal supervision over the released offender. It appears also that some courts adopted the practice of adjourning certain cases, giving the offender bail for a period, and at the same time asking the police court missionary, the police, or the Industrial Schools officer to report on the offender's recent conduct when the case came up again.[32]

There is, however, no directly traceable connection between these various experiments involving supervision during the nineteenth century and the introduction of an official system of probation in England in 1907. They are examples of the imaginative and unconventional use of existing provisions which sometimes occurs when changes in attitude and other circumstances give rise to frustration with prevailing legislation, rather than of practices which had a direct influence on subsequent developments. A more direct connection is evident between early experiment and official action in the development of probation in the State of Massachusetts; and it is to this American example that the introduction in this country of a probation system can be most directly traced.

In Massachusetts the key person in the first experiment in probation was not from the judiciary, but was a Boston cobbler, John Augustus. From 1841 till his death in 1859 Augustus stood bail for offenders brought before the Boston courts, and undertook their supervision between suspension of sentence on bail and recall for judgment which the courts made nominal on evidence of reformation. This was a development of the common law practice of

6

using bail to delay judgment and sentence which, as in England, was being used increasingly by judges in search of alternatives to imprisonment for young and first offenders.[33] Augustus chose his cases with care having regard to previous record, age and home circumstances and other such indicators of possible reformation. He promised the court to 'note their general conduct', and report impartially upon them when called upon.[34]

In the court's use of suspended sentence and the possibility of judgment on recall, and in the selection, careful supervision, record keeping and reporting, this experiment in Massachusetts exhibited most of the elements of modern probation systems. An important difference was that Augustus, whilst making undertakings to the court about his work, was not in any sense an agent of the court.

During the ten years following his death the Boston cobbler's work in the courts was carried on by voluntary workers though not always, according to Chute, with the same rigour.[35] Then in 1869 the State provided for the statutory appointment of an Agent of the Board of State Charities amongst whose responsibilities was the supervision of probationers. Thus the missing element, direct control by the court, was supplied.

Mounting dissatisfaction with the limitations of existing alternatives to imprisonment for young offenders led to government interest in possible new ways of disposal. On the return of the Liberals to power in 1880 Gladstone's new Home Secretary, Sir William Vernon Harcourt, concerned at the ill-effects of imprisoning children and conscious of 'a great body of opinion that in some form or other the parent should be made responsible for the child',[36] asked Chairmen of Quarter Sessions, Recorders and Magistrates to consider 'in what way the law ought to be amended, especially with a view to the prevention of imprisonment of young children, whether on remand or after conviction' and to send him their views.[37] Nor did he stop short at this domestic enquiry. Through the Foreign Office, he arranged to obtain from a number of other countries information about their methods of dealing with young offenders.[38]

The reports accumulated from various sources were subsequently published by the Home Office. The extensive replies of the judiciary, whilst revealing a widespread dislike of child imprisonment, produced no suggestion that a system of probation might be tried.[39] It was the Howard Association which furnished the Home Secretary with an account of the system of probation in operation in the State of Massachusetts.

The Association, anxious 'to utilise the increased public attention now directed to the matter', had itself been collecting information about various ways of dealing with juvenile offenders.[40] Up-to-date details of methods used in other countries had been received from their correspondents abroad. They had also studied the returns submitted by many countries to the Stockholm Prison Congress of 1878.[41] From these they had concluded that the most promising method not yet tried in this country was the Massachusetts system of probation. Impressed with the nature of this system, and the success claimed for it, they forwarded their information about it to the Home Secretary.[42]

In a pamphlet on the subject of Juvenile Offenders, the Association invited the attention of the public, and 'especially of people in authority' to the novel, 'preventive' system practised in Massachusetts since 1869.

The Massachusetts Legislature, it explained, had set up a special 'State Agency' to be responsible for the care of juvenile offenders. It was the duty of the State Agent or his assistants to make investigations into the cases of all children under seventeen charged with an offence, before they came before the court. If he thought it appropriate, the Agent could then ask the court to make a sentence of 'probation'. This formally gave him the oversight of the offender who continued to live in his own home.

The authorities in Massachusetts proclaimed themselves highly satisfied with the system. It was less costly to the State than institutional treatment, and it had proved successful as a preventive measure. By the early 1880s, nearly one-third of all the children convicted in the State were being dealt with in this way, and it was claimed that only 10 per cent of these were charged with further offences within twelve months, and 'very few at all in after years'.

Such a system, the Howard Association suggested, might well be adopted in England, at no extra expense, by utilising the services of existing officials. The Home Secretary could request one magistrate in each locality to direct his sole attention to young offenders. To assist him he might have the services of one or two policemen, or 'better still', one or more voluntary helpers, who would watch over the cases of any criminal or neglected children requiring 'authoritative influence'.

> The chief purpose would be, in the first place, to give parents or relatives of the said children such oversight or guidance as might enable them to discharge their responsibilities aright, and to avoid the necessity for further compulsion. But persuasion failing, fines or other compulsory influences would have to be used.[43]

The Association was no doubt gratified when the substance of this pamphlet was reproduced in an official publication containing the results of the Home Secretary's enquiries both at home and abroad.[44] Any hopes they entertained of early government action on their suggestion were doomed, however, to disappointment. The government's immediate concern seems to have been with the problems presented by the cost and administration of industrial and reformatory schools, especially in the light of the prevailing emphasis on parental responsibility; a Royal Commission to enquire into these schools was set up in 1882.[45] There were also indications that crime was on the decline[46] which may have reduced the incentive to take action.

The Howard Association did not allow the matter of probation to be entirely forgotten. In his evidence to the Royal Commission Joseph Sturge of Birmingham, a well-known magistrate and member of the Association, took the opportunity to mention the Massachusetts system which he had seen in operation the previous year.[47] And although the Commission did not mention this in its report, the Association in its invited comment reminded the Home Secretary of the information about probation supplied in 1881, and suggested its adoption as part of any revised arrangements the Home Secretary might be thinking of making for 'the disposal of neglected and criminal youth'.[48]

The Parliamentary Under-Secretary's reply promised every consideration of their suggestions but it is clear from its *Annual Report* for the following year (1885) that the Association was not surprised at the ensuing lack of action in view of 'the political events of the year, connected with dangers of war at one period, and with administrative and electoral changes at other times'. The question of Home Rule for Ireland dominated domestic politics and a ministerial crisis had followed Gladstone's defeat in June 1885. From the short-lived Tory administration there was no sign of action. The first initiative to introduce legislation dealing with probation came in the following year, 1886, from a private Member, Colonel C. E. Howard Vincent.

A former Director of Criminal Investigations at Scotland Yard, Vincent embarked in 1884 on a voyage round the world. In its course he visited Boston, Massachusetts, where he was much impressed by the working of their probation system.[49] When, on his return to England, he was elected Member of Parliament for Sheffield,[50] he determined to try to get a form of probation introduced into this country.[51]

He expounded his ideas at a meeting of the Social Science

9

Association,[52] an important platform for reformers of the time, and in 1886 presented a Probation of First Offenders Bill to Parliament. This proposed that, in any case where a person was convicted of a first offence for which he could be sent to prison, a court might

> instead of sentencing him at once to any punishment, or ordering him to enter into recognizances to come up for judgment when called upon, direct that he shall be subjected to police supervision as provided by the Prevention of Crime Acts of 1871 and 1879, for any period not exceeding the longest term of imprisonment to which he might have been sentenced.[53]

Its sponsor assured the Commons that he had not framed the Bill in any spirit of sentimental philanthropy towards hardened criminals, but solely 'to meet the case of those guilty of first offences of a minor character'. Like many others, he was concerned at the detrimental effects on the character of an offender which could result from a prison sentence. At the present time, he told Members, 'an unbroken career of crime, a constant battle with society, ending in a long sentence of penal servitude . . . too often succeeds the few weeks' or months' imprisonment given for a trivial first offence'; for, he observed, 'there is nothing more difficult to wipe out than the taint of prison—it hangs like a mill-stone round the neck to the very edge of the grave.'[54]

Vincent appears to have been greatly impressed with the work of the police force in carrying out supervision under the Prevention of Crime Acts. Only this can explain why he was prepared to utilise the provisions of these Acts for first offenders. For the Prevention of Crime Acts provided for police supervision of released convicts under what had become known as the ticket-of-leave system. Subjection to this arrangement carried with it a stigma probably more injurious than that inflicted by a normal prison sentence.[55]

Vincent was convinced of the importance of an element of official supervision in a probation system. In his opinion, the power of dismissal under the Summary Jurisdiction Act, 1879, was unsatisfactory because 'all further knowledge of the prisoner is lost to the public authorities; he has no great incentive to reform; and there are no means of bringing him up for judgment if his conduct is unsatisfactory.'[56]

Commending his proposal to the Commons, he claimed that it could benefit the community in a number of ways. A decrease in the prison population would result in financial saving. (The economical nature of this method of treatment was to be stressed again and again in the speeches and writings of its protagonists.) What was more, the use of such a system would

> hinder the manufacture of habitual criminals (and) gain to the State many honest citizens, by establishing powerful incentives to reform and giving first offenders the hope of leading useful lives, without absolving them from the consequences of crime or diminishing the safe-guards demanded by the social order.[57]

Although the Bill was introduced in January, it was apparently circulated only a day or two before the debate on the second reading in June. Mr. Childers, the Home Secretary in what was now Gladstone's third administration, pleaded shortness of time to consider the proposals because of the late circulation of the Bill, and requested an adjournment. Extra time having been granted,[58] Childers began to sound opinion outside the House.[59]

The Assistant Commissioner of the Metropolitan Police, Monro, when consulted about Vincent's proposal, showed no inclination to have the responsibilities of the police extended in this way. He considered the ticket-of-leave system 'quite out of place' for beginners in crime. Whilst effective when applied to habitual criminals, it would be 'most harassing and vexatious to the incipient offender'. And, in his opinion, harassment and vexation were not likely to be conducive to the reform of a first offender.

Provincial representatives of the police force—the Chief Constables of Liverpool, Manchester, Stafford and Birmingham—on the other hand, expressed no objection to the idea. But the members of the judiciary consulted by the Home Office were of much the same opinion as Monro. The Chairman of Lancashire Quarter Sessions considered such a 'horrible penalty' as supervision under the Prevention of Crime Acts 'wholly uncalled for in the case of first offenders', and the Chief Metropolitan Magistrate, whilst agreeing that committal to prison of minor offenders should be avoided, thought 'the infamy of being deemed to be ticket-of-leave men would be more injurious to their character and prospects than a long term of imprisonment.'[60]

While these consultations were taking place, the date arrived for the resumption of the debate on the second reading. Not only does the government appear to have been unready for this,[61] but, assuming that no further progress would be made with the Bill because of the proposed dissolution of Parliament, Childers left London to canvass his constituents in Edinburgh. His Parliamentary Under-Secretary was also away and, in their absence, the Bill passed its third reading in the Commons.[62]

11

In the Lords, its sponsor, the Earl of Belmore, referred to the successful operation of the probation system in the United States. He understood that 'two of our most important colonies', Victoria and New Zealand, had decided to try the experiment, and he asked their Lordships to pass the Bill as readily as the House of Commons.

By this time, however, the government had gathered its thoughts on the matter, and Lord Sudeley supported by the Law Lords, Halsbury and Herschell, called for the Bill's rejection. If passed, it would involve a large increase in the police force and other 'very considerable alterations in the working of the Criminal Law': changes which should not be wrought in a hurry. Halsbury considered the Bill 'unworkable'; Herschell that much more guidance would have to be given to courts than was contained in Vincent's Bill. Under this pressure, Belmore agreed to go no further with the proposal.[63]

Annoyed and bewildered at the attitude shown by the government, Vincent addressed a letter to *The Times* protesting at the treatment given to his Bill by an administration which he had understood to be sympathetic towards the introduction of a system of probation.[64]

Undeterred by his Parliamentary rebuff or by Monro's warning that there would be 'an outcry' if police supervision was introduced for beginners in crime,[65] Vincent was determined to re-introduce his proposals. From time to time during subsequent months he pressed the Home Office for its views. There, Godfrey Lushington, the Permanent Under-Secretary, considered the burdens laid upon the criminal under the ticket-of-leave system too great to inflict upon first offenders; and pointed out that the very heavy penalties laid down in the Prevention of Crime Acts for failure to report, would never do for those convicted of minor offences.[66]

In response to Vincent's pressure, Lushington sounded the new Home Secretary, Henry Matthews, for his opinion of the scheme. The Minister recorded his approval of 'some kind of police supervision or probation', though not as known under the Prevention of Crime Acts. He thought it might be dangerous to entrust such discretion to some courts, but that this was worth risking.

Although thus sympathetic and aware that what was required was 'something between imprisonment and discharge on recognizances', Matthews had nothing to suggest in the way of an alternative kind of supervision.[67]

In the meantime, the Earl of Belmore, who had maintained an interest in the Bill was able to re-introduce it in the Lords[68] whilst Vincent still awaited an opportunity in the Lower House. The first

12

reading took place in January 1887,[69] but the Bill was quickly replaced by a similar one brought in by the Earl of Erne.[70] By that time, however, Vincent had procured a first reading in the Commons of an amended version[71] of his original Bill and the Earl of Erne withdrew his in its favour.[72]

Vincent now made a concession to the opponents of police supervision. He proposed that, whilst courts should be able to direct that first offenders be 'conditionally released upon probation of good conduct', police supervision under the Prevention of Crimes Act should only be applied to them at the discretion of the court.[73]

During the second reading, Matthews, the Home Secretary, expressed horror at the proposal to apply police supervision under the Prevention of Crime Acts to first offenders. If the courts avoided this, the Bill then added nothing to the powers already available under the Summary Jurisdiction Act, 1879. At the suggestion of one of the Bill's supporters, he agreed to re-shape it and make it more acceptable to the government, if Vincent would allow.

The latter expressed his readiness to fall in with the government's attitude,[74] but did not withdraw the Bill so that it might be re-introduced later in a new form. He did, however, by arrangement with Matthews, consult with the Parliamentary Counsel, and came to the Committee Stage with a number of amendments which he hoped would render the Bill more acceptable to the House.

One of these sought to give more guidance to courts about the kind of case to which the new system might be applied. Regard was to be paid, for instance, 'to the youth, character and antecedents of the offender, to the trivial nature of the offence and to any extenuating circumstances under which the offence was committed.' It was also proposed that courts should be able to lay down conditions which the offender would be expected to observe. Failure to do so could result in his being brought back before the court for sentence.

Then Vincent proposed to substitute for supervision under the Prevention of Crime Acts supervision by some 'authority'—either an official bound to obey the orders of the court, or some other person or organisation willing to undertake this responsibility. It would be the duty of this 'authority' to report to the court, as required, on the behaviour of the released offender, to report immediately any breach of the conditions laid down by the court and, in such cases, to take or assist in taking any steps necessary for bringing the offender to justice.

Questioned about the nature of these 'authorities', Vincent suggested that Secretaries or Managers of Discharged Prisoners' Aid

13

Societies, clergyman or priests might be willing to supervise offenders, and that in some cases Police Superintendents would be suitable.[75]

Although the Bill passed the Commons, in the Lords the government dissociated itself with its form, suggesting that it required considerable amendment. As a result, the clause providing for an 'authority' was dropped in order to get the Bill through, and it thus reached the statute book with no vestige left of the principle of supervision.[76]

The first measure purporting to arrange for the Probation of Offenders had passed into law, but during its passage through Parliament it had lost any resemblance to the Massachusetts model which had the systematic supervision of the offender as its main principle.

No further attempt to introduce a system of official supervision was made for some years. The Howard Association contented themselves with efforts to encourage the courts to make liberal use of Vincent's Act. To this end they communicated with newspapers and, in 1892, five years after the passing of the Act, despatched a leaflet on the subject to Members of Parliament, magistrates and magistrates' clerks. They were of opinion that the Probation of First Offenders Act was 'worthy of far more practical recognition on the part of magistrates' than it had so far obtained.[77]

In the same year they enlisted the help of one of their 'Parliamentary friends', Mr. Samuel Smith,[78] who asked the Home Secretary to make the matter the subject of an official circular.[79] As a result, a circular dealing with both the Summary Jurisdiction Act, 1879, and the Probation of First Offenders Act, 1887, was issued the following month, April 1892. The Acts, it stated, were 'not so fully taken advantage of as they might be'. The Home Secretary hoped that they would be more frequently applied in those areas where they were so far little used.[80]

This government action was probably also prompted by the recent Report of the Prison Commissioners that the Governors of some local prisons were 'not aware of the Act having been applied at all'.[81]

The failure of the courts to use Vincent's Act can probably be attributed to three main factors.

Magistrates and judges were naturally reluctant to dismiss some offenders without any effective surety as to their future behaviour. There was no way of detecting any lapse in conduct until further crimes were discovered by the police.

There also existed a reluctance in some quarters to take a course

14

which involved recording a conviction. Giving expression to this in 1896, the Rev. W. D. Morrison, a prominent contributor to discussion of the treatment of offenders, thought it most important that in some cases the court should not proceed to a conviction 'inasmuch as a conviction, even if not accompanied by imprisonment, is often a serious impediment to the future career of the young'.[82] The Howard Association considered that

> the necessity of recording the conviction often constitutes in itself a hindrance to the application of the Act. For, in the cases of many persons charged for the first time with offences of a trivial nature . . . it is very desirable to avoid even the recording of a conviction.[83]

Since the use of the Probation of First Offenders Act involved the recording of a conviction, some magistrates preferred to continue the older custom of dismissing offenders under the Summary Jurisdiction Act, 1879, without the necessity of this.

Thirdly, if later experience in connection with the Probation of Offenders Act, 1907, can be considered relevant, it is very probable that a great many magistrates had never heard of the new Act; at best they were probably apathetic. And apart from the efforts made by the Howard Association and the one circular from the Home Office, nothing appears to have been done to increase their interest and awareness.

This was understandable. As a Home Secretary was to tell Vincent in a Parliamentary reply in 1901, there seemed 'no particular reason to urge courts to use this Act, rather than other Acts, when the practical effect is the same'.[84] By failing to provide for supervision, the Probation of First Offenders Act had added virtually nothing to the existing methods of dealing with young and minor offenders. Once this was fully appreciated, the search was resumed for other alternatives.

The chief arguments so far advanced in favour of the introduction of a probation system—mainly by Vincent and the Howard Association—were its value as a preventive measure and its economy compared with institutional treatment in prison or reformatory school.

The Howard Association now produced others which coincided with two aspects of current thinking. A French visitor to England was said to have exclaimed, 'What a country this is, where almost everyone is putting someone into an institution and paying for it'. This was, in the opinion of the Association, a disturbing tendency. 'It was incomparably better', they thought, 'to keep [both adults and

15

juveniles] from needing prisons and workhouses than to have to commit them thither.' They quoted with approval the complaint of an American writer that the practice of sending people to institutions was 'tending not only to burden the taxpayer, but also to increase a pauper spirit, and greatly to relax the parental sense of responsibility.[85] A probation system then would save public money and prevent any erosion of responsibility—considerations likely to appeal strongly to the public of the day. What was more, it was a method consistent with the ideas of those who felt with Morrison that 'a very indifferent home is better for the future welfare of the young than the best of institutions.'[86]

With these additional arguments, the Howard Association were now very strongly advocating the introduction of a probation system.[87] In 1898 they published the result of an enquiry conducted by them among about seventy 'practical authorities and acquaintances'—Chairmen of Quarter Sessions, magistrates and Chief Constables—as to the best ways of dealing with juvenile offenders.[88] The enquiry had been set on foot, they said, because of the existence 'of certain difficulties which have of late years been increased by changes in public opinion and in magisterial practice—but which have not yet been obviated by the needful collateral changes in legislation or administration'.

They enumerated the limitations of existing methods of dealing with young offenders. Public opinion, 'supported by official concurrence', disapproved of child imprisonment; magistrates were less inclined than previously to commit children to reformatories because of the 'growing and well-founded feeling' that widespread use of these institutions encouraged reckless and drunken parents to 'throw their offspring upon the honest taxpayer for support'; the use of the whip was a controversial issue which had not found favour with Parliament; and a simple admonition under the Probation of First Offenders Act was in some cases insufficient. The Association thought the courts' reluctance to use these methods, because of their inadequacies, was tending to 'produce a sense of impunity among many young persons'.

The 50 per cent response to the Association's enquiries revealed a general dislike of child imprisonment among the respondents, and a determination to avoid its use as far as possible. But no one suggested probation as an alternative. It remained to the society itself to advocate probation as a helpful step towards the solution of the existing impasse. It would meet the requirements of those who wished to enforce parental responsibility, and of those who were anxious that the novice in crime should not be further contaminated by a sojourn in prison or reformatory. It was more constructive and a better safeguard for society than a mere admonition; and it was very economical.[89]

Before Parliament opened in the following year, the Association again addressed a memorial to the Home Secretary asking him to give consideration to a number of matters which they thought worthy of legislation. Amongst these were the appointment of probation officers and the establishment of special courts for children.[90]

For the next few years the movement for a probation system merged with that for children's courts. The one reform was rarely called for without the other. This may have added impetus to the campaign for probation, but it possibly detracted from the realisation that probation was a method applicable to adults as well as to children. For many years after its introduction the use of probation for adults tended to be affected by, amongst other things, its association in the judicial mind with child offenders.

The Association's memorial had no apparent effect on the Home Office, but, during the next few years, they continued their advocacy of the probation system by the publication of further pamphlets. In *Probation Officers and the Gift of Guidance* they called upon 'many social reformers in the United Kingdom, and elsewhere, to consider the subject, and, as opportunity may present, to press it upon the attention of legislators and jurists, for practical adoption in greater or lesser degree'.[91] They also published a very perceptive account of the probation system in America, by Miss E. P. Hughes, former Principal of a Cambridge Training College for Women Teachers. Miss Hughes spent the winter of 1900–1901 in the United States and made investigations there on behalf of the Howard Association.[92]

She was greatly impressed by 'the admirable character and conduct' of the American probation officer, which she attributed to the fact that 'the initiators of this reform realised that the whole success of the scheme depended almost entirely upon the kind of probation officer chosen'. In some cases, the introduction of the system had been postponed until the right kind of officers were found—and not only found, but trained:[93] a prudence and thoroughness not emulated when this country later adopted the system.

She found the probation officer well-paid, and allowed great discretion in his handling of cases. 'He had the immense advantage', she wrote,

of being able to consider each case on its own merits. He need

17

not think of stern and equal justice and of strict impartiality. He was not an administrator of the law, like a policeman, but he was primarily an educator. He could afford to be very human, very brotherly, very individual in his treatment.

The authorities had assured her that an ex-policeman or ex-soldier was 'just the kind of man that was not wanted, for neither have been trained to be educators'.

Miss Hughes advanced several new arguments in favour of the probation method. Treatment could be adjusted to the individual case; self-respect could be better developed; and the family unit could be kept together. Where the offender was a wife, her place in the home could be retained. A male offender would not lose his job, or his skill, or the discipline of regular work.

Keen to see a similar system introduced here, Miss Hughes suggested that some voluntary agency might, with government approval, finance an experiment in two or three cities and be responsible also for recruiting and devising a year's training for suitable persons wishing to act as probation officers.[94]

The Home Office had had a recent informant of its own on the American system. At the Prison Congress of Paris in 1895, Sir Evelyn Ruggles-Brise, Chairman of the Prison Commissioners, had been invited to visit the United States to see the penal systems in operation there. In doing so, he paid special attention to the probation system.[95]

His Report, *Some Observations on the Treatment of Crime in America*, was submitted to the Home Secretary early in 1898.[96] Ruggles-Brise was favourably impressed by the success of probation in America. He pointed out that the Probation of First Offenders Act, 1887, whilst having borrowed the phrase 'probation', made no effective provision for supervision, or for the making of enquiries before trial into the prisoner's character and antecedents, which he saw as an important element in the probation officer's function.[97]

His views were echoed by Rosa M. Barrett in her Howard Medal Prize Essay, written in 1900. She pointed out that the proper application of the 1887 Act obviously required preliminary enquiries into the character and circumstances of an offender, yet the machinery for making these was entirely missing.[98]

Ruggles-Brise doubted, however, whether public opinion in England would tolerate this preliminary 'inquisition' of yet untried prisoners. He also thought he saw the possibility of conflict and rivalry between police and probation officers. And, unlike others, he was not struck by the economy of the system. In fact, he

18

considered it expensive.[99]

Nevertheless, when in 1903, probably because of continued reformist pressure in the country and on the government, he was asked to comment on a proposal to introduce probation in England, Ruggles-Brise showed himself greatly in favour of such a step and offered suggestions about legislation. This, he thought, should enable courts to order the discharge of a prisoner conditional upon his entering an institution or upon his being placed under the care of a specified person or of a probation officer. There should be power to bring the offender who did not adhere to the terms of his order back before the court to be sentenced to the term of imprisonment for which he had originally been liable.

Any legislation should provide for the appointment of probation officers, whose duties would be defined by the Home Secretary. To Ruggles-Brise the police authority seemed to be the most suitable for appointing probation officers, who would in many cases, he thought, be members of the police force.

He expressed no doubts about the suitability of policemen for this work. He already had experience, he said, of conflicts between rival charitable authorities over one case. This predisposed him to think that these agencies should not be given prime responsibility for supervision. He recognised, however, the 'invaluable service' rendered to magistrates by agencies like the Church of England Temperance Society,[100] and considered that the best arrangement would be to retain the services of these organisations, but to place their direction in the hands of an officially appointed probation officer. He hinted at the possibility of 'vested interests in the shape of existing agencies' blocking the way to the operation of an efficient system.

As Chairman of the Prison Commissioners, he saw in probation officers a means not only of dealing with offenders in the community but also of reducing the number of persons sent to prison in default of payment of fines. (At this time more offenders were going to prison for non-payment of fines than were committed direct by the courts.) The probation officer could be used to collect fines by instalments and help to check this scandalous situation.[101]

On receiving such favourable comment from Ruggles-Brise, the Home Office decided to seek more detailed information about the operation of the probation system in New Zealand and the Australian colonies. The only report forthcoming was about the New Zealand system, and this was examined by officials and passed to Ruggles-Brise.[102]

Soon afterwards they received a considerable number of letters from local authorities calling for legislation to establish children's courts staffed by probation officers.[103] These were the outcome of an attempt by a relatively new, vigorous organisation, the Committee on Wage Earning Children, to put pressure on the government. The Committee had recently organised a conference of philanthropic societies interested in children. The various representatives had agreed on the need for separate courts for children to which probation officers would be attached.[104] Following up this venture, the Committee had despatched a memorandum on the subject to local authorities, pointing out the need for legislation. The letters received by the Home Office were a direct result of this communication.[105]

They led the Permanent Under-Secretary, C. E. Troup, to observe that

> it might ... be well to ask the Magistrates of each Court (in
> the Metropolitan area) to report what are the arrangements for
> dealing with children in cases heard at the court, and whether
> any improvements could be suggested; and for observations
> generally on the subject.[106]

The replies of the magistrates were 'pretty conclusive against the provision of Courts for Children in London' and, although one or two mentioned the police court missionary, none suggested the employment of probation officers.[107]

At about the same time, the Home Office asked for the observations of Curtis Bennett, a Metropolitan Magistrate, on a paper entitled 'The System of Children's Courts and Probation Officers in the United States', written by N. C. Walsh, an official at Great Scotland Yard lately returned from America. Curtis Bennett, whilst agreeing with Walsh that there was much to be said for an organised probation system in this country, considered that in the Metropolitan Police Court District they were already enjoying, through their use of police court missionaries and School Board Officers, many of the benefits of a probation system.[108]

The work of police court missionaries was known to Curtis Bennett not only through his work as a magistrate but through his family's connection with the Church of England Temperance Society, which had at that time just over a hundred such missionaries spread over twenty-six Anglican dioceses.[109]

Founded in 1862 as the Church of England Total Abstinence Society, the society was renamed the Church of England Temperance Society ten years later, when it took as its objects, 'the

Promotion of Habits of Temperance, the Reformation of the Intemperate, and the Removal of the Causes which lead to Intemperance'.[110] One of the means by which it sought to further these was by employing agents to work in the cause of temperance amongst groups such as soldiers, seamen and railwaymen,[111] and in 1876, at the suggestion of Frederic Rainer, a printer, who wrote from Hertford, it extended its activities to the courts where, Rainer thought, practical help should be given to those in trouble whether through drink or other causes.[112] An agent or 'missionary' was appointed to visit some of the Metropolitan Police Courts. A further three were appointed during the following two years. Their principal duty, according to the Report of the Society for 1878, was

> to visit regularly the police courts for the purpose of dealing with individual drunkards, charged and convicted, with a view to their restoration and reclamation. They visit hopeful cases, and hand over such to Branch Societies, and work with the full consent in each case of the presiding magistrates.[113]

One of them, a Mr. Nelson, working in the Southwark and Lambeth districts, reported:

> I have been treated with the greatest respect, and afforded every facility for doing good, by the police court officials. I am glad to report that hundreds of men and women have listened to that one Divine instrument, the Gospel, in its simplicity, from my lips, as well as to advice to shun strong drink.

Of those with whom he had been in contact, 'Many', he wrote,

> simply sign the pledge, have a few words, and go on, refusing name and address. There are many that I have kept an eye upon, that are keeping their pledges, some are members of Parochial Branches [of the Society], some are attending Church and other places of worship.

Police court work did not occupy the whole of the missionaries' time. Their main interest was to increase temperance and they sought out drunkards everywhere. Mr. Nelson quantified his work for the year ending March 1878, thus:

Police court visits	473	Large works visited	172
Prison visits	34	Railway station visits	90
Homes visited	754	Police station visits	38
Pledges taken	426	Fire brigade station	
Cab stands visited	1,143	visits	19[114]

21

Missionary work was soon extended to other Metropolitan Courts, and further to Rochester, Liverpool and Lichfield; and in 1883 the Society's aim was to attach a special missionary to every Metropolitan Police Court,[115] a goal achieved except in one case by the end of the century.[116] In 1887 a 'mission woman' was taken into its employ to render help to the missionaries in 'specially difficult female cases'.[117] At the same time some magistrates began to make use of the services of the missionaries in cases of social distress where the courts themselves were powerless to help, to exercise informal supervision over persons released under the Summary Jurisdiction Act, 1879, and similar measures.[118] It was to this kind of arrangement that Curtis Bennett referred in his comment to the Home Office on Walsh's paper on the American system.

Other visitors to the United States in 1904 were Edward Grubb, who had succeeded Tallack as Secretary of the Howard Association, and Howard Vincent, who had received a knighthood in 1896. On his return, Grubb's 'Notes of a Personal Enquiry' into American penal methods, including probation, were despatched to the Home Office along with his Association's latest pamphlet, *Children's Courts and the Probation System*.[119] [120] Grubb also obtained publicity for his findings in *The Times*, which published two articles by him on American penal methods, and supported, in a leading article, his plea for the establishment of children's courts and a probation system.[121] Less than two months later, the paper's readers were provided with a further account of the merits of the Massachusetts system in a letter from Howard Vincent.[122]

By this time, Vincent was as interested in the establishment of children's courts as in the introduction of a probation system. In February 1905, he presented to the Commons a Bill which sought to allow magistrates to exclude the public from trials of children under sixteen.[123]

This was withdrawn when Vincent gave his support to a more comprehensive Bill introduced by a Mr. Tennant.[124] Tennant not only proposed separate courts for children, but also that courts should have the power to release young offenders for a period of supervision under 'such an authority . . . as the court may direct.'[125] The clause defining the 'authority' was similar to the amending clause proposed by Vincent during the passage of his 1887 Bill. In a memorandum on the Bill, Tennant envisaged that children might be supervised by 'an official of the court, the court missionary or some society willing to undertake the work.'[126]

It was clear to the government that this Bill could not pass before the end of the session so, noting that if it was re-introduced in the next session they would have 'a good deal to say about it in the way of criticism', they took no action. At the same time it was acknowledged at the Home Office that there was certainly 'a strong case for some more effective machinery for "probation"' than existed under the 1887 Act.[127]

When the same Bill re-appeared in 1906, official comment dubbed it 'shapeless and wanting in precision',[128] and it was not accorded a second reading. Nor was another Bill brought in by Vincent with the support of Viscount Helmsley,[129] father of Lord Feversham, who, thirty years later, played an important role in the affairs of the National Association of Probation Officers. Vincent hoped by his Bill to fill the gap in his 1887 Act by arranging for the police authorities to appoint probation officers,[130] and to make his proposals more acceptable by allowing a court to erase a record of conviction after a satisfactory report on a probationer.[131]

At the Home Office, however, the situation was ripe for a decision to be taken to introduce a government Bill to bring in a system of probation. A Liberal government had come to power on the resignation of the Balfour administration in December 1905. Herbert Gladstone, youngest son of W. E. Gladstone, and Herbert Samuel came to Whitehall, as Home Secretary and Under-Secretary, there to make a significant contribution to penal administration. 'With a splendid opportunity before us, and with energies released after so long a period of exclusion, the Ministry', Samuel wrote later, 'set to work all along the line.'[132]

During his father's last administration, Gladstone had been Chairman of the Departmental Committee on Prisons,[133] which had recommended radical changes, including the espousal of reformation as one of the purposes of imprisonment. His main interest on appointment to the Home Office was to continue with the implementation of these recommendations, already set in motion under the previous government. To his young Under-Secretary he gave 'a free hand to work on similar lines'.[134]

Two days after Samuel's appointment, the State Children's Association wrote to the Home Office in the hope of enlisting sympathy for their proposal that probation officers should be appointed for children. They marshalled all the arguments and their plea struck one senior official as 'a very reasonable one'. He recalled the existence of a file containing 'much interesting information' about probation systems abroad. The Permanent Under-Secretary, C. E. Troup, who earlier in the year had acknowledged that a strong case existed for a proper probation system, minuted that he thought 'something might be done in this matter at once', and thereupon

23

sketched proposals for its possible organisation. He appears to have been well aware of all the voluntary organisations who might be willing to provide probation officers, and to have had the idea that if they planned in the first place for the Metropolitan Police Courts, they would afterwards be able 'to suggest the same arrangements to courts throughout the country'.

When the file reached Samuel, he found the suggestion a valuable one.[135] It does not appear that he knew anything about probation before coming into office. There was a wealth of material available in the files for his perusal, however,[136] and he was much impressed, he said later, by what he read of the success of the American experiment.[137]

The Liberals having been confirmed in power at the January general election, Samuel presided in March over a small meeting to discuss what legislation should be introduced by the Department. In attendance were Chalmers, the Permanent Under-Secretary, his deputy Troup, Fenwick, the Chief Magistrate and his colleague Curtis Bennett, and Henry, the Commissioner of the Metropolitan Police.[138]

Probation was the first item on the agenda. The various officials summoned to Samuel's meeting had all had recent opportunities to learn something of the system. Fenwick had heard an account of the working of the system in New York from the Chief Magistrate of that State who had visited London in the previous year.[139] The Home Office had sought the views of Curtis Bennett[140] and Henry[141] on previous occasions, and Troup had been giving his attention to the subject from time to time over a number of years and had already formed ideas about the operation of a system in this country.[142]

All seem to have agreed with Samuel that some arrangement should be made for the appointment of probation officers, and also that the system should 'in certain cases' be used for adult as well as young offenders. It was necessary, of course, for them to consider where probation officers would come from, and in this there was less accord.

Curtis Bennett, the supporter of the Church of England Temperance Society, strongly urged that the police court missionaries, already engaged in social work in some courts, should be employed as probation officers, and that some payment should be made for their services. On the other hand, Fenwick, the senior magistrate, feared that, admirable as was the work of the missionaries and also of the School Board Officers, they would not be able to give the intensive supervision he thought desirable. 'The

24

police court missionary has at present quite as much as he can properly discharge without further burdens being cast upon him', he wrote in a paper which he left at the Home Office. In his view, probation involved more than the sort of work already being performed by these agents of voluntary societies. And he was doubtful about the wisdom of employing as probation officers persons who were responsible to and paid by bodies entirely independent of the courts. He thought that carefully selected retired policemen, such as were employed by the National Society for the Prevention of Cruelty to Children, would make the best probation officers.[143] Perhaps he had been influenced by his conversations with the Chief Magistrate of New York where ex-policemen were responsible for the supervision of probationers. Fenwick's suggestion was opposed, however, by the Commissioner of the Metropolitan Police. Prepared to admit that in some cases retired policemen might be suitable, Henry considered that, in others, a visit from a one-time member of the force, albeit in plain clothes, would be very much resented. In his opinion the best probation officers would be recruited from among 'men and women of higher class, such as now give their services gratuitously to the Charity Organisation Society.'[144]

This discussion about the most suitable people to act as probation officers was a microcosm of one which was to go on for a number of years, some people taking the view that the missionaries were best qualified, others that the police could most suitably carry out the necessary duties, and, still others, that what was needed was highly educated persons with an interest in social work.

At this early stage it was decided that none should be specifically excluded, but that

> in any system introduced there should be a great deal of elasticity as to the choice of probation officers and that, in London at any rate, it would be well that there should be . . . a panel of officers from which the magistrates could select the officer best able to deal with each case.

It was agreed that any payment to probation officers should come out of the same funds as those from which were drawn the expenses of the police force; the details could be regulated by the Home Secretary or the local authority as the case might be.[145]

No time was lost. On the following day Samuel settled with the Permanent Under-Secretary that the heads of a Bill providing for the appointment and payment of probation officers should be prepared.[146]

In the interest of order and convenience, it was thought expedient to bring together in the Bill all the provisions for the dismissal of offenders, with or without supervision. This would involve the repeal of the Probation of First Offenders Act, 1887, and of Section 16 of the Summary Jurisdiction Act, 1879.[147] This ostensibly sensible consolidation of the law relating to methods of dismissal unfortunately gave rise to subsequent misapprehension about the real nature of 'probation' which persisted to the detriment of the system's development.[148] The phrase 'dismissed under the Probation of Offenders Act' could imply the mere dismissal of a charge, the making of an order for the release of an offender on recognizance, or the making of a probation order proper which officially placed the offender under the supervision of a probation officer, or other suitable person, for a specified period.

Vincent had never intended his Act to be used for more than minor offenders. The Liberal Bill, however, proposed to allow the use of probation in connection with both indictable and non-indictable offences. Nor was the probation system to be restricted to first offenders. The Liberals proposed to give courts the opportunity to use it in a wide variety of cases if, having had 'regard to the character, antecedents, age, health or mental condition of the person charged, or to the trivial nature of the offence, or to the extenuating circumstances under which the offence was committed', such a course was deemed expedient.[149] In framing this guidance, the government followed closely the wording of Vincent's Act,[150] although the word 'youth', which appeared in that Act, was altered to 'age', probably because Ruggles-Brise, who naturally hoped the probation system would reduce the prison population, pointed out that the use of the former might lead to the Bill being considered applicable only to young offenders.[151]

At the suggestion of Home Office officials, the words, 'health'—'it would be useful to have the power, for example, in the case of a pregnant woman'—and 'mental condition' were added.[152] It was also made more evident than in the 1887 Act that these were indeed alternatives and that it was necessary for only one of them to be fulfilled in order to invoke the Act.[153]

One of the criticisms levelled at the 1887 Act was that its use required the recording of a conviction. It has already been noted that there was a body of opinion which considered that this should be avoided if possible in the case of young offenders.[154] In deference to this opinion which in 1906, according to Troup, held the balance, the requirement was omitted in the new Bill,[155] except in the case of orders made by the higher courts.[156] (This distinction was considered necessary because in Courts of Assize and Quarter Sessions, the question whether the charge is proved is in the absence of a plea of guilty—a question to be decided by the verdict of a jury; and the verdict of a jury is tantamount to a conviction).[157]

As in the Massachusetts system, and again following the 1887 Act, the Bill proposed that the courts should retain the sanction of being able to recall and sentence for the original offence any offender who failed to observe the conditions of his recognizance.[158]

These then were the principles upon which the Liberal Government proposed to base the new method of dealing with offenders. Their Bill also included simple machinery for operating it. The justices of each petty sessional division would have the power to appoint probation officers to serve the courts in their area.[159] No special arrangements were to be made for the appointment of probation officers at Assize Courts or Quarter Sessions; where they wished to use probation, these courts would be at liberty to employ the officer from the division from which the offender had been submitted for trial.[160]

The appointment of probation officers would be purely permissive.[161] The person named in a probation order need not necessarily be an officially appointed probation officer or the probation officer for that particular area.[162]

The Bill provided for the payment, by fee for each case, of probation officers or others undertaking the supervision of probationers. The amount of the fee was to be determined by the Justices subject to a maximum laid down by 'the authority having control of the fund out of which court expenses are paid.'[163] In the boroughs this was the borough council; in the counties it was the Standing Joint Committee[164] composed of representatives of the justices and of the county council.[165] This proposal to place ultimate control over the remuneration of probation officers in hands other than those of the justices who were to appoint them led later to disputes and even difficulties in some divisions.[166]

The proposal that payment should be by fee per case suggests that the government saw the job as likely to be a part-time rather than a full-time one. It was a reasonable beginning in view of the fact that no one knew how much use would be made of the system. They were quite prepared for courts to use the agents of voluntary societies as probation officers and the Bill even provided that in these cases the fees might be paid direct to the relevant society.[167] It is also clear from the Bill that there was no intention of debarring the police from appointment as probation officers.[168]

By the time the draft Bill had been circulated to a number of

27

officials, chief constables and other interested persons, all of whom gave it their general approval,[169] it was too late to hope that it would pass right through the Commons before prorogation. It was decided to introduce it, notwithstanding, probably to make the government's intentions known,[170] and the Home Secretary himself presented it to the Commons in December 1906.[171]

As expected, it got no further, but it was re-introduced early in the next session.[172] Even earlier with a Bill, however, was Howard Vincent, making his last attempt to 'amend the Probation of First Offenders Act, 1887, and to authorise the appointment of Probation Officers', and obstinately insisting on restricting the system to first offenders.[173] His Bill failed to obtain a second reading.

The new government Bill closely resembled that introduced in the previous session, except that it made provision for probation officers to be paid, where the court so desired, a salary rather than a fee for each case.[174] It had been brought to the attention of the Home Secretary that in Birmingham, where they were already experimenting with an unofficial form of supervision undertaking by 'probation officers', the latter were receiving salaries. The Bill was accordingly adjusted so that this and any similar arrangement might continue undisturbed.[175]

Even yet, however, the Bill was not safely on its way through Parliament. A technical mistake in the wording led to its early withdrawal,[176] but an amended version, the Probation of Offenders (No. 2) Bill, 1907, was presented the very next day, the 19th March.[177]

Although Gladstone sponsored the Bill,[178] it was his Under-Secretary, Herbert Samuel, who moved the second reading[179] and who was responsible for guiding it safely through its various stages. Opening the debate on the second reading, Samuel said the Bill was of a non-controversial nature—the Government had heard not a whisper of opposition to it from any quarter of the House. Its purpose was to enable courts to appoint probation officers and pay them salaries, so that certain offenders whom the court did not think fit to imprison, on account of their age, character or antecedents, might be placed on probation under the supervision of these officers whose duty it would be to guide, admonish and befriend them.[180]

As Samuel later observed, 'the Bill attracted very little attention, either in Parliament or outside, and passed through all its stages almost without discussion.[181]

There was some parliamentary interest in who should be appointed as probation officers. Mr. George Cave, member for the Kingston division of Surrey and later Home Secretary, wanted an assurance that there would be no objection to the appointment of police court missionaries. Mr. Cochrayne, noting that the Bill did not preclude the appointment of police constables, wished to be sure 'that these persons charged with the supervision of probationers should be carefully selected for the delicate duties they would have to perform.' Women, he thought, should be employed to supervise girls and young children, and specially trained persons for offenders released on account of their mental condition.[182]

Attempts were made, during the Committee Stage, to amend the Bill to specify the kind of person to be employed in certain circumstances. It was proposed, for instance, that in all districts where the number of juvenile offenders justified this, it should be necessary to appoint separate probation officers to deal with children's cases; that it should be mandatory to employ a female officer to supervise female offenders; and that the employment of police officers to deal with school children should be forbidden.[183] The government was opposed however to any move to fetter the discretion of the courts in the appointment of officers,[184] and all the amendments to this end were either withdrawn or defeated.[185]

The government took the opportunity in the Committee Stage to introduce a number of amendments of their own. They proposed that Courts should be given power to insert in a probation order conditions, over and above submission to supervision, by which a probationer would have to abide. It was suggested that the courts should be able to add conditions with respect to all or any of the following matters:

(a) for prohibiting the offender from associating with thieves or other undesirable persons, or from frequenting undesirable places;
(b) as to abstention from intoxicating liquor, where the offence was drunkenness or an offence committed under the influence of drink;
(c) generally for securing that the offender should lead an honest and industrious life.

And also that they should be able to vary these conditions during the period of supervision, or even discharge the order before due time if the conduct of the probationer warranted it.[186]

It was also thought advisable at this stage to include in the Bill some description of the work of a probation officer. The clause inserted in Committee in this 1907 Bill long remained the basic statement of the work of the probation officer in so far as it concerns the supervision of offenders. The officer would be expected 'to visit or receive reports from the person under supervision at such reasonable intervals as may be specified in the probation order or, subject thereto, as (he) may think fit; to see that he observes the conditions of his recognizance; to report to the court as to his behaviour; to advise, assist and befriend[187] him and, when necessary, to endeavour to find him suitable employment'.[188]

The most important government amendment was probably that which gave the Home Secretary power to make rules for carrying the Act into effect.[189] This was the only element of central control provided for in the Bill. There seems to have been no question at this stage of a government grant towards the service—and, therefore, no justifiable reason for giving the Home Secretary substantial controlling powers. But the power to make rules did vouchsafe to the Home Office some possibility of influencing the way in which the system was to develop.

The government were defeated on one issue in the Commons. Mr. Leif Jones's success in obtaining the deletion of the words allowing remuneration for the services of an agent of a voluntary society to be paid direct to the society,[190] suggests that there was a considerable body of members wary of the participation of the voluntary bodies in this new venture.

The one departure by the government from their policy of keeping the terms of the Bill as wide as possible was made at the Report Stage. They successfully introduced an amendment, providing that where circumstances permitted there should be appointed 'special probation officers, to be called children's probation officers, who shall, in the absence of any reasons to the contrary, be named in a probation order made in the case of an offender under the age of sixteen.'[191]

The inclusion of this clause was considered regrettable by Hugh R. P. Gamon, the young author of a contemporary study of the London Police Courts commissioned by the Toynbee Trustees. Writing 'An Appreciation and Criticism' of the Probation of Offenders Act, 1907, in the *Law Magazine and Law Review*, Gamon contended that the clause was incongruous with the general breadth of the Act. 'It is the tone of the clause that is at fault', he said; 'it purports to be directory, though the unfettered discretion of the magistrates, even on the much more vital question of the employment of policemen as probation officers, is the salient feature of the whole Act.'[192]

In the Lords, the government, in response to a request from the Howard Association, introduced a further amendment which gave courts the power to order an offender placed on probation to make restitution up to the limit of £10 for damages caused by his misdemeanour.

The Lords had even less to say about the Bill than the Commons. The Earl of Meath observed that the Bill could 'hardly be called a first-class measure in the ordinary sense of the term,' but 'there can be no doubt whatever that (it) will prevent crime and, to a large extent, empty our jails.'[193]

With this easy passage behind it, the Bill received the Royal Assent on the 21st August 1907.[194]

As Gamon observed in his contemporary criticism, the Act had a general breadth, it having been the government's policy to keep the terms of the measure as wide as possible. Many years later Samuel claimed that he had always held the view that the administrator of tomorrow is more likely to know what powers were needed to fit prevailing conditions than the legislator of today.[195] It is clear that neither the administrators at the Home Office, nor the legislators of the day, had very much idea what arrangements were required for the successful operation of the system in the years immediately following its inception. Their measure was dependent for its success on the co-operation of the magistrates, but they were ignorant as to the reception which would be given to the new system by those in the provinces. At the time there was no group such as the Magistrates' Association which might have been brought into consultation, and the views of the professional magistracy in the Metropolitan Police Courts could not necessarily be taken as representative of those of the lay magistrates in the rest of the country. They also assumed that the work of supervision could adequately be performed on a part-time basis by people without specific training.

Nevertheless the Liberal government must be credited with bringing to a constructive conclusion a long period of discussion about the merits, and suitability to the British situation, of a probation system of the kind introduced as many as thirty-eight years earlier in Massachusetts; and with allowing plenty of room for experiment in the early stages of its application.

Against a background of concern about the level of crime, dissatisfaction with existing penal measures, and a shift in penal policy towards dealing with crime through the 'rehabilitation' of offenders, the persistence of pressure groups and individuals and of the Prison Commissioners had stimulated interest and discussion and built up a fund of information within the Home Office. The catalyst was provided by the advent of a new administration in which the Home Secretary had a particular interest in the application of the principle of reformation and in schemes for

31

dealing with young offenders, and the complementary resourcefulness of the permanent officials in bringing forward the necessary papers.

CHAPTER TWO

EARLY DAYS
AND FIRST ASSESSMENT

The Home Office had deliberately arranged that the Act should not come into operation until the 1st January 1908.[1] 'If the Act comes into force before arrangements have been made', Troup had minuted, 'things will go wrong and discredit will fall on (it).'[2] The summary courts needed time to appoint their probation officers; the local authorities to sanction their remuneration.

The Home Secretary himself had to make these arrangements for the Metropolitan Police Court District, since he was the authority empowered to appoint and pay the clerks to the justices in the Metropolitan Police Courts.[3] This was a provision which was to be of considerable importance in the development of the probation service. The Home Office gained first-hand experience of the problems involved in administering the service at the local level. It was also able to use London as an experimental area and to make recommendations to the provincial courts with a confidence rooted, not only in authority, but in experience.

In addition to making arrangements for the introduction of the system in London, the Home Secretary had to consider what rules he should issue under the Act, and whether he should give any additional guidance to the courts to see that the new system got off to a good start. To advise him on these various steps he appointed a small domestic committee composed of Samuel, Fenwick, the Chief Metropolitan Magistrate, Troup, the Permanent Under-Secretary, and two or three other Home Office officials.[4]

Troup anticipated 'a good many difficulties' in making probation officer appointments. There were considerable differences of opinion as to the proper persons for the job, though it seems to have been generally accepted that the choice, if one was to be made, lay between the police—or police pensioners—the police court missionaries, and other persons unattached to any particular organisation but interested in social work.

The chief exponent of the case for the employment of police officers was Sir Evelyn Ruggles-Brise, Chairman of the Prison

Commissioners. He still considered that probation officers should in all cases be drawn from the ranks of the police force and that, if missionaries and others were to be used at all, it should only be in an assistant capacity.

Ruggles-Brise's attitude was understandable. His interest in the probation system stemmed chiefly from a desire to reduce the number of persons committed to prison. The imprisonment of children being by that time unusual, he was very concerned that probation should be used for adult offenders. Yet it seemed to him that most of the vociferous advocates of the new system had a very particular interest in the welfare of children. He probably felt the need to counter the opinions of these persons and organisations. His anxiety was expressed in a letter to the Home Secretary:

> There is a great confusion in the mind of many people who write articles on the subject of probation (many of them benevolent ladies). They seem to think that probation is merely a device for rescuing children of tender age—this appeals to their pity. But, 'probation' in the real sense is a State Scheme for furnishing an alternative to commitment to prison, with all that that implies, of that vast multitude of offenders who commit trivial and unimportant offences . . .
> This great work is for the State, and not for that large class of philanthropists . . . who can state the want of a system of probation glibly enough in the Press but have never, as far as my reading goes, suggested a system which shall be effective for the purpose above stated. I do not mean that a system of probation shall exclude all juvenile offenders. My only desire is that the comparatively easy task of providing for the care of juvenile offenders shall not jeopardize the whole system, which might be made one, I am convinced, of incalculable benefit to the State.'[5]

Whilst not wishing to deny to others the opportunity of using policemen as probation officers, the Home Office had never itself supported the idea. What is more, the Commissioner of the Metropolitan Police had made it clear on more than one occasion that he opposed such an arrangement. 'The disadvantages of placing probationers . . . and especially juvenile offenders, under police supervision' seemed to him 'to be obvious and to militate against the success of the experiment.'[6]

The philanthropists to whom Ruggles-Brise referred were as firmly against the employment of policemen in probation work as he was in its favour, and there was considerable opposition from other quarters also. Courtney Lord, Chairman of the pioneer Children's Courts in Birmingham, when consulted by the Home Office about their Probation Bill in 1906, took the opportunity to express his views about the use of police officers. Whilst prepared to acknowledge that supervision by carefully selected policemen would probably prove successful for adult probationers, visits from the police to child offenders might, he thought, cause the latter to be looked upon as criminals. He was most anxious to see this avoided.[7] Charles Russell, known for his youth work in Manchester and his interest in young delinquents, also told the Home Secretary, 'No average boy could be brought to consider the man in blue his personal friend, and unless the probation officer looks after his charge in the light of a friend, he will . . . achieve very little.'[8]

The two bodies whose interest in probation arose out of their wider interest in the welfare of children—the State Children's Association and the Committee on Wage-earning Children—were both opposed to the appointment of policemen as probation officers. Indeed, the State Children's Association urged the Home Secretary to avoid making any arrangements which would appear to identify the new system with any existing bodies dealing with offenders—such as the police, the police court missionaries or the school attendance officers—or with organisations like the Church and Salvation Armies already associated in the public mind with attempts to reclaim the degraded.[9]

These various reformers hoped that the Home Secretary would encourage the appointment as probation officers of well-educated individuals, of good social standing and with an interest in social work. Charles Russell and L. M. Rigby, for example, advocated the use of 'independent gentlemen, with leisure at their disposal'.[10]

'These gentlemen', Russell told the Home Secretary,

> are usually persons rendering whatever service they can to
> the community entirely voluntarily and are not, in any way, the
> servants of any philanthropic agencies that exist, and for this
> reason are peculiarly fitted for the work of probation officers
> as they have not primarily to consider the particular views of
> any particular society.[11]

In *The London Police Court Today and Tomorrow*, the report of a study commissioned by the Toynbee Trustees, Hugh Gamon advocated that probation officers should be 'better educated than the missionary . . . have the salary and prospects, at least, of a clergyman and his social rank.' Eminently suitable for the work in his view were the kind of persons then employed as secretaries to the branches of the Charity Organisation Society.[12]

There was also to be considered the claim of the Church of England Temperance Society for the appointment of their missionaries as probation officers. The Society's offer represented a considerable resource—more than a hundred workers already familiar with the courts—and the possibility of administrative and financial backing. The police court aspect of the Society's work appears to have been able to attract financial and other support from people outside the Anglican and the Temperance movements who had no particular interest in the primary prevention of intemperance which was the main aim of the Society.[13] In the 1890s the missionaries had consolidated their position and the magistrates of some of the London courts had made use of their services in a variety of ways, among them the making of enquiries during remand, supervision of young and elderly people after binding over and discharge, the finding of work for offenders, and not only in cases involving intemperance[14] (although at that time these would have been a greater proportion of all cases than is the situation today). It was usual for a magistrate to pay public tribute to the work of the Society's agents at its various annual meetings. At one such in 1894, R. O. B. Lane, Magistrate at the North London Police Court, said of the missionary's work:

> . . . the distinction and the note of such a work as this is that it has to be done by the individual and with the individual; that no case can be treated as one of a great class, but must be treated by itself, and for a reason that is obvious. When once people have fallen into crime . . . their moral courage has fallen to a low ebb, their hope has fallen to a low ebb, and their outlook must necessarily be gloomy, and dark, and weak. Now the police court missionary is the person who comes to deal with them when they are in that state of feeling. He meets them as they step out of the dock, takes them to his home, and follows them into their homes; he provides assistance for them, brings to bear upon them all that amount of sympathy without which it would be impossible to carry on this work; binds up the broken reed; he teaches them to look with the eye of hope for the future, and when he has found them a new life to start in, and a safe work to do, he does not leave them there; he still keeps in touch with them—still follows them to watch, to counsel, to see there is no relapse.

The work required 'the consecration of a lifetime' and 'agents who by sympathy, by discrimination of human nature and character, are specially fitted for the task.'[15]

Although the Society had a vigilant sub-committee charged with watching legislation and active as a pressure group whenever a subject related to the drink question was mooted or discussed in Parliamentary circles, it at no time took note of or considered any of the proposals put forward by the reforming bodies, or by Howard Vincent, which it might have recognised as a possible way of strengthening the position of the missionaries in the police courts.[16] However, in April 1906, before the Liberal Government's Probation of Offenders Bill was published, the Secretary of the Society reported to the Executive Committee that it had been represented to him that 'there was movement on foot for the appointment by the Government of certain officers, for dealing with cases of adult offenders,' and that the work would probably be given into the hands of a philanthropic society. The London Diocesan Branch was intending to approach the Home Secretary to offer the services of its Mission for this work.

As a result of this intimation it was resolved to appoint a deputation 'to wait upon the Home Secretary to offer the services of the whole Society in carrying out the work of the proposed probation officers.'[17] The following month the deputation was received by Samuel at the Home Office. They expressed their Society's willingness to fall in with any arrangements that might be made about court probation officers and pointed out that the Society, being a ready-made organisation and having well over a hundred agents already familiar with police court work, could easily provide probation officers, and indeed find voluntary workers to give assistance. They had a hundred and nine missionaries employed in the work, and in addition sixteen lady missionaries. Although its management was in the hands of the Temperance Society the police court work was, they claimed, 'absolutely unsectarian'.

Samuel replied that he had been impressed when he came to the Home Office to hear the high expressions of approval of the work done by the missionaries. He thanked the deputation for their offer, said it would be a misfortune if any system was set up in such a form as to exclude the services of their missionaries from the magistrates, and referred to a proposal that there should be a list of people of various kinds from which the magistrate would be able to select a suitable officer for a particular case.[18] Having made their offer the Society then had to await events.

Whilst the missionaries were not without their advocates in official quarters, the claim that they were eminently suitable for the work had been, and continued to be, challenged from various sources. A contemporary picture of the London missionary and his interests was drawn by Hugh Gamon who was amongst those who saw considerable drawbacks in his appointment as a probation officer. 'The C.E.T.S. missionary', he wrote,

> is the paid servant of some one of the local branches affiliated to the parent body . . . He is not in orders, but he affects not infrequently a semi-clerical costume. . . . He is liable to be called upon by his branch to be a propagandist, to aid in the general work of the society by delivering lectures and addresses on temperance and his special experiences, which form an inexhaustible fund of anecdote and terrible warnings.
> But his proper sphere is the police court to which he is assigned, and there he does the great body of his work. He has a special commission to work in the cause of temperance; the number of pledges that he has secured figures prominently in his reports. He has plenty of opportunity for producing his pledge book, but he has also a general commission of philanthropy and social enterprise and his reports speak of visits received and paid, persons met at prisons, situations found, men, women and children sent to homes, restored to friends, letters written and the like.[19]

In the course of his study of the police courts Gamon had found the missionary self-educated 'at best'; a disadvantage, he thought, in his contacts with the magistrates and the police. His association with the temperance movement and with denominational societies was likely to hamper further his effectiveness as a probation officer:

> Temperance is the primary object of his society and the society chooses its instruments in conformity with its ideas. But a [probation officer] of the highest type must possess qualities that a temperance advocate can afford to lack. What wonder then, that sometimes the police court missionary is well-intentioned but narrow-minded, zealous but inclined to preach. . . . As agents of a denominational society they are tainted with the sectarian brush.[20]

This writer also advanced the argument put earlier to the Home Office by Fenwick, the Chief Metropolitan Magistrate. The missionaries owed allegiance to bodies outside the courts. Their employing societies paid them and could dismiss them. Gamon doubted whether the magistrates could be completely at ease in employing 'another's henchman'. The missionary probation officer might also find himself in a difficult situation if he could not feel

38

certain of his society's approval when he sank all other considerations in an attempt to deal with his probationers in an enlightened way.[21] He knew of one court where the magistrates and the society disputed over the agent's body and where the magistrates had now raised the missionary's salary and could command his whole services without question.[22] Here the young lawyer certainly anticipated problems which were later to arise in connection with the system of dual control.

There was some opposition to the missionaries on the ground that they were fully occupied with existing duties. The Liverpool Stipendiary Magistrate, W. J. Stewart, who was consulted about their Bill by the Home Office, was an appreciative user of the services of the missionaries in his own court. But in his opinion it would be 'almost impossible for them to exercise the systematic supervision of probationers' in Liverpool. They were too few and already had many calls upon their time.[23] Another of the same mind was Thomas Holmes, recently appointed secretary of the Howard Association. Holmes had himself served as a police court missionary in the London courts for twenty years and told Mr. Gladstone during a visit to the Home Office that a missionary's duties were too heavy to allow him sufficient time to perform the additional work which would be involved in supervising probationers.[24]

Criticism on yet other grounds came from Russell and Rigby who doubted the wisdom of employing as probation officers the agents of a religious body, who would be 'under a certain obligation to promote its cause', and might be suspected by the probationers of trying to 'get at' them for religious purposes.[25]

In the face of all these pressures and possibilities the Home Office had deliberately avoided any attempt to pre-judge this issue as their Bill passed through Parliament. And now, when the time had come for actual appointments to be made, this small committee recommended for the Metropolitan Police Court District a policy of diversity.

The success of the system would depend, they thought, upon the selection of an appropriate officer for each particular case. It was therefore proposed that each Metropolitan Magistrate should be provided with a list for his court of officially appointed probation officers of different types and backgrounds, with a note as to the kind of case each was prepared to take.[26] They had already consulted with various individuals and interest groups—denominational bodies and voluntary societies—including those which, like the Church of England Temperance Society, were already engaged in

39

missionary work in the courts.

The Home Office Committee expressed themselves satisfied that the missionaries were well suited for the work. 'They are in constant attendance at the courts, have had much experience and are in touch with other philanthropic societies, with whom they work harmoniously,' ran their report. They recommended that the Society's agents should certainly be appointed probation officers in the London courts. The Society was eager to assist. Indeed they were prepared to forgo payment for their agents' probation work.

Three other religious bodies—the Church Army, the Federation of Local Free Church Councils and the Roman Catholic Westminster Education Fund—were prepared to nominate persons for appointment as probation officers. So too were the National British Women's Temperance Association and the Reformatory and Refuge Union.

In spite of their recommendation in favour of diversity, the appointment of policemen or ex-policemen was not considered by this committee. The Commissioner of the Metropolitan Police had, of course, never favoured the idea, and the Home Office, whilst unwilling actively to stifle the discretion of other appointing authorities in this matter, never seem to have been persuaded of its soundness.

An offer to provide probation officers was received from the Royal Society for the Assistance of Discharged Prisoners. This was declined, Samuel and his advisers fearing that suspicion would fall upon probationers supervised by agents of a society already dealing with ex-prisoners. Nor, after some deliberation, were they disposed to recommend the appointment as probation officers of the Industrial School Officers of the London County Council, whom they understood to be already fully occupied with their existing duties.

Reasonably sure that they could arrange through the various agencies for sufficient officers to supervise adult offenders, the Committee was less satisfied that they could guarantee the availability of persons suitable to take children's cases. The Act had not, of course, made mandatory the appointment of special children's officers, but these were to be employed 'where circumstances permit'.[27] As the appointing authority in a densely populated area, the Home Secretary could hardly omit to make such appointments.

Among those consulted by the Committee were two women active in social reform movements of the day. Mrs. Humphrey Ward, novelist and pioneer of the play centre movement, agreed to

40

recommend two or three of the Superintendents of her Play Centres as officers for children of school age. And Miss Adler, Secretary of the Committee on Wage Earning Children, suggested that they might try to enlist the help of some of the people 'connected with the Social Settlement in the East End'. In their report to the Home Secretary, the Committee consequently recommended that two or three experimental appointments of Children's Probation Officers should be made. 'Ladies and gentlemen fitted for this work could probably,' they indicated, 'be found at the University Settlements.'[28]

As well as making recommendations about the appointment of probation officers, the Committee drafted the first Probation Rules to be issued under the Act, and suggested that a Memorandum should be issued to all the authorities concerned to acquaint them with the existence of the Act and give some guidance as to its use.[29]

All the Committee's recommendations were accepted by the Home Secretary. In the Metropolitan Police Court District each Magistrate was supplied with a list of probation officers appointed for his courts. From this he could select as he liked; on the other hand he was quite free to place an offender under the supervision of a person not so appointed.

Almost all the officially appointed officers in London were agents of voluntary societies, the majority of them being the police court missionaries working for the C.E.T.S.[30] It was convenient that they were already in full-time employment with organisations prepared to allow them to take probation cases, for those on the lists were expected by the Home Office to regard their probation work as part-time only and to supplement their earnings from some other source.[31]

They were to be paid a fee and expenses for each case undertaken. It was thought impracticable to pay salaries at this stage because of the difficulty of estimating the extent to which the magistrates would espouse the new method.[32] Whilst the fee method certainly ensured that money was not expended if officers were not used, the Home Secretary's decision to adopt it in the Metropolitan Police Court District later proved to have been short-sighted.[33]

The scale of fees was acknowledged to be low, but the Receiver for the Metropolitan Police Court District, who had charge of the funds out of which the officers were to be paid, had pressed the Home Office to keep them as low as possible. He was anxious, he said, to spend as little as possible, as receipts from fines, which formed the basis of his fund, had fallen considerably in the previous year. What was more, he submitted, if the initial payments proved unsatisfactory, it would be easier to raise than to lower them.[34]

An exception from the method of payment by fee was made in the case of two special children's officers appointed in accordance with the committee's advice. Miss Ivimy and Miss Croker-King were paid a part-time salary worked out on similar assumptions to those used for the scale of fees (and therefore low), and were expected to give one-third of normal working hours to probation work.[35] They appear to have had independent means. Miss Ivimy was recommended to the Home Secretary as 'a lady who had much experience of work among the poor'.[36] She was said to have given up 'a lucrative position' to devote her energies to probation work.

The choice of officer and any supervision of probation work was left to the magistrate responsible for making the order. In a conversation with the Home Secretary, Canon Barnett of Toynbee Hall had suggested the appointment of Superintendent Probation Officers. The Canon feared that magistrates might fail to give sufficient attention to the choice of officer for each case. A Superintendent with a good knowledge of the various officers under him would be able to advise the magistrate on this point; and could also be used as an inspector of the work done.[37]

It was a proposal upon which the Home Office had an open mind. The Chief Metropolitan Magistrate was told that if he or any of his colleagues wished to experiment with such an arrangement, the Home Office were willing to make an appointment. However, the Chief Magistrate thought it best to begin on the simplest of lines and to leave this question to be reconsidered in the light of further experience.[38]

The Act empowered the Home Secretary to make rules for carrying the legislation into effect, and 'in particular for prescribing such matters incidental to the appointment, resignation and removal of probation officers, and the performance of their duties, and the reports to be made by them, as may appear necessary.'[39]

In accordance with this power and on the advice of the Committee, the Home Secretary issued the first Probation Rules, brief in comparison with later issues. They provided that the justices of each Petty Sessional Division were to meet in January of each year to make probation appointments, which were not to be for more than one year in the first instance.[40] As a result, it became the practice to appoint probation officers from year to year, the resultant insecurity being greatly resented by the officers. It was the first grievance which they succeeded in having righted when later they formed an organisation of their own.

The duties of the probation officer outlined in the Act were stated in more detail in the Rules. He was to be familiar with the Act and the Rules and to see that the probationer clearly understood the conditions of the probation order. Emphasis was laid upon the visiting of probationers by the officer rather than on a system of reporting by the offender. Weekly visits were to be made for the first month, after which their frequency would depend 'on the conduct and mode of life of the offender'. In the case of school children, the officer was also to visit the school. The use of a police court or police station as a centre where probationers reported to their officers was forbidden by the Rules which, in similar spirit, specified that probation officers were not to wear uniform.[41]

The probation officer was to report 'as to the conduct and mode of life of the offender and his observance of the conditions of his recognizance' as directed by the court making the order, and he was to bring to the notice of that court any failure by the probationer to observe the conditions of the order.

Rules for annual returns to be made by each probation officer to his Justices' Clerk, and by the Clerk to the Home Office, made possible the compilation of rudimentary national statistics relating to the new system. These were to give particulars of persons placed under his care, of the duration and conditions of their probation orders, of their conduct and progress in school or work, and of 'the result' of their probation—whether it had been 'satisfactorily completed', extended for a further period, or terminated because of failure to observe the conditions laid down.[42]

The Rules carried the force of law. A Memorandum on the Act,[43] which was sent to Justices on the advice of the Committee, was a purely advisory document. The considerations involved in a Home Office decision to issue a circular of advice to magistrates have since been discussed by Sir Alexander Maxwell, Permanent Under-Secretary of State. According to Maxwell, the question has to be asked whether the subject is one on which the Home Secretary, by reason of his position as central authority, is in a better position to form a judgment than magistrates. Care must be taken not to interfere with independent judicial discretion. If these principles are borne in mind, it is quite proper for the Home Secretary to bring to the notice of the courts general information and general considerations which they should have in mind when dealing with offenders of various types.[44]

Gladstone's Memorandum of 1908 was formulated along these lines. It made clear to the courts that the Act provided a new alternative to imprisonment: one which afforded greater security than the use of Vincent's Act. The new system and its method of operation were explained in some detail, and it was pointed out that

43

much would depend on the character and qualifications of persons appointed as probation officers. Here the Home Office first made use of its special position with regard to London to point an example to other areas. In London, the magistrates were told, the Home Secretary expected to be able to

> obtain the services of a sufficient number of persons who have
> already had a considerable experience of the kind of work that
> will fall on the probation officers, and whose qualifications have
> been already tested by the services they have rendered to
> various philanthropic societies.

He trusted that justices in other parts of the country would be able similarly to avail themselves of 'the officers of voluntary agencies engaged in assisting the necessitous, repressing mendicancy or reclaiming criminals and in the case of children, of these agencies which are devoted to promoting the welfare of children.' The influence which could be exerted by such persons was likely, on the whole, he thought, to be stronger than any which could be exerted by 'persons officially connected with the police'.

The Home Office had been persuaded by Miss Adler, to whom the draft Memorandum had been shown, to give it as the Minister's opinion that female officers should be appointed for boys and girls of school age and for female probationers over sixteen; to hope that 'rarely, if ever' would it be necessary to place children under the supervision of police constables; and to indicate that in all cases, probation officers should be 'persons of good education ... having some knowledge of the industrial and social conditions of the locality'.[45] As a guide to provincial courts, the Home Secretary outlined the method of payment and the scale of fees he intended to use in London. The adoption of the fee system and a similar rate of pay by many of the provincial courts interested enough to appoint probation officers can no doubt be attributed to this Memorandum. Unfortunately it later proved more difficult for the Home Secretary to persuade some local authorities to abandon the method or to increase the rate. It is clear from the Memorandum that the Home Office hoped to keep down the cost of the new service, not only by paying poorly, but by making use of honorary officers, both in London and the provinces.

The Home Office realised from the beginning that the interest and co-operation of the magistrates was vital to the successful operation of the system. They were told that Mr. Gladstone was of opinion that much good might result from the new Act, 'if the justices on whom the responsibility for carrying it into effect will

most rest, will give the matter their serious and careful attention.'
The qualification was significant. The making of probation orders
rested entirely with the individual courts and the appointment of
probation officers was permissive not mandatory, again depending
upon the interest of local benches. Where it was decided to make an
appointment, the choice of officer was theirs entirely. Apathy and
misunderstanding on their part could be disastrous.

On the 1st January, 1908, the experiment began.

The Home Secretary had made his arrangements for London
and could assess their effectiveness at close quarters. Only from
hearsay, and from the correspondence of such authorities as
troubled to communicate with him on the subject, could he gauge the
extent to which officers were being appointed and probation orders
made in the rest of the country.

Hopes that the Act would be quickly and uniformly brought into
operation[46] were not in fact realised. In many petty sessional
divisions the justices made no move to appoint an officer. In a good
number probation was never tried.[47] Many indeed appear to have
ignored both Act and Memorandum. The justices of Launceston did
at least write to ask whether the appointment of a probation officer
was compulsory, thus providing the Home Secretary with the
opportunity to encourage where he could not command. Whilst
acknowledging that there might be initial difficulties in finding a
suitable person for the post, he hoped that they would 'make every
effort to carry out the intention of the legislature in this Act'.[48]

Where police court missionaries were available, the courts
appear to have given them the appointments, probably following the
guidance given by the Minister in his Memorandum which happily
concorded with the easiest course available. In December 1907, the
C.E.T.S. reported that almost all the one hundred and twenty agents
of their Diocesan Branches had been appointed probation officers in
preparation for the coming into force of the Act.[49] The case of the
Liverpool Justices was possibly typical. 'We considered very
carefully', their Clerk recounted, 'how we should make use of (the
new Act), and ... came to the conclusion that we had better make
use of the existing police court missionaries. The missionaries were
already there,' he explained, 'being sent by four societies, the
C.E.T.S., the Catholic Aid Society, the Wesleyan Mission and the
Liverpool Ladies Temperance Association'.[50]

The Liverpool bench appointed the Chief Constable as a
probation officer, as well as the missionaries. They were quite at
liberty to do this. It is clear, however, that the Home Office did not
regard with equanimity the appointment of policemen, even for adult

cases. When the Beverley magistrates, for instance, wrote to ask the Home Secretary to approve the appointment of the Borough's Chief Constable as their probation officer, he replied that, whilst the matter rested entirely with them, in no way requiring his approval, he would ask them to bear in mind 'the desirability on general grounds of appointing as probation officers persons who are not officially connected with the police'.[51]

A novel arrangement was made by the five justices of Wenlock who appointed themselves probation officers. Entirely legal, the appointments, when brought to the notice of the Home Office, were allowed to stand on the assumption that the magistrates did not intend to claim any remuneration for their probation work.[52]

A number of other queries were raised, as was to be expected. The Salvation Army had to be assured that their agents might wear their uniforms whilst doing probation work.[53] (The Rule stated that uniforms should not be worn but this referred to those which might denote that the wearers were probation officers.) A group of justices who appointed the agent of a branch of the National Society for the Prevention of Cruelty to Children also asked about this and were told that, whilst it was a matter for their own discretion, the Home Secretary did think that 'visiting the homes of children in the uniform of the N.S.P.C.C. may not be altogether conducive to the friendly influence which it is hoped that probation officers may be able to exert.'[54]

It had to be made clear that the out-of-pocket expenses provided for in the Act were not intended to cover the cost of material aid given to probationers, which the Home Secretary said he could not regard as a necessary part of a probation officer's duty. The Sheffield City Justices had written to point out that it was sometimes necessary for the probation officer, in his work of assisting and befriending a probationer or helping him to find employment, to provide him with food and clothing.[55] The Home Office also made it known that they considered undesirable the use of probation officers as collectors of fines imposed on offenders by the courts.[56]

A more serious difficulty was raised in April 1908, when the Harrogate Borough Justices told the Home Office that the Town Council had refused to sanction the payment on the scales suggested in the Memorandum on the Act of the member of the Church Army they had chosen as probation officer. The Act provided that the final decision on the rate of remuneration of probation officers should rest with the authority having control of the fund out of which the salary of the clerk to the justices was paid. In boroughs this was the Town Council; in county divisions, the Standing Joint Committee, composed of members of the county council and representatives of the justices.[57] In neither case, therefore, was the paying authority identical with the bench which was the appointing body.

The Town Clerk suggested that the justices should appoint an honorary probation officer rather than one who they would have to pay. The justices saw no adequate reason for doing so, and both sides being adamant, matters, in the words of the Justices' Clerk, had 'reached a deadlock'. Since the Act made no provision for resolving such a dispute, the Home Secretary could only advise the magistrates to look for an honorary officer and to renew their application to the Town Council if their search proved unsuccessful.[58]

A similar reluctance to finance the new system was shown by a number of other local authorities. It was understandable, and the argument used by the local authorities has been advanced on other occasions in parallel circumstances. The new service for which they were now asked to pay had as part of its objectives the substantial reduction of prison sentences. The central government could be expected to benefit by a fall in the cost of the prison service. Should they not, therefore, make some contribution towards the cost of probation, rather than transferring the burden to the local authorities?

This point was taken up by the Penal Reform League who suggested an Exchequer grant towards probation. But, whilst the substance of the argument was acknowledged at the Home Office, Treasury agreement to any such proposal was considered remote in view of the 'present condition of the Exchequer'.[59]

The Penal Reform League had recently been formed to obtain and circulate information about criminals and their treatment, to promote a sound public opinion on the subject, and to help to bring about a more complete and effective co-operation between the public and public servants for the reclamation of criminals by a curative and educative system.[60]

The other societies which had campaigned for the introduction of a probation system retained probation among other interests such as the improvement of the juvenile court system brought in by the Children Act, 1908. The Howard Association, the State Children's Association, the Committee on Wage Earning Children, together with the Penal Reform League, and a number of specially interested individuals (who were often members of one or more society) were keen observers in those early months and were soon communicating their anxieties and suggestions to Whitehall. The Penal Reform League and the Committee on Wage Earning Children both sought information about the working of the Act by the questionnaire method.[61]

All were disappointed that magistrates were not making more use of the new alternative. Courtney Lord, the Birmingham pioneer of juvenile courts, and the Penal Reform League[62] wrote of the unfortunate apathy with which many magistrates appeared to regard the innovation. The State Children's Association claimed that they had received information from many quarters, 'that a large number of magistrates (were) in complete ignorance of the possibilities of the Act'.[63]

The problem of stimulating the imagination of the justices in regard to probation was alluded to by Miss Lucy Bartlett in a personal letter to the Home Secretary. Miss Bartlett, a leading member of the Penal Reform League[64] and, according to Ruggles-Brise, a lady 'of great intelligence and with a deep enthusiasm (for) this work', was even more concerned, however, with the need for magistrates to learn how to use probation with discrimination. 'The first half of the work lies with them, as the second half lies with the probation officer' she told the Minister; 'The right choice of cases in the first place is as important an element in probation as the right supervision of them afterwards.'[65]

These observers also found much to criticise in the choice of probation officers made by many courts. The Howard Association and the Committee on Wage-Earning Children began to draw attention to the need for using 'trained' personnel. The former feared that 'the wholesale appointment of volunteers, regardless of training or capacity' would jeopardise the system's chances of success;[66] and the latter asked the Home Secretary to call the attention of the magistrates to the importance of appointing trained social workers as probation officers.[67]

The two organisations expressly concerned with the welfare of children considered many of the officers who had been chosen to deal with young offenders far from suitable for the task. The State Children's Association criticised in particular the appointment of police court missionaries who, they alleged, were too busy to be able to undertake 'the detailed and continuous enquiry and oversight absolutely necessary to the success of child probation'. The missionaries had rarely, the Association said, had any training in the orderly keeping of records; and moreover, their long experience of adult 'failures' was likely to have produced in them a mental attitude, which would be a positive disadvantage in an officer dealing with young delinquents.[68] The Penal Reform League, too, suggested to the Minister that in many cases probation work was suffering in quality by being combined with the other duties expected of police court missionaries.[69]

In the opinion of the State Children's Association, courts had appointed the missionaries because they could obtain their services cheaply.[70] All these critics stressed the need to pay more generously for the work so as to be able to recruit suitable people.[71]

Not only were these bodies dissatisfied with the quality of the probation officers; they also complained of a lack of organisation of their work and suggested the creation of a supervisory grade—chief probation officers who would be responsible for organising and overlooking the work of any other officers and voluntary helpers. Such an arrangement, it was contended, would go far towards ensuring a high standard of work. It would also enable the most economical use to be made of the available effort.[72]

The Chief Metropolitan Magistrate had declined to experiment on these lines in London in the first few months of the Act. In August 1908, at the Home Secretary's request, he and his colleagues reconsidered a proposal to appoint superintendent officers in the Metropolitan Police Court District. Although admitting that they themselves had so far no means of knowing whether their individual probation officers had more cases than they could effectively manage, they decided against the appointment of superintendents on the ground that only two or three courts could be covered by any one superintendent because of the considerable distance between them.[73]

It is unusual for an official Committee of Enquiry to be set up only a year after the introduction of a new system. However it had all along been Gladstone's intention to review the arrangements after one year's operation so that any defects could be remedied in the early stages.[74]

By the end of February he expected the statutory returns from the courts under the Probation Rules. This would give, among other information, the number of cases put on probation by each court during the first year. A Departmental Committee on the Probation of Offenders Act, 1907, was accordingly appointed in March 1909, 'to enquire whether full advantage has been taken during the past year of the powers conferred by the Probation of Offenders Act, 1907, and, if not, what are the difficulties which have stood in the way of their more general use.' In the case of the Metropolitan Police Courts, where the appointment of probation officers rested with the Home Secretary, the Committee was also to advise whether existing arrangements for their appointment and remuneration were satisfactory, and 'whether any steps should be taken to secure the better organisation of their work, and their more frequent employment in suitable cases'.[75]

It was decided that a small committee could suitably make the review; and that in fact the one which had made the arrangements for the Metropolitan Police Courts could well be revived to form a nucleus. Samuel was again in the Chair and Troup, Permanent Under-Secretary, preserved the continuity, along with another Home Office official, who served as Secretary. Fenwick, the Chief Magistrate, having retired, his successor John Dickenson replaced him on the Committee. It was decided to add to the original membership the Earl of Lytton, Chairman of the State Children's Association, and R. D. B. Acland, K.C., Recorder of Oxford and Vice-Chairman of Berkshire Quarter Sessions.[76]

Having heard the evidence of twenty-nine witnesses—'rather a small number . . . for the purpose of such an enquiry', in the opinion of a contemporary commentator—the Committee reported in December 1909. In its opinion the system had already proved of value in many cases. It promised, indeed, to become 'a most useful factor in our penal law'. During its first year of operation 8,023 persons had been placed on probation, one-ninth of all those brought before the summary courts for indictable offences.

There was however very great variation in the extent to which it was being used by courts in different areas,[77] and this being the case, it was part of the Committee's task to ascertain what had prevented its use in some places. Witnesses provided a variety of explanations in the course of the Enquiry. One of these concerned the conditions which the Act allowed courts to attach to a probation order. Some magistrates who had been accustomed to binding over offenders under the Summary Jurisdiction Act, 1897, with whatever conditions they thought fit, had found the possibilities in the new Act too limiting. They could not, for example, attach to a probation order a condition that the probationer should reside for a period in an institution. So there had been a tendency to use the old rather than the new method, the magistrate sometimes placing the offender at the same time under the informal supervision of a missionary.

Appreciating this cause of dissatisfaction and agreeing that wider powers to make conditions would enhance the usefulness of the measure, the Committee recommended that the law should be amended to allow the inclusion of a condition of residence in a probation order.[78]

They saw less substance in three other explanations of the failure to make probation orders. The feeling existed, they were told, that the visits of a probation officer represented an unwarranted and certainly unwelcome intrusion into the private life of an offender; they were, therefore, unlikely to help bring about his reformation. Other evidence, the Committee reported, suggested that such fears were groundless.

Nor could they agree that there was any justification for the Act not being used merely because it imposed additional work on the magistrates' clerk, or because it added to the local rates. In their view the increased labour for the clerk and the increased cost were 'small in comparison with the immediate gain to the offender, and with the ultimate gain to the community'.[79]

Whilst agreeing that these difficulties accounted to some extent for the restricted use of the Act, the Committee thought magistrates' misapprehension about its scope or their ignorance of its existence, provided by far the most likely explanation. 'The title of the statute which is superseded—the Probation of First Offenders Act—and the fact that the probation system has been actively advocated by those who are specially interested in the treatment of juvenile offenders' had led to a widespread misapprehension that it applied only to first or young offenders.[80] The Committee attributed lack of knowledge of the Act to its novelty. 'Here and there', they reported, 'a justice of the peace may be found who is interested in its working, but many are still unfamiliar with its provisions, and the question of applying (it) is often not present in their minds.'

The new system was obviously not being given a trial in some areas, and the Committee recommended that the Home Secretary should attempt to increase its use by sending a separate communication to all justices of the peace, drawing attention to the provisions of the Probation of Offenders Act and suggesting their more frequent application.[81]

The Committee do not appear directly to have attributed the variation in the use of probation to the failure of the justices in many divisions to appoint a probation officer. Later Committees recognised that the use of the Act was heavily dependent upon the presence of a probation officer.[82] Nor did the Committee seem to consider that geographical or demographic factors, or even the organisation of the summary court system itself, might account for the failure of some courts to appoint officers and place offenders on probation. Justices in small towns and country areas dealt with a very small number of cases each year, and it was unlikely that they would show as much interest or see such relevance in the new system as those working in busy courts. The organisation of probation work may well have appeared more difficult to magistrates in courts serving rural areas and dealing with occasional offenders from remote villages. Many of them would not have had the benefit of advice about the provisions of new legislation such as would probably have been available to courts in large towns and cities, since they would have been served by part-time Clerks without the time or opportunity to keep abreast of such new developments.[83]

The Committee did regard the employment of at least one paid probation officer for each district as 'indispensable to the proper administration of justice', and the personality and efficiency of the officer as crucial to the success of the system. Some witnesses had testified to the unsuitability of some persons who had been given appointments. The appointment of police court missionaries was deprecated by the representative of the Penal Reform League, who claimed that they had not enough time to give to the work, and that they were not suitable persons to undertake the supervision of child probationers. Pressed by members of the Committee for an assessment of the work performed by missionaries in the London courts, he agreed that he would not like to say this had not been done satisfactorily; he insisted, however, that 'it might be done more satisfactorily'. His organisation wanted to see a least one properly salaried officer in each area, paid wholly out of public funds and able, therefore, to give undivided loyalty to the magistrates.[84] The Birmingham magistrate, H. C. Field, who said his own missionary had 'done very well', nevertheless wanted 'somebody appointed as a probation officer and nothing else'.[85]

Others, however, including the Metropolitan Magistrates Henry Curtis Bennett, John Rose, and John Dickinson, were obviously satisfied with the missionaries' work as probation officers. Mr. Rose's evidence provides another picture of the London missionary of the time:

> He is of the educated artisan class, a man of intelligence and a clear, cold mind, who investigates cases without sentiment, but thoroughly and efficiently. . . . He is altogether an excellent man for the post, because being of the artisan class, he knows what questions to put, he knows the sore places, and his judgement is good.'[86]

The representatives of the London and Southwark Branches of the C.E.T.S. told the Committee that in their opinion the missionary had a readier influence than the non-missionary officer. 'The missionary has a place in the public mind. . . . He is known to be a person who is essentially a friend.' In response to questions about the relationship between probation work and other missionary duties, they claimed that they had 'practically given our workers to the magistrates to use', and that it was understood that 'a man's police court work comes before anything else'.[87]

The Departmental Committee made no criticisms in its report of the type of person appointed, thus approving by implication the employment of the missionaries. They considered the courts fortunate to have obtained the services of such a large number of suitable people.[88] They were not however prepared to endorse wholeheartedly the employment of police officers, in spite of the evidence of the Clerk to the Justices of Liverpool where a branch of the Chief Constable's Department was still responsible for some probation work.[89] They adhered to the opinion, expressed by the Home Secretary in his Memorandum on the Act, that though the employment of policemen should not be prohibited, 'it should be very exceptional'.[90]

Appreciation was expressed of the voluntary probation work done by 'some young men who have had much experience of social work among working lads' and of the work of special children's probation officers.[91] The Committee found that only a very few courts outside London had appointed special officers for children. Their decision not to advise that such appointments should be made 'where circumstances permit', as the Act provided, probably had considerable effect on the subsequent organisation of probation work. In spite of the intention of the legislators in 1907, only in London and a few other areas did it become the custom to appoint separate officers for work with children.

The Report contains an account of some of the ways in which the Committee expected the probation officer to attempt to guide his charges 'out of the groove that leads to serious crimes'.

> He assists the man out of work to find employment. He puts the lad into touch with the managers of a boys' club. . . . He helps to improve the bad houses which are the breeding ground of child offenders. He persuades the careless to open accounts in the savings bank.[92]

The Committee warned against the danger of 'regarding the provision of relief in money or in kind as a chief element in the probation officer's duty'.[93] To influence the offender's character through the medium of his own personality was regarded from the first as the primary aim of the worker—an appreciation which was doubtless a considerable asset when the time came for a more conscious application of case-work method to probation work. The Committee disagreed with a proposal that probation officers should be used to collect fines, taking the view that the collection of fines was 'foreign to a probation officer's functions and likely to detract from his influence'.[94]

Consideration of the work done by probation officers under the Probation of Offenders Act—any other social work performed by them was not included in its terms of reference—led the Committee to conclude that the scale of fees in operation in London[95] was too low and unlikely to attract the type of person needed for the service.

It was realised that when the scales had been drawn up no account had been taken of the time that officers would sometimes spend making enquiries in cases where probation orders were never made. Whilst the Committee saw 'certain disadvantages' in the practice of making preliminary enquiries, they agreed that they might be useful especially in children's cases. They were certainly of the opinion that since probation officers had a duty to make these enquiries when requested, this should be taken into account when calculating their rate of pay. It was one of the factors which led the Committee to report that they considered it preferable to pay probation officers salaries rather than fees.[96]

Some witnesses who considered that probation work was badly organised advocated the appointment of chief probation officers, but the Committee rejected this proposal on the ground that in many districts the volume of work would not justify such an arrangement. They considered, moreover, that the appointment of a superintendent would weaken the responsibility of the probation officer and restrict the individuality of his approach. It was also possible that the introduction of another level in the hierarchy would mean that the magistrates would completely lose track of the progress of individual probationers.[97]

They allowed, however, that more supervision of the work of individual officers was desirable and were very anxious that the magistracy should take a greater personal interest in the operation of the probation system. In their opinion, 'there could be no greater encouragement to a probation officer and no more potent means of contributing to the success of the probation system than for the magistrates themselves to show . . . interest (in the work)'.

To these ends they suggested that in each Petty Sessional Division one or two magistrates should undertake informal oversight of probation work. The justices could also make a contribution by assisting in the formation of local committees to co-operate in probation work.[98] These two suggestions foreshadowed the later introduction of probation and case committees.

The Penal Reform League were dissatisfied with the organisation of the work at the national as well as the local level, and proposed that the duty of over-seeing the whole service should be placed in the hands of a semi-official Probation Commission such as existed in New York State. It would also be able to collect and disseminate information on probation matters, and arrange for the training of probation officers.[99]

Lucy Bartlett, the League's 'leader and instructor in these matters', thought a Commission composed of officials and people from various parts of the United Kingdom would ensure the co-operation of government and private citizen in redemptive work. The members of the Commission could use their semi-official position to make enquiries about and possibly influence probation in their own areas, and through personal contacts introduce others to an interest or participation in the work. 'It is an absurdity to think that one man in the Home Office can do all this.'[100] As Gordon Rose has pointed out, the League saw even at this stage that to establish probation as a profession of standing it was necessary to have a central body responsible for its promotion.[101]

They were unable to persuade the Committee, however, that the setting up of such a body would be a sufficiently helpful factor in the development of the service to warrant the necessary financial outlay. 'The expense of establishing such a commission would be quite disproportionate to the value of the work it would perform' they reported; but as a modest counter-proposal they suggested that it would be valuable to have one official at the Home Office specially charged to keep in touch with the development of probation work throughout the country. (This did not necessarily mean any change; by their own admission, an informal arrangement of this kind already existed at the Home Office.)[102]

Two useful practical steps which could be taken by the Home Office to improve the quality and organisation of the work were suggested in the Report. It could draft model forms for use in probation cases,[103] and it could issue and subsequently be responsible for revising a directory of all probation officers attached to courts in England and Wales.[104] A directory would facilitate the transfer of probationers who moved out of one Division into another. It would also be of great assistance to anyone who might wish to follow up the Committee's further recommendation for the improvement and maintenance of standards, 'that nothing would be so likely to provide the stimulus (needed to maintain the efficiency of probation work) as the formation of a society comprising and managed by the probation officers themselves'.[105]

A reviewer of the Report for the *Penal Reform League's Monthly Record* expressed disappointment that its recommendations were not more enterprising, although it did breathe 'an atmosphere of goodwill to this new system'.

It was not to be expected that a Committee of this composition would recommend far-reaching changes so shortly after the introduction of the system. It had been the intention of the Home Office that the inquiry should be primarily concerned with whether the 'provisional' arrangements made by them for the London area, intended to serve only for about a year, required alteration. An inquiry covering the whole country in equal depth would have taken too long to suit this purpose. It was in any case too soon to begin a large-scale inquiry, Troup had minuted. They would have to be very sure of their ground before they interfered with the very varied arrangements adopted in different districts, and he was therefore inclined to think that it would be best to 'set our own house in order first'.[106] This probably accounts partly for the fact that although it was seen as important that more interest and action should be taken by magistrates in some parts of the provinces, the Committee's only recommendation to this end was the despatch of an individually addressed circular. There would probably also have been a reluctance to suggest any action which might be interpreted as an attempt by the executive to put pressure on the judiciary.

Although there was some indication that cost was a contributory factor to the failure to use the system, the Committee does not appear to have considered the question of a government grant. The Penal Reform League had, early in 1909, suggested that this would assist the proper development of the system, which would in turn lessen the number of prisoners to be maintained at the government's expense. The force of this argument had been acknowledged in a Home Office minute but the observation was made that no authority existed for such a payment to be made and it was doubtful if Treasury agreement would be gained for such a proposal 'in the present condition of the Exchequer'. This had been seen by Samuel who obviously made no move to pursue the matter.[107]

Although some witnesses had criticised the policy of employing as probation officers the agents of voluntary societies, the Committee seemed satisfied not to recommend any change in this respect. The police court missions were the most obvious source of workers. Their missionaries were readily available in the heavily populated areas where the new system was probably most needed to reduce the number of custodial sentences. Even in the London courts the work was expected to be part-time, so that probation officers required to have some additional source of income such as was available to police court missionaries by virtue of their employment by the missions. The Committee did, however, connect level of payment with the recruitment of suitable probation officers and made a necessary contribution to the development of the service by reporting that the existing payments in London were too low to attract the type of person required.

CHAPTER THREE

A PERMISSIVE SERVICE

When the Departmental Committee on the Probation of Offenders Act reported in December 1909, the Liberals had been in office for four years. As Home Secretary, Gladstone had been able to put through an impressive programme of penal reform, in which he had taken a particular interest since his term as Under-Secretary of State at the Home Office in the 1880s and his subsequent Chairmanship of the Departmental Committee on Prisons. In addition to the Probation of Offenders Act, 1907, the government successfully introduced the Children Act, 1908, which dealt with the prevention of cruelty to and neglect of children and introduced mandatory separate courts for children, and the Prevention of Crime Act, 1908, which set the seal of government approval on the borstal system. According to Gladstone these were all part of 'a definite scheme for dealing with young offenders'.[1]

The introduction of separate courts for children, though these were rudimentary in the first instance, established the principle of difference on which further developments were built. As far as the probation system is concerned it is probable that the existence of children's courts had a beneficial influence on the rate of use, in that probation may have come more readily to mind in the new setting. Probation had also been closely linked with children's courts in the literature and speeches of the reformers, though how wide an impression these had made it is impossible to know. The making of social enquiries for which the probation officer was often employed certainly made more progress over the years in the juvenile than in the adult courts.

Only two months after the Committee on the Probation of Offenders Act, 1907, had reported, Winston Churchill succeeded Gladstone as Home Secretary in the Liberal administration. The new Minister was said to be much impressed with the benefits which could accrue, both to individual offenders and to the community, through a proper use of probation.[2] Within a comparatively short time of the publication of the Report, the Home Office acted upon those recommendations which it already had the power to implement.

The Committee had reported a very uneven use of probation up and down the country and had recommended that the Home Secretary should communicate with every justice, drawing attention to the Probation of Offenders Act and suggesting its more frequent application in suitable cases. It was not usual for the Home Office to send copies of circulars to individual justices.[3] Indeed, to do so was looked upon as no easy task by the administrators.[4] The Home Office decision to communicate directly with every magistrate about the use of this Act indicates its concern at the Committee's findings, and its recognition of the vital position occupied by the justices in the operation of the system.

Issued in April 1910, the circular made two points: a new method of treatment was available to magistrates under the 1907 Act—a method which could easily bring about a reduction in the number of short-term prison sentences; and the personal interest of the justices themselves in the work of the probation officer and in the progress of the probationer was very important to its success.

In an attempt to ensure that every justice would know something of the contents of the Committee's report, a selection of extracts was specially printed and enclosed with each circular. The Home Secretary hoped—and he could only hope—that each justice, in consultation with his colleagues, would 'be able to give effect to the recommendations of the Committee'.[5]

For its part, the Home Office complied with the Committee's suggestion that one official should be charged with the special oversight of probation work by giving this responsibility to J. F. Henderson who had been secretary to the Committee.[6] Henderson then set in motion the machinery for compiling a directory of probation officers which was published in 1911.[7]

There remained the Home Secretary's responsibilities as appointing and paying authority in the Metropolitan Police Court District. Although the Committee found little to criticise in the organisation of probation work in London—not surprisingly, for some of its members had been responsible for planning it—their assertion that the Home Office scales of pay for London probation officers were too low was unequivocal. Consequently, new rates were introduced in April 1910. Not only this; as a result of the Committee's Report, it was also decided largely to abandon the method of payment by fee in London and to make instead a fixed annual payment for the services of each probation officer.[8]

After two years' experience of the system, it was clear that the

Metropolitan Magistrates were making far more use of the missionaries of the Church of England Temperance Society for probation duties than of the agents of other societies or private individuals.[9] It was therefore arranged that fixed annual payments should be made to all C.E.T.S. missionaries as well as to the special children's officers appointed by the Home Office, and that the system of per capita fees, on a revised scale, should be retained for those who took an occasional case.[10]

The police court missionaries attached to the Southwark Diocesan Branch of the C.E.T.S., who served the Metropolitan Police Courts south of the Thames, had by this time begun to accept fees for their work. The London Branch, which worked north of the river, had continued to provide gratuitously the services of its agents, but now asked for payment.[11] Under the new arrangement, each male missionary received £40 a year, and each female £20, inclusive of expenses.[12] At this time the average salary for a male missionary employed by the London Branch was £157 a year, so that his earnings for probation work under the new system accounted for less than a quarter of his salary. Only one of the missionaries was employed full time on probation work.[13]

Some dissatisfaction was expressed in the Mission[14] when it became known that the new salary being paid to Miss Ivimy, one of the special children's officers—now employed in a full-time capacity—was £200 a year[15] which, even allowing for the additional hours to be worked, represented a substantial increase in salary. It happened that the Metropolitan Magistrates at the courts to which Miss Ivimy was assigned had been slower than some of their colleagues to try out the new method.[16] So the contention of the C.E.T.S. that Miss Ivimy, being paid £200 a year, had fewer cases than some of their male missionaries[17] whose services were recognised to the extent of only £40, was probably correct. The decision to employ this lady full time instead of one-third time, as previously, was a venture of faith on the part of the Home Office, which also took steps to encourage magistrates to make greater use of her services.[18] Miss Croker-King continued to give part-time services and two more women had been engaged on a part-time basis also to act as special children's officers. They were all paid at the same rate as Miss Ivimy according to the amount of time they were expected to give to the work.[19]

The Receiver for the Metropolitan Police District, who had urged that the original payment for probation work should be kept low, demurred at the salaries being offered to these women, but at least one Home Office official regarded them as none too high, in view of the personal qualification necessary for a good probation officer. Moreover, he minuted, 'the salaries given in London will serve as models elsewhere, and it is desirable that local authorities should strive to obtain the services of really good people'.[20]

The recommendation of the Departmental Committee that magistrates should be given wider powers to attach conditions to probation orders required legislation and, not being considered important enough to warrant a special Bill, had to await the accumulation of a number of related proposals. It was eventually placed before Parliament in the Criminal Justice Administration Bill, 1914.

The Home Office obviously thought it no part of their duty to foster the formation of the probation officers' society suggested by the Committee. Nor did the first move towards the implementation of this recommendation come, it appears, from a probation officer, but from a justices' clerk.

Sydney Edridge, Clerk at the Croydon court, and a former Mayor of Croydon, had interested himself in the probation system since its introduction[21] and had met a number of probation officers when he addressed meetings of police court missionaries in the Dioceses of Canterbury and Rochester.[22] In 1912 he met with a group of ten probation officers from the surrounding district in a private house in Croydon to discuss the formation of a national organisation.[23] As a result, the Town Hall, Croydon, was taken for an Inaugural Meeting under the Chairmanship of the Mayor. There some forty probation officers set up a provisional committee with Edridge in the Chair, to take the next steps towards the formation of a society. Among its members were Miss Ivimy and Miss Lance, two of the special children's officers directly employed by the Home Office.[24]

The Committee addressed a circular 'To the Probation Officers of England' asking for their support for the new venture.[25] (The recently published Home Office Directory of Probation Officers no doubt proved invaluable in making these contacts.)

By the time a meeting of intending members was held in the Caxton Hall, Westminster, in December 1912, one hundred and eighty officers had signified their interest. Seventy of them came to the meeting where they adopted a constitution. The National Association of Probation Officers took as its objects:

    a. The advancement of probation work;
    b. The promotion of a bond of union amongst probation
       officers, the provision of opportunities for social

intercourse; and the giving of friendly advice;

c To enable probation officers from practical experience by
collective action to bring forward suggestions on
probation work, and on the reformation of offenders.

Edridge was elected Chairman and George Warren, missionary probation officer at the Croydon court, Secretary. The Earl of Lytton, who had been a member of the 1909 Departmental Committee, accepted the Presidency,[26] but appears to have played only a passive role in the Association's work.

The Chairman devoted himself to the work of the Association with evangelical fervour. His dynamic chairmanship was complemented by the steady, untiring secretaryship of the equally dedicated Warren. For the rest of their active lives they both gave unstinting service to promote the development of the society.

In the early years they travelled a good deal to stimulate and assist in the formation of branches of the Association in various parts of the country.[27] Edridge also saw the need for a journal for probation officers and soon brought out a first issue of the Association's organ, headed 'National Association of Probation Officers'. He continued to edit this publication—which came out once or twice a year—for the next sixteen years. During this period it clearly reflected his personality and his own brand of enthusiasm: 'Bugle Calls not Lullabys' and 'United We Stand, Divided We Fall' were typical, frequently employed sub-titles. He was forthright in expressing his views and used the Journal as a vehicle for them.

In later years, when the Association had grown stronger, and when the service itself was better established, this professional association was to replace the reforming societies as the main pressure group concerned with probation. At this stage, however, the Penal Reform League, the Howard Association, the State Children's Association and the Committee on Wage Earning Children were still maintaining a watchful and lively interest in the progress of the new system.

During the two years which followed the issue of the 1910 circular, they expressed continued dissatisfaction with many aspects of its administration and with the failure of some magistrates to use it and of others to understand it.

At a Conference on Juvenile Courts and Probation convened in 1912 by the Penal Reform League, representatives from a number of voluntary societies, officials from the Home Office, and probation officers heard Courtney Lord call for more care in the selection of probation officers. He wished to see them rewarded by the payment of good salaries and pensions—an indication that he, at least, looked upon the service as one which had come to stay. At the same meeting the Manchester reformer, Charles Russell, objected to the employment of missionaries as probation officers on the ground that they put their missionary work before their probation duties.[28]

After the Conference the Penal Reform League sent a lengthy statement to the Home Secretary on the same subject. They were concerned about what they considered the poor organisation of probation work, and at the employment of 'persons ... mainly occupied in looking after adult offenders—inebriates, ne'er do wells, etcetera,' to supervise young probationers. They included also a suggestion that facilities for the temporary 'care and training' of probationers could be usefully provided.[29]

As Rose has noted[30] this was a period of increasing interest in the need for careful investigation and examination to be made before treatment of any kind was begun. This was connected to some extent with the concern at the time about the proper classification of the mentally retarded which was of course relevant to decisions made in the courts about their disposal. In their statement the League urged that preliminary investigations should be made by a probation officer in every case coming before a juvenile court.[31]

Commenting on this communication, an official noted that the League were 'not alone in looking to the Home Office to give magistrates a lead in the matter of probation.' The circular of 1910, for all its special treatment, had obviously not elicited the hoped for response from the magistrates. Now, only two years later, it was decided to supplement it with a further communication.[32]

Again the Home Office explained to the magistrates the intention of the Act. Again they suggested that it was still not being used to full advantage. And, probably as a result of the recent representations of the Penal Reform League, the opportunity was taken to affirm the value of preliminary enquiries, and to warn justices against possible misuse of the system.

They were urged to make sure that probationers received effective supervision from the probation officer. Whilst acknowledging that an officer's work could not fairly be judged by his written reports, the Home Office had received the impression from some of the reports lodged with them that they represented 'work of a merely formal and mechanical kind'. It was made clear to the justices that the responsibility for securing adequate supervision for probationers lay fairly and squarely upon their shoulders.[33]

In spite of this further effort on the part of the Home Office, the reformers continued to press their views upon it. Only six months after the issue of the circular, Charles Russell and Lord Henry Bentinck, both leading members of the Penal Reform League,[34] wrote jointly to the Home Secretary expressing concern at the failure of the magistrates to take a serious and enlightened interest in the establishment of a high quality probation service. The justices were not, for example, prepared to appoint full-time officers. They tended instead to rely on the agents of voluntary societies to do probation work. In any case, wrote Russell and Bentinck, the low rates of pay being offered for probation work were unlikely to attract good people into the service.

They also deprecated the courts' failure to make use of probation for adult offenders. And they reiterated the Penal Reform League's earlier allegation that many magistrates remained unappreciative of the need to make proper enquiries before deciding on the appropriate treatment for an offender, an attitude which could easily result in the misuse of the probation system.[35]

The two men were disappointed that more use had not been made of voluntary probation officers. Their regret was shared by their own and other reforming bodies and, to some extent, by the Home Office itself, although conflicting evidence had reached it as to the usefulness and the availability of voluntary workers.[36] Although it does not appear to have given any lead in this respect in London, the Home Office continued to draw attention over a number of years to the advantages to be gained from the use of voluntary workers.[37] Over most of its history, however, the probation service has tended to resist the employment of volunteers. This has no doubt been due in part to the weight of legal responsibility inherent in probation work. Magistrates preferred to entrust the supervision of probationers to readily available officers, over whom they could exercise some control, rather than to voluntary officers. Probation officers, for their part, appear to have preferred to carry out their responsibilities under the probation order without risking delegation to voluntary helpers.

This question was discussed at the time by Cecil Leeson in *The Probation System*, the first book devoted entirely to probation to be published in this country. Leeson considered that, whilst a probation system which relied entirely on voluntary workers might become haphazard and irresponsible, carefully selected and well-instructed volunteers, under the supervision of a salaried officer, could well supply 'the intensive work which makes probation real'. He was aware, however, that in England it was 'too often the custom of professional probation workers to look askance at the use of volunteer probation officers.'[38]

Leeson had first-hand experience of the operation of the system, having himself worked as a probation officer.[39] He had also had the opportunity of studying probation in the United States and other countries—an experience which seems to have considerably influenced his thought. (He had seen for example, the employment of voluntary helpers in America.)[40] Soon to become Secretary of the Howard Association and subsequently of a newly formed Magistrates' Association, Leeson was to render through the medium of these offices, as well as through his publications, an important contribution to the development of the probation service in this country.

From his book it is clear that, in 1914, Leeson was not wholly satisfied with the organisation of the service, either central or local. To improve its central administration, he suggested the formation of a special branch of the Home Office which would be charged with the general oversight of the service and to which would be attached peripatetic supervisors of probation work. The quality of the local service, on the other hand, could in his view be much improved by the appointment of chief probation officers (again as in the United States), especially if each chief officer was himself responsible to a committee of magistrates, or even to one or two specially designated justices, rather than to the whole bench.[41]

Leeson drew attention to the need to recruit persons of good education and was among the first to stress that officers should have a suitable training. Whilst agreeing with the Departmental Committee of 1909 that the probation officer's personality was of prime importance, Leeson feared that the emphasis laid upon this had tended to obscure the need for special training.[42] He himself had been one of the first to take the Diploma in Social Studies in the University of Birmingham,[43] and this experience no doubt led him to suggest that 'as the system expands ... and the demand for probation officers increases, it may be found possible to modify the Social Study Courses already possessed by most of the newer universities, to meet their special needs.'[44]

Leeson's book was published in 1914. In the same year an opportunity arose for the Home Office to include in a wide-ranging Criminal Justice Bill the amendments to the law on probation recommended by the 1909 Committee.[45] The new Bill sought to allow the courts more discretion in deciding the conditions to be contained in probation orders. It proposed to substitute for Section 2(2) of the 1907 Act, which specified the conditions which might be inserted in an order, one allowing the use of such additional conditions with respect to residence, abstention from intoxicating liquor, and any other matters as the court may, having regard to the particular circumstances of the case, consider necessary for preventing a repetition of the same offences or the commission of other offences.[46]

The government also wished through the Bill to make it clear that a court could vary the conditions of an order, or diminish or extend the period of probation shown in the original order, though not so that the total duration of the order would exceed three years.[47]

The two proposals passed easily through both Houses. A third evoked some discussion. The government had apparently decided that the appointment of a probation officer for every court might well be achieved if the supply of suitable persons available for appointment was increased as a result of an improvement in the remuneration offered for probation work. It also appears to have been prepared to subsidise the salaries of probation officers; but not, as might perhaps have been expected, through the local authorities who were responsible for any payment, but by means of a grant to voluntary societies.

In the Bill it was proposed that any society which was formed and had as its objects the care and control of persons under the age of twenty-one whilst on probation . . . or of persons whilst placed out on licence from a reformatory or industrial school or Borstal institution, or under supervision, should be able to apply to the Home Secretary for recognition. And that the government should be able to make grants to recognised societies under such conditions as the Home Secretary might recommend.[48]

The Home Secretary himself told the Commons that he thought that by subsiding societies they could ensure the supply of a competent probation officer for every court in the country, and also of persons ready to undertake after-care. With the help of the proposed subsidies, they envisaged the creation of 'a philanthropic network over the whole country'.[49] Although this intention was not made public, the clause related to a scheme being contemplated at the time for the formation of a central body to provide workers to supervise probationers and persons released from all types of penal institution.[50]

In spite of the approval of voluntary effort implicit in this proposal, the C.E.T.S. saw in it a threat to their own position in the existing service. The phrase 'if a society is formed' seemed to suggest that the proposed provision would apply only to new and not to established societies. They accordingly sought the assistance of one of their supporters, William Johnson-Hicks, M.P., who went to the Report Stage prepared to propose the omission of the whole clause in order to preserve the society's position.[51] Assured, however, by the Home Secretary himself that the government had no intention of excluding existing organisations, he successfully put instead an amendment indicating that a society 'already in existence' would also be eligible to apply for recognition.[52]

No one in the Commons questioned the advisability of subsidising the service through voluntary societies. Only the Marquis of Salisbury, in the Lords, asked why so much responsibility should be handed to societies over which there would be no effective public control. Although they did good work, he said, 'philanthropic societies are dominated by men who have very strong views on certain questions, and views which are not altogether approved ... by what are called men of commonsense outside.' In his opinion it would be very dangerous to allow such bodies to have control of the country's probation system.[53]

The clause was carried in spite of his disapproval and when the Bill received the Royal Assent[54] a few days after the outbreak of the first world war, it seemed as if the future role of voluntary societies in the probation service would be both assured and extensive.

The policy envisaged in these provisions of the Criminal Justice Administration Act, 1914, was never carried out. The Home Office later claimed that action upon this section of the Act had been deferred as a result of pressure of work during the war years.[55] This is understandable, but does not explain the failure to make use of it when peace once more returned. It can only be assumed that the Home Office underwent a change of heart in relation to this proposal. During the war an increase in juvenile delinquency focused the concern of government and public on the need to provide services for children aimed at prevention, and to improve methods of dealing with young delinquents.

The Home Secretary, for example, called a meeting of organisations concerned in any way with child welfare, to discuss the prevention of delinquency, and by the end of the war local Juvenile Organisations Committees representing such bodies had been set up to co-ordinate activity.[56] Also, the Penal Reform League in 1917 held a conference on Juvenile Delinquency at which a resolution was passed stressing the community's responsibilities towards children and parents and calling for more provision to be made of recreational activities for children and young people. A Committee appointed by this Conference subsequently drew up detailed proposals which the League published in *A National*

Minimum for Youth, 1917. Among other suggestions were a considerable number dealing with juvenile courts and probation. These repeated many of the reforming societies' concerns, such as the need for a Probation Commission, thorough investigation of cases before decisions are taken—carried out by probation officers but 'supplemented where necessary by medical, neurological and psychological expert opinion' (an indication of the progress made by this time by the discipline of psychology).

It was also suggested that probation officers should be recruited 'from among those who have been through courses of social study at Universities, such, for instance, as that provided at the London School of Economics, and have practical experience in social work'. They saw the probation officer as an investigator and adviser 'on whose experience and counsel Magistrates should largely depend,' and wanted salaries and prospects to be 'such as to attract men and women from the Universities'. A career structure was suggested which the authors of the publication thought would, with better salaries, attract the sort of person required for such a position.

An earlier suggestion, that homes or other institutions could be used in connection with probation,[57] was repeated; and the use of public funds for this purpose was advocated. The need to increase central government pressure on 'recalcitrant localities' and to provide incentive to efficiency were the reasons given to justify their most radical suggestion, that the cost of probation should be shared by the Treasury, 'say to the amount of 35 per cent, with additions up to 50 per cent, according to the efficiency of the work in each locality.'[58]

During this war-time period, considerable criticism was being voiced to the Home Office, directly and in print, about the work of the police court missionaries and the system of dual control. It is possible that the high level of concern about juvenile crime on the one hand, and this criticism on the other, had a considerable bearing upon the abandonment of the policy framed in 1914 to work through voluntary bodies.

An important attack on the system of dual control was made in 1915 by William Clarke Hall, the Metropolitan Magistrate, son-in-law of Benjamin Waugh and celebrated in his own right for his great interest in the welfare of children. His book, *The State and the Child*, dealt with the welfare of children and, among other things, stressed the value of the probation system as a method of dealing with delinquent children. So also did two other wartime books, Douglas Pepler's *Justice and the Child*, which appeared in 1914, and a second book by Cecil Leeson, *The Child and the War*, published in

68

1917.

Clarke Hall had obviously been influenced[59] by a recently published American text-book, *Juvenile Courts and Probation*,[60] in which the authors, B. Flexner and R. N. Baldwin, asserted that probation work could properly be carried out only by well-trained, well-paid, full-time officers of good academic background.[61] Whilst Clarke Hall had unreserved praise for the work of the London probation officers—missionaries and special children's officers alike—he considered that the British service could be staffed in the desirable way advocated by Flexner and Baldwin only if the system of dual control was abandoned.[62]

Less favourable accounts of the work of individual officers than that given by the Metropolitan Magistrate reached the Home Office from a number of sources, among them the State Children's Association from which the Home Secretary, Sir George Cave, received a deputation in July 1917.[63] The group included Lord Lytton, who had been a member of the 1909 Committee and Lord Henry Bentinck, M.P., who five years previously had written to the Home Secretary about deficiencies in the probation service.

Their organisation was disturbed that all too often courts appointed as their probation officer 'an elderly police court missionary, fully occupied with other work, uninstructed in child psychology and with little, if any, knowledge of modern reformative methods': a practice calculated to destroy the effectiveness of the system. What was more, those 'educated voluntary workers' which the Association were keen to see used in the service would 'be reluctant to work under the direction of persons whose outlook (was) narrow and of a past generation'.

The deputation asked the Home Secretary to use his influence with the justices to secure the appointment 'of well-educated, trained persons . . . of high ideals and sympathetic insight with a knowledge of the best reformative methods'. They also advocated the payment to probation officers of adequate salaries instead of fees. Payment by fee, still very prevalent in spite of the lead given by the Home Office, encouraged officers, they said, to undertake the supervision of more cases than could properly be managed.

On behalf of their Association they also suggested to the Home Secretary that a committee of magistrates and experienced social workers should be available to advise probation officers at all children's courts about their cases.[64]

The visit of this deputation led the Home Office to take stock of the volume of criticism which had been reaching them.[65] Persuaded that there was some justification in the allegations about the poor quality of some probation work, the Home Secretary very soon issued a circular to magistrates drawing attention to a number of deficiencies in the service in some areas.[66]

Like the previous circular on this subject, it emphasised that responsibility for the quality of probation work lay with the magistrates themselves. The perfunctory way in which supervision appeared to be performed in some areas could well be attributed to overwork. Indeed, the Home Office had heard of probation officers in some large towns with anything from 120 to 200 probationers at a time. The justices were reminded that the 1909 Committee had considered 60 the maximum number of cases to be given to officers in urban areas. It was pointed out that the payment of fees sometimes led to probation officers having too many cases, and justices were recommended to pay fixed salaries instead.

In a further attempt to improve the quality of work by getting magistrates to supervise it more adequately, attention was drawn to the practice 'already adopted in some towns' where magistrates expected periodic reports on their cases from the probation officers, and took a personal interest in the progress of probationers. (Although in a number of respects this circular clearly reflected the views given to the Home Secretary by the State Children's Association, there was no mention here of the 'case committees' suggested by the deputation.)

Magistrates were reminded, however, that they could exert considerable control over the quality of probation work through their choice of officers. They should appoint 'suitably qualified persons': the qualifications referred to were subjective rather than objective—'intelligence' and 'real sympathy with those coming under their supervision'. The circular implied that not enough care was being taken in this matter. There was evidence, the magistrates were told, that some of those appointed were too old or 'without the necessary gifts'. For the first time in an official communication it was suggested that missionaries were not necessarily always the best persons to supervise all cases: 'although many of them do their work well, especially as regards adult cases, they are occupied with other duties, and they are often, owing to their want of reformative methods, not well fitted to deal with lads and girls'.[67]

The Chairman of the State Children's Association hurried to thank the Home Secretary for embodying their suggestions in the circular. A Bishop of the Church of England was less pleased. He called at the Home Office about the 'outrageous statement' concerning the police court missionaries. It would be catastrophic, he told officials, to replace the missionaries by persons well-versed in

70

modern methods but lacking the missionaries' desire to bring Christian influence to bear upon their charges.[68]

The Home Secretary denied that the circular cast any general reflection upon the work of the missionaries, but insisted that there were nevertheless some who were unfitted for the probation service. Even the Secretary of the Church of England Temperance Society had admitted that his committee was not satisfied with the suitability for probation work of some of its agents in the police courts.[69]

In 1915, probably as a result of their anxiety over Section 7 of the Criminal Justice Administration Act, 1914, which referred to the recognition of voluntary societies for the purpose of grant aid, the Church of England Temperance Society had taken steps to strengthen the organisation of their police court work by establishing a Central Police Court Mission. Until the formation of this new department, no national committee had dealt exclusively with police court mission as opposed to other temperance work. The Central Police Court Mission was now set up 'to represent the Diocesan Missions in national questions, and to control and administer all general matters in connection therewith'.[70] It sought 'to effect, by the Grace of God, the reformation of all, irrespective of creed, who pass through the Courts, special attention being given to those who owe their position to their own intemperance or that of others'.

The temperance aspect of the missionary's work was still stressed. Indeed, the regulations governing the appointment of missionaries, issued by the newly formed Central Mission, began 'The Missionary shall be appointed as Temperance Agent of the Diocesan Branch (and not merely as Police Court Missionary)'. His duty was 'to do all in his power to further the cause of Temperance and all the interests of the Society', to solicit and collect subscriptions when so directed and generally to 'assist in the maintenance of the funds of the Society whenever opportunity occurs'. The application forms issued by the Central Mission for use in recruitment by local missions were framed to discover whether would-be missionaries were abstainers and regular communicants of the Church of England.

The Central Mission attempted to introduce a measure of uniformity into the organisation of the Diocesan Missions. It also exhorted them to pay adequate salaries in order to obtain the best type of missionaries—those with training in evangelistic work.

Its determination to expand its work was reflected in its policy statement. Diocesan Missions were called upon to increase their staff wherever necessary, and to adopt a militant attitude, seeking to

71

'occupy' additional courts 'upon every opportunity'. If a probation officer's post, previously held by a non-missionary, fell vacant, the Society's worker at the Court was expected, 'to use every endeavour to secure the position.'[71]

Although the Howard Association and other societies had on many occasions expressed their dislike of the dual control arising out of the employment of agents of societies as probation officers, and Sidney Edridge, under the banner of the National Association of Probation Officers, was campaigning for the abolition of this system, the C.E.T.S. seem to have encountered little opposition from local benches. The latter appear to have been only too glad to be able to appoint a probation officer with little effort and without incurring much expense for their local authority. In London, the Home Office itself appeared satisfied to employ C.E.T.S. agents as probation officers for adult cases.

After the war, however, an increasing number of courts began to appoint their own full-time probation officers instead of employing the agents of voluntary societies.[72] There is no direct evidence, but it is possible that the circular of 1917[73] was responsible for this trend, which gave rise to two Parliamentary questions enquiring whether it was now the policy of the Home Office to encourage magistrates to appoint independent probation officers in place of missionaries, thus increasing the burden on the rates.[74]

Faced with the actual loss of probation officer appointments in a number of provincial courts, the C.E.T.S. now had to begin striving to keep its place in the probation service. In spite of the bold offensive policy adopted by its Central Mission in 1915, it found itself moving over to the defensive.

Symptomatic of this was its sudden concern that its efforts should be made more obvious. Late in 1919 the Society pointed out to the Home Secretary that there was no indication in the Home Office Directory of Probation Officers that a very large number of them were C.E.T.S. missionaries. It asked that this should be noted in future editions.[75] In 1919, probably as a result of its anxieties,[76] it held the first national conference of its missionaries and in 1920 adopted the policy of encouraging all police court missionaries to join the C.E.T.S. Guild of Police Court Missionaries[77] established at the Conference.[78]

The Society defended its desire to maintain its position in the probation service in its Annual Report of 1919. If the courts ceased to appoint missionaries, it contended, the probation officer would degenerate into a mere court official 'after the type of the police officer'. It was convinced that only a missionary could properly fulfil the tasks of the probation officer.

By the end of 1920 the Executive Committee considered the situation grave. The Manchester Diocesan Branch had 'lost the court at Bury' and 'only just preserved the one at Blackburn'. At other provincial courts missionaries had left the Society to take up posts as independent probation officers at their courts.[79] A particularly severe blow was suffered in 1920 by the Police Court Mission in Liverpool. At the end of 1919 an official of the Liverpool Women's Police told the Home Office that the city greatly needed 'a consistent co-ordinated system of probation'. The supervision of adult probationers suffered, she said, from lack of coherence because the officers responsible were agents of several voluntary societies. Supervision was inadequate. So too, she considered, were some of the missionaries: 'they are too overworked and, some of them, too untrained to have time or understanding to undertake real probation work and give it a fair trial'. For one of the C.E.T.S. missionaries, presumably Mr. Goldstone who was later employed as chief probation officer, she had abundant praise. He had, she said, for a long time desired to establish a properly co-ordinated system.

These comments were referred by the Home Office to the Liverpool justices who had about the same time received a suggestion from the Chief Constable that the supervision of juvenile probationers, at present undertaken mainly by his staff, might be better done by an officer unconnected with the police force. They had also recently received a request for an increased grant from the Liverpool Ladies Temperance Association who provided two probation officers.

With all these matters arising together, the magistrates decided to appoint a sub-committee to enquire into and report upon probation work in Liverpool. In its report the sub-committee recommended the abandonment of the method of dual control. Whilst acknowledging that the missionaries had given 'magnificent help' to the magistrates in enabling them to carry out the provisions of the Probation of Offenders Act up to the present time, the committee thought that, in view of a rise in the number of offences committed by young people, the time was now ripe 'for a decided improvement and development in the mode of applying the principles of the Probation Act'. They considered it 'a matter of first importance that probation officers should be placed under the direct authority and control of the Justices'. Thus the officers would be able to give to probation work the 'unremitting attention' not possible for agents of voluntary societies.

The committee suggested that the justices should appoint Mr.

Goldstone, a C.E.T.S. missionary, chief probation officer in their direct employ. The voluntary societies should be asked to continue with their missionary as distinct from their probation work, and to nominate a very limited number of people for appointment by the justices as full-time assistant Probation Officers paid entirely by the court and under its sole control.[80]

The sub-committee's recommendations were accepted by the whole body of justices. Under the new scheme the part played by the Liverpool C.E.T.S. in probation work was severely reduced. Attempts by the Society at both local and national level to persuade the Liverpool Bench to reverse its decision were unsuccessful, and they had to agree to adjust their work to fit in with the new situation.[81]

The Chairman of the C.E.T.S. opined in November 1920, that their work in the police courts was slipping from them into the hands of the state. The Secretary was instructed to consult with 'particularly interested and well informed persons' with a view to discovering 'the best means of preventing the loss of the Mission'.[82]

The C.E.T.S. was frequently blamed by Sidney Edridge for his own organisation's failure to recruit as members all those employed as probation officers. In the opinion of the Committee of the National Association of Probation Officers many missionaries were reluctant to join the organisation in case by so doing they incurred the displeasure of the societies upon whom they depended for their livelihood.[83] There is no evidence that the Missions forbade their agents to join the Association, but they could hardly be expected positively to encourage them to participate in the activities of a body whose Journal continually called for the abolition of dual control.[84]

Despite the disappointing results of its recruiting drives, and in spite of the war, the probation officers' organisation had lost none of its early enthusiasm. Annual conferences had been held in London without a break and there had been other gatherings in the provinces. The indefatigable Edridge had produced successive issues of the Journal.

The Association was heartened by a significant event which took place in 1918. For the first time the Home Office official charged with the oversight of probation matters, then Alexander Maxwell (later to become Permanent Under-Secretary of State), attended its Annual Conference. Recognising the importance of this move, Edridge called it 'A long step in the right direction'.[85] Maxwell told the assembled officers that the department was anxious to extend the probation system and to have the views and co-operation of those engaged in the work. They were well aware, he said, of the need for further action by both central and local authorities to improve the organisation of the work, and they sympathised with the need for more probation officers and for their better remuneration.[86]

The proceedings of its conferences and the contents of its Journal indicate that the Association had maintained a broad interest in probation and related matters. Its members discussed 'Institutional Life and Its Effect Upon Children'[87] and 'Gaming Machines in Sweet Shops: Their Relation to Juvenile Crime' alongside problems such as the organisation of social clubs for probationers[88] and the difficulty of explaining the complicated language of the probation order to the young offender.[89]

Naturally enough they were also concerned with their conditions of employment, both as it affected their own lives and also, they claimed, in the interest of the quality of the service itself. In particular they complained of the poor payment offered for probation work and of the unfortunate consequences of the method of payment by fee. Because of this system of remuneration some officers were reluctant to recommend probation in some suitable cases lest they be suspected of grasping at additional fees.[90]

Early in 1918, using a questionnaire, the Chairman of N.A.P.O. solicited information upon a variety of related matters from all the courts in the country. He was disappointed at the lack of response. Only 223 of the 1,387 courts co-operated. Analysis revealed that at the majority of these the probation officers were paid by fee. Edridge was especially shocked to find that a 'very large Northern city' still clung to this system: 'One would have thought that at all events in this city probation officers were paid by reasonable and proper salaries,'[91] he wrote.

The Home Office official, Maxwell, who had attended the conference of the National Association of Probation Officers, had told them that his department was aware that the position with regard to pay was unsatisfactory. A year later, in 1919, having made further contacts of this kind with probation officers, Maxwell was sufficiently disturbed by their assertions to bring their complaints to the notice of his seniors.[92]

At the Home Office it was considered unwise to contemplate any action without complete and first-hand information from the courts themselves. In order to obtain this the Probation Rules were amended to require all courts to send each year to the Home Office a statement of the total annual remuneration for probation duties of each probation officer, the method of payment, any other posts held by the probation officer and the remuneration received for these.[93] The data thus collected confirmed that many probation officers were

75

grossly under-paid.[94] In spite of the suggestion in the 1917 Circular a large majority were still paid by fee, many still on the scale of fees suggested by the Home Office in its first Memorandum on the Probation of Offenders Act in 1907. Although the Home Office had revised these scales for its own probation officers, the change had never been widely announced and, in the absence of any suggestion from the centre, some provincial courts had obviously given no thought to increasing the remuneration of their officers for a number of years.

Some areas paid their probation officers a small retaining fee which was quite unrealistic when compared with the number of cases actually supervised. A married couple who were also in charge of a boys' home were paid a fee of £10 a year for undertaking probation work. On the date the return was completed they were supervising between them eighty-three probationers. In a northern town a male officer with one hundred and twenty-four cases at a time received £50 a year which he was compelled to supplement by taking additional employment.

The pay of police court missionaries varied from place to place, but many full-time workers were paid at £60 to £80 for women and £100 to £120 for men, rates considered very low by the Home Office. War bonuses had been rare among probation officers, and it was clear that 'no substantial rise in salary' had been given 'to meet the rise in prices'.

Evidence suggested that some of the earlier suggestions by the Home Office that courts should review the remuneration of their probation officers had met with response in some areas. This very enquiry itself seems to have provoked some courts to act. The justices of Kingston-upon-Hull decided to raise the annual salaries of their officers by £39 bringing them up to £207 for men and £127 for women. And in Cardiff, where fees had been paid for the supervision of the only two probation cases in the last year, the bench decided to appoint a full-time officer at a salary of £200 a year.[95]

The Home Office now had definite information about the remuneration of probation officers throughout the country, and it was again reminded of the difficulties which could arise owing to the fact that in county areas whilst the justices appointed probation officers, the scale of their remuneration had to be approved by the Standing Joint Committee which provided the money. One or two benches had written to complain that their recommendations for an increase in the salaries of probation officers had been ignored or rejected by the Standing Joint Committee. They had resorted to the practice of supplementing the probation officers' pay out of the Poor Box. In these cases the Home Secretary had written to the relevant County Council asking them to give favourable consideration to the question.[96]

The Justices of Bingley in Yorkshire had recently written to the Home Office to suggest that power to fix the remuneration should now be vested in Justices rather than the Standing Joint Committee. With their suggestion they sent an account of probation work in their area. They had formed a committee which met monthly to receive probation officers' reports and to offer advice and assistance with difficult cases. This interest had, they claimed, resulted in more satisfactory supervision. Evidently they were setting high standards for their probation officers. For these they were willing and anxious to pay well. They argued that

> the basis of payment for preventive and reformative work is out of all proportion to money expended in carrying out sentences of convicted persons. A greater payment is made in some cases for conveyance to prison alone than is allowed for a period of supervision of a person who it is desired to prevent becoming a criminal.

The interest taken by this Bench in the remuneration of probation officers was 'unusual'[97] but it was not unique. At about the same time the Clerk to the Justices of Bolton, Lancashire, had written to the N.A.P.O. Journal claiming such sentiments for his employers, and calling for a Home Office circular designed to strengthen the hands of the Justices in getting the Standing Joint Committee to grant an adequate amount.[98]

The Home Secretary had no power to make specific recommendations to courts about probation officers' pay, and in any case the situation was not the same in every case. Some officers for example were also employed by another body to perform other functions. Some were well qualified, others had already been declared by the Home Office unfit to perform the work properly. In fact, the central authority was completely ignorant of the qualifications of officers outside London.

Nor could they upbraid magistrates for not always making good appointments, when there was no machinery in existence through which they could obtain the names of suitable persons seeking posts. Furthermore there was no means whereby such men and women could discover where vacancies existed for which they might apply. On several occasions trained social workers had called at the Home Office to ask how to enter probation work and, unless a vacancy happened to exist in the Metropolitan Police Courts, it had been found impossible to help them.[99]

Within a few years a highly unsatisfactory situation had unfolded itself to the Home Office. They were anxious to remedy it and to improve the quality of the probation service. It was recognised that this might well be done by making probation work the subject of a government grant with its usual corollary, greater central control over local administration. This line of thought must be seen against the wider background of relationships between central and local government, and in particular of the substantial growth in the use of grants-in-aid since the introduction of the probation system in 1909.

Since the payment of the first government grant in 1835, the amounts paid and the number of services involved had increased steadily with the recognition that the cost of services such as police and education, forced upon localities by the decisions of the central government, represented too great a burden for some areas. In addition it was increasingly appreciated that certain services, such as health and education, had national implications. Local government had undergone reorganisation in 1888 in response to the need for better administration of the growing number of services being thrust upon local bodies as a result of the expansion of government intervention in the course of the nineteenth century, and following that the amount expended on grants-in-aid by the central authority rapidly increased.

In 1914, five years before the Home Office began to consider the desirability of a grant for probation, the Departmental Committee on Local Taxation had recommended an increase in the use of grants, and the period following the publication of its report saw an even more rapid rise in the amount and number of grants.[100] It is not surprising, therefore, that at this time the reforming societies and the administration began to see the provision of a government grant with the concomitant central control as the way to improve the probation service and establish minimum standards throughout the country. The probation system had been in operation sufficiently long for its deficiencies to be properly identified, and in the atmosphere of public concern about delinquency during and after the war, anxiety about the quality of provision for probation began to outweigh considerations about cost to the Exchequer.

Nevertheless, the making of a grant was a considerable step to contemplate, and one which had so far received scant attention. More evidence of the need would have to be produced, it was thought, and the most suitable machinery for assembling this would be a Departmental Committee.[101]

CHAPTER FOUR

THE CASE FOR CENTRAL CONTROL

In November 1920, the Home Secretary, Edwart Shortt, announced the appointment of a Departmental Committee under the chairmanship of the Parliamentary Under-Secretary, Sir John Baird,

> to enquire into the existing methods of training, appointing and paying Probation Officers and to consider whether any, and if so what, alterations are desirable in order to secure at all Courts a sufficient number of Probation Officers having suitable training and qualifications; and also to consider whether any changes are required in the present system of remuneration.[1]

The Committee like that of 1909 was small and composed entirely of persons actively involved in the operation of the probation system. There was the same nucleus of Parliamentary Under-Secretary, senior Home Office official—on this occasion Sidney Harris, who had recently become Head of the Children's Branch which dealt with probation—and metropolitan magistrate. They were joined by a county justice and Miss Ivimy, one of the special children's probation officers employed in the metropolitan police courts. The preponderance of London-based members, all but the justice, is striking especially as the Committee's terms of reference, unlike those of 1909, in no way singled out the metropolitan district for special attention.

Neither the local authorities which supplied such public money as was spent on probation, nor the voluntary societies which provided most of the probation officers and part of their salaries had a voice on the Committee. The local authorities gave evidence through the County Councils Association and the Association of Municipal Corporations. Only two of the six principal societies supplying probation officers, the Church of England Temperance Society and the Central Discharged Prisoners' Aid Society, submitted evidence.

Sidney Edridge appeared for the National Association of Probation Officers and Margery Fry for the Howard League for

Penal Reform, the latter formed by the recent amalgamation of the Howard Association and the Penal Reform League.[2] A few probation officers and justices gave evidence on their own account.[3] No organisation yet existed to speak for magistrates as a body, though this situation was soon to be remedied by the formation of the Magistrates' Association.

The Committee's enquiry was limited to those aspects of administration regarded at the Home Office as the most pressing problems at the time.[4] The question of payment and appointment had long been a matter of fairly wide concern, training however had been seen as desirable only by those in the forefront of reform or acquainted with developments in other spheres of social work.

Struck by the continued variation in the use of probation by different courts, and seeing a connection between this and the fact that about a quarter of all summary courts still had no probation officer, the Committee expressed the view that every court should have the services of a probation officer at its disposal,[5] and framed its recommendations on the basis of that principle.

The two most controversial matters considered by the Committee were whether the responsibility for appointing and paying probation officers should remain with the local justices or be transferred to some other authority; and whether the courts should continue to employ the agents of voluntary societies or appoint their own officers to carry out probation work.

The Howard League for Penal Reform was still pressing for general responsibility for the probation service to be placed in the hands of a paid Probation Commission.[6] Shortly before amalgamating the Howard Association and the Penal Reform League had drafted a Bill, for introduction by a private member, proposing the establishment of such a Commission to supervise the operation of probation legislation, and with power to delegate the duty of appointing probation officers to local probation authorities.[7]

The Committee however found little support for the proposal among other witnesses and, in any case, it thought the creation of a new government department unlikely to be 'viewed with favour at the present time'. The country was beset by post-war economic difficulties which had led the government to ration departmental expenditure and to cut down its administrative apparatus by abolishing some of the ministries set up during the war.

The Committee's objection to a scheme of central appointment seems to have turned chiefly on its belief that close co-operation between the court and the probation officer was essential for the successful working of the system.[8] This was more likely to be achieved, it was thought, if the justices had a direct voice in the selection and control of their officers.[9] Also the desired relationship between the probationer and the officer—that of a friend rather than an official—might also be difficult to achieve if probation officers were to become a 'new class of Civil Servant'.[10]

The Committee reported in favour of leaving the appointment of probation officers in the hands of the local magistrates, but recommended that this responsibility should be channelled by each Bench into the hands of two or three of its members who would 'organise probation work, select probation officers and keep closely in touch with the progress of their cases'.[11] Here was the first official suggestion that the Bench's interest in probation work should be concentrated by delegation, and the seed of the Probation Committee system.[12]

The combination of county areas for the more effective execution of probation work can also be traced to a recommendation of this Committee, which found organisation rudimentary in small towns and villages where the number of probationers did not justify the appointment of a full-time officer. It commended to the consideration of other counties the example of Staffordshire where a Police Court Mission had been organised for the whole county. Independent of any other Society, its control was vested in a body which included magistrates from the various Petty Sessional Divisions. This arrangement enabled the appointment of full-time officers to act for several courts which could not separately have provided enough work for a full-time officer.[13]

That the Committee would have to consider the case for and against the continued appointment as probation officers of the agents of voluntary societies was inevitable. Opinion had long been divided about the merits of the existing system, and those who deplored and those who supported it seized the opportunity to present their case to the Committee and to counter that of their opponents.

Tradition, of course, was on the side of the Church of England Temperance Society, chief exponent of the employment of missionaries. Perhaps more importantly at this stage, and in view of the economic situation, it mustered a 'considerable amount of financial support' from voluntary sources which, contributed towards the salaries of missionaries giving all or much of their time to probation work, represented a substantial relief to public funds.[14]

It was still widely accepted that religious motives were essential to the successful pursuance of probation work. The C.E.T.S. argued that by employing their missionaries the courts secured the services of persons who had been led to take up the work by religious conviction. They further suggested that their missionaries, not being looked upon as officials of the court, were able to 'exercise a wider and more beneficial influence than would otherwise be the case'.[15]

Those who wished to see an end to the appointment of the agents of voluntary societies as probation officers levelled their criticism mainly at the C.E.T.S. They regretted that probation should still be associated to such a great extent with the activities of a temperance organisation, and that the Society's policy of restricting appointments as missionaries to members of the Church of England narrowed the field of recruitment to the service. This could result in deliberate rejection of some otherwise suitable candidates and might, it was suggested, account for what some considered the low standard of qualifications required by the police court missions. It was also pointed out that the geographical areas covered by the individual missions were inappropriate to the organisation of the probation service. The missions were based on ecclesiastical areas which did not coincide with petty sessional divisions or counties.[16] One of the major criticisms of the existing system was that it placed a missionary probation officer in the difficult position of owing allegiance to two masters—the court and the voluntary society.[17]

Whilst tradition was on the side of the C.E.T.S., the trend was with this other body of opinion. The Committee noted the growing tendency of courts in large centres to appoint their own probation officers without recourse to a voluntary society. Those who regretted this argued that such an arrangement might result in the probation officer being regarded by offenders as a court official rather than as a friend; an important feature of the probation system might thus be jeopardised. It might also prove difficult, they suggested, to obtain by this means the services of people with deeply held religious beliefs.[18]

The Committee thought it undesirable to recommend a uniform system. Both arrangements had their advantages and local justices should be free to adopt whichever they considered most suitable for their area.[19] Some observations were made about both methods. The Committee was anxious that courts appointing their probation officer direct should make provision not only for the execution of the statutory work of the probation officer, limited at this time to the supervision of probationers and to the making of enquiries for the courts in connection with possible probation cases, but also for the carrying out of other social work in the courts, traditionally performed by the missionaries, and often referred to as 'missionary work'. This was work 'of the greatest value to magistrates when they need enquiries to be made . . . and when a helping hand can be given, or a word in due season can be spoken,' and they urged that in appointing and fixing the remuneration of probation officers, courts and local authorities should not discriminate too narrowly between probation work and missionary work.[20]

In connection with the employment of missionaries as probation officers, the Committee issued what was tantamount to a warning to the C.E.T.S. Whilst reluctant to make any recommendation which might put any check on the development of the work of the voluntary societies, it had to admit that there was substance in the criticisms of those who attacked the C.E.T.S. 'Considerable changes in the constitution of the Society' were needed in order to encourage 'a more progressive spirit in probation work, and to attract better candidates to the service'.

The committee advocated the complete separation of the Police Court Mission from the temperance work of the Society, and its re-organisation on county rather than diocesan lines. Preference should be given to lay rather than clerical representation on the Mission's Committee, and magistrates and social workers should be prominently associated with both its central and local control. The Missions should now refrain from requiring their probation officer missionaries to engage in fund-raising and organising activities, and from restricting police court missionary appointments to members of the Church of England.[21]

The C.E.T.S. was born of temperance out of Anglicanism. In making these demands the Committee was asking of it no small sacrifice in return for the continued participation of its Mission in the social work of the courts. In view of the recommendations the Committee intended to make, the Society had been sounded before the publication of the Report to ascertain whether it would be willing to fall in with the suggestions.[22] Its acquiescence enabled the Committee to follow up its criticism with a more favourable reference to the Society. 'We understand', they reported, 'that the responsible authorities of the Society recognise the force of the criticisms and are prepared to reorganise their probation work on much broader lines.'[23]

Apart from the two main classes of probation officer—the missionary and the 'independent'—the returns disclosed

> a considerable number of persons of varied interests and qualifications who are employed on probation work, such as attendance officers, police officers, collecting officers, rescue workers, officers of the N.S.P.C.C., Poor Law, and other local officers, keepers of places of detention, and a number of other

83

persons engaged in various occupations . . . but remotely
connected with probation work.

Such appointments, and especially the appointment of police
officers, were detrimental, in the Committee's view, to the success of
the probation system.[24]

However, the majority of probation officers being employed on a
part-time basis, it was almost inevitable that they would also be
engaged in some other form of employment. Part-time employment
policies and the level of payment were obviously connected. The
Committee's terms of reference included the method of payment of
probation officers. It found that one or two counties and a few of the
larger towns were paying regular salaries on a full-time basis. But in
most cases the officer was either paid a small lump sum, varying
from about £5 to £20, for probation work, obtaining the rest of his
salary from other sources, or he was paid by fees.

The Committee recommended that the system of payment by fee
should be discontinued and that all regular officers, full-time and
part-time, be paid either a salary or a fixed annual sum. However,
although acknowledging that the remuneration of provincial officers
was often very inadequate, it found itself unable to suggest a
universal scale because 'so much depends on the circumstances of
the work and the cost of living where the officers (are) employed'.
Instead, it was suggested that local authorities might like to take as a
guide the scale of salaries they were recommending for the London
service.

The London scales had been revised as recently as 1919 and
further supplemented by a cost-of-living bonus. The Committee
considered adequate the starting salary of £200 for a male
missionary, but recommended raising the maximum from £250 to
£350. The officer should be able to look forward to achieving this
point by the age of 45. The special children's officers had continued
to receive 'considerably higher' salaries than the missionaries—an
indefensible arrangement in the opinion of the Committee.[25]

Although it considered the existing financial rewards inadequate
in many cases, the Committee made it clear that it did not regard
probation as 'in any sense . . . a profession in which persons can
expect to earn large salaries'. No more, apparently, did the
probation officers, whose moderate salary demands elicited a special
reference in the Report.[26]

According to Harris of the Home Office, they were fortunate that
the Committee thought fit to recommend any increase at all in their
pay. The Report had been written under the shadow of the 'Geddes

axe', the policy of stringency in public spending which followed the report of the Geddes Committee on National Expenditure. It had, said Harris, 'required a good deal of courage at this crucial time in the national finances to recommend any increase in the salaries of public officials'.[27]

The National Association of Probation Officers had been asking for 'a reasonable, legitimate living wage' and for a pension scheme.[28] 'Strong representations' had been made to the Committee on this subject. However, with only a small proportion of probation officers in the direct employment of local authorities, and in view of the number of other employers involved, the Committee was unable to see how a pension scheme embracing all officers employed wholly or mainly on probation work could be devised.[29]

That the Committee was asked to consider the training of probation officers indicates that the Home Office was inclined to pay some attention to the matter. The necessity for training had been stressed by the Howard Association and others who looked to America for a model when the introduction of the probation system was being considered and occasionally since, but administrative and other practical matters appear to have pushed the subject into the background. The Departmental Committee of 1909 did not discuss it at all.

At that time training for social work was not in any case very well developed. This had had its beginnings on both sides of the Atlantic towards the end of the last century,[30] a progeny of the social work then being carried out in voluntary organisations such as the Charity Organisation Society and the Settlements. The desire of the well-educated workers involved to pass on the principles which underlay this Victorian charitable work, and to maintain high standards, led them to start schemes of training within their own agencies or in co-operation with others. Thus Octavia Hill, and Margaret Sewell, Warden of the Women's University Settlement in Southwark, together started training through lectures and practical work for recruits to their fields of work. Training and discussion of training was also an important feature of the Charity Organisation Society's operations in the 1890s, and in 1903 the School of Sociology, an independent institution, had been set up in London by a Committee which severed itself from the Society. This School was amalgamated in 1912 with the London School of Economics, and the two-year course it had run for intending social workers continued to be offered.[31]

Meanwhile a School of Social Science offering a similar course had been established at Liverpool University in 1904, and a number of other universities also introduced the two-year social science diploma courses which Leeson and other reformers saw as suitable for those wishing to take up probation work. However the organisations engaged in social work saw these courses as useful only for providing the necessary background knowledge of the social sciences. They continued to arrange their own more practical 'professional' training as a necessary addition to a university course.[32]

Social work training, then, was in its infancy when probation was introduced in 1907. Interest in it was centred mainly in the university settlements and the Charity Organisation Society and its offshoots such as the Council of Almoners. The largest group of probation officers, the missionaries, were not of this stable. Where training touched them, if at all, was through schemes run by religious bodies for parochial workers.[33] Since the government had had little idea how and to what extent the probation system would develop it is not surprising that proposals about training, especially for part-time work done mainly by the employees of other bodies, were largely ignored.

Although training opportunities for social workers were still very limited, and available mainly to the well educated, by the end of the first world war interest in training for probation officers was growing amongst those closely involved with the work. In 1919 Cecil Chapman, the Metropolitan Magistrate, who gave evidence to the Departmental Committee, recommended intending probation officers to take the training in social work offered by the London School of Economics. 'The work of supervision', he said, 'involves a great deal more than tact and sympathy: visiting and the writing of adequate reports require strength of body and mind, and amateurishness of performance is a mere waste of time and money'.[34]

Another witness, T. W. Trought, a Birmingham magistrate greatly interested in probation, was also advocating higher education and systematic training for probation officers. He thought universities and colleges should be asked to provide academic education for those wishing to take up the work, and that the local Benches should 'furnish practical training under regular officers',[35] as was the case in training for other branches of social work.

At a meeting of probation officers in 1919, one of their number, who for twenty-seven years had served as a police court missionary, called for the introduction of training centres for probation officers. He claimed that many of his mistakes could have been avoided if he had had more guidance when he first took up the work. The courts ought not, he said, to be places where untrained and inexperienced officers conducted their experiments.[36]

Nevertheless, the Departmental Committee was particularly weak in its discussion of training. The Police Court Mission and the Church Army, it reported, both undertook the training of police court missionaries. The Report contained no description or criticism of these schemes. The two organisations, it was suggested, might give to selected candidates the opportunity to benefit from higher education and wider social work experience whilst in receipt of a salary.[37] But whilst acknowledging that there was a need in the service for people with a university background, the Committee do not appear to have given serious attention to the suggestion that the education and training afforded by the university social science courses was what was required for probation officers. An indication of its view of probation work can be gained from its comment that 'It must be remembered that men and women who go to the universities usually do so to fit themselves for a professional career, and it is doubtful whether a probation service organised on the lines we consider desirable would provide opportunities or prospects which would usually attract candidates of university training.'[38]

Although the Committee wanted the development of probation work to remain in local hands, it recognised that a central authority was needed 'to bring the importance of the work to the knowledge of magistrates, to keep in touch with and study its development both in this country and abroad, and to collect and publish information.' This was 'naturally' one of the functions of the Home Secretary. The 1909 Committee had suggested that an official at the Home Office should be specially charged with this kind of work and the Home Office had acted upon the recommendation. Nevertheless, over ten years later, this other Committee found that the staff of the Home Office had been 'so taken up with other duties that there has been difficulty in providing satisfactorily for the development of probation work'.

This should not be allowed to happen again, their report implied. The Children's Branch of the Home Office should be provided with sufficient staff to enable more time to be devoted to probation. It was also suggested that an annual Home Office report on the state of the probation service would be of use to magistrates, probation officers and to other social workers, a suggestion repeated years later in 1936 and 1962 by other committees on the probation service but not acted upon until 1966, although the Children's Branch of the Home Office did from 1923 bring out occasional reports on the whole of its work, including probation.

Another new recommendation was that the Home Secretary

should appoint a small, unpaid Advisory Committee in connection with probation work. Representatives of magistrates, local authorities and probation officers, and others with special knowledge or experience, should be asked to serve on such a body; and those from the London area should form an additional body to assist with the organisation of the work and the appointment of officers in the Metropolitan Police Court District.

Some witnesses advocated the institution of an inspectorate for the probation service, but the Committee wished to leave the development of the work very much in local hands. It did, however, want to see closer co-operation between central and local authorities and recommended that the Home Office should keep in touch with developments in all areas and discuss with local authorities the organisation of their schemes.[39]

Although the Committee did not recommend any immediate extension of central government control over the local administration of probation—except through the extension of advisory and information services—one of its most important recommendations did foreshadow an increase of supervision from the centre. This was the recommendation for which the Home Office had looked when the Committee was set up. The time had now come, the Committee considered, for the institution of a government grant towards the cost of probation:

> Having regard to the national importance of a good probation service, the direct saving to the Exchequer when probation is successful, and to the fact that the State already contributes to the cost of elementary schools, reformatory and industrial schools, places of detention and other public services, we strongly recommended that the Government should undertake— at any rate when the financial position is clearer—to pay half the cost of providing Probation Officers.

It continued:

> If a Government grant on these lines were agreed to, it should carry with it a certain amount of supervision without direct interference with the organisation of the work on local lines. When a County or Borough wishes to obtain the Government grant they should submit a scheme for the approval of the Home Office, giving particulars of the scheme and the number and qualifications of the Probation Officers they propose to appoint.[40]

When published early in 1922, the Report met with moderate

88

approval. It recommended steps which had been advocated in some cases over a good number of years by those interested in probation work: every court should have a probation officer at its disposal; the remuneration of probation officers should be improved; the government should provide a grant towards the cost of the service.

The newly constituted Magistrates' Association regretted that the Committee had not insisted that a government grant should be made available immediately.[41] This important new organisation had been founded by a group of justices, supported by the Howard League, while the Committee was sitting. Its purpose was to supply magistrates with useful information, to promote uniformity of practice amongst them, and to encourage the use of reformative methods in the treatment of offenders. 'To secure in England and Wales a thorough application of the probation system' was one of its immediate aims.[42] This was not surprising, Cecil Leeson being its first secretary.

Probation officers knew well how much the success of the probation system depended on the attitude of the magistrates. At their 1920 Conference, Alderman Wilkins of Derby, a justice who could not be accused of apathy, had said that there were still 'thousands of magistrates' who knew nothing of probation work.[43] The formation of this progressive-sounding body was greeted enthusiastically by Edridge who looked forward to the great benefits it would bring to the probation service.[44]

His Association was chiefly disappointed with the Departmental Committee's conclusions about a superannuation scheme.[45] The Howard League was particularly disappointed with its recommendations on training.[46] As for the C.E.T.S., they accepted the Committee's criticisms with what appeared to be a good grace and a determination to retain their place in the service by making some of the changes suggested in the Report.

The Home Office, for their part, had got from the Committee the recommendation and information they required for an eventual approach to the Treasury for money in aid of probation work. In the meantime, two familiar courses of action were pursued. Still having no power to direct, the Home Office again tried to encourage courts to make a wider and more efficient use of their powers under the Probation of Offenders Act; and action was begun upon those recommendations which did not require legislation. A copy of the Committee's Report was sent to all magistrates' courts, local authorities and Standing Joint Committees. The attention of the magistrates was drawn particularly to the Committee's recommendation that each Bench should appoint from among its number a small Committee to organise probation work. A good many courts, they were told, were already finding such an arrangement valuable. The Home Office suggested that such a Committee should

> undertake the important task of selecting suitable men and women as Probation Officers and consider questions of remuneration; hold periodical meetings with Probation Officers to receive their reports and supervise their work; and generally watch over the progress of probation in the district.

The Courts were also asked to review the remuneration of their probation officers in the light of the Report, and it was inferred that they would have the moral support of the central authority in their dealings with the local authorities, who were asked in turn to co-operate with the justices in providing adequate salaries. The Home Office were able to announce that it had already been decided to adopt for London the scales suggested by the Committee.[47]

The Report gave impetus to the work of the Home Office official in charge of probation matters. The question of probation organisation was taken up with a number of individual Benches and local authorities. Houston, who had served as Secretary of the Departmental Committee and who had this special assignment, told a gathering of the National Association of Probation Officers, that he found this aspect of the work no easy matter.[48] Houston also became Secretary of the Advisory Committee which was now appointed by the Home Secretary as a result of the Report. Sir John Baird, who had been Chairman of the Departmental Committee, was made Chairman of the new Committee. Harris of the Home Office also became a member, along with three Metropolitan Magistrates (Clarke Hall among them), three provincial magistrates, a justices' clerk, a county clerk, an official of the Police Court Mission, one of the Prison Commissioners, and three probation officers, one of whom was a missionary attached to the C.E.T.S.[49] All three probation officers were members of the National Association of Probation Officers, which quickly recognised in the Committee a new avenue for the expression of their point of view. Members were exhorted to keep the three probation officers well informed upon matters affecting their interests.[50]

The Home Office made use of the Advisory Committee as steps were taken to implement other recommendations in the 1922 Report. One of its first duties was to consider the amendment of the Probation Rules, mainly with a view to enabling the Home Office to obtain fuller information about local probation organisation. This

90

was needed, not only for general purposes, but also for the compilation of the annual reports it was hoped to issue in accordance with the Committee's suggestion.

Amended Rules were issued in June 1923. These prohibited, for the first time, the appointment of members of the police force or school attendance officers as probation officers. Even the engagement of persons retired from these occupations was only to be contemplated in very exceptional circumstances. Following a recommendation of the Departmental Committee, this instrument also abolished the system of annual appointment,[51] about which the National Association of Probation Officers had complained for so long.

The First Report of the Children's Branch of the Home Office came out in the same year. In it the Home Office acknowledged the greater interest now being displayed by the justices in the probation system and welcomed the attention being given to it by the Magistrates' Association.[52]

Those members of the Advisory Committee who were also concerned with the organisation of probation work in London met more frequently than the full Committee (which was criticised by the Howard League for meeting only twice in the first eight months of its existence).[53] The London Committee was directly concerned with the practical application of probation in the London Courts—the selection and appointment of new officers and general supervision of their work in the Metropolitan Police Court District.[54]

Soon after the publication of the Report, a deputation from the C.E.T.S. called at the Home Office to discuss in more detail the changes they were prepared to make. Introduced by the Bishop of London to Sir John Baird, they hoped that 'a definite understanding' could now be reached between the C.E.T.S. and the Home Office. They were prepared, they said, to meet Home Office requirements by dropping the Society's name from the title of the Police Court Mission; by basing the latter on county or Quarter-Sessional, rather than diocesan areas, and by increasing the lay membership of their Committees and including, where possible, local magistrates and philanthropists. Their police court missionaries would no longer be required to take an active part in raising funds; and the Missions would endeavour to improve their salaries, which the deputation admitted had been inadequate in the past.

There remained, however, two points of difficulty which were presented by the deputation. These concerned the 'religious test' and the temperance work of the Society, more basic to the pursuit of their objectives than the administrative matters on which they were willing to give way. The Society would have to insist, the deputation

91

said, on their right to appoint Churchmen as their agents. But if the Home Office was willing to recognise this right, they would undertake not to consider themselves bound to appoint an Anglican on every occasion, but to judge each case on its merits. An applicant otherwise well qualified by 'religion and vocation' would not necessarily be rejected on denominational grounds. Further, they would wish to insist on the right of their officers to 'propagate temperance work' if they so desired, although they could undertake that no missionary would be expected to do this against his will.

The deputation left with the asurance that the Home Office was prepared to accept their undertakings in these two instances, and that it was satisfied with the extent to which the Society was willing to fall in with the recommendations in the recent report.[55]

Two other gestures by the Home Office brought further reassurance. The Rev. Harry Pearson, Secretary of the London Police Court Mission, was invited to serve on the Advisory Committee;[56] and at a meeting held by the Society at the Mansion House, Sidney Harris said that, in his personal opinion, probation work could be more efficiently carried out by a religious society than by the government or the local authorities.[57]

In accordance with a suggestion of the Departmental Committee,[58] the C.E.T.S. Branches in the Dioceses of London and Southwark, which provided officers for the Metropolitan Courts, re-organised their police court work so that the whole area could be served by one undertaking entitled 'The London Police Court Mission'[59] (the term by which C.E.T.S. work in the London courts had long been colloquially known). Following the Committee's recommendations, it included on its Committee, besides C.E.T.S. representatives from the two dioceses, three Metropolitan Magistrates and two Middlesex Justices (it also served some courts in that county). Two prominent laymen, Lord Cave, the Lord Chancellor, and Sir Edward Troup, Permanent Under-Secretary of State at the Home Office, accepted invitations to serve as President and Chairman respectively.

Its work was described in its first Annual Report:

> The Police Court Mission has for its object the reformation of
> all offenders charged in the Courts. Its method is to apply the
> remedy of personal, sympathetic assistance instead of fines and
> imprisonment. Every endeavour is made to help first offenders
> and to save them from forming criminal habits. The
> Missionaries are at the service of all who desire their help . . .
> and whether professing any creed or none.

92

Further, they assist the magistrates by making enquiries into the circumstances of persons applying at the Courts for help and advice, and they deal with many cases of difficulty involved in domestic troubles.

They are responsible for the supervision of offenders placed on probation, as they have all been appointed to act as Probation Officers in their respective Courts. All their duties are carried out under the immediate direction of the magistrates.

It looked as if the recommendations of the Departmental Committee were being conscientiously followed by the C.E.T.S. in the London area. There was no reference to temperance in this statement; the title of the C.E.T.S. did not appear in connection with the London Police Court Mission and lay people were elected to its Committee. The Home Office was invited to send an observer to its Committee meetings and it undertook to pay its probation officers the salaries recommended in the 1922 Report.

Later it became clear that the severance of the Mission from the temperance movement was not complete. Although the holder of the two posts, the Rev. Harry Pearson, was at pains to maintain a distinction between them, the Secretary of the Police Court Mission was also the Secretary of the London Diocesan Branch of the C.E.T.S. The Mission's Annual Report was bound together with that of the parent body, and the number of pledges of total abstinence taken by the missionaries still figured in the summaries of their work.[60] This re-organisation in London seems, nevertheless, to have had a beneficial effect and perhaps accounts to some extent for the continuing strength of the London Mission when others began to decline.

The C.E.T.S. branches in the London area went further than its adherents in other parts of the country in carrying out the recommendations of the 1922 report.[61] Some attempt was made to improve the services of the provincial Missions. The Central Police Court Mission appointed a C.E.T.S. Diocesan Secretary as part-time organiser of the Mission work in each of the provinces of Canterbury and York (the ecclesiastical basis of the work persisted in spite of recent criticisms). The organisers could give advice to any diocese on police court mission work.[62] Throughout its existence, however, the central body was hampered by the extreme decentralisation written into its constitution, carefully guarding the autonomy of each Diocesan Branch.

The Central Mission revived the lapsed Guild of Police Court Missionaries and organised an improved pension scheme for the

Missions' employees.[63] By this time the National Association of Probation Officers can be assumed to have been well known, so that the decision to revive the Guild seems to indicate that the C.E.T.S. wished to foster a particular group morale amongst its missionaries. The Guild sought 'to deepen and strengthen the spiritual life of each member and to keep the true Missionary spirit among C.E.T.S. Police Court Missionaries.' It hoped to provide them with opportunities for social intercourse and by means of meetings and lectures 'to promote the greatest benefit to those placed under their care'.[64]

Whilst the Home Office and the C.E.T.S. were engaged in carrying into effect some of the recommendations which did not require legislation, the Magistrates' Association, the Incorporated Society of Justices' Clerks,[65] the National Association of Probation Officers[66] and the Howard League for Penal Reform[67] were urging government action to make mandatory the appointment of a probation officer for every court, to provide an Exchequer grant towards the cost of the probation service, to improve the salaries of probation officers and to make official arrangements for their superannuation.

In 1922, under the presidency of Lord Henry Bentinck, Chairman of the Howard League, a number of interested members of Parliament formed a Penal Reform Group. Soon afterwards a deputation from the Group called on the Parliamentary Under-Secretary at the Home Office to press for a government grant in aid of probation work.[68] In the following year, Bentinck, in a Parliamentary question, asked the Home Secretary whether he did not think that 'the only possible way of getting a more efficient system of probation is for the Government to give a grant towards the maintenance of proper probation institutions'. Mr. Bridgeman replied that he had no doubt that if the Government was prepared to spend money in this way, it might be usefully spent; but it was 'not very easy to go in for additional expenditure at the moment'.[69]

Towards the end of 1923, the Children's Department of the Home Office reviewed in some detail the progress of the probation service, possibly as a result of the pressure for a grant to be given. The review revealed clearly that although the Report of the recent Departmental Committee had aroused fresh interest in probation work, the practical response of the provincial courts to its recommendations had been disappointing. There were still too many courts without a probation officer and only a minority of the eight hundred serving probation officers were employed full time on work in the courts. The failure of the courts to respond to the Committee's

94

recommendations about remuneration was especially disappointing. And the Home Office was still hearing of local authorities who refused to approve the reasonable payment for probation officers suggested by the justices.

It was obvious that something more was required to accelerate progress than the existing arrangement whereby the Home Office official who was Secretary of the Advisory Council attempted through propaganda and occasional visits to encourage the development of a permissive service. Experience had shown that 'the attempt to organise the service by correspondence from Whitehall' had failed, and that closer personal contact between officials at the Home Office and the magistrates and probation officers in the courts was needed.

In view of the system's dependence upon the interest of the magistracy, the Home Office had so far considered it 'better to persuade than to coerce'. But clearly, encouragement and persuasion were not going to be sufficient to induce all courts to appoint a probation officer.[70] The situation required that the Home Secretary should be given a more authoritative role in the structure of the service.

The Departmental Committee had already pointed the way to this by strongly recommending that the government should make itself responsible for providing a grant to cover half the cost incurred by local authorities in the provision of probation officers. Such a grant would materially assist the system; it would also enable the Home Office to obtain greater control over such essential aspects of the service as the appointment and payment of the officers, without greatly hindering development on local lines.

Accordingly, the Home Office sought Treasury approval of the principle of a government grant.[71] As Bridgeman had indicated in the Commons, this was not an advantageous time for such a request. The Geddes Committee on National Expenditure[72] had recommended a reduction in the amount spent on government grants, and had condemned the use of percentage grants (which was what the Home Office had in mind for probation) on the ground that the central government was obliged to contribute in step with local authority spending over which it had no control.

However, it could be argued that in the case of a grant towards the salaries and expenses of probation officers, the Home Office would be able to control the level of expenditure by regulating the number and salaries of officers. What was more, the payment of a grant towards probation could have the effect of reducing the need for central government expenditure on institutional forms of

95

treatment.

Agreeing to the principle of a grant, and that the percentage system might be adopted experimentally, the Treasury stipulated that the Home Office 'must keep check on the numbers appointed and keep rates of pay down, and there must be no evidence that the government grant is killing voluntary assistance'.[73]

Parliamentary sanction for the proposed expenditure was now required. By this time the first Labour government had come into power and was preparing to introduce a Criminal Justice Bill to improve the administration of justice. Their Bill[74] closely resembled one which, in the previous session, had gone through the Lords and into the Commons, but failed to complete its passage on account of the general election.[75] It was now decided to add to the Bill a part dealing with the probation of offenders.[76]

A Memorandum on the Bill explained that the object of this part was

> to encourage the development of the probation system in the
> light of experience, especially by providing for the appointment
> of probation officers in each petty sessional division, by
> promoting the combination of petty sessional divisions
> for this purpose, and by improving the methods of super-
> vising and paying probation officers.

These proposals clearly reflected the recommendations of the recent Departmental Committee.

The Bill was introduced in the Lords by the Lord Chancellor, Viscount Haldane, who told his fellow peers that he had become well acquainted with the problems of the probation service through his connections with the Magistrates' Association. The government, he said, wished to make the system more effective by spending upon it a moderate sum of money. It proposed to make to local authorities, not an absolute grant, but a grant-in-aid to be given only on condition that probation work was being efficiently carried out.[77]

Viscount Cave, Lord Chancellor in the previous government, supported the Bill on behalf of the Opposition,[78] and the Church of England Temperance Society's spokesman in the Lords, the Bishop of London, expressed himself 'most enthusiastically in favour'.[79]

The Central Police Court Mission was somewhat alarmed,[80] however, at the government's proposal to repeal Section 7 of the Criminal Justice Administration Act, 1914, which gave the Home Secretary power to make grants to voluntary societies.[81] Although this power had never been used, the Mission considered that its deliberate omission would make it appear that the work of the voluntary societies was now being discouraged.[82]

The Bishop moved an amendment which sought to allow the 1914 provision to stand. He also proposed that a clause should be added to the government's Bill which would make it clear that 'nothing in this Part of this Act shall affect the right of voluntary societies to supply agents for the missionary work in any probation area, or for engagement as probation officers.'

Assured by Lord Haldane that the government had no desire to interfere with the work of the voluntary societies, he withdrew his amendments.[83] But the Missions were still uneasy, especially when they discovered that some interested people had received the impression that the Bill would terminate the participation of voluntary societies in probation work. Approached about this difficulty, the Home Office suggested that the Society should arrange for a question to be asked in the Commons to which the Bill had now gone; the reply would serve to dispel any misconception.[84] Sir William Joynson-Hicks, who had watched the Society's interests in Parliament on another occasion, put the question and received the desired assurance from the Home Secretary.[85]

The Bill's progress was hampered in the Commons by the weight of government business,[86] and then curtailed by the defeat of the Labour government and the subsequent general election. However, the Home Office could confidently look forward to the re-introduction of the Bill by the new Conservative government, which was known to be in favour of its proposals.

In any case the payment of a government grant was not held up. An arrangement made whilst the Labour government was still in office had secured that if the necessary legislation could not be passed that session, a grant towards probation for the coming year could be authorised by a Vote in the House of Commons. The sum of £22,250 was accordingly included in the Department's estimates for the year 1924–5 to cover a government contribution of approximately half the estimated cost of the probation service.[87] The money was voted and immediately distributed to local authorities in the form of a 50 per cent grant based on the actual expenditure incurred by each in the previous year.[88]

In March 1925, Joynson-Hicks, now Home Secretary, introduced into the Commons substantially the same Criminal Justice Bill, in which provision was made for the payment of a government grant towards the cost of the probation service:

There shall be paid out of monies provided by Parliament towards the expenditure of local authorities under this Part of

97

the Act . . . such sums as the Secretary of State, with the
approval of the Treasury, may direct and, subject to such
conditions as he may with like approval determine.[89]

Apart from this, the most important proposals in this part of the
Bill were those concerning the local organisation of the probation
service. The basic unit of organisation would be a 'probation area',
and the appointment of at least one probation officer for every area
would be mandatory.[90] Each petty sessional division would become
a probation area, though the Bill made an important exception in
providing that the Home Secretary should have the power to make
orders combining two or more divisions to form a single probation
area.[91] Courts of quarter sessions in counties would be able to
submit schemes to the Home Secretary containing proposals about
the constitution of combined areas.[92] Probation work in each
probation area would in general be the responsibility of a new
statutory body, the probation committee, composed of a number of
magistrates. In an area which comprised a single division, this
committee would be appointed by the Bench; in combined areas, by
the justices of the various divisions in a manner prescribed by the
Home Secretary in the combination order.

In combined areas, the probation committee would appoint and
pay the officers for the whole area, but their work with probationers
would be supervised in each division by a committee—also called a
probation committee—appointed for this purpose by the local
Bench. In other areas the whole Bench would retain the
responsibility for the appointment of officers unless choosing to
delegate this to its probation committee. The committee would in
any case pay the officers and supervise their work.[93]

The money for the salaries and expenses of probation officers
would continue to be provided by the local authorities: but, whereas,
under the 1907 Act, they had been able to refuse to pay the
remuneration suggested by the justices, this Bill proposed to give
them no such opportunity to interfere. The Bill provided that
remuneration should be fixed by the probation committee for the
area and would require the approval of the Home Secretary, to
whom any dissatisfied local authority could make representations.[94]

At the Report Stage, Mr. John Guest, who said he had the
interests of ratepayers at heart, convinced the Home Secretary that
the local paying authorities should have more say in the matter of
salaries. The Bill was accordingly amended to allow that, subject to
any regulations which might be made about remuneration and
expenses, these should be agreed between the probation committee

and the local authority. If the two bodies failed to agree, the amounts should be determined by the Home Secretary.[95]

As under the 1907 Act, the Home Secretary would have the power to make rules, but the new Bill specifically gave him the right to fix salaries, expenses and superannuation payments, to prescribe the qualifications of probation officers and to provide that appointments should not be effective unless confirmed by him.[96]

As well as making probable the improvement of the salaries of probation officers by proposing that the Home Secretary should have power to regulate them, the Bill sought to allow the Home Secretary to arrange for the introduction of a superannuation scheme for probation officers.[97]

The Departmental Committee had urged that women officers should as a rule be appointed to supervise women probationers and that specially qualified children's officers should whenever possible be attached to every juvenile court.[98] The Bill did not seek to make such arrangements mandatory, but proposed that they should be made 'where circumstances permit'.[99] The opportunity was also taken in the Bill to give local authorities power to contribute towards the maintenance of a person released on probation with a condition of residence.[100]

Opposition to these proposals was negligible. For a second time, however, the Police Court Missions were disappointed to find no allusion to voluntary societies in the Bill.[101] But on this occasion they had an important sympathiser in the Home Secretary, who, to demonstrate his goodwill towards the voluntary societies, moved an amendment when he opened the debate on the second reading, to the effect that 'it shall be lawful to appoint as a probation officer for any area ... a person who is the agent of a voluntary society, and any sums payable by way of salary, remuneration or otherwise ... to such an agent may be paid to the Society.'[102]

This proposal did not go altogether unchallenged. At the Report Stage, Mr. Westwood moved to leave out the clause, not, apparently because he was opposed to the principle of the appointment of agents, but on the ground that payment should be made direct to the probation officers themselves. Thus, he argued, 'we should have control in connection with these men who have been doing such splendid work, and we should be sure that they receive adequate remuneration for their work'.

Supporting the retention of the clause, Joynson-Hicks reminded the House that the voluntary societies had made a large contribution to the probation system. The government and the Treasury considered it 'no small thing' that these organisations now provided between £30,000 and £40,000 a year towards the work. He also considered it helpful that probation officers should sometimes be able to talk over difficult cases with some committee apart from the magistrates, and those attached to the voluntary societies had this opportunity.

The House decided that the clause should stand,[103] and thereafter this part of the Criminal Justice Bill passed easily through its Parliamentary stages and the measure received the Royal Assent on 22nd December 1925.

CHAPTER FIVE

A PERIOD OF EXPANSION

The increased control which the Home Secretary was now able to exercise over the probation service as a consequence of the grant-in-aid was evident in the longer and more detailed Probation Rules issued in 1926. For the first time the Home Office could claim to have some control outside the London area over the kind of person given a permanent appointment in the probation service. Although the initial selection of probation officers remained firmly with the local probation committees, the Home Office now had to be given notice of every new appointment and details of the age, qualifications, experience and salary of the new entrant. What was more, the continuance of any such appointment for more than one year was made dependent upon the approval of the Home Secretary.[1]

Unsatisfactory appointments were still undoubtedly being made and, as well as insisting upon the approval of appointments, the Home Office tried, through the Rules, to give some guidance to the magistrates making the selection. They were not to confine their consideration to those acknowledgedly primary qualities, strength of character and suitable personality, but were also to take account of a candidate's education, experience, training and physical fitness.[2] There was still no guidance as to what the justices should regard as suitable training for the work. So little, of course, was available.

The new Rules made twenty-five the lower, and thirty-five the upper, age limit for future entrants to the service, thus limiting to a very narrow age range the field from which courts could draw new probation officers. The decision to set such a low maximum age was connected with the Home Office plan shortly to introduce a superannuation scheme for full-time officers.[3] Retirement at sixty-five was also insisted upon—no doubt to ensure that standards should not be jeopardised by the employment of persons too old to perform the work efficiently.[4]

The fixing of salary scales by regulation was an important controlling function now assumed by the Home Secretary.[5] A substantial increase in the number of good quality candidates could not be expected without an increase in the salaries offered. The new Rules also allowed for the fixing, with the approval of the Home Secretary, of a special scale for Principal Officers and for probation officers with approved university qualifications.

Unfortunately, the scales of pay incorporated in the 1926 Probation Rules applied only to full-time probation officers, and therefore to a minority of those employed on probation duties. However, fixed salaries—intended to reflect the probable number of cases to be supervised and the character and extent of the district served—instead of fees, were now to be paid to all part-time workers.[6]

The salary scales for the full-time workers applied to both missionary officers and those in the direct employ of the courts. For some years it had been the practice in the Metropolitan Police Court District for the voluntary societies to be responsible for one-third of their agent's salary and for the Receiver, on behalf of the Home Office, to provide the remaining two-thirds. The Rules now extended this system to all other areas.[7]

A system for recording the details of probation cases, which had been introduced in London early in 1925,[8] was similarly made compulsory for all probation areas.[9] In this way, probation records, like the salaries of full-time officers, were standardised throughout England and Wales.

The constitution and duties of the newly created Probation Committees were laid down in some detail. In connection with their supervision of the work they were specifically enjoined to discuss with the probation officer 'from time to time' the progress of each probationer and to give such help and advice as they were able.[10]

The Committee of 1922 had suggested that Courts of Quarter Sessions could with advantage use probation more freely.[11] The Assize Courts also made very little use of the system. The Home Office hoped that a new rule making it clear with which area responsibility for supervision lay in any particular case, would encourage these higher courts to make more probation orders. The supervision of any offender placed on probation was to be undertaken by the probation officer for the area in which he resided, whether the order had been made by the local magistrates, those of another area, or by a higher court.[12] It was also more likely that a court would make probation orders if a probation officer was in attendance at its sittings. The new rules authorised Probation Committees to allocate the services of a probation officer to Quarter Sessions,[13] but omitted to provide in a similar way for Assizes.

In 1926, the Home Office greatly improved the employment conditions of full-time probation officers by introducing the superannuation scheme for which the Criminal Justice Act provided. The Committee which reported in 1922 had considered impracticable a general superannuation scheme for probation officers: but it was recognised at the Home Office that the officers greatly needed the security which such a scheme would impart, that a scheme would help to attract good candidates and would also ensure that officers were not retained beyond the age when they could be expected to render satisfactory service.[14] Accordingly, even before the Criminal Justice Bill was safely through Parliament, a small committee of Home Office and Treasury officials, probation officers, the secretary of the C.E.T.S. and a justice of the peace, was appointed to prepare a scheme.[15]

Introduced the following year, the scheme related only to full-time officers. Equal contributions to the Probation Officers' Superannuation Fund were required of the officer and his local authority. In the case of the missionary officers, contributions from each of these two sources were two-thirds of those for the independent officers. Their pensions were likewise to be two-thirds of their independent colleagues'.[16] It was hoped that their societies, already responsible for a third of their salaries, would assume a similar responsibility for providing a third of their pension. Some Missions already provided pensions for their agents.[17] Others, however, were to fail to make these expected arrangements and their agents to suffer in consequence.

It was arranged that officers who at the time were over fifty-five should receive small gratuitous pensions, the missionary ones two-thirds of those awarded to the independents.[18] Some members of the National Association of Probation Officers carried on, without success, a prolonged and poorly conducted protest against what they considered to be this shabby treatment of the older missionaries.[19]

That the Home Office was keen to inaugurate a superannuation scheme for probation officers supports the impression that work in the probation service was recognised as being inherently a full-time permanent undertaking, comparable in status with that of other public servants, such as local government officers, who already enjoyed the relatively rare fringe benefit of a superannuation scheme.

The promotion of combination schemes for the better organisation of probation, especially in county areas, became an important concern of the Children's Branch. By 1928, thirty-six of the sixty administrative counties in England and Wales had schemes approved by the Home Secretary, and three orders had been made directing certain boroughs and county districts to combine to form a probation area.[20]

The Home Office was disappointed to find, however, that combination did not in itself wholly achieve the desired ends. Not all combined areas were willing to provide enough probation officers adequately to perform the available work. A policy of stringency in public spending was being maintained in conditions of continuing economic recession. 'The need for economy has been reflected in these as in other matters' the Children's Department reported in 1928, consoling themselves, however, with the observation that to have created an authority responsible for probation work in areas which had hitherto been devoid of organisation was 'a notable development',[21] and no doubt hoping for improvements when the economic situation changed for the better.

The setting up of the combined areas had involved its staff in a considerable amount of travelling to provincial courts and local authorities. Personal contact between the Home Office officials and those involved in the probation service outside London was thereby increased. The officials had also interviewed all recent entrants during their first year in the service in connection with the rule that all new appointments should lapse after one year unless confirmed by the Home Secretary. Some other officers had also been visited, and thus, for the first time, the Home Office began to establish what they considered 'valuable contact with the personnel of the probation staff in districts outside the London area.'[22]

Despite this increased 'outside' activity, the department's knowledge of the state of probation work in some areas was scanty. It relied heavily for information upon annual reports voluntarily forwarded by the courts, and no doubt it was by the most interested courts that these were sent. Where reports were not forthcoming, the Children's Branch had to acknowledge that it was unable to 'give particulars of the local, as opposed to the general, development of the work outside London.'[23]

Although there was certainly more contact than previously between the Home Office and the provincial courts, the increased control given to the Home Secretary along with the grant-in-aid system had not been reinforced by the customary concomitant, the power of inspection. The Committee set up in 1920 had considered the question, but had not been prepared to go so far as to advocate inspection, even though it recommended the payment of a grant-in-aid. During the review of the system by the Home Office in 1923 however, Harris had minuted, 'The attempt to organise the service by correspondence from Whitehall has failed, and it is quite obvious that some form of inspection is essential.'[24] The matter was again considered by the Departmental Committee on the Treatment of Young Offenders set up in January 1925 by Sir William Joynson-Hicks on becoming Home Secretary in the new Conservative government, interest in the treatment of young offenders having been stimulated in the country by the report of a Departmental Committee on Sexual Offences Against Young Persons in 1925.

The new committee under the chairmanship of Sir Evelyn Cecil, later succeeded by Sir Thomas Molony, was given far broader terms of reference than had been customary for such enquiries, which had usually been limited to a specific method of treatment or problem. This breadth reflected developments in thinking about the causes of juvenile delinquency and the related espousal of reformation as a principal objective in dealing with young offenders, whose characters were seen as 'still plastic and the more readily moulded by wise and sympathetic treatment.'[25] This required a policy of careful diagnosis and the selection by courts of 'treatment' suited to the needs of the offender. Thus it was appropriate that a Committee of Inquiry should examine the system in the round.

As it was only three years since the Committee on the Training, Appointment and Payment of Probation Officers had reported, and as it was still too early to assess the effects of the recent Criminal Justice Act, the Young Offenders Committee did decide to limit its enquiries concerning probation to certain aspects of the system.[26] Its chief significance for the development of probation stemmed from its observations and recommendations about the role of the Home Office, arrangements for pre-trial enquiries, and the use of homes and hostels in connection with the probation system, and from its proposal that the supervisory work of the probation officer should be extended to the neglected, as well as to the delinquent child.

Although the Young Offenders Committee had received 'a good deal of evidence as to the need for much closer central control over the manner in which probation is carried on', inspection could not, in its view, 'very well be applied to probation . . . as to institutions'. The Home Office should however play a more positive part in the development and surveillance of the service, a role more consistent in the Committee's opinion with the administration of the government grant. If the department acted as a clearing house for ideas and methods, and provided increased opportunities for consultation and discussion, it would render considerable service to isolated magistrates and probation officers. The Committee recommended that the staff currently employed on probation matters at the Home Office should be extended and re-organised to enable this function to be adequately exercised.[27] It also suggested the reconstitution of the Advisory Committee on Probation and the extension of its terms of reference to include after-care, in which probation officers were becoming increasingly involved.[28]

The failure of some magistrates to obtain adequate information about the circumstances and environment of children and young persons before ordering treatment had been pointed out from time to time.[29] Recent enquiries made by the Home Office showed that there were still a few courts which never arranged to be provided with such information, and that others did so only when it appeared necessary.

In the majority of courts where reports of this kind were used, they were provided by the police force. However, a considerable number relied on the probation officer to provide information, either instead of, or in addition to, that given by the police. In a few areas the School Attendance Officers made the relevant enquiries.[30] The Young Offenders Committee regarded the provision of these reports as essential to the proper working of the juvenile courts and, through them, of the probation system. The police force, it suggested, was not necessarily the best agency to provide them; on the other hand, the reports of the School Attendance Officers, who were 'constantly visiting the children's homes', should always be available. Reports from these sources could 'usefully be supplemented by special enquiries made by the court's probation officers.'[31]

This implication that the reports of the School Attendance Officers were a necessity, those of the probation officers merely a useful addition, led to long-lasting confusion and disagreement about the responsibilities of the two types of officer in connection with cases appearing before the juvenile courts.[32]

A very practical recommendation made by the Committee in this connection was that the police should notify the Local Education Authority and the probation officers of every case scheduled to be heard in the juvenile courts, so that reports could be prepared.[33]

More than ten years had elapsed since the Criminal Justice Administration Act, 1914, had given courts the power to make residence in a specific place a condition of probation. Since the terms of reference of the 1920 Committee had not extended to this, the Young Offenders Committee was the first to look into the use which had been made of this power. It found that since 1915 there had been an increasing tendency to associate probation with institutional treatment. Sometimes this was done in an irregular way, and in the committee's opinion there was cause for anxiety about

106

this process.[34] Some magistrates were using a probation order with a condition of residence in cases where committal to a reformatory school would have been more appropriate. This was not always a result of inadequate knowledge of the offender's needs and circumstances, but, rather, a means of providing institutional treatment without recording the conviction necessary when sending a child to a school. Sometimes the method was adopted to avoid using the schools because the magistrates believed (mistakenly, in the Committee's view) that these institutions still clung to the primitive methods of earlier years.

In another part of its report the Committee was recommending that convictions should no longer be recorded in juvenile courts. It hoped that, if this was accepted, and if magistrates became better acquainted with the present methods used in reformatory and industrial schools, probation with a condition of residence would be restricted to the type of case for which it was originally intended.

An irregular use of residence sometimes arose as a result of magistrates placing on probation an offender whose home background completely frustrated the officer's efforts. The latter then sometimes resorted to the expedient of finding a Home which would look after his charge. The Committee pointed out that the adoption of its recommendation that home surroundings reports should be available in all cases would mean that this situation should no longer arise.

Some of the homes to which probationers were being directed were institutions whose purpose was to give a lengthy period of training, within their own walls, of a kind not unlike that provided by the reformatory and industrial schools. There was no statutory inspection of such places, some of them 'run on narrow and old-fashioned lines', and the Committee was alarmed by its discovery of an 'illogical and even dangerous situation in which a lad or girl can be sent to an uninspected Home for (say) two years, instead of to the institutions which have been specially provided for the training of these young people with the guarantee of government inspection.' There was a danger, they reported, that 'unless suitable safeguards are found, unsatisfactory forms of institutional treatment may grow up as part of the probation system.'[35]

The Committee, whose terms of reference ensured that it would see probation in the context of the existing range of methods for dealing with young offenders, helped to avert this possibility by insisting that the function of the probation system was to provide supervision in the open. The condition of residence attached to a probation order was not a means of providing institutional treatment

107

over a long period, but a device to remove an offender from an unsuitable home background for a relatively short period, giving him, at the same time, the benefit of a probation officer's help and advice. This type of treatment could best be carried out, the Committee thought, through residence in 'hostels' where probationers could lodge whilst 'pursuing ordinary work in conditions of freedom', rather than in 'homes' where they worked as well as lived. The probation system should not, they insisted, 'be associated with institutional training in the strict sense'.

Some homes, it suggested, could well be transformed into hostels and thus become more appropriate for use in connection with the probation system. This would help to alleviate the shortage of such accommodation, which should always require the approval and inspection of the central authority. It would be possible to give them some financial help under the Criminal Justice Act, 1925, which allowed local authorities and the Home Office to contribute towards the maintenance costs of persons released on probation.[36]

This Committee was concerned with neglected as well as delinquent children, hitherto treated separately both in legislation and in practice. Its recommendations laid the foundations of a different approach to the two classes based on its opinion that 'in many cases the tendency to commit offences is only an outcome of the conditions of neglect, and there is little room for discrimination either in the character of the young person concerned or in the appropriate method of treatment'.[37] This principle was reflected in the recommendation that the kind of supervision provided by probation officers could usefully be extended to the neglected child.[38]

Now that their functions and methods were becoming better understood and appreciated, and that probation officers were being appointed for every area, it was perhaps to be expected that use would be made of them in an increasing variety of ways. By this time it was common to find a probation officer carrying out after-care work on behalf of Home Office schools or the Borstal Association,[39] and the Young Offenders Committee's recommendations for the improvement of after-care services in no way envisaged a lessening of the probation officers' involvement in this work.[40]

Some courts had been using their probation officers to supervise offenders between the ages of sixteen and twenty-one who had been allowed time to pay fines. The Committee, anxious further to reduce the number of young people committed to prison in default of payment of fines, considered that greater use of the courts' powers[41] to place them under the supervision of some person until the fine was paid, could effectively contribute to this. Probation officers, it thought, were well qualified to undertake the work, but it did not advocate their invariable use for this purpose. Other suitable persons, it reported, could no doubt be found to assist the court by exercising this kind of supervision.[42]

The imagination of the Committee was caught by 'an admirable arrangement' pioneered in Cardiff where, since 1924, probation officers had been used instead of police officers to escort children to Home Office schools. The system had soon been adopted by the Home Office in the Metropolitan Police Court District and by a number of other areas.

In approving of this and other additional duties for probation officers, the Committee warned that Probation Committees should take these into account when determining the number of staff needed for their area. For, like earlier committees of enquiry, it had heard of work badly executed as a result of the over-burdening of officers. This could of course be avoided, the Committee pointed out, if Probation Committees would exercise 'constant and effective supervision' over the work.[43]

Some witnesses advocated the appointment of Chief Probation Officers to organise the work and to supervise the other officers. The Probation Rules, 1926, did in fact provide that an authority might pay a higher salary to a principal probation officer 'appointed to supervise the work of other probation officers'.[44] However, the Committee found 'the general trend of opinion' to be 'against any creation of different ranks of probation officers'. It was feared that such an arrangement might interfere with the special and important relationship which should ideally exist between the magistrates, the probation officer and the probationer.[45]

As to the quality of the officers themselves, the Committee expected the new salary scales and pension scheme to attract more suitable candidates, and expressed themselves interested to see how many people possessing university qualifications would come forward. The new scales allowed for the payment of such people on a higher salary scale than that for those with more modest qualifications,[46] but even these rates should not, the Committee considered be regarded as final.[47]

Not all magistrates were yet taking very seriously the appointment of their probation officers, for the Committee found it necessary to recommend that in future 'all vacancies ... should be advertised ... and ... candidates interviewed personally by the appointing authorities'.

The abolition of dual control was again demanded by a number of witnesses. Not yet, however, was a Committee prepared to approve the abandonment of the voluntary element in the probation service. Once again the long connection of the voluntary societies with the social work of the courts, and the financial advantages gained from the employment of their agents, counted in their favour. Besides, the Committee confessed itself none too sure that it would be possible to staff the service without the missionaries—though many of them would surely have turned 'independent' in the event of the abolition of dual control. There was also the useful service rendered by voluntary societies in making money available for certain aspects of the work which could not suitably count as legitimate public expenditure.

The imposition of denominational tests, which might preclude the recruitment of some good candidates,[48] was seen by this Committee as the main risk accompanying the continuance of the system of dual control. After the 1922 Report had recommended that the Church of England Temperance Society should help to widen the field of recruitment to the probation service by allowing non-Anglicans to serve as its agents, the Society had insisted upon their 'right' to appoint only Churchmen, but promised to consider all future applications on their merits and not necessarily to reject a good candidate on denominational grounds.[49] But many, if not all, branches of the Society, failed to act upon this undertaking.[50] In *Children's Courts*, published in 1926, William Clarke Hall severely censured the Missions for their use of denominational tests. He called upon them to forgo this practice and to place their organisation at the service of the public instead of continuing 'to regard it as a mere annexe to their own particular church, to use for its own propaganda'. In the magistrate's opinion, this 'great public' work should not be entrusted to an organisation which imposed religious tests upon any of its workers.[51]

The Young Offenders Committee seems to have found the use of tests much less disturbing than Clarke Hall. The risks, it thought, could effectively be neutralised if Probation Committees always selected the best available candidate, whether missionary or independent.[52]

Few changes in the law relating to probation were proposed by this Committee, though it deplored the fact that the Probation of Offenders Act, 1907, grouped together three different methods of dealing with offenders—dismissal, binding over without supervision, and supervision by a probation officer. This had contributed to the prevalence of the idea that probation was tantamount to a dismissal or let-off, and the Committee considered that in any new legislation it would be advisable to reserve the term 'probation' strictly for release under the supervision of a probation officer.[53] It also recommended that courts of assize and quarter sessions should no longer be required to record a conviction before making a probation order.[54] An inconsistency would thus be removed, for the courts of summary jurisdiction were already in this position.

The report of the Young Offenders Committee set the principles upon which policy in relation to young offenders was based for many years. The emphasis on 'treatment', and the improved juvenile court arrangements which followed the Committee's report[55] provided a setting highly conducive to the application of probation, and to the development of the social work of the probation officer.

Whilst the unfavourable economic climate of the years immediately following the publication of the Report of the Committee on Young Offenders frustrated the prospects of early legislation to implement some of its recommendations, so far as the probation service was concerned much could be done by administrative action.

Using the Report as a reference point, the Home Office despatched a succession of circulars to the courts during the next few years. Attention was once more drawn to the prevalent misconceptions about probation,[56] and courts were advised against using probation time and time again for the same offender.[57] The need for careful selection of officers was stressed and the magistrates were told that vacancies should be advertised and candidates interviewed by the appointing authority before an appointment was made. The Home Office decided to try to fill a gap by undertaking to keep a record of persons wishing to enter the probation service, and asked to be notified of vacancies so as to be able to put candidates in touch with possible employers.[58]

The recent Committee's recommendation that female offenders should be supervised by officers of their own sex[59] was brought to the notice of magistrates, who were reminded of the reference to this in the Criminal Justice Act, 1925. Unfortunately for those who held this to be a matter of some urgency, the Act insisted on this arrangement only 'where the circumstances permit'.[60] At the beginning of 1929, 480 of the country's 1,028 Petty Sessional Divisions were still without the services of a woman officer. By no means all of these Divisions were in the sparsely populated areas, where there might have been some excuse for failing to make an appointment of this kind owing to the limited number of female offenders placed on probation.[61]

The several suggestions made by the Committee about ways in

which probation officers could with advantage be employed were drawn to the attention of the courts in this series of circulars: as escorts for children going to Home Office Schools,[62] for after-care work,[63] for home surroundings enquiries and reports (as a supplement to those of the Local Education Authority),[64] and to supervise young people who had been given time to pay fines.[65]

The Home Office also urged greater use of hostels in connection with the probation system, especially as an alternative to imprisonment for young people. The Home Secretary already had power to contribute to the cost of maintenance of young people sent to a home or hostel under a condition of residence.[66] It was decided to use this in order to encourage the use of suitable establishments for this purpose, and to exercise some control over the length of time for which offenders were committed to them. The Home Secretary was ready, it was announced, to pay half the cost of maintaining any probationer of either sex between the ages of sixteen and twenty-one in a hostel, and any girl in this age range, in a home, to a maximum of seven shillings and sixpence a week, provided the local authority would contribute a similar amount. To discourage long-term committals, the grant for each individual was limited to a period of six months and, to protect probationers from some of the unsuitable homes alluded to in the report, and no doubt also to encourage a raising of standards in these places, it was only to be payable where the home or hostel had been approved by the Home Secretary and was subject to his inspection.[67]

As the Committee had intimated,[68] it was no easy matter to find suitable residential accommodation for use in connection with probation. Many existing homes for girls specialised in long-term rather than short-term training. It was hoped that the hostels for ordinary working lads and girls which existed in some areas might take probationers. Where no such provision existed, the Home Secretary suggested that 'the Justices should discuss with representative bodies engaged in social work the possibility of meeting the need without incurring any undue expense'. He regretted that no help could be given by the government towards the capital cost of any such enterprise.[69]

The reconstitution of the Advisory Committee on Probation to enable it to deal also with problems of after-care, as suggested by the Committee, was possible without legislation, as this was a non-statutory body. In March 1928, the appointment of an Advisory Committee on Probation and After-Care was announced. It gave greater representation to the provinces than its predecessor and included justices, senior Home Office officials, an official of the

National Police Court Mission, William Clarke Hall, the Metropolitan Magistrate, a Prison Commissioner, a Justices' Clerk, a Director of Education, a Chief Constable and two probation officers.

The Committee met two or three times a year over the following seven years and dealt with a wide variety of subjects referred to it by the Home Secretary or raised by its own members. These included the employment of part-time officers, the duties of Probation Committees, the approval of probation homes and hostels, probation officers and the superior courts, the employment of women probation officers, and the supervision of young offenders given time to pay fines.[70] From time to time, representatives of local Probation Committees were invited to its meetings to discuss the operation of the probation system in their own particular areas.[71]

The Advisory Committee was concerned with the introduction in 1930 of an important experiment—an official training scheme for persons wishing to enter the probation service.[72] Credit for the first real attempt to provide probation officers and would-be officers with a suitable training must go to the C.E.T.S. who, four years earlier, in 1926, arranged for their London headquarters to become an Extension Centre where missionaries and others could study over a period of four years for the London University Diploma in Economics and Social Science. It remained in existence for a number of years, and in 1930 the Society extended similar help to those outside London by arranging with Ruskin College, Oxford, for the provision of a correspondence course leading to the same qualification. The Society was willing to pay the fees of any of its missionaries who took advantage of the scheme.[73]

The training scheme initiated by the Home Office set out to provide a small number of selected candidates with a period of practical training under experienced probation officers, and the opportunity to visit reformative institutions. In addition, those who 'had not received the advantages of a liberal education' were to be given the chance to obtain a university qualification in social science.

The scheme was publicly advertised and the trainees selected by a committee appointed by the Home Secretary. By arrangement with the local Probation Committees, successful candidates were then attached as Assistant Probation Officers to departments in Manchester, Birmingham or Liverpool, where they received practical training whilst also attending the social science course at the local university. The trainees' salaries and expenses ranked along with the other expenses of the local Probation Committee for the 50 per cent government grant.[74]

113

The setting up of a training scheme was consistent with developments in the broader sphere of social work. The almoners, trained initially by the Charity Organisation Society had established an Institute to regulate entry and to provide training, including attendance by some of its trainees at a university social science course.[75] And the first course of professional training for psychiatric social work was estabished at the London School of Economics in 1929.[76]

In spite of the declared intention of consecutive governments,[77] a government Bill to implement some of the recommendations of the Young Offenders Committee was not produced in Parliament until the end of 1931, probably because of a pre-occupation with problems arising out of the continuing economic depression.

In the meantime, the Howard League for Penal Reform, impatient of official inaction, drafted its own Children Bill.[78] Introduced into the Commons in July 1930, under the Ten Minute Rule,[79] by one of the Penal Reform Group, many of its provisions closely followed the recommendations of the Committee. In relation to probation it sought to give statutory recognition to the probation officer's new task of escorting young people to Reformatories or Industrial Schools; to do away with the need for higher courts to record a conviction before making a probation order; and to ensure that all vacancies for probation officers were advertised and candidates personally interviewed. The reformers also proposed that the employment as probation officers of agents of voluntary societies should be made illegal and that no candidate for the post of probation officer should be subject to a religious test.[80]

The voluntary societies were naturally alarmed at this threat to their position. A private conference of the societies was called by the Church of England Temperance Society and met under the chairmanship of Joynson-Hicks, now Lord Brentford. The meeting decided to ask the Home Secretary to receive a deputation (as influential as the societies could muster) to protest against the offending clause.

Fears were temporarily allayed when Lord Brentford received from the Home Secretary the assurance that the government was currently preparing its own Bill on the subject and that there was no longer any occasion for the proposed deputation.[81] As a result, presumably, of the same intelligence, the promoters of the Children Bill decided to abandon any attempt to take it further.[82]

On the 11th December 1931 the government's Children and Young Persons Bill was introduced in the Commons, its proposals stemming mainly from the report of the Young Offenders

Committee. Among them was the introduction of a 'supervision order' placing a child or young person found 'in need of care or protection' under the supervision of a probation officer.[83] At a later stage, this proposal was amended to cover the making of a supervision order in cases found 'beyond control' as well as those in need of care or protection.[84] The government also sought to make it possible for courts to make a supervision order concurrently with an order committing a child or young person into the care of a 'fit person'.[85]

The probation officer would have similar responsibilities towards this new class of charges as he had towards probationers. A child subject to such an order would be able to be brought before a juvenile court at any time, so that the court might, if it was considered in the child's interests, make an approved school order or a fit person order removing the child from the custody of his parents.[86]

Following up the comments of the Young Offenders Committee and the subsequent official circular on the use of conditions of residence, the Home Office now sought to amend the relevant section in the Criminal Justice Administration Act, 1914. The new Bill proposed that it should not be possible to send a child or young person to an institution not subject to Home Office inspection, unless whilst there he was to be employed or seek employment outside its walls. It also sought to make mandatory notifications to the Home Secretary of the terms of any orders which included a requirement to take up residence in a non-inspected institution; and to give him the power, if he considered it in the offender's interest, to cause an application to be made to the court which might then either omit the condition of residence or name in it an alternative institution.[87]

A provision was included that, in all but trivial cases, juvenile courts should be provided with information about the home surroundings, school records, health and character of the children and young persons brought before them. Probation officers, however, were alarmed to find that under the Bill it was the local authorities which were to be informed of cases coming before the courts and given the duty of seeing that this information was available.[88]

It is not absolutely clear from the Report of the Departmental Committee on the Treatment of Young Offenders whether it considered that the reports from the education authority, which it declared so important, would be compiled solely from information already in the files, or whether it regarded it also as part of the

115

authority's responsibility in some cases to arrange that homes were visited for the purposes of gathering the required information.

During the debate on the Bill in the House of Lords, the Earl of Feversham, President of the National Association of Probation Officers, said that he understood that Clause 20, which stressed the responsibility of the local authority to supply reports, was framed for the purpose of seeing that they supplied courts with information in their possession at the time they received a notification that a case would be heard. 'But', he continued, 'the Government, in their enthusiasm to win the co-operation of the local authorities, omitted to remember the important work of investigation carried out by the probation officer.'[89]

The National Association of Probation Officers threw all its efforts into trying to get amendments to the Bill giving probation officers a statutory place in the machinery for making enquiries and reports in all cases coming before the juvenile courts. It had the active support of the Penal Reform Group, the Howard League,[90] and the Magistrates' Association.[91] Representations were made direct to the Home Office, and the help of Members of Parliament was enlisted.[92]

As a result, the clause providing that when a child or young person was to be brought before a court of summary jurisdiction, or a juvenile court, a notification of the time of the appearance and the nature of the charge or application, should be sent by the police to the local authority for the district in which the young person resides, was successfully amended so that a similar notice would be sent to the probation officers for the probation area in which the court was to sit.[93] The Home Secretary also undertook to introduce an amendment indicating that although the duty was laid upon local authorities to make enquiries and to report to the court, these authorities were not to be under an obligation to make investigations into home surroundings in any petty sessional division where the justices had directed that this work should be performed by the probation officer.[94]

This was cold comfort to the probation officers, who were not at all confident that, short of legislation, their magistrates would think of employing them for this purpose. As the government pointed out,[95] the Probation Rules gave justices the power to direct the probation officer to make preliminary enquiries, including enquiries into home surroundings, in cases where the making of a probation order might arise,[96] but the probation officers feared that not many magistrates would be conversant with the Rules, which gave the officer no power to proceed with enquiries on his own initiative.

116

Not having entirely achieved their objectives whilst the Bill was in the Commons, the headquarters staff of the probation officers' Association abandoned all other work in an attempt to get the Bill further amended in the Lords. The support of members of the Upper House was assiduously canvassed and there took place 'a rapid succession of interviews and meetings ... in the House of Lords, in the House of Commons, and at the houses of Parliamentary members.'[97]

The Association was in a better position than ever before to try to influence legislation. Some of its leaders were persons able to canvass potentially influential support in an informal way. It also possessed a London office and a full-time Secretary of ability.[98] It even had its enthusiastic and involved President, the Earl of Feversham, in the House of Lords. In a maiden speech, he contended that the amended clause was now so ambiguous that it was certain to lead 'to considerable doubt and endless confusion as to the roles of the education authority and the probation officer in the making of preliminary investigations'. Agreeing that the education authority had an important part to play, he nevertheless considered it essential to successful probation work that the probation officer should himself make enquiries concerning persons for whose reclamation he would be held responsible by the court.[99]

He proposed an amendment to limit the local authority's duty to the supplying of any relevant information in its possession at the time it received notification of a case (unless asked by the court to provide further material), and to give probation officers the duty 'to make such further investigation and supply such additional information ... as the court may require and direct'.

For the government, the Lord Privy Seal, Viscount Snowden, was not prepared to support the amendment. He considered it extremely likely that the education authorities would call in the assistance of the probation officers in making their reports. His optimism was not shared by Lord Feversham, who failed, he said, 'to see in the justices, the local authority and the probation officers the happy trium-virate' taken for granted by Lord Snowden; but his amendment was negatived.[100] The primary responsibility for furnishing reports was thus placed in the hands of the local authorities.

The National Association of Probation Officers had limited success in amending this Bill, but in other spheres it was enjoying considerable influence and support. During the late 1920s its leadership had undergone a radical change. Sidney Edridge, in whose hands it had firmly remained for the first sixteen years of the

Association's existence, retired in 1928 on account of old age.[101] In spite of his outspokenness and tendency to dogmatise and to dominate the Association, his leadership seems to have gone unchallenged throughout these years. The probation officers may well have been thankful to have such an indefatigable champion of their cause, more influential than many of them could hope to be and able to speak with fewer inhibitions than those who depended for their livelihood upon the probation authorities. Without the justices' clerk, it is possible that the Association might never have survived its early testing years. In all its work it had been greatly hampered by lack of money. The poor remuneration of many probation officers compelled it to keep its subscription low,[102] and even when augmented by subscriptions from Associate Members, its income was a very small one with which to attempt to build up a national organisation for a scattered group of people.[103]

The year before Edridge retired from the Chair, the Association gained the interest and active support of Gertrude Tuckwell who, in 1920, had been made the first woman justice of the peace,[104] and of the young Earl of Feversham,[105] recently returned from a two-year visit to South Africa where he had worked, under an assumed name, as a probation officer. The former became President in 1928 and Feversham, wishing to maintain his interest in probation work and make some contribution to its further development in this country, agreed to become a Vice-President[106] thus, like Miss Tuckwell, beginning a long association with the probation officers' organisation. A year later they were joined by William Clarke Hall, who accepted an invitation to follow Edridge in the Chair.[107]

These three became the national leaders and spokesmen of the Association. Through their many contacts they were able to canvass interest and support for the Association's work in social territory productive in terms of both influence and money. It was not long before the Association was accorded a civic reception at the Mansion House;[108] other receptions took place in great houses at the time of the Annual Conferences, and on the occasion of its twenty-first anniversary in 1933, delegates were invited to an At Home at 10 Downing Street.[109]

The change in the Association's leadership was reflected in its journal. A new start was made. It took the name 'Probation' and assumed a different character, less colourful and evangelical, but with a style which was probably more widely acceptable than that of Edridge.

The first Chairman had often raised money to finance an issue of the Journal.[110] This new 'Probation' was even more dependent upon the financial help of one of the leaders. In the first issue, Lord Feversham expressed himself happy to meet the expenses of the Journal in the hope that it would be a means of encouraging all probation officers to join the Association and of bringing about better co-operation between them.[111]

Lord Feversham has said that on his return from Africa he was dismayed to find the probation service in England and Wales in an inferior condition to the one in which he had gained his experience.[112] It was important, in his opinion, to get the support of the general public for probation work, and he was anxious that the National Association of Probation Officers should undertake vigorous propaganda to that end.

His vision of the part which could be played by the Association in the advancement of probation work led him to go beyond giving time and energy for its existing work and money for its journal, and to put forward in the third issue of *Probation* a 'New Scheme for Further Development'. Seeing 'an urgent need for the establishment of a properly equipped office where the valuable but disconnected work ... being done by voluntary officials might be consolidated', he offered to guarantee to the Association, for a period of five years, the services of a full-time secretary, an assistant secretary and a central office. He had been promised a large sum of money towards this by a Mrs. William Carrington of New York,[113] and he was also prepared to contribute from his own resources.[114]

His offer was accepted by the Association, which also agreed to the condition that he should have the right to choose the new full-time secretary.[115] H. E. Norman, South Africa's first probation officer who was at this time Senior Probation Officer for the Witwatersrand,[116] was nominated and elected in May 1930.[117] It was under Norman that Feversham had worked during his sojourn in Africa.[118] Impressed by his ability and personal qualities he considered him the best man to build up the organisation in the desired way.

To give Feversham the fullest opportunity to carry forward his plans, Miss Tuckwell resigned the Presidency in his favour and continued her work for the Association in the office of Vice-President.[119]

Only two years after the initiation of this ambitious scheme, the Association faced an unexpected crisis. Financial misfortune compelled Mrs. Carrington to discontinue her grant. However, the influence of its leaders stood it in good stead, for Miss Tuckwell and Lord Feversham, together with Sidney Harris, head of the Children's Branch of the Home Office, obtained from the Pilgrim

Trust a promise to furnish the Association with £1,000 a year for two years.[120]

It was obvious, however, that the organisation could not expect such substantial help for very much longer and that it would have to bring its expenditure, which had reached £1,600 a year, nearer in line with the £400 which was the most it could hope to raise from its membership.[121] Clarke Hall (who had been knighted in 1932)[122] put forward a number of alternative plans for the future. Among them was a proposal that the Association should give way to a new body, a National Probation Association, with a membership open to all interested in probation.[123] The Association's Branches were being sounded on this matter, when news came of the sudden death of Clarke Hall on his yacht on the Norfolk Broads.

Whilst the Association and the probation service were the poorer for his death, out of it came a solution of the former's financial difficulties and a new body devoted to making known his ideas about probation and the juvenile courts. He had been an outstanding pioneer and supporter of the more modern methods of dealing with offenders. Those who shared his interests were therefore surprised to read in *The Times* a less than laudatory obituary. Their indignation fired them with a determination to see that appreciation of his work should assume a concrete form.[124]

A small group of some thirty 'influential persons', among them Lord Feversham, Miss Tuckwell and the Archbishop of York, met at the home of Sir Herbert Samuel—until recently Home Secretary—and formulated a scheme which was announced to the public in letters to *The Times* and other papers in December 1932.[125] It was proposed

> that there should be a Clarke Hall Fellowship to which may belong all those who are concerned with the treatment of the offender. The Fellowship will concentrate on those two sections of the field which Clarke Hall made peculiarly his own. It will endeavour in the first place to make known throughout the country his conception of the Juvenile Court by arranging for Clarke Hall lectures; . . . in the second place (it) will do everything possible to put the National Association of Probation Officers upon a sound financial basis, for the modest salaries of the officers themselves cannot furnish all the necessary administrative costs.[126]

The public appeal brought forward generous contributions towards a Trust Fund from which the National Association of Probation Officers was given substantial financial help for a period of twelve years.[127]

As a result of its increased income, central office and full-time staff, the activity of the Association increased tremendously. Very successful efforts were made to recruit more members; after a few months, the Association claimed as members 63 per cent of full-time officers and by 1935, 95 per cent.[128] Norman also set out to expand its contacts with other organisations and to build up a relationship of confidence between the Association and the Home Office. That he was successful in doing this was partly due no doubt to the fact that its leaders were *persona grata* at the Home Office, but Norman himself appears to have won the respect of the senior official Sidney Harris.

The Association was also able to bring to the notice of the Advisory Committee on Probation and After Care matters, such as the conditions of employment of part-time probation officers, about which it was concerned, since both Clarke Hall and Feversham were members of that body.[129] The Committee itself occasionally consulted the Association or asked it to forward information on particular subjects.[130] The Association was also in close contact with the Magistrates' Association which had a similar policy on probation matters.[131] Cecil Leeson[132] continued his interest in the probation movement after becoming secretary of the Magistrates' Association, Clarke Hall was its Chairman from 1930 until his death, Gertrude Tuckwell was a member of its Executive Committee and Feversham, who was made a justice in 1931,[133] served on its Council.[134] In 1932 the two Associations arranged a conference of magistrates, justices' clerks and probation officers which considered the social investigations made by probation officers, their case loads, the use of voluntary workers and the function of magistrates in the probation system.[135]

In the 1920s and 1930s probation officers were concerned, as were other social workers, with social problems such as unemployment arising out of the depression.[136] By the late 1920s they were also taking an interest in 'the theory and practice of probation,' and in the application of psychology, and of what are now recognised as case-work techniques, to the social work of the courts.[137] Cyril Burt's work, *The Young Delinquent*, published in 1925, had aroused interest in psychological aspects of crime and in the relevance of psychological knowledge to social work; and developments in social casework in America were being reported by returning visitors and were imported at the end of the decade by early psychiatric social workers.[138] The probation officers' journal carried articles such as 'The Psychology of the Criminal',[139] and at

121

its conference in 1929 sessions were devoted to 'The Technique of Probation' and 'The Unconscious Motive of the Delinquent'.[140] The following year a paper on probation in America read by W. H. Chinn, a Birmingham probation officer, contained what must have been one of the earliest references to 'case-work' in the history of probation in Britain.[141]

In the decade following the Criminal Justice Act, 1925, considerable growth took place in the size, functions and status of the probation service. The mandatory employment of probation officers led to an increase in their number, a development which in turn affected the potential size and influence of the National Association of Probation Officers.

The number of persons placed on probation likewise increased (from 15,094 in 1925 to 18,934 in 1933) as did the proportion of offenders disposed of by this method.[142] This can be attributed to the wider availability of probation officers, greater knowledge on the part of magistrates, and probably also to a change in public attitude towards institutions[143] and the closure of a number of reformatory schools,[144] though in these respects it is impossible to distinguish cause from effect.

The scope of the work had also expanded as a result of the introduction of the supervision order, the provision for the making of social enquiries for juvenile courts, and the commendation by the Young Offenders Committee of the employment of probation officers to escort children travelling to institutions.

Better conditions of employment for probation officers had been provided by the introduction of salary scales and a superannuation scheme. The growing belief that a good educational background and specialised training were desirable if not indispensable qualifications for the work was reflected in the provision for the payment of higher salaries to persons with university qualifications and the institution of an experimental training programme. And among probation officers references to probation work as a profession began occasionally to be heard.[145]

CHAPTER SIX

A MAJOR REVIEW

The National Association of Probation Officers claimed that it was largely due to Feversham and Norman that a government proposal to set up a committee to consider matrimonial proceedings in the summary courts was extended to enable a review to be made of the whole of the social work of the courts.

In January 1934, Feversham had been made Lord-in-Waiting in the National government, an office which, according to the Association's Annual Report, was to carry with it responsibility for measures connected with the social services of the courts.[1] Soon afterwards, Lord Listowel introduced a private member's Bill proposing the establishment of special courts for dealing with domestic cases, and of a definite procedure for matrimonial conciliation.[2] The National Association of Probation Officers decided to declare itself in favour of the Bill on condition that it could be amended to provide the probation officers with a statutory place in conciliation work, in which by this time they had become widely involved. Its Committee agreed that Feversham should speak to the government about this.[3] During the Bill's second reading, the Lord Chancellor, Viscount Sankey, told the House that the Home Secretary would be willing to have examined the possibility of changes along the lines proposed. With this promise of an enquiry, Listowel withdrew his Bill,[4] and a few weeks later, on the 25th July, the Lord Chancellor announced that the Home Secretary had decided that, since in many courts matrimonial conciliation was undertaken by probation officers, and since these officers were also performing other work for the courts, any enquiry of the kind promised should take their position into account. Many of them were fully employed already, and, indeed, it might be as well to consider whether, in view of the increase in probation work itself, adequate arrangements existed at all courts for the supervision of offenders placed on probation.

The Home Secretary had therefore concluded that the promised enquiry ought to be directed not just to arrangements for conciliation, but to the general question of providing the courts wit adequate means of carrying out the whole of these social service He proposed to ask a Departmental Committee

> to enquire into the social services connected with the
> administration of justice in courts of summary jurisdiction,
> including the supervision of persons released on probation and
> in suitable cases of persons ordered to pay fines; the
> application of conciliation methods to matrimonial disputes;
> and the making of social investigations on behalf of the court
> and other work falling, or likely to fall, upon probation officers
> and to report on the above questions and as to what changes ar
> required in the existing organisation of probation services and
> otherwise.[5]

The Head of the Children's Branch of the Home Office, Sidne Harris, was appointed Chairman of this Departmental Committe on the Social Services in Courts of Summary Jurisdiction.[6] Th departed from the arrangements in 1909 and 1920 when th Parliamentary Under-Secretary, and not a permanent official, ha been in the Chair. Harris had now been connected with the operatio of the probation system for about fifteen years and had been member of the Departmental Committee on the Trainin, Appointment and Payment of Probation Officers which reported i 1922 and of the more recent Young Offenders Committee.

Once again, almost all the members of the Committee wer directly connected in some way with the probation service. Lor Feversham was a provincial magistrate and President of th National Association of Probation Officers. Miss Madeleir Symons, a well-known speaker on delinquency, and Samuel Osbor of Sheffield were also magistrates, the latter Chairman of his loc: Probation Committee. Other members included the Deputy Clerk the Peace for Surrey, E. J. Hayward, one of the leading justice clerks, and Miss J. I. Wall, from the staff of the Children's Branch the Home Office.

One hundred and twenty-six witnesses were heard by th Committee. They included representatives of the executive of th National Association of Probation Officers, of its several Branche and of the Magistrates' Association. Seven probation officers an eight magistrates gave independent evidence, and the Committe also interviewed four Metropolitan Magistrates, a Stipendiar Magistrate, a High Court Judge and representatives of the Society Clerks of the Peace of Counties, the Incorporated Justices' Clerk Society, the Chief Constables' Association, the Howard League fc

enal Reform, the Police Court Missions, the Charity Organisation
Society and the Joint University Council for Social Studies. The
Archbishop of York was a distinguished individual witness.[7]

A large amount of information and opinion was amassed in this
way and was complemented by the results of an enquiry made by
questionnaire of representative courts throughout the country.
Considering its volume, and variety of sources, the evidence
provided on the whole a very uniform picture of the state of the
service, and the same suggestions for improvement recurred
throughout. Only on a very few matters was there any divergence of
opinion amongst witnesses.

As far as the probation service was concerned, the Committee
saw its task as the consideration of what was mainly an
administrative problem. This was the organisation of the service for
its now varied functions—the practice of conciliation in
matrimonial disputes, the supervision of persons placed on
probation, and the carrying out of other social work of the courts.[8]

The evidence produced for its consideration led the Committee
to conclude that 'the most important need of the probation service
(was) an improved system of organisation.'[9] Since 1925, the service
had passed through a period 'of continuous growth and steady, if
slow, improvement in methods of organisation, in technical
efficiency and in the standard and conditions of service of the
probation officers'. But it was now 'suffering from growing pains'.[10]
The number of probation cases had been increasing, and the range of
duties expected of probation officers was extending. The Committee
thought this expansion of work was proving too much for the
existing organisation.

It was not, they pointed out, that drastic changes in the law were
required. The courts already had the necessary powers, and the
administrative framework had already been set down, for the
operation of a satisfactory service. The trouble was that so many
benches had neglected 'to carry out the intentions of the legislature,
either in the letter or the spirit'.[11]

An outstanding feature of this disregard for the law was a
widespread failure of courts, after ten years of opportunity, to
appoint the probation committees made mandatory by the Criminal
Justice Act, 1925. In some areas the justices had gone through the
motions of appointing a Committee but, in spite of the rules about
frequency of meetings, it had never met to carry out its duties under
the Act. In other places, Probation Committees kept to the letter of
the law by holding meetings, but evaded the spirit of the 1925
legislation in a number of other respects.

125

Some, for instance, failed to establish and maintain adequat contact with their probation officers. The Committee reported 'Many probation officers complain that they have never met thei Committees and that they carry out their work without supervisio criticism or encouragement.'[12] The Sussex Branch of the Nation Association of Probation Officers had said that the practice in it area was for the Clerk to the Justices to present the probatio officer's report to the Probation Committee. If the officer wa summoned to attend the meeting, he usually only waited outside th door on the chance that he might be called in to discuss a speci case.[13]

This failure of the Probation Committee arrangement, 'intende to be the pivot of the system of organisation set up by the 1925 Act was a serious one. It indicated the level of ignorance or apathy i regard to probation which still existed in some places. The result wa that the local service was without direction or supervision and th whole responsibility for probationers was left in the hands of th frequently isolated probation officer.

Another way in which Probation Committees had ignored th intention of the Act was in appointing part-time rather than full-tim officers, and by failing to appoint women officers to supervis women and girls. The service was still mainly a part-time one. Of th 858 officers employed in 1935, 559 were part-time workers.[14] Thei salaries were in many instances purely nominal—over 200 of the received £20 a year or less—and, as the Committee pointed ou they could not be expected to undertake any work for the court apa from the supervision of probationers. So the courts to which the were attached were often without a probation officer at their sitting and other social work now being performed by full-time officers the busier courts remained undone.

Like the 1922 Committee, Harris and his colleagues found tha the part-time officers followed 'a great variety of other occupations and usually 'lacked the necessary qualifications for probation work Some of them were in other forms of social work, but others we engaged in work quite unrelated to probation, such as greengrocer or undertaking. In spite of the Probation Rule which mad retirement compulsory at sixty-five, 50 of the part-time workers wer above this age and some of them were over seventy and even eighty.

In those areas where unqualified and inexperienced people wer giving a small proportion of their time to probation work, the servic was obviously only a shadow of what had been intended in 1925. some places, however, the service was more comprehensive than th probation officer's conditions of employment would have suggeste

Some of the part-time officers were giving a lot of time to the work for what the Committee considered inadequate financial reward.[16] The National Association of Probation Officers, which claimed 63 per cent of the part-time officers among its members,[17] had for some years been calling attention to their situation, and its Branches gave the Committee evidence of many cases of probation officers giving almost full-time service for very small salaries.[18] The questionnaire returns confirmed that such cases were not uncommon, and the Committee included in its Report illustrations showing that there were some officers giving four days a week to probation work for which they received anything from £25 to £80 a year. It appeared, the Committee reported, that there existed 'serious exploitation of part-time officers'.[19]

The full-time officers did not suffer in the same way, for their salaries were now regulated by the Home Office. In their case, it was the quality of the work that the Committee found disturbing. There was evidence that a great many were seriously overworked and from this the Committee inferred that work with individual probationers must inevitably be suffering.

The returns made to the Home Office for the year 1934 showed that in the provinces there were 'no less than 42 officers, including three women, with over 100 cases, including one with over 300, two with between 200 and 300, and four between 150 and 200'.[20] And this in spite of the statement by the Committees of 1909 and 1920 that 60 to 70 cases seemed to be as many as men in most districts could properly supervise, and that women should normally have rather fewer; and despite a number of Home Office circulars asking courts to ensure that the work of their officers did not suffer as a result of their being overburdened with work.

The majority of male officers appeared to be supervising from 60 to 80 cases and the majority of women between 50 and 70. The position, the Committee stated, was 'neither fair to the probation officers, nor to the probation system'.[21]

Another serious deficiency was the absence of a woman probation officer in over three hundred petty sessional divisions. In spite of pressure from the Home Office, the Magistrates' Association and the National Association of Probation Officers, here again the spirit of the 1925 Act was being evaded by the probation committees. Admittedly, the Act only insisted on such appointments 'where circumstances permit', and many of the divisions in question were in sparsely populated areas, but the Committee could find no excuse on this count for at least sixty-eight of them.

The Committee were adamant that it was necessary to have a

woman probation officer in every area. Apart from the risk incurred in putting a woman on probation to a male officer, a woman, the Committee thought, could deal more effectively and with more freedom with the case of another woman or girl than could a man. There were other tasks too, such as the making of social investigations and matrimonial conciliation, where in some circumstances a woman probation officer could give useful assistance to the court.[22]

The Committee saw improvement in the organisation of the service as the best remedy for 'these serious deficiencies', and made important recommendations to this end. It wrote, in fact, of the need for 'radical changes in the organisation'.[23] However, the majority of its suggestions called for what amounted to greater acceleration in the pace of changes which had already been set in motion, so as to ensure maximum efficiency in the more complex situation produced by the growth of the work. The Committee indicated, for example, the need for a further increase in central control and its more effective application, for more combination of petty sessional divisions, for a clarification of the local administrative arrangements, and for the abolition of dual control. Only in its uncompromising stand on the last question could its recommendations properly be described as proposing radical change.

Increased Home Office participation in the organisation of the service had been advocated by previous committees, and there had been some re-organisation and increased activity in Whitehall in response.[24] A particularly large step in this direction had been taken through the Criminal Justice Act, 1925, which added considerably to the erstwhile negligible power of the Home Office to control the service. However, it was evident to this Committee that, in spite of these increased powers and of more Home Office contact with provincial courts, many local services were operating at a standard well below that envisaged in the Probation Rules and in Home Office circulars. It considered that the service would benefit from still further direction and supervision from the centre. 'In its present stage', it reported, 'the probation service, which is now developing rapidly, needs the direction and guidance of an active central authority to ensure efficiency, to act as a clearing house for new ideas, and to co-ordinate the work of the various authorities. There is much to be done in the next few years and no step is more likely to contribute to the development of an efficient service than that the Home Office should accept greater responsibility for its general administration, supervision and direction.'

In that event, it would be very necessary for the Home Office to

128

maintain adequate contact, through visits and in other ways, with those concerned with probation work in the local courts.[25] The Committee saw no reason why this should not be the duty of an official inspectorate. For nine years, local authorities had been receiving grants in aid of probation work, which, in theory were subject to the maintenance of standards of work which were satisfactory to the Home Secretary. The Committee could not conceive how, without a system of inspection, the government could exercise through the grant system any control over the maintenance of standards.

A form of inspection had in fact been in operation for some years. The Children's Branch of the Home Office had arranged for the inspectors it employed for other purposes to visit and interest themselves in the work of probation officers; and since 1926, they had been making recommendations about the retention of officers after the completion of a probationary year.[26] These inspectors gave evidence before the Departmental Committee and advocated increased powers for inspectors who might be concerned with probation. Their visits, they asserted, had almost invariably been welcomed. Probation officers and Clerks had appreciated this interest on the part of the Home Office, and the opportunity to talk to someone about their work and its problems. For some of the more isolated officers, these visits were the only source of information about the operation of the service as a whole. The inspectors claimed that, as a result of the contacts they had made in the provinces, they had received hundreds of enquiries about many aspects of probation work.

Apart from examination on behalf of the Home Secretary of the work of full-time recruits during their first year in the service, the inspectors' work within the probation service had included giving advice to local courts about the number of staff they should employ and about suitable offices and equipment. They had suggested the appointment of women officers, made recommendations about remuneration, and persuaded some of the Missions to make contributions towards the superannuation of their missionary probation officers. 'Undesirable practices' had been noted and reported within the Children's Branch, and information about new developments which might be of general interest had been collected. Sometimes they had been able to gain the ear of a Clerk to point out some of the probation officer's difficulties, where the latter might not have been successful.

They had been frequently told, they said, that 'official' inspection would be welcomed. Moreover, occasions did sometimes arise when it would have been helpful to have been able to insist on seeing records or making more searching enquiries.[27]

Their confidence that statutory inspection could be successfully introduced into the probation service was borne out by the evidence received from the National Association of Probation Officers, the Magistrates' Association, the Incorporated Justices Clerks Society and individual probation officers and magistrates who would be closely affected. All were positively in favour.[28] The sole objection was in fact put to the Committee by the Home Office Inspectors themselves, in order that they might refute it. It was possible that inspection in this field might be seen as an infringement of the principle that the Executive should not interfere with the work of the Judiciary.[29] Unimpressed by this suggestion, the Committee pointed out that it was not proposed to give the Home Office any right to criticise judicial decisions, and that inspection 'would be concerned only with the execution of these decisions by the probation officers and the organisation of the social services of the Courts'. It was thinking of inspection 'not in the narrow sense in which it is sometimes regarded, but primarily as fulfilling functions of advice, encouragement and stimulation,' and it recommended that the Home Secretary should be given a general power of inspection to satisfy himself, before the payment of a grant, that a reasonable standard of efficiency was being maintained.[30]

Recognising the force of the argument put by some witnesses that the association of probation work with Children's Branch encouraged the prevalent misconception that probation was only for children, the Committee suggested that the Home Office should consider internal re-organisation with this criticism in mind. In its opinion probation also deserved a periodic report of its own, independent of those occasionally issued by the Children's Branch. The Committee recognised that probation work could benefit considerably from more public interest—the fostering of which had so far been undertaken by the National Association of Probation Officers and the Clarke Hall Fellowship—and considered that a report reviewing the progress made in the work in various parts of the country would stimulate interest both in the courts themselves and among the general public.[31]

In connection with the Home Secretary's functions in the service, the Advisory Committee, reconstituted in 1928 on the recommendation of the Young Offenders Committee with terms of reference which included after care, had, in the Committee's opinion, proved its worth. Since 1928 it had considered and advised on over thirty different aspects of the work of the probation service.[32]

A further broadening of its terms of reference to take in all the social services of the courts performed by probation officers was now suggested. It should still be representative of all relevant interests, and appointing authorities, in particular, should receive adequate representation 'in order to ensure close contact with the actual operation of the system'. It was a measure of the Committee's recognition of the National Association of Probation Officers' claim to represent those employed in the service that it saw no reason for the Home Secretary to continue the practice of appointing probation officers individually to the Committee if the Association was represented upon it.[33]

The contribution which the Association had made to the probation service was given substantial recognition in the Report. It had not only assisted in raising the status and improving the techniques of the officers themselves; it had also brought the nature and value of their work to the attention of magistrates and the public. The Committee considered that a large measure of the Association's success was due to the fact that it had 'taken a wide view of its functions and ... not confined its activities to the improvement of the material conditions of its members'. It allowed, however, that the latter was a legitimate part of the organisation's work.

The Committee commended the Association's recent publication of a *Handbook of Probation*.[34] The preparation of this manual had been initiated under the chairmanship of Clark Hall and impetus had been given to its production by the appointment in 1934 of the Departmental Committee. The material for the book was contributed by officers and members of the Association and by specialist sympathisers. It dealt, among other things, with the law relating to probation, the administration of the service and the techniques which were being developed in the work. The Clarke Hall Fellowship helped to finance its publication and to procure as editor an experienced writer, Mrs. Le Mesurier.[35]

When the Departmental Committee considered the operation of the probation system at the local level, its findings led it to recommend that many more petty sessional divisions should be combined to form probation areas. Indeed, it went so far as to say that this principle of combination should be applied to every division except those comprising the larger county boroughs.

Since combination was introduced in 1925 half the divisions in the country had entered into combination schemes. Five hundred and ninety-six of them had formed forty-eight probation areas. But in twenty counties the divisions remained uncombined. A county, the Committee held, was usually the most effective unit for combination: it was the largest local government area, a unit for the appointment of justices of the peace, and, through the Standing Joint Committee, the authority responsible for financing the local probation service.

The case for combination was 'unassailable', and where tried had proved 'highly advantageous'. A division which remained separate could not usually provide sufficient work for a full-time officer, and its probation committee was unlikely to possess enough knowledge and experience to make a good choice of staff or to supervise the work. From the officers' point of view, experience in a single division was likely to be narrow, and specialisation and promotion in the locality highly improbable.[36]

For the running of local services the Committee saw no reason to depart from the probation committee system introduced, like the principle of combination, by the 1925 Act. Indeed, no better method had suggested itself to the members of the Committee than that committees of the justices themselves should control the administration of the service, directing and encouraging the work of the officers and keeping in close touch with the social services of the courts.[37]

As might well have been foreseen, the Committee's enquiries revealed some confusion in the combined areas about the functions of the two kinds of 'probation committee'.[38] The probation committees of some of the divisions had been claiming the right to organise the work of the probation officers attached to their courts, as well as to give their detailed attention to the work with individual cases. To concede this function to them, the Departmental Committee reported, would be to sweep aside the very purpose for which combination had been arranged—the centralisation in the hands of one authority of the responsibility for organising the work in the whole area.

In spite of this conflict, the Committee saw the divisional committees as important to the proper functioning of the system. With their intimate knowledge of their own division, these bodies were far more suitable than the probation committees for the whole of combined areas to examine in detail the cases being supervised for them by the probation officer, and to give the latter help and advice.

The Report suggested that the misunderstandings should be resolved by re-naming the divisional probation committees 'case committees'. This would distinguish them from the area probation committees and at the same time indicate their very different functions. The probation officer needed the support of a case

132

committee to which he could turn for advice, which might be able to 'throw new light on some of (his) problems' and even 'become a source of strength and inspiration'. The case committee should also interview probationers, where necessary, to give encouragement or admonition. It should give advice about the variation or discharge of probation orders and should supervise the use made of conditions of residence. Such a committee could also be associated in a similar way with other of the probation officers' duties. These committees might fulfil their functions even more effectively, it was suggested, if they could call in the assistance of persons who were not members of the Bench. Persons with 'experience of public assistance administration, education or public health and representatives of voluntary societies and other social workers' could extend the committee's own breadth of experience.[39]

As a move towards increasing the contact between the committees and the probation officers, which it had found to be lacking in some places,[40] the Committee recommended that a probation officer should act as secretary to the case committee. The Clerk to the Justices, who often filled this post, should be made ex officio a member of the committee in order to keep in personal touch with its work.

Because it considered the case committee just as essential to the successful operation of the system in single as in combined areas, the Committee suggested that there its functions might be made the responsibility of Case Sub-Committees of the Probation Committee. Here again, a probation officer might be appointed secretary to the sub-committee.[41]

The appointment of probation officers was one of the important functions of the probation committees in combined areas and of Benches or their probation committee in single areas.[42] Although on this occasion none of the witnesses advocated that responsibility for appointments should be in the hands of a national authority, the Committee, like its predecessors, considered whether it should in fact remain with the local magistrates. It chose to agree with its predecessor of 1922 that good co-operation between magistrates and probation officers was essential, and since it was most likely to be effected when the magistrates selected their own officers, appointments should be left in their hands. The Committee thought that in single, as in combined, areas the probation committee, rather than the whole Bench, should select the officers. And, although so much in favour of local appointment, it did not doubt the need for the central authority to 'impose certain restrictions as to age, education and training'.

It was acknowledged that selection by the central government would not be without certain advantages. One authority was more likely to maintain a uniform standard of personnel than many authorities making their own appointments. One particular difficulty stood out, however. If probation officers became, in a sense, government officials, the use by courts of information stemming from them 'would inevitably raise questions of interference of the Executive with the Judiciary'.

The transfer of the probation system to the local authorities had not been considered by previous committees. Its consideration now probably reflected the growth of local authority activity in personal social services since the beginning of the century. It was recognised by the Committee that such an arrangement would have the particular advantage of bringing probation officers into closer touch with services administered by these bodies. But it was open to the same important objection as transfer to the central government.[43]

The appointment of probation officers could not be considered without reference to the recurring question of the employment of agents of voluntary societies. The Committees of 1909 and 1922 had endorsed—the latter with some reservations—the principle that, if the justices so desired, nothing should prevent their appointing as probation officer a police court missionary or other similar agent. The Social Services Committee dissented from this view. Whilst acknowledging the great debt owed to the voluntary societies for their provision of personnel and money, it considered that the time had come for the probation service to become a wholly public one. The aim of many of its recommendations was an improved system of organisation, and it did not think that the necessary improvements could be brought about whilst responsibility for the appointment and control of probation officers remained divided.

It was a subject upon which strong views were still held. Some witnesses fervently pleaded for the retention of voluntary societies in the probation service; others were equally anxious to convince the Committee of the absolute necessity to place the service on an entirely public basis.

When the National Police Court Mission heard of the government's intention to set up the Committee of Inquiry, it appointed a special sub-committee to watch the progress of events. Evidence was prepared, the signatures of magistrates in favour of the retention of missionary officers were collected and forwarded to the Committee, and consultations were held with the Archbishop of York who agreed to appear before the Committee on the Mission's behalf.[44]

The London Police Court Mission also began the preparation of evidence. The Missions were not without appreciation of the possible effect which the Report of the Committee might have upon their work. The Secretary of the London Mission warned that the Committee's recommendations 'would have far-reaching results which would affect the whole conduct, and possibly the existence itself, of the Police Court Mission'.[45] This possibility was probably further brought home to the supporters of the Missions when it was pointed out in the Annual Report of the London Mission for 1934 that among those appointed to the Committee there was no one, except the Chairman, who could be considered a friend of the Church of England Temperance Society.

The weighty arguments adduced in separate evidence by the Church of England Temperance Society, the London Police Court Mission, and the Archbishop of York[46] were summarised thus by the Committee.

> (1) the 'missionary spirit', a sense of vocation based on religious conviction, which leads men and women into the work regardless of material prospects in the simple desire to help their fellows, is no less necessary in the future, and can only be assured by the continued association of the Mission with the probation service.
>
> (2) Greater flexibility is possible under a voluntary than under an official system. It is one of the probation officer's greatest assets that he is regarded by the public as friend rather than an official, and it would be serious if this relationship were endangered.
>
> (3) The missionary officer received valuable support from his attachment to a religious organisation, spiritual help, advice in difficulties and the interest and friendship of a wide circle of persons in sympathy with the Mission.
>
> (4) Substantial relief is afforded to public expenditure by the voluntarily subscribed funds of the Mission.[47]

On the other hand, those who opposed the continuance of the present system also had considerable arguments to support their point of view, and on this occasion they were, amongst those who gave evidence, in the majority. They included that long-standing opponent of dual control, the Howard League, and also the Magistrates' Association, the Incorporated Justices' Clerks Society, the Inspectors of the Children's Branch of the Home Office, the National Association of Probation Officers and individual probation officers, some of them missionaries.[48]

Their argument was presented thus by the Committee:

(1) Valuable as has been the help of the Mission in this direction in the earlier stages of development, what is now an established public service should be wholly financed from public funds and should be under undivided public control. The limited resources and restricted organisation of the Mission are a hindrance to the full development of an expanding service.

(2) The dual control which is inherent in a system whereby the responsibility for appointments and the payment of salaries is shared between the Courts and voluntary societies is open to objection in theory and has given rise to serious difficulties. In some areas the direction of the probation officer's work has in practice been largely delegated to the Mission, while in other areas the division of responsibility between two authorities has deprived the work of any effective supervision or direction. In some instances the result has been friction between the Courts and the Mission. Probation officers have told us that they find this dual loyalty a source of embarrassment.

(3) Admission to a public service should not depend upon membership of a missionary or other voluntary society. This requirement is said to deter some candidates with excellent qualifications from becoming probation officers, and some of the missionary officers, especially the younger ones, dislike the restrictions which are sometimes imposed on their personal freedom in matters of conduct, such as temperance, church attendance and amusements.

(4) One essential condition of the participation of a missionary society in the organisation of a public service must be the attainment of a responsibile standard of efficiency. Though there are notable exceptions, the branches of the Police Court Mission as a whole do not reach the necessary standard, and some of them are in financial difficulties. Our notice was drawn to some who have been in arrear in the payment of salaries and superannuation contributions, and we have been told by some probation officers that this is a genuine source of anxiety to them.[49]

The Social Services Committee was greatly impressed by the almost unanimous opinion of the National Association of Probation Officers that the service should be divorced from the Mission. It understood that at the Association's Annual Conference in 1935, only six members had dissented from a resolution to that effect[50] (an assertion later disputed by the Church of England Temperance Society).[51] What was more, the quickening tendency for courts to 'desert the local Mission' and appoint independent officers[52] had furnished no evidence that the service had suffered in any way. On the contrary, the Committee had found general agreement that the standard had improved in recent years.[53]

The spokesmen for the Missions had drawn the Committee's attention to the appreciation expressed in the 1922 Report of their contribution to probation work. They had pointed to the favourable attitude taken by that Committee towards their continued participation in the service.[54] This was, however, a two-edged argument, for the Missions had done their cause considerable disservice by failure to re-organise along the lines then suggested.

Harris and his colleagues found, for example, that the separation of the Mission from the temperance work of the Church of England Temperance Society had been effected in theory, but not in practice. The National Police Court Mission and the Temperance Society were housed together, served by the same Secretary, and issued their Annual Report between the same covers, the Mission being described as a department of the Society. As a consequence, they were still closely identified in the public mind. The provincial Missions had clung to the diocesan areas and failed to re-organise on county lines, and denominational barriers to recruitment had not really been removed. The Committee understood that their missionaries were

> sometimes expected to participate in the raising of funds, by speaking or preaching, by organising flag days and bazaars, and in some cases, we are told, by such unsuitable methods as collections at football matches and other sporting events and entertainments.[55]

The Midland Branch of the National Association of Probation officers told the Departmental Committee, in their evidence, that the missionaries employed by the Staffordshire Police Court Mission (an independent body, the formation of which had been favourably mentioned in the 1922 Report), were harassed by the difficulty of raising money and by fears of dismissal should they fail to collect a certain quota towards the funds.[56]

The Committee did not leave this question without suggesting what might be the future contribution of voluntary organisations to the social work of the courts. A number of useful projects remained to be undertaken. The voluntary societies could encourage people possessed of a sense of vocation derived from religious belief to enter

137

the probation service and they could possibly help to provide the necessary training. They could perhaps form groups of voluntary workers, and provide assistance to probationers referred to them for help. A shortage of probation homes and hostels persisted, and the Committee suggested that by providing some of these, the Missions could 'perform a great public service'. In such ways the Committee argued 'the religious spirit in probation work, which it is their chief anxiety to preserve, far from being lost, may be guaranteed and preserved.'[57]

It was now time, the Committee reported, to place the probation service, not only on a fully public, but also on an entirely full-time basis. This principle dovetailed into that of combination. The Committee considered that a combined area would normally be large enough to employ a group of full-time officers of both sexes.[58]

The possibility of creating groups of this kind probably made the Committee's consideration of the need for more supervisory posts rather more realistic than it had seemed earlier. Its recommendation that principal probation officers should be appointed to supplement the supervisory work of Probation Committees[59] marked a departure from the views of the Young Offenders Committee.[60] A few areas had already made such appointments, and if the evidence of witnesses can be taken as a guide, there had been considerable change of attitude between 1927 and 1936 towards such a structuring of the service. Whereas the 1927 Committee found scant support for the idea, it was now advocated by the National Association of Probation Officers and the Magistrates' Association.[61] The craving on the part of many witnesses for better organisation and supervision in the service seems to have overcome any distaste they might have had for the placing of an intermediary between the probation committee and the probation officer.

The definition provided by the Glasgow Probation Committee of the duties of a principal probation officer was approvingly reproduced by the Committee. He was

> To advise the Probation Committee on all technical details of the probation system. To be the executive of the Probation Committee in the organisation and administration of the system.
>
> To supervise field work and all case records of all probation officers in the area.
>
> To act as liaison between Probation Committee and Education Committee in questions of Probation—Approved Schools, Approved Homes, Remand Homes, etc.

138

To co-ordinate the activities of the Probation Department with the Police, Charitable Organisations, Social Services, Clinics, etc.

To encourage by frequent reports and observations the promotion of effective methods for the fullest development of Probation.

To arrange the duties of probation officers interested in other forms of social work, that they, fortified and equipped by their probation experience, may help such kindred activities; in this way broadening the basis of their social endeavours.

Not only did the Social Services Committee consider that the appointment of principal officers would improve organisation; it realised that the creation of these posts would introduce prospects of promotion into a service hitherto devoid of such attractions. This, in its turn, was likely to bring in good candidates, and to encourage efficiency among serving officers. Where the number of officers employed in an area did not justify the creation of a principal's post, the Committee recommended the payment of a special allowance to a 'senior probation officer' for carrying out supervisory duties.[62]

The duties performed by probation officers varied from court to court. Common to all was the supervision of probationers, but the proportion of time devoted to this work differed a good deal. This, the Committee insisted, was the probation officer's primary function, and no other duties should be allowed to interfere with its efficient execution. Whilst it thought that a probation officer should be present at every court sitting where he might be required, it suggested that the courts should try to use his time economically by grouping the cases which might need his attention. This would leave him time for visiting and other aspects of his work with probationers.

Some of the evidence heard by the Committee suggested that visiting and reporting tended to become perfunctory because the probation officer was overloaded with work. It described home visiting as normally an 'indispensable' element in probation work. Reporting by the probationer to the officer was also important, helping to emphasise that the offender was expected to make efforts as well as the officer, and ensuring that some interviews could take place away from the probationer's family. The Committee pointed out, however, the need for the methods of work to be varied to suit the needs of the individual probationer and urged that officers should be allowed a good deal of elasticity in arranging home visits and reporting.[63]

Whilst the supervision of probationers was the chief duty of probation officers, they also had the statutory duty under the Probation Rules to 'make such preliminary enquiries, including enquiries into the home surroundings, as the Court may direct, in respect of any offender in whose case the question of making a probation order may arise'.[64]

The Rules made it clear that the decision as to whether enquiries should be initiated was the court's entirely, and only referred to situations where probation was likely to be applied. On the other hand, the Children and Young Persons Act, 1932, repealed by the consolidating measure of the same name in 1933, gave the local authority the duty of providing the juvenile court with information about the home surroundings, school record, health and character of all children and young persons coming before it. The local authority was only relieved of the obligation to report on the home surroundings if the Court specifically arranged for the probation officer to do so instead.[65]

The Home Office appear soon to have recognised that some difficulties and misunderstandings might arise as a result of this provision. In an official circular of the 9th August 1933 it was suggested to the justices that they should discuss with the local authority the best way of allotting these duties between the probation officers and those of the local authority—the school attendance officers. Whilst the Home Office considered that the school attendance officers might well be able to provide information about home surroundings, it implied that in the case of young persons who had left school, the local authority's information could be supplemented by the probation officer.[66]

The circular also made a point put by Lord Feversham in the 1932 debate, but not considered by the government weighty enough to sway its decision at the time, that if a probation order is likely to be made, the probation officer should be able to advise the court on the basis of first-hand contact with the case, whether it was in fact a suitable one for this type of treatment.

The Committee found that the provisions in the Rules and in the 1933 Act had not ensured the full use of the probation officer as a source of information. Moreover, whilst they considered valuable the information which the local authority could provide about school records, health and character, they were of opinion that 'for the purposes of the Court, the probation officer is the best person to make enquiry into home surroundings'. It was 'right', they reported, that a Court should receive this information from its own officer, and they quoted it as the opinion of probation officers that contact with the offender and his family at this early stage laid a good

140

foundation for subsequent work under a probation order.[67]

They were evidently not greatly influenced by the evidence presented by the Association of Superintendents of School Attendance Departments, which was out to defend the position gained in 1932. Their departments, these officers claimed, were in a better position to provide information about the homes of children and young people because their areas were smaller than those of the probation officers and they were therefore likely to have a more intimate knowledge of the homes within it, and because they had greater resources in the shape of the schools and the school health service on which to draw for information. They also suggested that the visit of a probation officer for the purpose of making a report might give an erroneous impression to neighbours of the family concerned. Indeed, they went so far as to express the opinion that all child delinquents should be placed under the supervision of the education authority rather than a special officer of the court.[68]

A Money Payments (Justices Procedure) Act, 1935, passed whilst the Committee was sitting, further increased the investigation work of the courts. Its purpose was to reduce the number of persons sent to prison in default of payment of fines by providing that, instead of being automatically imprisoned, a defaulter was to be brought before the court so that consideration could be given to his reasons for failing to pay and for investigation into his financial circumstances. The Departmental Committee on Imprisonment by Courts of Summary Jurisdiction in Default of Payment of Fines and Other Sums of Money, which had made the recommendations embodied in the Act, had reported the need for every Summary Court to have an officer responsible for undertaking enquiries into the means of parties in maintenance order cases, or of persons who had failed to pay a fine. It considered probation officers suitable persons for undertaking these enquiries, provided always that an adequate staff existed to ensure that probation work and these investigations were properly performed.[69]

The Social Services Committee reported in the same vein. These investigations were best performed by a trained social worker and, in the Committee's view, it would be a mistake for courts to appoint a new class of officer for the purpose, when an increase in the size of the probation staff could enable the work to be effectively carried out.

The Money Payments (Justices Procedure) Act, 1935,[70] also extended to offenders of all ages the court's power to place under supervision those to whom it allowed time for the payment of fines, and the Committee agreed with the opinion expressed in a Home Office Circular of the 8th November 1935 that the training and

141

experience of the probation officer rendered him a suitable person to undertake this supervision work. It did not, however, think that probation officers should be employed by the courts to collect money from offenders—indeed it was exceptional now for this to happen—but it saw no reason why officers should not sometimes assist offenders by taking from them instalments to be given to the collecting officer for the court.[71]

Some probation officers were responsible for after-care work with young people released from Approved Schools and Borstal Institutions, and with ex-convicts and discharged prisoners. The Committee was opposed to the probation service becoming involved in responsibility for either statutory or non-statutory after-care of prisoners. Nor was it anxious for probation officers to undertake such work for the Borstal Association, partly because of the time it could take up and partly because of the risk of contamination of probationers through contact with persons who had been considered in need of Borstal training. However, a letter to the Committee from the director of the Borstal Association insisting that the continued employment of probation officers was vital to his organisation led to a reconsideration of the question,[72] and to the Committee's reluctance to 'suggest any general change of practice at present' in areas where probation officers were allowed by their Committees to do the work, and where sufficient staff existed.

It was satisfied that probation officers could, without detriment to their other duties, act, when requested, as local friends to boys and girls from Approved Schools, the primary responsibility for whom rested with the Schools themselves.

Enquiries made by the Committee indicated that it was the general practice throughout the country to employ probation officers as conciliators in cases involving matrimonial disputes. In fact about half the applicants for summonses of this kind went in the first place to the probation officer.[73] The probation officers advocated that this should become standard procedure,[74] but this, the Committee reported, had its dangers. It meant, as Mr. Claud Mullins, the Metropolitan Magistrate, who was taking a particular interest in attempts to introduce new arrangements for domestic cases, told them, that the probation officer became a buffer between the applicant and the court,[75] and might thus deny the applicant his right to have his case heard by the magistrate. It could easily lead to a denial of justice because of the over anxiety of a probation officer to feel that conciliation had been effected.[76] So that, whilst the Committee approved of the practice adopted by many courts of attempting conciliation, and considered that probation officers were the most suitable people to undertake it, it recommended that a magistrate, with the assistance of the Clerk, should see all applicants and decide whether conciliation should be attempted.[77]

Matrimonial conciliation by probation officers was unofficial; there was no statutory authority to pay for it out of public funds. Innumerable examples of this and other non-statutory or 'missionary' work had been given to the Committee. Typical was that submitted by the probation officer at the West London Police Court who advised parents how to deal with difficult children, gave advice about family budgeting, arranged for the reduction of hire purchase payments by personally undertaking to see that they would be regularly paid, advised applicants for affiliation summonses and helped them to get the necessary evidence. Others were helping people to find accommodation, dealing with disputes between neighbours, acting as guardian *ad litem* under the Adoption Act, 1926, dealing with applicants for assistance from the poor box, making enquiries for the court under the Guardianship of Infants Acts, or giving assistance to wives and relatives of persons sentenced to imprisonment.[78]

The probation officers were very anxious that their sphere of work should be properly defined and that many of these duties should be given official recognition.[79] Agreeing that much of this work was properly that of the probation officer, who was now, in its view, the court's social worker, the Committee considered unwise any attempt to define too closely the duties which he should perform. It was preferable that individual courts should decide this for themselves. But they should always ensure that their probation staff was large enough to be able to carry out the work satisfactorily.[80]

An important feature of this Report for the development of the service was its emphatic assertion that the possession of a sense of vocation and the right kind of personality was no longer sufficient to ensure the proper execution of the social work of the courts. The performance of the increased range of duties expected of the officer and the application of the appropriate techniques required the skill and knowledge of a properly trained social worker.

The importance of training was now 'generally recognised in all branches of social work'. The Committee had been able to study information about the training of hospital almoners, psychiatric social workers, and the Care Committee Organisers employed by the London County Council. It had received evidence from representatives of the Joint University Council for Social Studies[81] and the Charity Organisation Society had stressed to it the need to give probation officers more training in general case work.[82]

Most of the officers in the probation service had had no special training; they had 'had to pick up the techniques of court work as best they could in the actual performance of their duties'. Few people had come into the service from the university courses. The hope that improvement in salaries since 1925 would encourage more university-trained people to take up probation work, had not in fact been realised. The Home Office training scheme had been small in scale, and had so far provided only eighteen new officers for the service. Apart from these trained entrants, some serving officers had been able to acquire a qualification through the Police Court Mission's University Extension Courses. These sources of training were clearly inadequate for the provision of a fully trained service. 'Such a haphazard method of providing for a service of such public importance cannot be defended at the present day', the Committee reported.

It was clearly unrealistic to recommend that all new entrants should possess a university social science qualification, though the Committee seriously considered this step. The principle that the Home Office should have some training responsibilities having already been established, it is not surprising that the Committee saw it as the body most suited to undertake the training of a substantial number of new entrants; and it recommended the extension and improvement of the existing training scheme 'so as to meet the needs of the whole probation service'.

The representatives of the Joint University Council for Social Studies criticised the experimental scheme run by the Home Office on the ground that in the selection of trainees, insufficient attention was paid to academic ability. Some had found the university courses too difficult and had failed their examinations. Any difficulties these students had experienced in pursuit of a diploma had been exacerbated by the arrangement for them to gain practical experience of court work concurrently with their studies at the university.[83] It was understandable that the probation committees who were employing them as assistant probation officers, and paying half their salaries, would expect them to give some assistance in the day-to-day work in the court.

There was evidence, nevertheless, that those who had passed through the course had 'obtained considerable benefit'. It had also 'had the merit of emphasising the value of a broad training in social science in the probation officer's work'.[84] The Committee's recommendations for a new training scheme embodied the principle that this 'background in social science' should be imparted to all trainees. Those who were able should take a university diploma as part of their training; the rest—people 'with substantial social experience and good general education'—should be given this background through a specially designed shorter course. In addition all candidates would require a short specialised course dealing with the work of a probation officer. It was suggested that this 'Probation Course' should be organised in two parts, the one theoretical, the other practical. The former would consist of lectures on the law and procedure relevant to probation work; the latter of training under selected probation officers in different types of court, of visits to institutions providing treatment for offenders and to relevant agencies such as Child Guidance and Mental Clinics and Public Assistance Institutions.[85]

The Committee encountered difficulty in reconciling its belief that the selection of probation officers should rest as far as possible with local probation committees, with its conviction that all future entrants to the service should be trained for the work. Any training scheme would obviously have to be national rather than local, and some selection would have to take place before public money was spent on training persons who wished to become probation officers. Their proposal was that the Training Scheme should be seen as a co-operative venture between local probation authorities. All could have some part in it and benefit from it when they needed new officers. The Home Office should set up a Probation Training Board on which the local appointing authorities would be 'adequately represented'. This would select trainees from amongst applicants who responded to public advertisement of the scheme, local committees thus being involved at the first stage of selection through their representation on the Board. They should also be kept well informed of the scheme so as to be able to encourage suitable local people to apply for selection.

When a vacancy occurred, an appointing authority would inform the Board and would receive from it the names of a number of trained candidates from which to make a selection. The Committee hoped that most vacancies would be filled in this way, but some concession was made to the principle of direct local recruitment by allowing that, in special circumstances, an appointing authority might be given the opportunity of selecting a local candidate for the special consideration of the Training Board.

The local authorities would also be financially involved in the scheme which, it was suggested, should be financed by making a percentage reduction in the government grant to each authority. The candidates selected by the Training Board would be paid a subsistence allowance and expenses out of this fund.

145

In its concern that training should be provided for people wishing to enter the service, the Committee did not ignore the need to arrange some training for existing officers. The subject was one, it thought, which 'might usefully be examined by the Probation Advisory Committee with the object of raising the standard of work throughout the country to a higher level'. Opportunities of this kind would, it was convinced, be greatly appreciated by the probation officers themselves.[86]

Not only was the probation service still having to recruit untrained persons; it was heavily dependent on people with an elementary education. The Committee considered that the possession of a secondary education should ordinarily be the minimum requirement for applicants. A probation officer's work demanded enough education to enable him to prepare reports, keep records and conduct correspondence. In addition, 'the delicate task of adjusting other people's difficulties', required 'the breadth of outlook which a good education should provide'.[87]

Conditions of service and their effect on recruitment and efficiency also occupied the attention of the Committee. Particular difficulty had been experienced in obtaining the services of well-trained, well-educated men. Recognising that the cause lay, not only in the poor prospects of promotion, which would be improved by the introduction of more principal and senior posts, but also in the low maximum salary obtainable by the ordinary probation officer, it recommended the raising of the maximum, and indeed the minimum, salary. It also considered there should be power to give up to four increments for each year of age over twenty-six to enable suitable commencing salaries to be offered to older candidates with experience in other fields of work.[88]

There was also a need, it reported, for more attention to be given to holiday arrangements and hours of work for probation officers[89] and to the provision of clerical assistance, transport facilities, accommodation and equipment to enable the work to be done efficiently. Many officers had no office except their own homes, and the Committee had learned of workers who had to conduct interviews in the corridor, in the yard outside the court or in a neighbouring tea-shop.[90]

The age limits for new entrants to the service stood at twenty-five and forty. Since it was thought that some men and women who might otherwise have entered the probation service on completing a university course were deterred by the prospect of having to wait several years before they could even apply to do probation work, the Committee recommended that the minimum age should be lowered to twenty-three.[91]

The variation in the use of probation between different courts noted in the Reports of 1909, 1922 and 1927 was still very marked. The percentage of indictable cases placed under the supervision of a probation officer varied from 43·8 per cent in one district to 5 per cent in another. In some areas many offenders dismissed or bound over without supervision under the Act, or sent to prison or borstal institutions, could in the Committee's opinion more suitably have been placed on probation.[92] The same criticism could be applied to Courts of Assize and Quarter Sessions and the Committee recommended that the services of a probation officer should be available at these courts whenever the question of making a probation order was likely to arise.[93]

The misconceptions about the scope and nature of the system first noted by Samuel and his Committee in 1909 had similarly persisted, in spite of Home Office attempts to dispel them. Some courts were still under the impression that the system was only applicable to children, or to first offenders. Some failed to discriminate properly between probation and dismissal or binding over, and the practice continued in some places of binding over an offender and of placing him at the same time under the informal supervision of the probation officer.[94]

The Committee believed that an explanation for the wide variation in the use of probation was to be found partly in defective organisation, which it hoped would be improved as a result of its Report, and partly in misconceptions which could be cleared up by amendments to the law.[95] It therefore reiterated the recommendation of the Young Offenders Committee, that in future legislation the term 'probation' should be applied only to release under supervision, and not to binding over without supervision or to dismissal. This would not only dispense with confusion about the three different methods of treatment; it would mean an end to the appearance in newspaper reports of the phrase 'dismissed under the Probation of Offenders Act' which helped to encourage in the public mind the idea that probation was equivalent to being 'let-off'. This 'unfortunate' idea was further fostered, the Committee reported, by the words of the 1907 Act which suggested that probation might be used when 'it is inexpedient to inflict any punishment, or any other than a nominal punishment'.

The Report suggested that to omit 'age' from the circumstances to which the court was to have regard in deciding to make a probation order would help to banish the misconception that probation was only for young people; and that 'the triviality of the

147

offence and mental condition' should no longer figure among these circumstances, because the former was 'in most cases ... an argument against supervision' and the latter a condition unlikely to lend itself to successful probation.[96]

Apart from the issue of dual control, the most controversial question discussed by the Committee, and the only one on which it could not agree to make a unanimous recommendation was whether a conviction should be recorded before the making of a probation order by courts of summary jurisdiction, as was the case in higher courts. In Oaten v. Auty[97] in 1919, Lord Darling had called the phrase 'without proceeding to conviction' used in the 1907 Act 'unscientific, thoroughly illogical, and ... merely a concession to the modern passion for calling things what they are not, for finding people guilty and, at the same time, trying to declare them not guilty'. This does not seem to have influenced the 1922 Committee which had recommended indeed that the need to record a conviction in the higher courts should be dispensed with.

The majority of the Harris Committee, however, agreed that the pretence was misleading and injurious to the probation system, and were of opinion that the law should be amended to do away with it, provided that arrangements were also made to maintain the protection afforded to probationers found guilty by summary courts from any legal disqualifications arising out of having been convicted of an offence.[98] Miss Symons and Miss Wall signed the Report with reservations on this matter, the former asserting that it was contrary to the intention of the 1907 Act, and that there was no evidence that the existing practice had any unfortunate results on the system.[99]

To simplify the law on probation, the Committee recommended that the technical requirement that a person being placed on probation should enter into a recognizance should be dispensed with, and that the probation order itself should set out in simple terms the conditions to be observed by the probationer, and the consequences of failure to comply with them. 'The valuable element of consent' connected with the recognizance could be retained in the probation system if the court asked the offender whether he consented to being placed on probation.[100] The conditions themselves should be few and simple, and directed, 'to the special circumstances of the individual case'. There was a tendency arising out of the use of a form prescribed by the Home Office, which contained a list of suggested conditions, for courts to use these stereotypes somewhat automatically.

The shortage of suitable hostels and homes for use by probationers under a condition of residence had persisted. This

148

situation led the Committee to make the suggestion that, in the absence of places in approved probation hostels it might be of advantage to find places in ordinary hostels or in suitable lodgings for some probationers, and that the Home Office should in these cases provide a 50 per cent grant to local authorities contributing to the cost, as for hostels and homes.[101]

When the report of the Committee on the Social Services in Courts of Summary Jurisdiction was published in 1936 more than ten years had elapsed since Parliament had provided in the Criminal Justice Act for the appointment of a probation officer and the administration of probation work in every area of the country. Although the spirit of this legislation had been evaded in some places, the Committee found itself in agreement with the principles upon which the system and its administrative framework had been based. Strains had been put on the latter as a result of growth. The Committee's contribution was to recommend a strengthening of the structure and organisation through clarification of the roles of the various elements in the service, the removal of the inhibition and potential friction associated with a system of dual control, the more realistic application of central control over standards by the introduction of an inspectorate, and oversight of the day-to-day work of local services by principal probation officers.

A change of principle was involved only in the introduction of a supervisory grade of officer (hitherto regarded as undesirable on the ground that this might jeopardise the relationship between the court, the probation officer and the probationer),[102] in the recommendation that the service should be organised on a fully public basis rather than continue in its partial dependence on voluntary bodies, and in the view of some, in the proposal that conviction should always be recorded before the making of a probation order.[103]

Whilst the importance of efficiency, which was the keynote of most of its recommendations, must not be underestimated, the most significant feature of the report was its view of the probation service as an entirely public enterprise, and of the probation officer as a full-time, trained and well-educated social worker of the courts.

CHAPTER SEVEN

THE END OF 'DUAL CONTROL'

The Report of the Social Services Committee became the blueprint for the probation service for the next quarter of a century. There was virtually no opposition to most of its recommendations, which incorporated the main views of the National Association of Probation Officers and the Magistrates' Association,[1] representative of the staff and employers in the service. The principal Home Office official concerned with probation work had been Chairman of the Committee and the inspectors of his Branch had made observations[2] in which the Report concurred. Only the police court missions had cause for disappointment.

It was soon made clear that the government was prepared to act upon the proposals. Within three months of the publication of the Report a start was made by the creation of a separate Probation Branch within the Home Office, to direct the rest of the plan for probation. Its Head, B. J. Reynolds, announced that those of the recommendations which could be acted upon without legislation would be considered as soon as possible.[3] Harris was reported to estimate that re-organisation along the suggested lines would take about five years to accomplish.[4]

The establishment of the new branch was soon followed by the appointment of the first inspector for the probation service, Miss D. M. Rosling, previously employed as a missionary probation officer in the Metropolitan Police Courts.[5] She was joined a few months later, in June 1937, by two male inspectors.[6]

Further adjustments in the central administration of the probation service were made in the same year by the appointment of a new Advisory Committee and a Probation Training Board. The terms of reference of the Advisory Committee were extended beyond probation and after-care matters to include 'the other social services of the court', in accordance with the wider view of probation work taken by the Departmental Committee. Harris was appointed to the Chair and its membership included Reynolds, Head of the Probation Branch, representatives of justices and of the clerks who acted as secretaries of Probation Committees, one of the Prison Commissioners, a high court judge, a stipendiary magistrate and a representative of the National Police Court Mission.[7]

The Departmental Committee had suggested that one of the duties of the Advisory Committee should be to take an interest in the progress of any training scheme which might be instituted,[8] and interlocking appointments between the Committee and the Probation Training Board ensured its close contact with arrangements for training. The Board's responsibility was to provide facilities for the training of candidates for appointment as probation officers, and also of those already working in the service.[9]

The Report had urged that no time should be lost in launching a training scheme, and preparations were hastily made so that the first selection of trainees could take place in June 1937. A leaflet outlining the work and giving details of training facilities was issued during the year. There was no lack of interest; during the first year there were a thousand applicants for the fifty available places.[10]

The hastiness of the Board's preparations precluded much change in the arrangements for enabling the more academically able candidates to take a university diploma. Under the new scheme they were still appointed to the staff of probation offices in the neighbourhood of the university, and although Reynolds said that an endeavour would be made to free them from much of the practical work in the Courts and 'to extend their contacts with the practical side of other social services',[11] their vacations at least were devoted to probation work. They were thus deprived of the experience in other branches of work which was available to their fellow students.[12]

For trainees with university social science qualifications, and for those for whom a university education was not considered suitable, the Board now instituted a 'Short Probation Course' lasting from six to twelve months according to individual need. It included practical experience of probation work in different courts and a series of lectures on subjects considered appropriate.[13] One of the difficulties which presented itself during the early years of the training scheme was finding practising officers with sufficient training and teaching ability to undertake the supervision of the trainees' practical work[14]—a problem which was universal in social work over many years as demand for qualified workers increased and training programmes expanded.

In the first two years from 1937 to 1939 one hundred and seventeen men and forty women completed training under this new scheme and took up full-time appointments in the courts.[15]

Priority was given to the training of new entrants[16] but the Board also made a start with the training of serving officers by arranging half-day release courses extending over twelve months in conjunction with universities in various parts of the country.[17]

Simultaneously with this drive to constitute a pool of trained candidates from which the justices could make their own selections, steps were taken to improve the salaries of probation officers. Exactly in accordance with the recent Committee's recommendations, the Probation Rules, 1937, raised minimum and maximum salaries and gave probation committees power to give a limited number of extra increments to new entrants over the age of twenty-seven.[18] According to the Home Office, the new scale compared favourably with the Burnham scale for teachers in elementary schools.[19]

At the same time, the lower age limit for new officers was dropped to twenty-three and the upper limit raised to forty.[20] An amendment to the 1926 Rules permitted the appointment of senior as well as principal probation officers and provided that an annual allowance in addition to the ordinary salary could be paid to this new grade of officer.[21] In a circular explaining the new Rules, the Home Office pointed out that any senior or principal appointment required the approval of the Home Secretary, and expressed readiness to advise appointing authorities about the establishment of appropriate supervisory posts for their area.[22] By making Home Office approval necessary, the central authority established almost from the start control over the structuring being introduced into the service. The Home Office itself appointed, for the first time, a Principal Probation Officer for the Metropolitan Police Court District.[23] Soon afterwards three Assistant Principal Probation Officers were added and a senior appointment made in each Metropolitan Police Court.[24]

The furtherance of combination in county areas and encouragement of the appointment of full-time probation officers were important features of the work of the Probation Branch during this period. They also tried to stimulate greater use and understanding of probation in some areas[25] and prepared and issued a booklet, mainly for the use of magistrates, on the objects and organisation of the probation service.[26] Since experience had demonstrated that Higher Courts were more likely to make probation orders where there were clear arrangements relating to the system, the Home Office sought to increase its use by encouraging the appointment of a liaison officer for the whole of an area committing cases to a Court of Assize or Quarter Sessions. The attendance of a probation officer at these courts, the availability of home surroundings reports in cases where probation might be considered, the attendance of women officers when necessary, could all be ensured under this arrangement, suggested by the Social Services Committee and subsequently considered and approved by the Probation Advisory Committee and His Majesty's Judges. In a circular to Clerks of the Peace, the Home Office hoped that, since they appeared to be in the best position to organise this service, they would be willing to make the arrangements. It was pointed out that the officer selected for this liaison work should be a person of administrative capacity, with judgment and capabilities which would command the respect of the court, and who would be able to work harmoniously with his colleagues. The Clerks were asked to forward to the Home Office particulars of the arrangements made so that the liaison officers could be indicated in the Directory of Probation Officers.[27]

Through administrative action the Home Office was thus able to proceed with many of the Departmental Committee's suggestions. Some, however, had to await legislation. The recommendations dealing with the hearing of domestic cases and arrangements for conciliation were the first to be dealt with. Very soon after the publication of the Report the Home Office had commended to justices the Departmental Committee's view that whilst applications for summonses should not in the first place be made to the probation officer, he should be used as conciliator and his work in this field should come under the supervision of the Probation Committee.[28] Shortly afterwards some of the Committee's recommendations were embodied in the provisions of the Summary Procedure (Domestic Proceedings) Act, 1937. As well as providing for the separate hearing of domestic proceedings and for the constitution and conduct of the court in these cases,[29] the Act extended the statutory duties of probation officers to include conciliation work and the making of investigations for the court into the means of parties to domestic proceedings or those in any matter of bastardy.[30] Religious interests were taken into account in a section which provided that, when a court requested a probation officer to attempt to effect conciliation and the parties to the case were of the same religious persuasion, the court should where possible select an officer of the same persuasion.[31]

The passing of this legislation was a further step in the recognition of the probation officer as a social worker of the courts rather than as solely a supervisor of probationers. An important effect of the Act was that a substantial part of the erstwhile unofficial or missionary work being performed by probation officers became statutory duties, and therefore eligible to attract the government grant-in-aid for probation work under the Criminal Justice Act, 1925.

The significance of this change was missed by the Central and the London Police Court Missions. Disappointed by the recommendations of the Departmental Committee about the place of voluntary societies in the probation service, they mustered the strongest possible delegations to make a last attempt to put their case to the Home Office.[32] (The London Mission decided to act independently of the Central Mission, in the hope that the Home Office would be willing to consider making an exception in their case.)[33] However, it was made clear to the delegations that the government was convinced that the probation service should become a wholly public one. They were still further dismayed to learn that what they had assumed would be their last opportunity to oppose the decision—the passage of a Bill through Parliament to enable payment for 'missionary work' to be made out of public funds—had in fact passed them by. The Home Office pointed out that further legislation was unnecessary, the requisite power having been arranged under the Domestic Proceedings Act.[34]

The London Police Court Mission announced its decision 'to bow to the inevitable'. Its agents serving as probation officers in the Metropolitan Police Courts were transferred to the direct employ of the Home Office on the 1st July 1938[35] and some two years later the Middlesex Probation Committee took over complete responsibility for the Mission's agents working in the county area.[36] The Central Police Court Mission's resolution strenuously to oppose the recommended change[37] suffered a similar collapse after their representatives' visits to Whitehall.

In the conversations and correspondence which took place with the Missions, the Home Office adopted the Departmental Committee's view that much remained for the voluntary societies to do to help the probation service. In particular they were asked to consider the establishment of more homes and hostels for probationers and of a hostel in London for trainees under the Home Office Training Scheme.[38]

Both the London and the Central Missions appear to have adopted a realistic approach to the situation. A Sub-Committee set up by the Central Mission to consider the position after conversations with the Home Office reported,

the only way in which the Police Court Mission can exist in the future is by those controlling it being realistic at the present

154

time. It would be a grave disservice to Church and Nation if the Mission refused to continue at all because it could not longer occupy itself with all the functions which it has hitherto performed.[39]

Harris later commended the courage with which the London Mission faced the new situation and took up new aspects of the work.[40] Temporary accommodation was soon found for use as a Trainees' Hostel in London and the first students took up residence in July 1938. The Mission assumed primary responsibility for the project[41] which was to make an immense contribution to the training of probation officers over many years.

The Police Court Missions also expressed readiness to assist the Home Office to increase the number of probation homes and hostels.[42] Concerned that the use of conditions of residence in hostels had been restricted owing to the lack of this type of accommodation, the Home Office began to consider what steps might be taken to encourage an increase in its provision. In the meantime it took up a suggestion of the Social Services Committee,[43] and offered grants similar to those under the homes and hostels scheme towards the maintenance of probationers boarded out or placed in lodgings under a condition of residence. The grant was only to be given on condition that the local authority agreed to make a similar contribution; that great care was exercised in the selection of lodgings; that the probation officer paid frequent visits to them; and that care was taken to see that the grant was diminished as the wages of the probationer rose and enabled him to become gradually self-supporting.[44]

The opportunity to incorporate in legislation more of the changes suggested by the Departmental Committee occurred in 1938 when the government allowed time for a Home Office Bill of some importance to consolidate and extend existing legislation dealing with a wide range of penal matters. Over the previous few years recommendations by Committees of Enquiry into various aspects of the penal system had been accumulating. Gordon Rose has pointed out that 'by the middle thirties the reforming organisations were once more becoming restive' and the appointment as Home Secretary of Sir Samuel Hoare, scion of a family of reformers, 'made it almost inevitable that something would be done'.[45]

Announcing the forthcoming introduction of the Bill to a conference of the National Association of Probation Officers, Sir Samuel said it would 'bring together into a single, easily manageable form all the principal enactments connected with probation'. The inclusion of basic provisions for probation in a Criminal Justice Bill such as this would 'make the probation system appear in its right function as an integral and essential part of all (the) many problems of social reformation'; and he expressed 'the confident hope' that by the time the Association met again one year hence, the Bill would be on the statute book.[46]

The Criminal Justice Bill was introduced into the Commons in November 1938.[47] Its Memorandum explained that the provisions relating to probation gave effect to the recommendations of the Committee on the Social Services in Courts of Summary Jurisdiction.

By referring to probation proper in a clause separate from that which referred to the two other methods,[48] it was hoped to allay the longstanding confusion arising from the association of probation with dismissal, and with binding over without supervision, in the 1907 Act.[49] Another persistent misconception, that probation was applicable only to young offenders, would hopefully disappear as a result of the omission in this Bill of any reference to age as a circumstance of which courts should take account when considering probation for any particular case.[50]

The procedure for placing a person on probation was simplified by the provisions of the Bill which dispensed with the need for a recognizance and merely stated that

> where a court by or before which a person is convicted of an
> offence for which the court has power to pass a sentence of
> imprisonment, or to impose a fine, is of opinion that, having
> regard to the circumstances including the nature of the offence
> the character and home surroundings of the offender, it is
> expedient to place him under supervision, the court may, in
> lieu of sentencing him, make a probation order.

The element of consent on the part of the offender implicit in a recognizance, was preserved by a provision that the court should explain to him 'in ordinary language' the effect of an order and the consequences of failure to comply with its conditions, and should not proceed to make one unless he expresses his willingness to comply.[51]

The opportunity was also taken to include a stipulation that a condition of residence in an institution should not have effect for more than twelve months and should always be notified to the Home Secretary.[52] The Bill provided also for the inspection of institutions to which probationers were sent,[53] and gave local authorities the power to make grants towards the capital costs of probation hostels or homes in their area.[54] A clause regularising the inclusion in an order of a condition that a probationer submit to mental treatment, resident or otherwise, for a period of not more than twelve months[55] reflected the increased interest being shown in this aspect of penology.

In the provisions dealing with administrative machinery the Bill aimed at distinguishing more clearly between the functions of the probation committee for the probation area and the committee (designated 'case committee' in the Bill) for each petty sessional division. As under the 1925 Act every probation area, single or combined, was to have a probation committee composed of justices and appointed in the same manner as previously, to be responsible for the local administration of the service and for appointing probation officers.[56] A case committee for each petty sessional division would take the personal interest in the work of the officers with individual probationers[57] which was regarded as so important to the system. In uncombined areas this committee was to consist of the entire probation committee or of a group appointed by it from among its members; in divisions which formed part of combined areas, the case committee was to be appointed by the justices for the division from among their number.[58] No provision was made for the co-option of non-justices suggested by the Social Services Committee.

The power of appointing authorities to select as probation officers the agents of voluntary societies was to be removed by the repeal of the relevant section of the Criminal Justice Act 1925. They were to be under an obligation to appoint not merely a probation officer for their area, but a sufficient number to ensure that at least one man and one woman could be assigned to each division.[59] (The Head of the Probation Branch had recently said that the Home Office was 'growing tired of the explanation that there was no work for a woman officer to do'.)[60] In every case where a woman or girl was placed on probation, the officer was to be a woman.[61]

The importance of training, and the government's responsibility for seeing that it was provided, was recognised in a clause permitting the use of central government funds for the training of probation officers or of persons for appointment to the service.[62]

No attempt was made in the proposed measure to define in any detail the duties of a probation officer, who was 'to undertake the supervision of probationers and other persons placed under their supervision, and to perform such other duties as may be prescribed or ... imposed by any enactment'.[63]

157

The National Association of Probation Officers was deeply disappointed, however, at the government's failure once again to include in proposed legislation a statement to the effect that one of the duties of the probation officer was to make social enquiries for the court.[64] The probation officers found this omission hard to understand in view of the recommendation of the Social Services Committee that the law should be amended to ensure that courts should give priority to consideration of probation as a method of treatment and, before making a probation order, take into account any information which the probation officer might be able to provide.[65] Even more recently, the *Fifth Report on the Work of the Children's Branch of the Home Office* had pointed out the advantage to be gained by the use of probation officers to make home surroundings reports: where a child was put on probation, the co-operation of the parents was more easily secured if contact had been made whilst the case was before the court. The Home Office had hoped that, as a result of the Departmental Committee's report, 'this important practical point (would) be more widely recognised'.[66]

Puzzled by the apparent change of heart, the Secretary of the National Association of Probation Officers suggested that, since the Home Office had always appeared to accept the wisdom of this particular recommendation of the Committee, and since Mr. S. W. Harris had been chairman, it could only be construed 'that very great pressure must have been brought to bear on the Home Office before those vital recommendations ... were omitted from the new Bill'.[67] No doubt he was referring to some pressure exerted by education authorities anxious to continue their association with the juvenile courts.

Before the Bill went into Committee the Executive Committee of the Association put its view to the Head of the Probation Branch who attended one of its meetings to answer questions on the matter. When it appeared that the Home Secretary was unwilling to adopt its proposals that the Bill should be amended to include statements that the making of social enquiries was a duty of probation officers, and that before making a probation order courts should consider any reports made by a probation officer, the Association sent circular letters to Members of Parliament and personal letters and briefing notes to selected Members asking for support for amendments which Mr. Godfrey Nicholson had promised to put in Committee.[68]

Speaking on Mr. Nicholson's amendment on the subject of social enquiries, Sir Samuel Hoare said he was ready to consider the re-working of the amendment before the Report Stage, but he thought it ought to be made clear that the enquiries were to be made only on the direction of the court.[69] He subsequently promised, as a result, the Association claimed, of its representations and of the pressure applied in the Committee,[70] to incorporate into the Bill at a later stage an amendment to the effect that it would be the duty of a probation officer 'to make, in accordance with any directions of the court, enquiries as to the circumstance or home surroundings of any person with a view to assisting the Court in determining the most suitable method of dealing with his case.'[71]

Referring to that part of Mr. Nicholson's amendment to the effect that magistrates should take into account any information about the offender's home circumstances which the probation officer might be able to provide, the Home Secretary proffered three reasons why it should not be accepted. The amendment, he said, would have the effect of limiting such enquiries to probation cases, when there were others where they were just as necessary; it would be difficult to apply such a provision in the High Courts; and thirdly, there were still some backwaters where efficient probation officers did not yet exist. He thought it better to deal with the matter by means of a circular. Various Members pointed out that magistrates might ignore or might not even see such a communication and Sir Samuel promised to look again at the question, although he could not see any way of surmounting the difficulties which he had put to the Committee.[72]

The section of the Bill relating to probation which attracted most attention in the Commons was that which proposed to make proceeding to conviction a necessary preliminary to the making of a probation order.[73] Almost all the speakers except those in the government considered this a retrograde step[74] in spite of the presence in the Bill of a clause designed to ensure that no legal disqualification would be suffered by probationers as a result of the change.[75]

When, in Committee, an amendment was put to avoid the need for conviction before dismissal and binding over, a division resulted in its defeat. However, the following clause, dealing with conviction before the making of a probation order, was discussed early the next morning before the arrival of many of the government's supporters, and a similar amendment was carried. It was assumed that the government would have its way during the later stages of the Bill.[76] But the length of time taken over the Committee Stage, and the deterioration in the meantime of the international situation, resulted in postponement by the government of further debate. Questioned on a number of occasions about finding time for the Bill, the Home

Secretary was unable to say whether this would be possible.[77] War was subsequently declared and soon afterwards the House heard that the government had reluctantly come to the conclusion that time could not be found for the Bill without prejudicing 'the effort on which all our energies must now be concentrated'.[78]

Another ten years was to pass before the opportunity arose to introduce a Bill of a similar nature. But although the outbreak of war frustrated this attempt to amend and consolidate the legislation relating to the probation system, and although wartime conditions put new difficulties in the way, the development of the probation service nevertheless continued as far as possible along the lines proposed in the 1936 Report.

In planning for the eventuality of war, the government had anticipated more disruption in the work of the courts than did in fact occur.[79] The war naturally brought some problems and changes, however, some of them connected with the day-to-day work of probation officers.

Evacuation played havoc with their supervision work. Some lost contact with their probationers when the latter moved to reception areas, and the attempt to re-establish it was sometimes made difficult by parents' reluctance to give their child's new address if it meant that foster parents would find out about the probation order. Sometimes parents threatened to bring home their offspring if this had to happen.[80] There was also some confusion about the transfer of cases to officers in the reception areas. Obviously their work would be considerably increased if all cases were transferred. Eventually it was decided that difficult ones should be formally transferred, the rest notified to the officers in the areas where they were accommodated. Some of the reception areas experienced an increase in delinquency, which itself resulted in more work for the local probation officers.[81] Where offences were committed by evacuees, there were unusual difficulties attached to making enquiries into their home surroundings.[82]

To help with probation work, and generally to assist in dealing with difficult children, the Home Office sent out a number of probation officers from the Metropolitan Courts to the reception areas.[83] Those who were left behind in London, and those in other industrial areas which experienced heavy raids, had their own particular difficulties. Whilst there were daylight as well as night-time raids, it was not easy to maintain arrangements for reporting by probationers. Home visiting also posed problems where many people were away from home in public shelters or at work.[84]

For officers all over the country the departure of some of their probationers to the forces made for difficulties in keeping in touch and in trying to carry on some form of supervision. Some courts discharged the orders of probationers who went into the forces; others did so after a period, on receipt of a satisfactory report from the probationer's unit.[85]

The domestic and matrimonial difficulties thrown up by the separation of husbands and wives by military service was a source of additional work for probation officers, whose offer to help with army social work of this kind[86] was officially accepted. Army Welfare Officers were instructed to use probation officers to make enquiries for them at the homes of men who had come to them with domestic problems. In many cases the enquiries were devoted to estimating the possibility of successful conciliation in matrimonial disputes; others involved reporting what help or advice was needed where difficult children were the problem. The Home Office stressed to Probation Committees the value of this kind of work in war-time and hoped they would encourage their probation officers to undertake it. For the purpose of the Exchequer grant towards probation, it was to be regarded as part of the normal conciliation work of the service.[87]

Like other services, probation lost some of its young men to the armed forces. Probation was considered essential enough to rank as a reserved occupation, at first for all men over thirty-five, and before long for all over thirty years of age.[88] Even so, a quarter of the full-time male officers soon departed the service, for a good number of young men had been recruited in the drive following the 1936 Report.[89] In spite of this loss, the number of full-time officers, which had increased from 299 in 1935 to 509 in 1939 continued to rise. By 1945, there were 750 employed in the service.[90]

The Probation Branch itself suffered the loss of experienced officials including, for a few years, B. J. Reynolds, its Head.[91] Nevertheless, under central direction progress was made even during the war years in bringing about combinations, establishing principal and senior posts, increasing the number of full-time officers, and the employment of more women officers.

Between 1936 and 1943 9 combined areas were constituted, bringing the total to 47. During the same period 14 new principal posts and 65 senior posts were established; so that by 1943 one in seven probation officers was receiving remuneration above the basic scale. The Social Services Committee had found 300 courts without the services of a woman officer. Seven years later, less than 100 were in this position.[92]

The shortage of male officers at the beginning of the war led to the employment, on the advice of the Home Office, of women to do most of the matrimonial and kindred social work of the court and to supervise boys up to fourteen, as well as women and girls, so that the available manpower could be used where it was most necessary, for the supervision of adult males.[93]

Although the Advisory Committee on Probation and the Probation Training Board ceased to meet, the Probation Branch continued, with the help of some members of the Board, to train prospective officers.[94] For a few months at the beginning of the war, training was limited to practical work, although the London Police Court Mission, in whose hostel the trainees continued to reside, provided, with the concurrence of the Probation Branch, a number of lectures to help to supplement the practical training.[95] In 1941, however, the training scheme was extended and theoretical work re-introduced.[96]

Between 1940 and 1944 172 people were trained for entry into the service in spite of war conditions.[97] In 1945 the Parliamentary Under-Secretary at the Home Office, the Earl of Munster, was able to announce that 50 per cent of the 750 full-time officers in the service had been initially selected and trained under the official training scheme.[98]

The Home Office appears, in fact, to have been deflected not at all from its determination to carry through the policy recommended in 1936. Opinion at the time considered that the war placed them in a strong position to do this, and the manner of carrying it out gave rise to resentment and an atmosphere of insecurity within the service.[99] The National Association of Probation Officers was led by a series of personal incidents, reported by members, to make a formal protest about the methods of inspection and what it considered the unwarranted interference of the Home Office in local matters.[100] The Home Office appeared to the Association to have allowed their anxiety to produce an efficient service to lead them into trying to effect the transfer of experienced officers to senior posts in new areas without reference to their existing employers. The Association detected, it thought, a change in the balance of power between the central authority and the local probation committees.[101]

The lack of security prevalent in the service at this time can perhaps be accounted for in part by the general uncertainty attached to living under wartime conditions. It was probably aggravated further by discussion in the mid-war years about the future organisation of the growing social services in the post-war years and the apparent keenness of the education authorities to envelop all the services concerned with children.

Reynolds himself, on his return to the Probation Branch in 1943, told a conference of the National Association of Probation Officers that he thought the day would come when a survey would be made of all the separate services dealing with the personal needs of individuals. Would, he wondered, 'some of the educationists succeed in establishing a monopoly of all youth services and take over from Probation and other departments the care and supervision of all persons under eighteen?'[102]

Within the service, too, the question of financial responsibility for probation work was being seriously discussed.[103] A vote taken at a Conference of the National Association of Probation Officers showed that the majority of probation officers were satisfied with the existing arrangements for finance and control. Those who wished to see the whole responsibility for the finance of the service transferred to the central government considered that the greater uniformity in service conditions, salaries for senior posts, size of case-loads and standard of work expected which would follow would benefit the officers and improve the quality of work performed by the service as a whole. Others, however, feared a change in the public's image of the probation officer if he became a kind of civil servant. They saw the probation officer cramped by official regulations and denied a sufficiently free hand in his work. Local control, they argued, meant that those responsible knew the needs and circumstances of the area in which their probation officers were working. The advocates of national control denied that membership of a nationally operated service was incompatible with a sense of vocation, and that a central authority could not appreciate the needs of the various districts. Inspectors travelling about the country could see and compare the needs of different localities and view them in relation to the needs of the service as a whole.

There was even some discussion of the merits of placing a centrally financed service on a regional basis. Some thought this might be more acceptable to the courts and the probation officers than control direct from Whitehall.[104]

The unease within the probation service did not escape the notice of some of the most enthusiastic advocates of the probation system. During the summer of 1944, at the instance of Gertrude Tuckwell and Margery Fry a small group of magistrates from both London and the provinces met to discuss their concern about the probation service. They were aware of something unsatisfactory in the relationship between the probation service—the probation committees and the probation officers—on the one hand, and the Home Office on the other. They understood that officers and committees were disturbed at the extent to which the Probation Branch was exercising control over the service and at the manner in which this was being done.

There were complaints that the Home Office was trying to influence the deployment of experienced personnel by encouraging, without reference to the employing committees, some officers to apply for new senior posts in other areas; and that the probation inspectorate was not sufficiently mindful of the position of the probation committees in the administration of the service to make contact with them when visiting and inspecting the work of their officers. It also appeared that the desire of the Home Office to build up a fully trained service sometimes led to differences between them and probation committees about the appointment of new officers.

Since it was their opinion that this matter should be brought to the notice of someone other than the officials directly concerned with the Probation Branch, the group prepared a memorandum and planned that, with the help of an even more influential sympathiser, Miss Tuckwell and Miss Fry should make a confidential approach on its behalf to the Permanent Under-Secretary. These two were aware, however, that the Home Office was very much busied with other affairs and that it was important to wait a suitable opportunity to broach the subject.

Whilst their plans were being consolidated, it was announced[105] that the Home Secretary had appointed a new body, an Advisory Council on the Treatment of Offenders, of which Miss Fry and the Permanent Under-Secretary were both to be members. With this intelligence, they decided to send their memorandum to the Chairman of the New Council, Sir Norman Birkett, who they were convinced would give it careful consideration.[106]

It happened that the first subject which the Council was asked to consider was 'what more can be done to develop the probation service as a highly skilled profession requiring not only a missionary spirit but training and expert knowledge'.[107] The magistrates' memorandum was laid before it, and evidence was also received from the Magistrates' Association[108] and the National Association of Probation Officers. The Probation Officers' Association was then invited to send a deputation to meet the Council. The five representatives who took part were questioned particularly about their views on the practical exercise of Home Office powers of control over the probation service. These they expressed frankly, helped, no doubt, by the sympathetic questions of Miss Fry and others.[109]

The Council's report to the Minister was not made public nor any consequential action announced. Probably some adjustment was made within the Probation Branch itself. Perhaps further discontent was obscured by or forgotten during the period of readjustment to peacetime conditions at the end of the war. At any rate, the National Association of Probation Officers, which had made no secret previously about its unsatisfactory relations with the Home Office, reported at the end of 1945 that its relationship with the Home Office throughout that year had been a happy one.[110]

The Association had been re-organising its affairs during the previous few years, and adopted a new constitution in 1945.[111] The period of outside support and leadership was now virtually at an end. Lord Feversham, though maintaining his interest and continuing as President, was away on active service during the war and on his return assumed a more passive role in the Association's affairs. Gertrude Tuckwell had retired from the Chairmanship in 1941 and the Association, after one or two unsuccessful approaches to other 'outsiders',[112] departed from precedent and appointed a probation officer in her stead.[113] Its members were now better remunerated and greater in number, and by 1945 it was able to dispense with the financial support of the Clarke Hall Fellowship except in connection with its Journal, which it shared with the Fellowship.[114]

The war over, the Association looked forward to the time when the government would again introduce penal reform legislation. It set up a sub-committee to reconsider the provisions of the 1938 Criminal Justice Bill, and began to compile a list of interested Members of the new Parliament to contact when necessary.[115] It moved into the post-war years independent of patronage and more fitted to assume the role of a modern professional organisation.

CHAPTER EIGHT

SOCIAL CASEWORK FOR
THE COURTS

In the years immediately following the end of the war, the new Labour administration, with a clear mandate for reform, was occupied with an ambitious legislative programme and consequent administrative reorganisation, including the introduction of a national health service and a comprehensive social security programme. It was not until late in 1947 that time was given to a Criminal Justice Bill.

Introduced by the Home Secretary, Chuter Ede, the Bill contained proposals very similar to those of 1938, among them the abolition of imprisonment by summary courts of persons under 17,[1] and by higher courts of under 15s, and restrictions on imprisonment of persons between 17 and 21. Two new sentences for children and young offenders emerged from the proposals. Attendance centres, a feature of the 1938 Bill, were at first omitted but later proposed and accepted in the Lords.[2] The inclusion of a proposal for the establishment of dentention centres, not included in the 1938 Bill, may have been influenced by the prevailing public concern at the rise in the number of indictable offences[3] and by the experience gained during the war of military detention centres.[4]

The proposals relating to probation sought, as in 1938, to consolidate the relevant legislation and to amend it in accordance with some of the recommendations of the Social Services Committee.[5] A clear distinction was made in the Bill between probation, dismissal, and binding over, and all references to age, antecedents, health, mental condition, the trivial nature of the offence, and extenuating circumstances, as justification for the courts' use of probation, were omitted. The wide scope intended by the government for the application of probation was made plain: probation could be used for any offence where the sentence was not fixed by law.[6]

The need for a recognizance was to be dispensed with, but it would be necessary for the court to obtain the consent of offenders over fourteen years of age to the making of a probation order.[7] In spite of the protests made in 1939, there was again no reference to the making of a probation order 'without proceeding to conviction', which had applied to the making of probation orders by summary courts since the introduction of the system; as in the previous Bill, a provision was included to exempt probationers from any legal disqualification arising out of having been convicted of an offence.[8]

One year was to be the minimum period for which an offender could be placed on probation,[9] and the maximum for which a probationer could be required to reside in an approved home or hostel.[10] It was again proposed that courts should be given a specific power to insert in a probation order a requirement that the probationer should undergo mental treatment for a period not exceeding twelve months, though only on medical evidence that the offender's mental condition required and might respond to treatment, and that it was not such as to justify certification under the existing Lunacy or Mental Deficiency Acts.[11] In general the insertion of requirements was left to the discretion of the courts.

Following the recommendation of the Social Services Committee,[12] the government made a proposal symptomatic of the growth in the use of probation and the desire for greater efficiency, that in future the name of the petty sessional division in which the offender resided, instead of the name of an individual officer, should be inserted in the probation order. The offender would be required to be under the supervision of an officer appointed for, or assigned to, that division.[13]

Whilst confirming broadly the existing arrangements for the local administration and supervision of the service, the Bill, as in 1938, drew a clearer distinction between the duties of probation and case committees.[14] It also incorporated the suggestion made by the 1936 Committee, but not taken up in 1938, that case committees should be able to co-opt non-justices who might be able to contribute to their work.[15] Probation committees were to appoint a sufficient number of probation officers to enable the services of both a male and female officer to be allotted to each petty sessional division;[16] and women and girls placed on probation were always to be under the supervision of the woman officer.[17]

To the relief of the probation officers, the making of social enquiries for the courts was included in the Bill's definition of their duties:

> It shall be the duty of probation officers . . . to inquire, in
> accordance with any directions of the court, into the
> circumstances or home surroundings of any person with a view

167

to assisting the court in determining the most suitable method of dealing with his case.[18]

Here, the principle insisted upon by Sir Samuel Hoare (now Viscount Templewood) when Home Secretary in 1939, that the court should be the directing authority,[19] was preserved. The making of enquiries was not to be automatic but left to the initiative of the court. However, this provision was important in drawing attention to the fact that the probation officer was properly available to courts for this purpose; and also in relation to stipulations in other parts of the Bill that courts would have a duty, in the case of certain categories of offender, to consider information about circumstances, character and physical and mental condition.

New proposals for the conditional release on licence of young prisoners and persons serving the proposed sentences of preventive detention and corrective training implied the need for additional after-care provision, and the supervision, 'in such cases ... as may be prescribed', of persons released from custody, was included among the duties prescribed for the probation officer.[20] This indicated that the government, in contrast to the Social Services Committee, saw the probation service as being an appropriate agency for dealing with ex-prisoners.

Under the 'Administrative Provisions as to Probation', the Home Secretary's existing powers to prescribe the constitution, procedure, powers and duties of probation committees, and the salaries and qualifications of probation officers were to be retained, and the further power sought to regulate the conditions of service and duties of probation officers.[21]

As in 1938 permission was sought for the payment of government grants towards the cost of enlarging, improving, or carrying on approved probation homes and hostels provided by voluntary societies or individuals,[22] though in the Memorandum on the Bill, the government made it clear that new homes and hostels would be provided gradually and that it was impossible to say what expenditure would be required for these. It estimated that £250,000 of central government money and a similar amount from local authorities would be required to help existing institutions of this kind.

Debates on the Bill were largely dominated by discussion of proposals to alter the prison system and to abolish corporal punishment. By contrast those dealing with probation were generally welcomed by both the Commons and the Lords. It was clear that the system was by now thoroughly accepted and established as one of the principal methods of dealing with offenders.

It was the proposal to record a conviction before making a probation order which again aroused most controversy. Most of those in the Commons who referred to this clause regretted the change, and wished to see the existing exemption retained in spite of its illogicality. It was defended, for the government, by the Solicitor General on the grounds that to have proved that a person had committed an offence and then not to convict them was 'wholly anomalous' and misleading to prospective employers and others interested in a person's record.[23]

An attempt to defeat the government's intention was unsuccessfully made in the Standing Committee.[24] In the Lords objections to the proposal were again raised. Lord Holden, for example, suggested that many people had succeeded in re-establishing themselves in society just because no conviction had been recorded against them. He knew that the London probation officers, with whom he had some contact, disapproved of the move to change the existing arrangement.[25]

The government, unwilling to give way entirely on this question, compromised to some extent during the Committee Stage in the House of Lords, when the Lord Chancellor moved an amendment that although a conviction should be recorded before a probation order was made, it should not be deemed to be such once the order was made, unless the probationer was subsequently brought back before the court and sentenced for the original offence; and, in the case of those under seventeen, not even then. The amendment, he said, had been designed to enable former probationers who applied to go abroad to say that they had not been convicted on an offence.[26]

In their advances to interested members of both Houses, the National Association of Probation Officers had expressed objection to the proposals to introduce conviction with probation, and to replace in the probation order the name of the probation officer by that of the petty sessional division. They also wished to see included in the new Bill's definition of their duties the words 'advise, assist and befriend' which had figured in the 1907 Act, and for which they no doubt felt a sentimental attachment.[27] The government allowed the inclusion of the phrase during the Committee Stage,[28] but was unwilling to accede to the Association's request that the name of the probation officer should appear in the probation order. In the Upper House, Lord Raglan said that the Association considered that the inclusion of the officer's name helped to establish, right at the start, the necessary personal relationship between the officer and the probationer. Lord Chorley, for the government, insisted that the proposed change would in no way impair the relationship and would certainly introduce more flexibility by enabling a change of officer to be made, in the event of the original one being unable to continue, without further recourse to the court.[29] In 1964, sixteen years after the change was made, probation officers observed that the fears expressed in this respect had so far proved groundless.[30]

Viscount Templewood wanted consent to the making of a probation order to be necessary in the case of offenders under fourteen, as for those over that age. However, the Lord Chancellor, whilst agreeing that consent was an important feature of the system, did not wish to see this emphasised so much as to prevent courts from placing under the supervision of a probation officer a child who would not give his consent.[31]

The Bill received the Royal Assent on the 30th July 1948, the provisions relating to probation coming into force on the 1st August 1949. The Criminal Justice Act 1948 replaced previous measures as the basic legislative framework for the probation service. By this time the struggles to get the system known, understood and used by the courts, to evolve an administrative structure which would retain the desirable element of local interest and yet allow of organisational efficiency, to make probation into a public service employing full-time staff, and to build a strong and active probation officers' organisation, were largely over. As was to be expected in view of the different social climate of the post-war years and of the changes which had taken place in the probation service since 1907, new concerns and problems emerged.

The subsequent development of the service has been inextricably bound up with changes in penal policy influenced by dissatisfaction at the failure of existing methods to stem the upward movement of crime rates and by pressures within the penal system arising out of the increase in the numbers committed to prison; and with changes in personal social service provision and organisation in response to new thinking about ways of preventing crime and of delivering social work services.

As a result of changed economic conditions and improved social services, problems of poverty and unemployment loomed less large among the concerns of social workers. Relieved of much of the need to find sources of help, they now required a knowledge of the more complex social services and the ability to help their clients to use and communicate with them.

Greater attention was being paid in social work to the non-material aspects of clients' problems. Psychological research and wartime experiences had been important factors in the widespread adoption of a view of the family as a highly important social unit,[32] a trend which influenced the work of the child care, and to a lesser extent, the probation service. With the growth of the social services there was an increased likelihood that more than one service and possibly more than one social worker would be involved with a family. The need for, and the problems connected with, co-operation were increasingly recognised.

A shift to a more family-oriented approach in social work, strongly influenced by the recently published findings of John Bowlby on the relationship between maternal care and mental health,[33] was further reinforced by the explanations being produced for the rising crime rate which distressed and puzzled the country during the immediate post-war years. Amid the varied explanations expounded in the absence of research—the war, the cinema, the decline in church-going, the loosening of parental discipline—there was a growing conviction that a secure family background was likely to contribute to sound emotional development and the prevention of delinquency. In a joint circular on juvenile delinquency issued in 1953 the Ministers for Home Affairs, Health and Education observed that important among long-term causes were unsatisfactory home conditions involving bad housing, family conflict, neglect and lack of affection and parental interest.[34] The probation officers, however, appear to have been more reluctant than some other workers to move away from their traditional concentration on the individual.[35]

Other fields of social work were being expanded to meet demands arising out of increased social welfare provision, and the recognition that social work had a peculiar contribution to make. The post-war legislation had also produced a new kind of social worker, the child care officer employed by the local authority Children's Committees set up under the Children Act, 1948. Government-backed training schemes led to the rapid build-up over the next decade of this new group of workers with their own professional organisations, the Associations of Child Care Officers and of Children's Officers. Conceived mainly to help children deprived of a normal home life by the provision of alternative care, this new service, with its training and concerns focused on the needs of children, was, inevitably, given the influence of Bowlby's findings, to develop strong interests in preventive work with children and families in their own homes—a sphere of overlap with probation officers. Probation officers, however, saw no threat to the development of their service or to their professional interests.

171

The Children's Department had replaced the Education Department as the body responsible for carrying out the local authority's responsibility under S. 35 of the Children and Young Persons Act, 1933, to provide the juvenile courts with home surroundings reports. Although it was in fact very rare for courts to ask child care officers to provide reports, when the opportunity arose in 1952 with the introduction of the Children and Young Persons (Amendment) Bill, the National Association of Probation Officers made strenuous efforts through their Parliamentary contacts and by representations to the Home Office, to have an amendment passed which would ensure that only probation officers could be used to obtain and present home surroundings reports in the juvenile courts.[36] They thus revived the controversy of 1931.[37] Lord Merthyr agreed to put such an amendment but withdrew it when the government gave an assurance that measures would be taken to avoid overlap.[38] There followed informal discussions at a high level about liaison arrangements between the children's and the probation services whereby, according to the National Association of Probation Officers, in the interests of saving manpower, probation officers would present the information supplied by the probation service.[39]

Later the Association tried to persuade the Ingleby Committee, set up in 1956 to review the operation of the juvenile courts and related matters, that the probation officer was the most appropriate person to present all the information, being always in attendance at the court.[40] But the Committee considered that, on the whole, the children's departments, 'having regard to their functions and experience and to their responsibilities for many of the children as a result of court proceedings', should present reports, except that the probation officer should present the home surroundings report where he had made the relevant enquiries.[41]

The Children's Department of the Home Office was much occupied with the setting up of the exciting new children's service, and its reports for 1951 and 1955 reflect this pre-occupation. The Probation Division continued steadily with the main tasks of the central authority for probation, which were to bring out Probation Rules under the new Act, to ensure that the intention of the Act with regard to local administration was carried out, to improve the administrative efficiency of the service by pursuing a policy of combining areas, to carry out its responsibilities in relation to recruitment and training, and generally to exercise the greater control over the service recommended in 1936.

The greater length of the new Probation Rules issued in 1949 reflected the development of central control and more complex administrative arrangements. Some omissions were an indication of the maturity of the service. It was no longer considered necessary, for example, to give guidance to probation committees about the qualities to be looked for in a prospective officer, or to prescribe that uniforms should not be worn. On the other hand, it was necessary to include new rules relating to the duties of senior and principal officers, a reflection of the movement towards a hierarchical structure. The duty of a senior officer was to

> include the supervision of and advice upon the work of probation officers, and in particular a senior probation officer shall organise the office work and the distribution of work between probation officers, and examine and advise upon the manner in which they keep their records and the manner in which their working time is used.[42]

Similar duties were laid down for a principal officer but he was also to undertake the organisation and supervision of the service in his area, and to advise the probation committee on technical matters relating to the service.[43]

Greater experience of the manner in which work with probationers was best carried out, and appreciation of the highly individualised nature of social casework, no doubt accounted for the more general terms in which the probation officer's duty towards probationers were couched. The officer was now to 'keep in close touch with the probationer, meet him frequently, and unless there is good reason for not doing so ... visit his home from time to time and require the probationer to report to him at stated intervals.'[44] The specific direction that he was to encourage all under his supervision or towards whom he had some duty to perform 'to use the appropriate statutory and voluntary agencies which might contribute to his welfare'[45] set the probation service in the context of the broader social provisions of the post-war era.

In accord with the intention of the Act, the new Rules extended the supervisory duties of probation officers to cover prisoners released on conditional licence. The after-care aspect of the work of the service was further emphasised by including among its statutory duties voluntary after-care, on official request, of persons released from prisons and the new detention centres, and the work already being done in supervising youths and girls from borstal at the request of the Central After Care Association, and from approved schools at the request of the managers.[46]

It was necessary to prescribe in the new rules the constitution and procedure of probation committees and case committees and to define clearly their respective responsibilities.[47] An earlier provision authorising probation committees to allocate probation officers to quarter sessions was now made mandatory and included assize courts,[48] an amendment designed to encourage greater use of probation and of social enquiries by the higher courts.

Effecting the combination of more probation areas proved to be a lengthy and sometimes difficult task. The further away in time from the 1936 Report, of course, the more likely was the Probation Division to be dealing with areas either reluctant or uninterested. The policy of the Home Office was not to use its power to combine probation areas unless there were some measure of local agreement.[49] Thus time had to be given to convincing at least some of the authorities concerned of the benefits to be had from combination. The fact that compulsion was used on some occasions[50] indicates that the Home Office was serious in its intentions to improve the administration of the service by creating units of a more efficient size. For example the petty sessional divisions, the boroughs, and all but three of the county boroughs of Lancashire were in 1959 combined into three probation areas at the insistence of the Home Office. Feeling about this was strong enough to bring forth more than a passing mention when the Permanent Under-Secretary addressed the Annual Conference of the National Association of Probation officers.

'I know well', he told the assembly,

> the difficulties which many of those most anxious for the well-being of the Service felt about this reorganisation; and the decision to bring it about was not lightly taken. The Home Secretary fully understood the reluctance felt by some officers, as well as by magistrates, to see the former organisation of the Lancashire service disturbed; and he would not have insisted upon the new scheme had he not been convinced that it was right. His decision was not in any way a reflection on the loyal work that has been done by Lancashire officers, often under a pressure greater than in most other parts of the country.

The creation of larger units for the purpose of local administration was, he continued, always difficult and controversial; but the advantage of local interest, perhaps more readily assured in smaller units, had to be balanced against the greater organisational efficiency of larger units. It was after balancing these factors that the Home Secretary had concluded that in Lancashire the creation of larger groups, sustained by local committees, would enable a service

174

which had already done invaluable work to tackle its growing problems with even greater efficiency.[51]

Between 1947 and 1959, the 292 probation areas in England and Wales were reduced to 104.[52] Combination was mainly between the various areas in a geographical county. By 1959 only 9 separate county petty sessional divisions, 34 county boroughs and 3 other cities, and the metropolitan magistrates' courts area remained uncombined.[53]

The progress made in combination and a general increase in work and the number of officers in the service led to the creation of more principal and senior posts recommended by the 1936 Committee. By 1962 there were 62 principal probation officer posts in the service.[54]

Further expansion of the inspectorate in the Probation Division of the Home Office enabled it to exercise the greater leadership and control which the 1936 Committee had insisted was necessary. By 1959 the establishment of inspectors was 11 and the inspectorate was now the chief point of contact between the central authority and the rest of the service. It was customary during this period for a full inspection of each probation area to be made every few years, giving the representatives of the central authority the possibility of checking on standards, preferring advice and criticism, disseminating information, and making valuable personal contact with both magistrates and probation officers. Many *ad hoc* visits were also made to probation areas on Home Office business or at the request of the local committee, and, in accordance with the Probation Rules, a visit was paid by an inspector to each new officer before the confirmation of his appointment. There was thus a good measure of opportunity for building up knowledge and relations between the central and local authorities. After 1957 full inspections of areas had to be curtailed in the face of rapid expansion, but the other points of contact remained.[55]

The continuing rise in the volume of serious crime during much of this period put the correctional services, including probation, under considerable pressure. The absolute number of probation orders rose with the number of offenders, from 32,543 in 1948 to 39,623 in 1958, but an interesting feature revealed by analysis of the wartime and post-war statistics was that a change had taken place in the rate of use of probation by the courts. Whilst the number of persons placed on probation for indictable offences rose fairly consistently in the decade after the war, varying more or less with the total volume of crime in any one year, the percentage of offenders treated by the probation method fell consistently,[56] in spite

175

of the restriction on the imprisonment of persons under 21 by the Criminal Justice Act, 1948, which might well have been reflected in an increased use of probation. Between 1938 and 1960 the percentage of juvenile offenders convicted of indictable offences placed on probation decreased from 51 to 35 per cent. In the case of those over seventeen there was also a fall between 1938 and 1947 from 22 to 11 per cent, but the rate recovered somewhat during the 1950s and was 15 per cent in 1960.[57]

The range of alternatives had of course been widened by the introduction of attendance and detention centres. Some evidence suggested that the decline in the use of probation was complemented to some extent by an increase in fining.[58] There is no evidence to suggest that magistrates were disillusioned with probation and the trend was, and remains, difficult to explain. The higher courts were actually more ready to apply probation for the more serious cases than were the justices,[59] so an explanation did not lie in that direction. It is possible that the rate could have been influenced by a feeling of reluctance on the part of magistrates to add to the burden of overworked officers.

Concern at the great decline in the proportion of offenders placed on probation was expressed to the magistrates at the annual conference of their Association in 1948 by Sir Alexander Maxwell, Permanent Under-Secretary at the Home Office who thirty years earlier had been the governmental official charged with the oversight of probation matters. He also drew attention to the continued variation between areas in the use made of probation and asked justices to consider the situation in their own districts.[60] A study by Max Grünhut, Reader in Criminology in the University of Oxford, of juvenile delinquency and the treatment practice of the courts in different areas of England and Wales, published in 1956, revealed that considerable variation persisted.[61] Whilst, as Grünhut pointed out, practice must be considered in relation to such local factors as the incidence of delinquency, the marked variation of some areas from the norm suggests that there probably was room for a more frequent use of the method by some courts.

The considerable increase in the absolute number of probation orders made by the courts, together with an expansion of other work, increased the demand for probation officers. Between 1950 and 1959 the number of full-time officers in the service rose from 1,006 to 1,502.[62] In accordance with previous trends and with government policy[63] the number of part-time workers continued to fall, most of those who remained being employed in sparsely populated areas of Wales.[64]

In 1949 the Probation Advisory Committee and the Probation Training Board which had been revived after the war were replaced by a Probation Advisory and Training Board, the Home Secretary being of opinion that 'at the present state of development of the service' it was more desirable that a single body should consider the training and work of the service and the general administration of the system.[65] The Board was mainly concerned during this period with the training scheme for which it selected candidates[66] (using the guidance provided by the National Institute of Industrial Psychology in 1946).[67] As had been the custom, the Board was composed of persons with a wide range of interests connected with the courts such as lay and stipendiary magistrates, probation officers, Home Office officials, clerks to justices, clerks of the peace, recorders, and criminologists.[68]

Although it had been the aim of the Home Office that new appointments should be confined to persons trained under its auspices, this had by no means been achieved because recruitment through the training scheme had not kept pace with the demands arising as a result of the increased work-load. During the period from 1946 to 1961 about one in four was untrained, a 'direct entrant' to the service.[69] This has been attributed by some to the failure to expand the training scheme sufficiently to keep pace with very rapid expansion of demand in the late 1950s. One feature of the problem was said by the Home Office to be the scarcity of suitable candidates.[70] They had engaged in some publicity, notably the sponsorship of a film *Probation Officer* in 1949,[71] and the issue of a booklet about the service in 1952.[72] The number of applications for training far exceeded the number actually accepted which ranged, in the ten years from 1949 to 1959, from 41 (in 1955) to 131 (in 1958).[73] In 1959 the Permanent Under-Secretary of State at the Home Office, Sir Charles Cunningham, claimed that the recent rise in the number accepted for training was due to increased publicity on the part of Home Office and the service which had resulted in a greater proportion of suitable applicants. Moreover, he said, 'In the last two or three years, the Selection Committee of the Probation Advisory and Training Board have taken special precautions to ensure that no suitable applicant should be turned away, while resisting any general lowering of the standard set for acceptance.'[74]

This suggests that the earlier pursuit of such a policy might have produced equally good results. In considering the question of recruitment at this time it is necessary to recognise that the service faced increased competition from other fields of social work, as well as from other 'helping' occupations such as nursing and teaching, for

177

what may have been a limited pool of interested and suitable people.

The continued increase in crime led not only to pressure on the correctional services and some necessary expansion, but also to greater public and official interest in causes and remedies, exposing, in an era when attempts were being made to apply scientific principles and methods in the study of social phenomena, a formidable lack of reliable research findings.

It is clear from the *Memorandum on Juvenile Delinquency* sent jointly by the Home Secretary and the Minister of Education to Chairmen of County Councils and to Mayors of County Boroughs in 1949 that there was concern in official quarters at the inability to pronounce on the causes of a problem with such a nuisance and publicity value. The Ministers referred to their appreciation of the need for 'scientific enquiry', to which they were giving their attention. Hope was placed in the results which might be expected from the scientific approach being developed in the disciplines of psychology and sociology.[75] In 1951 the Home Office claimed that indeed 'the problem of improving methods of diagnosis and treatment by the application of scientific principles to the study of causation has been in the minds of many for some time past.'[76]

The Home Office had in fact instituted one of the few studies in this field already undertaken in Britain, a statistical investigation carried out in 1938 by Carr-Saunders, Rhodes and Mannheim of the London School of Economics, who pointed out in conclusion that the proper use and limits of the statistical method in this field were not fully understood, and that the analysis of statistics could only provide pointers to the direction in which causation might be looked for.[77]

In Britain as in the United States there had been a considerable growth of academic interest in crime,[78] and, faced with much current divergence of opinion on how to tackle the problems,[79] the Home Secretary called together in 1950 a number of psychologists and sociologists from the universities to advise on what lines research might best be pursued.[80] Under the Criminal Justice Act the Home Secretary had power to spend money on research[81] either directly or by giving financial support to work being done outside the civil service, and having received the required expert guidance,[82] the Home Office embarked on 'a small planned programme designed to encourage studies in the universities with a view to increasing scientific knowledge on the subject of delinquency, as well as to producing results of practical value.'[83]

In criminology interest had begun to move from the causation of crime to the effects of treatment.[84] Probation, as an established form of treatment with a uniform system of recording certain basic data about probationers, was, as Grünhut observed at the time, 'an excellent field of observation'.[85] In 1947 the Home Office had been forward-looking enough to arrange that data which could later provide information about the results of probation should be collected in the Greater London area. Under the Home Secretary's newly instituted programme of support for criminological research in universities, the Cambridge University Department of Criminal Science undertook an analysis of this material for the years 1948 to 1953[86] inclusive, producing general success rates for probation of 62 per cent of the juveniles and 74 per cent of the adults. The findings also indicated that the method was particularly successful in the case of female offenders.[87]

A small supplementary survey of probation data from Oxfordshire, Buckinghamshire and Berkshire produced very similar findings to those for the Greater London area, but also made a further contribution to probation research by considering the relationship between social characteristics and success on probation,[88] an area also explored by E. W. Hughes in Coventry[89] and by Grünhut.[90]

So far there had been no attempt to assess the effectiveness of probation as compared with other ways of dealing with offenders except by the comparison of crude 'success rates' of various methods on the particular group of offenders for which they were selected. Fresh ground was broken by Leslie Wilkins of the newly established Home Office Research Unit who, in a small project reported in 1958, studied reconviction data for matched groups of offenders to which different treatment methods had been applied. His results revealed, however, no significant difference in success as between probation and other methods.[91]

The Home Office gave financial and other support to a study started by Grünhut in 1955 of the use made of Section 4 of the Criminal Justice Act, 1948, by which mental treatment could be made a requirement of a probation order. Since this provision had then been in operation for several years it was possible to obtain data about reconviction as well as about the characteristics of offenders and the practice of the various courts. Teething troubles had been thrown up in the course of practical application of this new provision, not the least being (as had been anticipated by the Home Secretary in 1949)[92] the shortage of examination and treatment facilities,[93] the limit of one year put upon the requirement for treatment, the relationship between the psychiatrist and the probation officer, and the problem posed by the case in which it was obvious that no progress could be made.[94] The subject had been made topical by the recent appointment of a Royal Commission on the Law Relating to Mental Illness and Mental Deficiency which would no doubt consider the question of probation with a requirement of mental treatment. Grünhut found from his survey of all relevant cases recorded in 1953 that the chances of successful treatment did not on the whole appear to be impaired as a result of having been ordered by a court, and that two-thirds of those to whom such orders were applied successfully completed their period of probation. Whilst it was not possible for Grünhut statistically to compare his reconviction results with those of the study carried out by Cambridge University, he suggested that his figures supported the assumption that the success or failure for offenders with mental inadequacy or disturbance was not much different from that of probationers in general.[95]

Although a serious beginning had been made, it could not be expected that research, of this relatively primitive nature, would have any effect on practice, though it may have helped to ward off any possibility of complacency and to emphasise the value of well-designed and accurately maintained records. Magistrates continued to have to base decisions about the suitability of cases for probation or other methods on past experience, common sense, the advice of probation officers and current pressures of various kinds.

Research and other developments in psychology, and particularly theories concerned with the development of personality and human behaviour, had a greater effect on probation, through its relationship to social work, than did work in criminology. In the first book published in Britain on 'social casework',[96] an approach to social work first developed in the U.S.A. mainly by psychiatric social workers, Eileen Younghusband, a leading British social work teacher, commented, 'It was inevitable that the advances in psychology should sooner or later shatter the old secure framework of every profession involving close personal relationships.' The social worker's expertise now had to reach beyond a knowledge of the social services.

> It is now demanded of her that she shall seek to understand the person in need not only at that particular moment in time, but in all the major experiences and relationships which go into making him the person he is, with conflicts of whose origin he may be unaware, with problems whose solution may be less in external circumstances than in his own attitudes, with tensions, faulty relationships, inabilities to face reality, hardened into

forms which he cannot alter unaided.[97]

The exponents and practitioners of 'social casework' had been accumulating 'a body of knowledge' comprising principles and methods of practice considered vital to the proper execution of social work. The transfer of this knowledge, both academic and practical, was the main objective of the separate courses of specialised training for the various forms of social work then existing and in particular for medical and psychiatric social work. Not all probation officers admitted that social casework was useful or indeed new, but in general the service, as one critical officer put it, 'enthusiastically backed this horse of progress'.[98] It afforded a theoretical framework highly appropriate to their work with individual offenders. Many saw in it the possibility of learning more in depth, of acquiring and developing new techniques and thus of being more successful in helping their probationers. Moreover, the existence of a body of knowledge, capable of being studied and expounded, provided them with an important additional bolt for the building of a 'professional' image.

In contrast to the *Handbook* published by the Association in 1935 in which the term 'social casework' did not appear, *The Probation Service*,[99] produced to replace it in 1958, devoted a quarter of its pages to an explanation of the principles and methods of social casework and their application in probation and supervision work. It was acknowledged, however, that

> though casework training is a modern innovation and
> systematic casework principles have only recently been widely
> recognised, many probation officers are realising that the type
> of help they have been giving to their clients over many years
> has in fact been based on such principles.[100]

In exploring the usefulness and applicability of generic casework methods and principles in their own particular setting, probation officers did encounter some difficulties, for example how to reconcile the principle of self-determination for the client with the authoritarian relationship with which they were presented by the probation order and the sanction of return to the court.[101] There was also the time-honoured phrase 'advise, assist and befriend' in which their statutory duty was still couched. A contributor to *The Probation Service* wrote that 'Giving "advice" has been a subject of controversy among social workers, but agreement seems to have been reached that advice in the form of telling a client what he should do has little place in modern casework.' It was possible,

181

however, to argue that advice could mean, in the casework context, not 'telling a client what he should do', but the giving of information with the object of 'clarifying the issues confronting the client and . . . lowering his anxiety'.[102] Similarly to 'befriend' was interpreted as to offer 'a special type of friendship, *viz.* the professional casework relationship in which the probation officer's warm and sincere concern fertilizes the probationer's capacity for growth and change'.[103]

These developments had inevitably a considerable influence on the content of training given to intending probation officers. The lecture content remained basically the same—law, criminology, social administration, human growth and development, and special aspects of probation work such as after-care and matrimonial conciliation. But the adoption of casework theory aroused interest in the integration of theory with practice. The Principal Probation Inspector in the Home Office, F. J. Macrae, saw the closer integration as being 'due to a growing confidence that theoretical principles are demonstrable in practice'.[104] Another outcome was a change in the nature of practical training. The student was no longer merely to observe and discuss the activities of an experienced officer, but was required to try out for himself the knowledge imparted in the theoretical part of his course, being given cases of his own to deal with under the supervision of the tutor officer. This in turn led to a change in the image and responsibilities of the tutor officer who, according to Macrae, 'no longer regards himself simply as a demonstrator of his own highly individual methods of probation work and a provider of opportunities for other observation: he knows that he is rather a teacher of the specific skills common to sound casework practice'.

The Home Office along with probation officers gave considerable thought to the qualities and supplementary training needed by officers undertaking what in other fields was known as 'casework supervision'.[105] Following American practice this was becoming accepted as an essential part of training in casework and, indeed, by the end of the 1950s an important feature of provision for its trained staff by agencies seeking the highest standards in casework application. As well as arranging courses for tutor officers the Home Office provided opportunities for serving officers, trained and untrained, to become acquainted with casework principles and practice; and, no doubt to ensure that they appreciated the new requirements arising out of these developments, all principal and senior probation officers were called to short courses 'designed to give them an understanding of the principles and purposes of casework supervision'.[106]

The acceptance of the need for a new type of supervision led not only to the requirement for more training for tutor officers but to a request by the National Association of Probation Officers for other special arrangements for them, such as more opportunities to meet together and smaller case-loads.

Alongside these new developments came an upsurge in the aspiration of probation officers to professional status. In her address to the Association's Annual Conference in 1956 Miss E. P. Corner, the first woman probation officer to be elected Chairman, referred to their good fortune 'to be living and working at a time of such intense interest in the sphere of probation casework'. 'It is,' she went on,

> this gradually accumulating, and continually modifying body of knowledge on casework which, together with the professional standards built up through the years . . . entitles us to our claim to constitute a profession, and which is indeed the hallmark of our particular profession.[107]

During the 1930s there had been references of a rather unconfident kind to probation as a profession. Now, however, probation officers seemed more determined to have their claim to professional status recognised. One factor accounting for this was no doubt the increased proportion of officers with university degrees or diplomas or with training which involved academic study, such as the Home Office course. Almost all officers were now employed in a full-time capacity and naturally saw the career aspect of the work in a different light from earlier workers, many of whom were part-time. Also whilst the number of persons in social work generally was increasing, they were to some extent operating in a seller's market since the demands for them and recognition of their usefulness were increasing. Probation officers were conscious[108] however that their claim to a body of knowledge and particular skills suffered somewhat from the fact that none had expressed this in writing, and the publication by their Association of *The Probation Service* in 1958 was intended to remedy this deficiency.[109]

Other indicators of their professional aspirations during the 1950s were their demands to share in the selection of recruits,[110] to have a greater say in training arrangements,[111] and to have entry restricted to trained personnel;[112] their desire to raise the standard of probation work generally;[113] their preoccupation with the drawing up of a professional code;[114] and their dalliance with the idea of an Institute of Probation.[115] Some social workers—the hospital almoners for example—had already achieved some of these goals,

183

but probation officers and most other groups were at the stage of formulating and discussing rather than of achieving their aims.[116]

Changes in the work of probation officers during this period stemmed not only from the conscious adoption of casework principles and methods, but also from the further extension of their social enquiry, matrimonial conciliation and after-care functions. The growth of social enquiry and matrimonial work was on the whole a continuation of existing trends. Whilst these aspects of the work increased in volume partly as a result of government action and encouragement, another contributory factor was initiative on the part of the courts in making use of the probation officer as an aid to their own functioning. On the other hand, the significant extension of after-care work, which did not arise out of the business of, and which was of no direct value to, the employing courts, can only be attributed to the usefulness of the service to the central government in the execution of its penal policies—and the complementary view of the probation officers, as expressed through their Association, that this was an appropriate function for them to perform,[117] being specialists in casework with offenders in the community.

A feature of post-war penal policy has been the provision, whenever this proved possible, of compulsory after-care. This was seen not only as a possible safeguard for the community, but as a means of continuing and reinforcing any rehabilitation effected by the institution, and of providing support at the time when the offender again faced the stresses of life outside.

Before 1948 compulsory after-care for persons over seventeen was provided only for young men and women released from borstal and was the responsibility of the Borstal Association (for boys) and the Aylesbury Association (for girls), both of which frequently used probation officers as their agents. With the increase in the amount of after-care likely to be required as a result of the provision in the Criminal Justice Act 1948 for the release on licence of prisoners under twenty-one on conviction, men and women sentenced to preventive detention or corrective training, and persons serving life imprisonment,[118] arrangements for statutory supervision were rationalised. The Central After-Care Association was set up by merging the Borstal and Aylesbury Associations and the Central Association for the Aid of Discharged Convicts. Financed from public funds but under unofficial management it was responsible for arranging after-care for prisoners and borstal detainees released on licence. Whilst it had some staff of its own to work in the London area and with special cases, in the provinces it was to rely, as had its predecessors, on associates, many of them probation officers, to

184

carry out the work,[119] which was made one of their duties, on request, under the Probation Rules, 1949. As the Prison Commissioners later observed, the government at this time took 'the important decision to improve the effectiveness of after-care in the field by arranging for it to be carried out by the only nation-wide body of social caseworkers qualified to do it'.[120]

As has already been indicated, the decision to make the probation service the primary agent for the after-care of adult prisoners was all the more significant in that it was contrary to the recommendations of the Social Services Committee, which had been reluctant to accept the proposal that probation officers should supervise persons released from borstal and had been altogether against their use for adults released from prison. In the case of borstal after-care, the objection had been based, however, not on any fundamental incompatibility of function but on the fear of the possible contamination of probationers, and on the amount of time which would require to be devoted to such difficult work. The Committee was less explicit about its reasons for recommending against the use of probation officers for the after-care of adult prisoners.[121]

Obviously the countrywide coverage of the service and its commitment to the rehabilitation of offenders weighed heavily in favour of the decision. By this time also both Home Office and public had confidence in the probation service. (Alternatives would have been to create a new service; to second to the Central After-Care Association a number of probation officers to work exclusively on after-care;[122] to rely on voluntary bodies such as the Discharged Prisoners Aid Societies which did not exist in all areas and were not then regarded as doing their work particularly satisfactorily; or to give the responsibility to the police, which would have smacked too much of the ticket-of-leave system and not accorded well with the policy of rehabilitation.) The decision was highly significant for the future of the service in setting it on a course of development destined in the long run to alter the balance of its work and to carry it closer to the custodial elements of the penal system.

Supervision by probation officers, at the request of school managers, of boys and girls on licence from approved schools had never been questioned. However, as a result of changes within the boys' approved school system and as a wartime expedient, a system of special Approved School Welfare officers, stationed mainly in urban areas, had come into existence.[123] After-care for girls, and for boys living out of reach of one of the Welfare Officers, was usually carried out, on request, by a probation or a child-care officer.[124] In

185

1954 approved school welfare officers were providing after-care for 62 per cent of the boys on licence, the probation service for 15 per cent, and the children's departments for 19 per cent. The girls' schools were using children's departments in 51 per cent, probation officers in 30 per cent, and their own staff, not welfare officers, and others in 19 per cent of cases (there being no approved school welfare officers for girls).[125]

During the late 1940s and the 1950s there was some dissatisfaction with the after-care of approved school boys.[126] The Magistrates' Association and individuals such as the Metropolitan Magistrate, Basil Henriques, who wished to see a suitably expanded probation service as agent for the managers, argued that, however good the approved school welfare officers might be, it was impossible for them to cover contact with the boy and the home at the same time. The absence of schools in some districts and the fact that in many parts of the country the boys' homes were widely and thinly distributed meant that the appointment of a welfare officer for all districts of the country could not be justified. On the other hand 'the whole country is covered by the probation service'.[127]

Spokesmen for the other view claimed that many managers and heads preferred to use the special officer where available and that the system was working very efficiently, though it had 'never been given a fair chance owing to lack of numbers'. Moreover, boys leaving approved schools often wished to have nothing to do with the probation officer whom they regarded as an enemy rather than a friend. They should be given a fresh start away from the shadow of the court.[128]

The Home Office was obviously concerned about the state of approved school after-care for it arranged regional conferences in 1951 and 1952 with Heads of Schools to discuss ways of improving the arrangements, and in 1955 issued a long Memorandum for the guidance of Managers and Staff of Approved Schools and of persons appointed as their agents.[129] Soon afterwards, it was considered by the Ingleby Committee which found that the approved school welfare service had 'certain obvious shortcomings', lack of trained workers, of adequate supervision, and of sufficient contact with other services concerned with the family. In spite of the contrary view of the managers and staff of the schools, it recommended that the principal agents for carrying out the work should be the probation service and local authority children's departments, and that there should be a gradual run-down of the special welfare service.[130] No immediate action followed this recommendation, for by this time, late 1960, the whole question of both statutory and voluntary after-

186

care was under consideration at the Home Office and about to be referred to the Advisory Council on the Treatment of Offenders.

Voluntary after-care for prisoners (still the great majority) discharged from prison without any obligation to accept supervision had for many years been in the hands of local Discharged Prisoners' Aid Societies which assisted prisoners coming out of local prisons in their area, mainly by giving financial aid.[131] In return for their contribution to prison welfare and after-care work the Societies received financial assistance from the Exchequer. When, after 1948, after-care was being taken more seriously, it was understandable that a closer look should be taken at the functions and finance of these societies, and that consideration should be given to the parts to be played in the future in the welfare and re-establishment of discharged prisoners by the state and the voluntary societies.

A committee for this purpose was set up by the Home Secretary in 1951 under the Chairmanship of Sir Alexander Maxwell, then in retirement. Composed solely of persons connected with the Societies and the Prison Commissioners, the Committee was asked also to consider the question of extending after-care provision, the financial requirements of the work and the principles which should govern the division of cost as between the state and voluntary funds, and changes that might be required in the organisation and staffing of prisons or Societies for the more effective prosecution of the work.[132]

There was already a body of opinion which considered it time that full-time trained social workers were employed in the prisons to keep in touch with prisoners' families and to link the home and the returned prisoner with local social agencies. The Aid Societies, it was claimed, did not seem able to undertake the necessary work and lacked trained staff.[133]

The report made by Maxwell and his Committee in 1953 revealed that the local Societies had not kept abreast of modern developments in the application of social casework methods to work with offenders and their families,[134] and suggested that the emphasis of the Societies' work should be changed from the giving of material aid on discharge (a need which could now be met by statutory bodies such as the National Assistance Board), to the provision of after-care supervision of a casework kind for discharged prisoners.[135] The Societies' employees at present based in the prisons could be moved outside to form the nucleus of a field-work staff.[136]

This seems to have been a suggestion designed to get the local Societies out of the prisons, especially since it was also recommended that there should be appointed to the prisons prison welfare officers who would be employed by a central body, the

National Association of Discharged Prisoners' Aid Societies, and appointed in conjunction with the Prison Commissioners. Among their duties would be the selection and referral to the local societies of prisoners in need of after-care.[137]

In the light of subsequent events, it is significant that the model suggested by the Committee for the proposed new prison welfare officer was the probation officer. The welfare officers they asserted should have qualifications similar to probation officers and salaries at least as good. Indeed they expected 'that suitable candidates for these posts might often be found from within the ranks of the probation service'. There should also be no loss of pension rights on such a transfer.[138] The intention was obviously to improve social work within the prisons by the introduction of qualified officers, whilst allowing continued participation by voluntary effort through a more responsible body.

As far as work outside the prisons was concerned, the Committee referred to the help already being given to the Aid Societies by probation officers in dealing with ex-prisoners living beyond the Societies' reach, hoped that this assistance would be continued and extended, since using the probation service was 'one of the most valuable and effective methods by which the network of after-care can be extended to districts which it might be difficult, if not impossible, to cover.'[139]

After considerable delay, apparently due to protracted discussions between the authorities and the Aid Societies, it was decided that the Prison Commissioners should be authorised to initiate an experimental pilot scheme for the appointment of prison welfare officers at three or four larger prisons, but only in areas where the local Aid Society was prepared to accept this re-arrangement.[140] Not all the local societies were anxious to move along the lines suggested by the Maxwell report. In 1956 the Prison Commissioners were

> somewhat disturbed by the slow rate of progress in some of the Discharged Prisoners' Aid Societies in implementing those recommendations of the Departmental Committee which were intended to lead to a more constructive use of the resources of the Societies for positive after-care.[141]

The Commissioners reported themselves pleased, on the other hand, with the work of the new prison welfare officers[142]—though actual appointments had in fact been few owing to financial restrictions—and by the end of 1961 these officers were working in all prisons except the central establishments served by the Central

After-Care Association.[143]

The Maxwell Committee had observed that statutory after-care might well be extended to other groups of prisoners when more experience had been gained.[144] Four years later, in 1957, the appointment of R. A. Butler to the Home Office, to quote a contemporary commentator, 'raised hopes of a new approach to the treatment of offenders'.[145] Among his early actions in the office was to ask his Advisory Council on the Treatment of Offenders to consider the basic question of whether compulsory after-care for prisoners should exist, and if so to what categories it should be applied.[146] In spite of interest shown by previous holders of the office, Butler himself was very dissatisfied with the amount of research going on in the criminological field and set it high on his priorities for action.[147] In its subsequent report the Council regretted forcibly that it had had to form its opinion, that the extension of compulsory after-care was desirable, without having available any objective evidence in the form of research findings.[148]

Guided by the principle that any extension should be concentrated on those in special need who would also be likely to be diverted from crime as a result of help, the Council recommended that equal first priority should be given to adult prisoners serving a sentence of imprisonment of twelve months or more who had served only one previous sentence of imprisonment; and adult prisoners serving a sentence of four years or more.[149]

There appears to have been doubt that the existing arrangements for carrying out compulsory after-care should be continued in the event of any extension. Countrywide coverage and existing expertise were again considered important factors. 'The probation service', the Council observed,

> combines like no other organised body, the two essentials for
> effective after-care. It is composed of trained social workers,
> and we agree with out witnesses in their emphasis on the need
> for a professional approach. Secondly, it is so spread over the
> whole country that a discharged prisoner will seldom live more
> than a few miles from his supervisor, with the result that if a
> crisis occurs in his rehabilitation, help and advice are readily
> available.[150]

The Home Secretary, having accepted the Council's recommendations awaited the opportunity to introduce the necessary legislation. In the meantime more evidence of Butler's interest in research and treatment, and also of concern at rising crime rates which after fluctuation had moved on upwards for three years, appeared in the form of a White Paper, *Penal Practice in a Changing Society*, which reviewed the problems, announced plans for more research and an Institute of Criminology, and put forward for discussion various proposals for changes in the penal system. 'It is a disquieting feature of our society', the paper began, 'that, in the years since the war, rising standards in material prosperity, education and social welfare have brought no decrease in the high rate of crime reached during the war: on the contrary crime has increased and is still increasing.'[151]

There was particular concern at the 'startling increase in convictions of young men between sixteen and twenty-one,' especially since this group was responsible for more than its share of the disturbing and persistent increase in crimes of violence since the end of the war. This had led to a reconsideration of existing provision for the treatment of this age group, and suggestions made by the Prison Commissioners, whose borstals, detention centres and young prisoners' centres were under great pressure, were referred to the Advisory Council on the Treatment of Offenders for its advice.[152] Among the Council's resulting proposals for the development of a custodial system for young offenders, separate from that for adults over 21 and based on borstals and detention centres, was the recommendation that all sentences of custodial training for this age group should be followed by a period of statutory after-care.[153] For the probation service—taken for granted by the Council as the appropriate agency to carry out the after-care[154]—this particular recommendation would mean the addition to their work of the compulsory after-care of offenders released from detention centres, an aspect of the penal system itself to be expanded.

The Advisory Council's proposals on both after-care and the treatment of young offenders were embodied in a Criminal Justice Bill introduced to the Commons by Butler in November 1960. The Bill proposed enabling powers for the Home Secretary to extend compulsory after-care for twelve months to persons released from detention centres; persons serving prison sentences of four years or more; or sentences of six months or more where a previous sentence of corrective training, preventive detention, borstal training, or three months' detention had already been served, or where a person was under 26.[155] Introducing the second reading debate, the Home Secretary said the intention was 'to provide supervision and support during the crucial period after discharge. Nothing we can do for a young man whilst he is in prison is of any value unless we can negotiate the readjustment to freedom successfully.' He recognised that the probation service would have to carry 'a much heavier burden as a result of the compulsory after-care introduced in the Bill', and a number of Members referred during the debates to the need for expansion of the service. 'This idea of after-care for prisoners is very greatly frustrated by the shortage of probation officers', said Mr. Patrick Gordon Walker.

The government recognised that the extra work involved could not be undertaken immediately. After-care was to be extended to the various categories as it became clear that the probation service was sufficiently prepared. In view of the new organisational problems likely to be created by the extension of after-care, the Home Secretary intended, he told the Commons, to ask his Advisory Council to review existing arrangements for the organisation of both statutory and voluntary after-care.

In the debates there were warnings about the need to expand and improve the pay and conditions of the probation service, but the only controversy aroused by the proposals relating to after-care was the machinery for recall if a prisoner flouted the conditions of his licence. However, as a result of subsequent changes in policy, the provisions for extending statutory after-care to new categories of offender[156] were never brought into operation, except for that relating to persons released from detention centres,[157] and were repealed by the Criminal Justice Act, 1967.[158]

The policy of making the probation service responsible for the after-care of adult prisoners, affected not only its size but the nature of its clientele, now likely to comprise a greater proportion of older and more experienced offenders and of people with home backgrounds less conducive to their rehabilitation than that of most probationers. The adult discharged prisoners with whom probation officers had previously worked were mainly those who had accepted supervision willingly or who had sought them out. The Report of the Liverpool Probation Committee in 1951 indicated that the extension of after-care under the 1948 Act had involved the service in that city in the supervision of about three hundred persons over 17, 'the majority of whom have more experience in crime than those normally placed on probation'.[159]

Another important feature of post-war penal policy was the restrictions placed by Parliament on the imprisonment of certain categories of offender, with the intention of avoiding the disadvantages attributed to incarceration and of relieving the pressure on the prison system. This policy had an effect on the social enquiry work of the probation service in the adult courts. Many courts had so far called for a report only when a probation order was being considered. The Criminal Justice Act 1948 prohibited the

191

imprisonment of persons aged between 17 and 21 unless the court considered no other method appropriate, in which case courts of summary jurisdiction and courts of quarter sessions had to state reasons for this opinion. In order to assist them to determine the appropriate sentence, courts were to obtain and consider information about the offender's circumstances, and to take into account any information about his character and physical and mental condition.[160] Similar restrictions were placed on the imprisonment of first offenders in 1958.[161] Although these enactments did not make it mandatory for courts to call for a probation officer's report, the nature of the factors to be taken into account and the need to give reasons for a decision involving imprisonment were strong indicators and incentives for the court to ask for a social enquiry report.

With the movement away from the tariff system and the consequent extension of the range of sentencing objectives there was already a trend in the adult courts towards greater consideration of the circumstances of offenders. There was also fuller awareness by the courts of the presence and functions of the probation officer, a factor which could influence the rate of requests for social enquiries. In spite of this, and of various legal requirements, the adult courts were still not making as much use of remands for full enquiry as was considered desirable by the Home Office,[162] or indeed by the Magistrates' Association.[163] The Advisory Council on the Treatment of Offenders in their Report on Alternatives to Short Terms of Imprisonment, in 1957, recommended that suitable steps be taken to draw the attention of the courts to their powers in this respect.[164]

Greater emphasis on the use of reports for adults gave rise to discussion about the actual scope of the expertise of probation officers and the content of their reports, and probation officers were brought up more forcefully than in the juvenile courts (where the welfare of the child was a dominant factor) against the problems faced by sentencers in relation to the expectations of society and the purpose of penal sanctions.

There was also controversy about the timing of social investigations. Some thought it in the interest of accused persons that reports should be at the disposal of the court at the trial, so that decisions could be taken without delay and offenders spared the anxiety of waiting to hear sentence later. Others saw pre-trial enquiries as an infringement of personal liberty.[165] There was also criticism of the speed at which some enquiries were made. It was contended that some, especially after trial, were made so quickly that they could not be regarded as a sound basis on which to make a decision.[166]

Government insistence on the consideration of alternatives to imprisonment and the taking into account of social factors for certain categories of offender increased the need for adequate provision of information. By this time, it was common for this to come from a number of sources such as the police, probation officers, prison governors and medical officers and, in the juvenile courts, local authorities. Since the Prison Commissioners' proposals for changes in the treatment of offenders aged 17 to 20, which would involve the courts in deciding between detention centre and longer custodial training on the basis of its assessment of the needs of the individual, were then under consideration, it is understandable that reports for the courts were in the Home Secretary's mind. A system of the kind envisaged would depend for its success partly on the supply of full information about offenders. In a written answer on the 21st February 1958, he announced that, with the Lord Chancellor, he had come to the conclusion that arrangements for bringing offenders to trial needed to be examined with particular reference to the problem of providing the courts with the information required in determining treatment. They proposed to set up an inter-departmental committee for this purpose. In the following June the Committee was appointed with Mr. Justice (later Lord) Streatfeild in the Chair. It was restricted by its terms of reference to the criminal, or higher, courts, but it being the first enquiry into arrangements for providing courts with information necessary to enable them to select the most appropriate treatment, its recommendations were acknowledged to have relevance to other parts of the system.[167]

Sentencing had become, the Committee pointed out, 'a more complex task'. Courts were called upon to decide between the competing claims of a number of sentencing objectives, and between a wider range of sentences, than was the case several decades previously.[168] The Committee sought to make recommendations which would help to clear up some of the existing anomalies and difficulties such as the duplication of information, and lack of knowledge on the part of those closely involved of the court's policy about the timing of enquiries or the content of reports. The cardinal principle underlying its deliberations was that 'sentences should be based on reliable, comprehensive information relevant to what the court is seeking to do'.[169]

The National Association of Probation Officers gave both oral and written evidence to the Committee and, when the report was published in 1961, found in it much about which to be pleased.[170]

The different nature of the enquiries leading to the statement of antecedents provided by the police and the probation officer's report was clearly stated. Whilst acknowledging that, as well as information about previous convictions, education, employment and date of birth the police statement might also contain concise information about domestic and family circumstances, the Committee emphasised

> that in dealing with individual cases it should be borne in mind that the antecedents statement provided by the police cannot be an adequate substitute for a probation report where the court needs a detailed study of the offender's social and domestic background. Before the development of the probation service, the court rarely looked for more than a brief picture of the offender from the police officer in charge of the case. But courts now place increased emphasis on the offender's social and domestic background, particularly where he is young or has no previous convictions, and there has been a corresponding increase in the amount of such information which they wish to to have, particularly as it is also thought to be relevant to the court's assessment of what is most likely to deter or reform the offender before it.

In the Committee's view a probation officer was able to provide information relevant to the court's assessment of an offender's culpability and to its consideration of how his criminal career might be checked. He could also, provided he had relevant and substantial experience, helpfully furnish the court with an opinion on the possible effect of a particular type of treatment, not necessarily probation, on the offender. This was not usually available from any other source, and the Committee considered it essential in some cases if the sentence was to be based on adequate information.[171]

Consideration was also given to the timing of social investigations, and the extent to which pre-trial enquiries should be made. There was wide variation in the attitudes and practice of courts in these respects. Some witnesses argued that pre-trial enquiries should only be made where the accused was to plead guilty—a fact not always known with certainty until the time of trial. There seemed also to be wide differences in the attitude of defendants, whether intending to plead guilty or not, to pre-trial enquiries. The Committee, recognising the advantages of having information prepared beforehand, recommended that probation officers should be entitled to make such enquiries (even when there was a plea of not guilty) where the defendant, after having their nature and purpose explained and having been given ample opportunity to object, agreed.

Accepting that to attempt to make pre-trial enquiries in every case coming before the higher courts would be impossible given existing resources, the Committee considered that some minimum standard of coverage should be set. It suggested that this should comprise defendants under thirty, those not previously convicted of an offence punishable with imprisonment, and other defendants recently in touch with the probation service.[172] The Committee recognised that such an arrangement would 'substantially increase the number of enquiries made by an already hard-pressed service', and that a shortage of probation officers might delay its full implementation.[173] From the point of view of the probation service, the Streatfeild Committee's exposition was an important acknowledgment of the probation officer's expertise in social investigation and its relevance to current policies for relating treatment to individual needs in the case of adult offenders.

The extension during this period of the matrimonial and related duties of probation officers likewise represented a continuation of an existing trend. The revival of interest in the family as an important social unit and the increase after the war in applications for divorce, and in divorces obtained, gave rise to a number of official enquiries concerned with various aspects of marriage and divorce. In 1946 the Committee on Procedure in Matrimonial Causes had been set up by the Lord Chancellor, under the chairmanship of Mr. Justice (later Lord Justice) Denning, to examine among other things, 'whether any (and if so, what) machinery should be made available for the purpose of attempting a reconciliation between the parties, either before or after proceedings have been commenced'.[174]

The Committee had noted the increased interest, during and since the war, in conciliation arrangements and efforts to provide means for reconciliation—for example in the armed forces during the war. It had praised the work of probation officers, officially recognised since the Summary Procedures (Domestic Proceedings) Act, 1937. 'The probation officers', it reported,

> have done their work so well that they have gained the confidence of the public. The applicant in these cases, usually the wife, sometimes approaches the probation officer direct, on being referred by a friend or by some social agency. More often an application is made to the court for a summons against the husband for a matrimonial offence. The applicant, if willing, is commonly invited first to see the probation officer, with a view

195

to reconciliation. Sometimes a case is adjourned more than once during the hearing, if there appears to be any possibility of reconciliation.[175]

The work of the Marriage Guidance Council, set up in 1938 and re-constituted in 1943, had also been warmly commended as the 'most striking development in recent times' in this sphere. The Council had 'treated marriage guidance on a scientific and specialised footing'.[176]

A recommendation of this Committee that the state should financially assist and sponsor, but not run, a Marriage Welfare Service, led to the appointment a year later of a committee to consider how marriage guidance could best be developed with the assistance of Exchequer grants.[177] The Chairman, Sir Sidney Harris (then recently retired) having for many years been directly concerned at the Home Office with the probation service, the possible contribution of the service in the development of marriage guidance facilities was fully considered. Would not, for example, the extension of the probation service be the 'easiest and best way of providing marriage guidance?' The Committee thought not, advancing three reasons for this view. The probation officer's connection with the courts would prevent some classes of person from consulting them:

> there are many persons who would never look for guidance, if they could find it only by applying to officials ... whose main duty is to supervise offenders or to act as conciliators where the marriage difficulties have reached the Magistrates' Courts;

probation officers do not normally deal with persons seeking guidance before marriage; nor was it desirable that probation officers should undertake an indefinite amount of work of this kind, especially when that work must occupy a great deal of time if it is to be done with any hope of success. The service could not, in the Committee's view, be expected to deal with all the matrimonial problems brought to its notice and would indeed benefit if it could refer some applicants to an organisation specialising in marriage guidance.[178]

Here, therefore, was a suggestion that to enlarge the probation officer's responsibilities in the matrimonial sphere to enable a comprehensive marriage welfare service to be provided would be to give it work which in amount was beyond its capacities. This was a consideration not given the same weight in relation to after-care. But the first of the Committee's points which implied recognition of the stigmatising effect of the service's association with the courts was perhaps the one which counted most against the adoption of the service as the primary state supported agency for marriage guidance. Certainly the probation officer's matrimonial, like his other work, lay among persons 'mainly of the lower income groups',[179] who came to him, it has been suggested, because they had not the means to consult a solicitor.[180]

As a result of the Committee's report, Exchequer grants were made to the National Marriage Guidance Council, the Catholic Marriage Advisory Council, and the Family Welfare Association. The National Marriage Guidance Council was able to develop and expand its work and assist with the formation of more local Councils.[181] Probation officers were found, from the start of the movement, among those who initiated action to form Marriage Guidance Councils.[182] There is some evidence, however, that during this period some probation officers felt that the service's contribution in this field tended to be over-looked and to lack public appreciation in comparison with the more publicised work of the Council.[183]

Whilst the Denning Committee had recommended against a deliberate extension of the work of the probation service in marriage guidance, it had proposed that the service should be responsible for the provision of conciliation facilities which it found lacking in the Divorce Courts. The existing matrimonial work of probation officers had arisen out of their summary court duties. At the Divorce Courts, where the parties intended much more final action in relation to their marital affairs, there was no social work advice available to judges, applicants or respondents. They had consequently recommended that one feature of the state-sponsored service should be the appointment of Court Welfare Officers to give guidance to people who resort, or contemplate resort, to the Divorce Court. Such officers should be, the Committee reported, 'of such education, sympathy and understanding as to be able to obtain the confidence of all sections of the community'. They saw the possibility of the government's making an immediate start in the matter by selecting the first such officers from the probation service. Indeed, they saw 'no reason why the new service should not be developed from the existing probation service', which they considered sufficiently flexible to allow for expansion and strengthening to deal with such new responsibilities and having personnel 'so selected and trained that they are well suited for the work'. An added—and important—advantage was that the service had a countrywide network which would be invaluable in matters such as the making of enquiries.

The Committee saw important work for the Welfare Officer in

197

cases involving dependent children, and had recommended that the Court should be able, at any time after the petition had been filed, to refer such a case to the officer for enquiry and report on the welfare of the children.[185] In any case, it suggested, the Welfare Officer should be available to give advice and guidance to parents seeking divorce, and to those who have been divorced, on the welfare of their children.[186]

As a result of the Committee's recommendation a tentative beginning was made in 1950 with the appointment of a Court Welfare Officer to be available to the judges in the Divorce Court in London. For an experimental period of six months a member of the Probation Branch of the Home Office was seconded to the London Probation Service to undertake this work, which was later continued by the Deputy Principal Probation Officer for London on a part-time basis. The Home Office was no doubt anxious to provide a person acceptable to the judges to ensure that the scheme would get off to a good start.[187] The work appears to have been restricted to making enquiries connected with the children in divorce cases, when called upon by the judges,[188] and was therefore much more limited than that envisaged by the Denning Committee. As time went on, the need was felt to increase the number of officers available to be called on by the Court and in 1952 two women probation officers were nominated to assist with the work at the London Court.[189]

Arrangements for conciliation and for the welfare of children in matrimonial proceedings were considered again by the Royal Commission on Marriage and Divorce appointed in 1951 following the introduction by Mrs. Eirene White of a Bill[190] to extend the grounds for divorce.

Like the Denning Committee of 1946 the Commission wished to see the State giving encouragement to existing conciliation agencies rather than setting up an official conciliation service. It recommended a modest increase in Exchequer grants to voluntary bodies, contemplating 'that the valuable work already being done in the area of the magistrates' courts in England and Wales by the probation officer will continue'.[191]

The Commission also considered the question of the welfare of children in matrimonial proceedings which many witnesses claimed was inadequately provided for. A large number considered that there should be some means of ensuring that someone was specially charged to look after the children's interests; and many that the responsibility should be placed upon the court to consider arrangements for children in every case, whether custody was contested or not. It had been suggested that a system of court

198

welfare officers would be needed throughout the country to ensure that reports were available about home circumstances and proposed arrangements.

The Commission rejected on practical grounds as well as on principle, a proposal that reports should be prepared in all cases where children were involved. It preferred to have parents reminded of their continuing responsibility to the children by the requirement that the petitioner should submit a written statement setting out proposals for the care of the children, rather than risk creating the impression in their minds, by having independent investigations made in every case, that the decision about the future of the children was largely to be taken out of their hands. Furthermore, if all cases were to be investigated 'a very large number of officers would be necessary'. The possible benefits did not justify this expense, apart from which an adequate number of experienced social workers would not be made available. Whilst considering a service of court welfare officers essential, the demands likely to be made upon it did not indicate to the Commission the need to set up a special service. Instead, the 'valuable development' which had taken place in the Divorce Court in London should be extended to all forty-two towns in the provinces where divorce cases were tried. In the provinces similar arrangements should be made through designation of a probation officer to act part-time as court welfare officer. He would receive all requests for reports from judges trying cases in the town and would either provide these himself or arrange for investigations to be carried out by fellow officers in other areas.[192]

In spite of the existence of the London model, any discussion at this time concerning the welfare of children could not ignore the existence of the eight-year-old child care service. (Indeed as early as 1947 the Denning Committee had considered the proposed children's service as a possible source of court welfare officers, but had concluded that welfare work of the nature envisaged, which had as its main purpose the making of a once and for all decision in the best interest of the child, was different from the day-to-day supervision necessary for the deprived children who were to be the main concern of the new children's service, and that 'the Children's Officer and visitors should not be expected to act as Court Welfare Officers'.)[193]

The Royal Commission therefore considered the relative advantages of the two services for the purpose, concluding that

> often officers of either service would be equally suitable, but the
> balance of advantage seems to us on the whole to lie with

the probation service, since the work is more closely allied to much of the probation officer's present duties. The probation service has more experience than has the children's service of proceedings in the magistrates' courts bearing on the custody of children, and of attendance at the higher courts.

It consequently recommended that the probation service should be given these responsibilities in every case, there being advantage, they considered, in confining the work to a single service.[194]

On the other hand, in the case of its recommendation that the court should have the power, on making an order for custody, to place the children under the supervision of a welfare officer for such time as it thought fit, the Commission saw the two services as equally suitable. The important thing here was that supervision should be carried out by an officer stationed near the child's home.[195] This recommendation was embodied in the Matrimonial Proceedings (Children) Act 1958, for the Divorce Court,[196] and the Matrimonial Proceedings (Magistrates' Courts) Act, 1960, for the domestic courts.[197]

When the former legislation was introduced by a private member, Mr. Arthur Moyle, it was proposed[198] that the probation service should carry out supervision. However, during its passage Miss Joan Vickers said that since the Royal Commission had decided that either service was equally suitable for this work she would like to see the court having discretion to use either, and she was successful in obtaining the inclusion of the children's officer as a possible supervisor.

In December 1956, a few months after the publication of the Report of the Royal Commission, the Lord Chancellor announced that the government intended to extend the work of the probation service in the divorce courts.[199] The Probation Rules were amended in 1959 to make this work a statutory duty for probation officers.[200]

The development of probation service work which took place in the Divorce Courts during this period amounted to the provision of facilities for the making of social enquiries connected with children at the request of the judges. They fell short of the conciliation service envisaged by the 1947 Denning Committee,[201] where the responsibility of the officers would have included the provision to appellants on request of advice and of casework help if necessary.

The growth of matrimonial work and the change in its nature were used by the National Association of Probation Officers as one of a number of arguments supporting its claims during this period for improvements in salary rates.[202] The Association, led now by practising probation officers elected for three-year periods, showed a relatively more active concern with remuneration and conditions of service than before the war, understandably since most of its members were now full-time officers whose level of income was wholly dependent on the official salary scales.

From 1948 until his retirement in 1967 it was served ably and devotedly by its general secretary, Frank Dawtry. Employed earlier by local Discharged Prisoners' Aid Societies, and with experience of welfare work at Wakefield and Maidstone prisons, Dawtry had already developed a considerable interest in penal affairs. Immediately before his appointment by the Association he had spent two years as secretary to the National Council for the Abolition of the Death Penalty which conducted a vigorous campaign before and during the passage of the Criminal Justice Bill, 1948.[203] A born campaigner, he also brought to the Association the benefit of his recent practical experience of pressure group activity and the connections made through this. Whilst his position with the Association gave him additional opportunities to increase his knowledge and to extend his influence in the penal field, his own connections and the ability he displayed, helped to publicise the views of the Association and to raise its prestige.

Whilst even greater consultation might well have been welcomed, the Association was now being asked from time to time by the Home Office for its comments on matters such as the framing of Probation Rules,[204] training,[205] records,[206] and legislative[207] and research proposals[208] relevant to its interests. It continued, on its own initiative, to make known to the central authority and to the Probation Advisory and Training Board its views on topics such as training and qualifications[209] of particular concern to it at the time.

Early in 1949, having received from the Association a number of requests for changes in salaries, the Home Office decided that the time had come for pay and conditions of service of probation officers to be settled with the help of formal negotiating machinery,[210] as had become the practice in other public services. The Association, while deprecating the consequent delay in settling their outstanding claim, agreed to constitute the staff side of the new negotiating body. The Joint Negotiating Committee for the Probation Service was duly set up in 1950, with an employers' side composed of representatives of the County Councils Association and the Association of Municipal Corporations (as county councils and county borough councils financed probation committees), the Home Office (in its capacity as the London probation authority), and the Magistrates'

Association[211] to afford representation of probation committees. The Negotiating Committee's function was to discuss, and where possible agree on, proposals for changes in salaries and conditions of service and to make recommendations thereon to the Home Secretary. Under its constitution either side might refer a dispute to the Minister of Labour for submission to an appropriate form of arbitration—in practice the Industrial Court. The statutory power to prescribe salaries still lay, however, with the Minister, though an assurance was given when the machinery was established that its recommendation would not lightly be ignored.[212]

The initial meetings of the Committee were marred, from the Association's point of view at least, by the policy set out in the government's White Paper on Personal Incomes which obviously made difficult any recommendations for equal pay (one of the Association's demands) or for salary increases of an appreciable size.[213]

Some of the bases of the claims made by the Association during this period are of interest as illustrations of the way it saw and wished others to see probation work—although the emphasis put on any particular argument was naturally determined by the likelihood of achieving the desired result. They stressed the independence of the service from local government, its position within the judicial system, and the particularly high degree of individual responsibility carried by probation officers, though they wished to be seen as social workers in so far as this indicated that education and training were required. Emphasis was placed on the growing number and proportion of officers with training and university qualifications.[214]

A number of adjustments to the salary scale were achieved during the first half of the 1950s based, in the Association's opinion, either on the cost of living or on comparability with other social workers, and not on the changes in their responsibilities and professional standing,[215] though the employers claimed that all the circumstances were in fact considered.[216]

In view of the failure to get satisfaction through the negotiating machinery, support grew among members for the suggestion that a grand enquiry into the work of the service by a Committee such as that which reported in 1936 might produce the required evidence, and in doing so carry the necessary weight to produce action. It was suggested in the Executive Committee in 1954 that in order to obtain a complete revision of salaries the Association should continue its attempts to establish the professional status of the probation officer, increase its publicity, contacts with other bodies, and participation in public enquiries 'until it could be shown that the probation service now stood in a position very different from that of a few years ago'. It would then be possible to press for an enquiry competent to review the whole work of the service and to make recommendations about salaries.[217]

The subsequent activities of the Association suggest that this policy was adopted. In the Negotiating Committee requests continued to be made for a general review of salary scales.[218] Evidence was prepared for the many official enquiries into matters in which probation officers had some interest, and statements of the Association's views were made to the press at appropriate times. From 1955 onwards it was usual for the Chairman to refer at the annual conference to the need for an enquiry.[219] The following year, 1956, saw the campaign carried into Parliament. Anthony Greenwood, one of the Association's contacts in the Commons, asked during a debate on the work of the Home Office whether serious consideration would now be given to a complete review of the service.[220] A question put down to follow up this request produced the written reply from the Home Secretary that the work of the service was under constant survey by his Department, which had the help of the Advisory and Training Board and of various experts on policy and practice relating to training.

'In addition', he continued,

> various aspects of the work of the probation service have been recently or are likely to be the subject of recommendations by bodies appointed to inquire into matters with which the service is concerned. On the information at present before me, I do not consider there is a need for a general review, but I shall be glad to consider any matters which the hon. Member may wish to bring to my notice in this connection.[221]

Later in 1956, there was some disappointment among probation officers[222] with a salary award made, after arbitration, to officers on the basic scale. Subsequent negotiations with regard to scales for senior grades, held over until the result of arbitration on the basic scale, led to a recommendation for an increase of 10 per cent, which the Home Secretary, tied at the time by the government's wage-freeze policy, refused. Instead he awarded $8\frac{1}{2}$ per cent, the rate of the recent increase at the maximum of the basic scale, but considerably less than the 18 per cent given at the lower end.[223] In spite of protests and parliamentary questions the Home Secretary stood firm, though permission was granted for representatives of the staff and some of the employers' side to meet with him to discuss and justify the reasons for the recommended 10 per cent increase.[224] The

Association was infuriated by the fact that earlier readiness to wait to negotiate the senior salaries, had resulted in reduced chances of getting the recommended amount by virtue of running into the period of wage-freeze; and by the failure of the Home Secretary (though within his rights) to accept the negotiated settlement.[225] At this time recruitment was not keeping pace with increased demands on the service, and officers particularly hard-pressed,[226] and already disgruntled, felt the blow keenly.

Determination to secure a full review was now reinforced and the Association set up a special sub-committee concerned with arousing interest in, and support for, the demand for an enquiry.[227] The following year was 'one of intense parliamentary activity'. Notes on salaries, recruitment, and other matters supporting the demand for an enquiry were prepared for Members of Parliament known to be interested in the service.[228] Parliamentary friends did not let the matter of salaries rest and took the opportunity to draw attention also to the various difficulties facing the service.[229] Still the Home Office insisted that an enquiry was unnecessary, the Advisory and Training Board being 'as well qualified and equipped to deal with this question as any Departmental Committee could be'.[230] Pressure by the M.P.s, some drawing on a forceful article by Dawtry outlining the justification for an enquiry,[231] was maintained throughout the year. The reporter for the Association's Journal considered the Commons very sympathetic towards the service on these occasions.[232] Referring, at the 1958 annual meeting, to the recent Parliamentary activity the Association's Chairman saw signs that, after the 'beating of a lone drum' over some years, 'an orchestra is beginning to form'.[233] The Home Office, however, appeared unmoved. They had the feeling, said the Parliamentary Under-Secretary, that the demand for a committee was prompted by a desire for higher pay for which there was negotiating machinery; as to the other problems, such as recruitment and training, the position, he argued, was improving.[234]

In December during a debate on supply, Anthony Greenwood asked whether the Home Secretary would receive an all-party deputation on the question of an enquiry into the probation service.[235] This was agreed, [236] but before the meeting took place, a decision was taken in the Home Office to institute an enquiry. Whilst outlining the government's policy on penal affairs set out in the White Paper, *Penal Practice in a Changing Society*, the Home Secretary announced, to the great satisfaction of probation officers, that the time was ripe for an enquiry into all aspects of the service.[237]

CHAPTER NINE

SOCIAL WORK
IN THE PENAL SYSTEM

The terms of reference of the Committee of Enquiry set up in May 1959, under the chairmanship of Ronald P. Morison, Q.C., were to inquire into and make recommendations on:

(a) all aspects of the probation service in England and Wales and in Scotland, including recruitment and training for the service, its organisation and administration, the duties of probation officers, and their pay and conditions of service having regard to their qualifications and duties and to pay and conditions of service in related fields; and

(b) the approved probation hostel system in England and Wales and in Scotland.[1]

Morison was acquainted with the legal and judicial systems of England and Scotland, the enquiry embracing the services in both countries. The appointment of an independent chairman was a departure from the precedent set in earlier enquiries into the probation service, which had been chaired by the Parliamentary Under-Secretaries or permanent officials.

The membership came mainly from spheres of interest directly concerned with or impinging upon the operation of the service, such as probation committees, the judiciary, the local authorities, and probation officers. The central departments were represented by Assessors, Miss W. M. Goode, Head of the Probation Division, acting for the Home Office. An appointment not falling so clearly into this pattern was that of T. A. (now Sir) Fraser Noble, then Secretary of the Carnegie Trust for the Universities of Scotland and subsequently Vice-Chancellor of Leicester University, a proved administrator, who later became the first independent chairman of the Probation Advisory and Training Board. Social work training was represented by Eileen Younghusband, lately chairman of an official working party on social work in local authority health and welfare departments.

The National Association of Probation Officers began to

organise the collection, preparation and presentation of its evidence, raising a special fund and obtaining a grant from the Joseph Rowntree Village Trust to finance the operation.[2] The greater number and wider interests of the organisations which provided evidence, compared with previous enquiries, illustrated the growth in importance of the probation service as well as the proliferation of organisations to represent particular interests. The Committee received evidence from among others the newly formed Central Council of Probation Committees, the local authority associations, the Magistrates' Association and the Justices' Clerks' Society, the Home Office, the London Police Court Mission (still directly concerned with the provision of a training centre), the Council of the Law Society, the Howard League for Penal Reform, the Joint University Council for Social and Public Administration, the Association of Headmasters, Headmistresses and Matrons of Approved Schools, the British Medical Association, the Royal Medico-Psychological Association and the Association of Chief Police Officers of England and Wales; and from many similar bodies with interests in the service in Scotland.

The Committee's report, published three years later and impatiently awaited by those concerned with probation, was a document which in the main approved the existing functions and organisation of the service and recommended continued development along lines already drawn by legislation and by the 1936 Committee.

Central to its findings was the Committee's conviction that developments such as the application of 'the highly professional approach described by the term "social casework",' and work in the behavioural sciences bearing on the understanding of delinquency, had resulted in

> the final and irreversible emergence of the probation service as a profession, requiring professional training and skill.

Casework was seen by the Committee as a central feature of probation work. Its adoption had resulted in 'major changes in the ways in which probation officers establish and use the personal relationships on which their success depends'. The difference between the supervision work of the probation officer of the 1960s and his counterpart of a quarter of a century earlier was, 'the appreciation of, and concentration upon, the probationer's ability to benefit from a developing personal relationship with the probation officer'.[3]

The extent to which a particular function was in fact 'social casework ... concerned with offenders and those who have come into the ambit of the courts'[4] was one of the criteria used by the Committee to assess the appropriateness of the various functions then being performed by probation officers. Another was consistency with their work with probationers. A further criterion—the ability of the service, compared with that of other services to carry out a particular task—was implied in its conclusion that 'the functions of the service have developed to meet needs which probation officers are best equipped to meet.'[5]

Since the Committee concluded that the major existing functions were being 'appropriately and desirably performed by the service',[6] its reported discussion relating to functions dealt mainly with operational problems such as barriers to adequate performance or with matters on which there was a difference of practice or opinion.

The Committee viewed favourably the growing use by the courts of probation officers to provide reports on adults. Although some were already calling for these reports in cases where probation was not necessarily being considered, the Committee thought it should be brought to their attention that the probation officer had a duty to prepare reports in such cases on request, and suggested that the term 'social enquiry report' should be employed, rather than 'probation report', which suggested limitation to cases being considered for probation.[7]

The 1936 Committee's recommendation, that magistrates' courts should always have to take into account information provided by a probation officer before making a probation order, had never been acted upon, and when the matter was again raised the Morison Committee would only go so far as to recommend that enquiries should be made wherever possible, since necessary exceptions might well arise.[8]

Although the question of the timing of enquiries had recently been discussed by both the Ingleby and Streatfeild Committees, the Morison Committee went over the ground again. It found itself, like the probation officers,[9] divided on whether enquiries should be made before trial, and was content to point out the considerations and to make no recommendations.[10] The expression by probation officers of opinions relating to the choice of disposal, and the kinds of disposal, if any, on which they should comment, were also matters upon which opinion and practice varied considerably.[11] The views expressed by the Streatfeild Committee on informed opinions volunteered by probation officers about the suitability of individual offenders for probation, were endorsed by the Morison Committee which was, however, less convinced about the other body's

207

'innovatory' proposal that a probation officer should offer opinions on offenders' suitability for other methods of treatment if he felt suitably informed and experienced. The Morison Committee, concerned more closely with probation work, contended that probation officers were not equipped by their experience, nor could research yet equip them, to assume a general function of expressing opinions to the courts about the likely effect of sentences.[12] Thus the Committee, for all its confidence in the probation officer's ability to perform a wide range of functions, showed itself appreciative of his limitations in the light of existing knowledge.

In dealing with the primary function of the service, the supervision of probationers, reference was made by the Committee to the continued decline in the number of probation orders in relation to the number of offenders found guilty of indictable offences. Whilst admitting that the reason could not certainly be stated without more research, the Committee saw no reason for thinking that the decrease reflected any loss of confidence in probation by the courts. They ascribed it to 'more discriminating selection as experience of the system has grown and as a wider range of alternative treatments has become available to the courts', and possibly to some reluctance to make probation orders when it was known that probation officers were under heavy pressure.[13]

An interesting trend which had to be taken into account when comparing supervision demands on the service with those of earlier periods, was the continual decrease since 1950 of one-year orders and a rise over the same period of three-year orders. It was possible, the Committee thought, that courts had decided out of experience that greater benefit would accrue from a longer period of supervision, and had also sought the greater control provided by longer orders. Its interests being in the efficient use of the service, and therefore in supervision lasting only as long as necessary, the Committee urged that the tendency to make longer orders should be matched by 'good use of the courts' power to discharge orders before their full term'. While there was evidence that there had been an increase in the use of discharge powers, the Committee recommended that it should be further encouraged by the removal of the legal provision that only the court which made the order, and not the supervising court, had power to discharge. The law should be amended so that the power to discharge an order would lie with the supervising court unless a superior court which had made an order had reserved to itself the power to discharge it.[14]

The Morison Committee approved the other supervisory duties of the service, criticising however the indiscriminate use of probation officers in some areas to supervise fined offenders. In some places also the collection by probation officers of fines by instalments had not wholly disappeared, and the Committee considered that every effort should be made to avoid the use of a probation officer for this duty, which was 'not in keeping with the other functions for which he is appointed and trained'.[15]

Like most of its witnesses the Committee considered that after-care, not only of approved school children but also of persons released from borstal and prison, was an appropriate function for the service. It fell into the 'broad band of social casework which probation officers can appropriately undertake because it is concerned with offenders and others who have come within the ambit of the courts'.[16]

In its discussion of arrangements for after-care the Committee was inhibited to some extent by the knowledge that the Advisory Council on the Treatment of Offenders was carrying out a complete review of the matter. It drew attention, however, to the considerable expansion which would be required to carry out the policy of extending after-care to further categories of prisoner, and to take over the duties of the Approved School Welfare Service if this was run down as suggested; and to the fact that, whilst probation officers were 'generally anxious to retain their after-care work', it was nevertheless 'the cause of considerable anxiety'. After-care suffered, along with certain other functions, from the tendency for work other than that of supervising probationers to be regarded as something extra to be fitted in where possible. The difference in clientele and the intensive work often involved immediately upon a prisoner's release, called, in the Committee's view, for support from committees and supervising officers, and for preparation during training.[17] The Committee could appreciate that those probation and case committees which were not making sufficient allowance for the work, and not, perhaps, giving probation officers the necessary support in this sphere, 'may have felt less concerned with this than with the other work because it is not placed upon probation officers directly by the courts, and ... may have doubted their jurisdiction over it because of the probation officer's responsibility to a third party'.

About one-fifth of the matrimonial conciliation work being performed by probation officers was directly referred to them by the courts, and the Morison Committee had no doubt that conciliation at the court's request should remain in their hands: 'The service by which this delicate work is undertaken must be one of social caseworkers to which the courts have ready and constant access and in which they have proven confidence. The probation service meets these requirements and no alternative to it is available.' It was not the case, in the Committee's view, that this work was extraneous to probation. It had a valuable preventive function on the grounds that work resulting in the preservation of, or help to, families 'reduces the risk of delinquency and other maladjustment'. Matrimonial work might well come into supervision work, and the problems and techniques of matrimonial conciliation were 'not of a different order from those associated with probation work'.[18]

A much greater proportion of the matrimonial work of the service (27,713 out of a total of 43,398 cases in 1960)[19] came to it as a result of a direct approach to the probation officer by persons with marital difficulties. Some of these may have gone to the officer in the knowledge that this was the first step towards starting proceedings in that particular area, but some were known to be merely seeking help and to have no intention of taking legal action.

It had been suggested by some that this part of the work should be undertaken by other agencies, but the Committee considered that such an arrangement would result in 'an undesirable and artificial distinction'. There was obviously a demand; the probation service was known in many areas as the agency able to help with such difficulties; it was trained for the work; and many people would have no alternative available. Even where alternatives were made available or their facilities increased, some people needing help would feel the probation officer 'particularly well placed and equipped for the handling of their difficulties'.

Again, however, there was the practical difficulty that matrimonial work, and certainly voluntary cases, was insufficiently allowed for by probation committees when deciding on the size of staff required. It had been suggested during the course of the enquiry that the propriety of 'voluntary work', and the need to provide for it, might be emphasised by making it a statutory duty, but the Committee did not 'think it would be right to impose a duty on probation officers to act as conciliators at the request of members of the public'—it could place the officer in difficulties. It would also prevent regulation of the amount of work by committees in the event of staff shortage. So it recommended that work at the request of courts or public 'should be recognised as a desirable and appropriate function of probation officers', that the demand for this service should be taken into account in planning by committees, and that subject to any direction by the committee—presumably about the time available for the work—it should be left to each officer to decide in voluntary cases upon the scope for conciliation.[20]

A wide variety of other voluntary applicants for help unconnected with the work of the courts were still being dealt with by the service either as a result of direct approach, request by the courts, or reference by the police. The problems represented defied analysis, the Morison Committee found, but among the most frequent were 'requests to the probation officer to give advice and assistance to an unmarried expectant mother; to resolve a quarrel between neighbours; or to supervise a difficult child as a "voluntary" case and advise his parents how to handle him'. On this subject it took a similar view to the 1936 Committee: people should certainly not be turned away without being seen, but officers using wide discretion should where possible refer cases to appropriate specialised agencies.[21]

Since practically all the existing functions of the service were found appropriate, there was 'no substantial scope for reducing the total load'. Indeed, the Committee pointed out, in most spheres the work was likely to increase. This was a factor which had to be borne in mind when it went on to examine the organisation and administration of the service. It also took into account the view it had formed of the nature of the service as 'essentially a social service of the courts'. The work arose mainly out of court decisions, and probation officers (unlike other workers in the penal services whose work also came through the courts), were assigned to the court to work under its direction. There was also a subjective element in the relationship between the probation service and the courts. The probation officer, the Committee observed, not only is, but 'feels himself to be' a court servant because of the source of his work and the fact that it came through judges and magistrates 'to whom he is very often, although not necessarily, personally known'.[22]

In considering the organisation and administration of the service the Committee was, in effect, evaluating the relevance to circumstances existing a quarter of a century later of the principles on which the Social Services Committee had based its recommendations.

Like that Committee it considered the arguments advanced in favour of a change to local authority or national administration. The Association of Municipal Corporations asked it to recommend the transfer of the probation service to the local authorities on the ground that the latter were financing a service over which they had no control. The concern of the decade with co-operation and co-ordination between social agencies was reflected in its additional argument that advantages were to be gained from closer integration of the service with local authority services. The Committee was unconvinced; closer integration would not necessarily achieve better co-operation, and the financial aspect involved consideration of principle rather than of efficiency, with which it felt itself mainly concerned.

The arguments for a national service were based on the advantages which this would produce by way of economy in administration, standardisation of local organisation and conditions, and a better distribution of manpower. Morison and his colleagues saw no need, however, for rigid uniformity, and regarded the existing central authority as capable of producing the necessary degree of standardisation.[23]

Evidence led them to the conclusion that the existing arrangements were already efficient, the lack of discontent with these at a time of great pressure being seen as a factor supporting this conclusion. They attributed the existing efficiency to the concern of the magistracy, its principal user, to the policy of combination into units conducive to sound and economic administration, and to the good relations between local authorities and probation committees. In the Committee's opinion the employer–employee relationship between magistrates and officers had been 'of prime importance in the growth of the probation system'. It had 'fostered the court's interest in probation and ... encouraged probation officers in their work by the assurance that their employers are people who are in daily touch with their practical problems'. The desirability of the retention of this relationship outweighed, in the Committee's view, all arguments in favour of change.[24]

Whilst local administration was an important factor in satisfactory administration, there remained a number of small areas whose efficiency, the Committee considered, could be increased by combination. It recommended that steps should be taken by the Home Secretary to bring this about in the case of areas unable to support a staff of a principal and six other officers, or a staff with two women officers.[25]

The operation of the probation committee system had proved so satisfactory that it was possible to recommend the abolition of a number of minor central controls over matters such as the delegation of functions to sub-committees, the frequency of meetings, and expenditure on decoration and repair of offices. This type of control, introduced by the 1925 Act, did not reflect, the Committee argued, what should now be the purpose of Home Office control, to ensure efficiency, to safeguard the Exchequer interest, or both of these. They were further influenced in favour of this decision in view of the principles relating to wider local responsibility embodied in the government's White Paper on *Local Government Finance*.[26]

Central control was lacking, on the other hand, over the size of local establishments, which was entirely in the hands of probation committees. Identifying this as a major factor in the planning of recruitment, training and distribution of officers, the Committee recommended that a 'key' central control over establishments should now be introduced.[27] This, of course, was more important than in 1936 because of the increased size of and demands on the service, and the greater emphasis on training.

The central authority had, in the Committee's view, played the part envisaged for it by the Social Services Committee. Its activity, and particularly that of the inspectorate, had been 'a major cause of the remarkable development of the service since the 1936 Committee reported'. Some, however, suggested otherwise, and it was clear to the Committee that 'in the last few years' relationships between the Home Office and other parts of the service had been strained. In addition there had been a lack of good public relations, the Home Office not always having succeeded in projecting to the service as a whole 'a full picture of its considerable activity and of its warm and genuine interest in the welfare of the service'. This, the Committee suggested, could partly be remedied by the 'reasonably frequent' publication of a report by the Home Office on the work of the service, 'bringing out the extent of its own activity'. Other difficulties of relationships should be helped, the Committee hoped, by its own recommendations on salaries, training, and central controls.[28]

For the inspectorate the Committee had considerable praise. It was 'in great measure to their credit that the service has kept abreast of the developments in knowledge and casework method that have enabled it to attain its present professional standing,' and it had been invaluable in making its experience widely available and in preparing the ground for combination. However, because of the additional work caused by rapid expansion, regular inspections of probation areas had not been taking place, and the Committee recommended that consideration should be given to increasing the establishment to enable three-yearly full inspections to be carried out. The abandonment of the system of confirmation of new officers' appointments to free inspectors for other work was considered, but rejected in view of the need to maintain minimum standards in the face of the continuing influx of 'direct entrants' who had not been through the central selection process. Suggestions were advanced that, in view of the growth of supervisory appointments within the service, the inspectorate should now act only in a consultative capacity, or concern itself solely with administrative matters; but the

Committee recommended no change in the inspectorial role.[29]

The supervisory functions of lay case committees were also questioned by some witnesses who found them inconsistent with the professional and technical nature of modern casework. However, whilst concluding that detailed supervision by case committees of the way in which officers carried out their work was no longer necessary, the Committee considered that the reduction of their role to an advisory one would represent an undesirable weakening of the link between the service and the magistrates. The work of case committees was helpful in giving magistrates an insight into the work and problems of probation officers, and in enabling them to 'gain experience of the scope for probation'. In the opinion of the Committee case committees should continue to give advice, help and support, 'with due regard to the availability of professional supervision'.[30]

Since 1936 the service had assumed a hierarchical structure, a development promoted by the policy of combination, the increase in the size of the service and the complexity of the work. It was the view of the Morison Committee, and of probation committees, that the existence of supervisory grades contributed to the quality of the service, and was also instrumental in attracting and retaining officers of high calibre.[31] The institution, common throughout professional social work, of the practice of casework supervision requiring 'a high degree of sensitivity and insight' was, in the Committee's opinion, a development which should, in the future, influence the choice of principal and senior officers and the proportion of supervisory posts.[32]

Although largely approving the existing administrative arrangements in the provinces, the Committee was less satisfied with the situation in the Metropolitan magistrates' court area. Pressed by the London probation officers, the metropolitan magistrates on the London Probation Committee, and the London Juvenile court panel, the Committee agreed with the overwhelming evidence it had received that the Secretary of State should cease to be the probation authority for the area.

The main arguments were that, the Home Office being its local authority, the needs of the London service had had to be subordinated to considerations of national policy; that the existing arrangements did not reflect the nature of the service, the magistrates having only advisory and not controlling functions; and that the Home Office was 'seen as essentially remote from the problems and interests of its probation officers and its administration as consequently inefficient'.[33]

214

Seeing no great evidence of inefficiency itself, the Committee found discontent with the administration much more prevalent in London than elsewhere. The apparent remoteness of the Home Office had been particularly unfortunate, it pointed out, in view of the atmosphere and conditions in which the London service works. 'The unremitting flow of work to the courts which ties officers to court duties for long periods; the drab neighbourhoods where many of the court buildings are sited and where most of the work is done; the distance which many officers must travel to work', together with the lack of internal cohesion which had resulted from the long-standing division of work between probation officers dealing with adults (the successors of the missionary officers), and with children (the successors of Miss Ivimy and Miss Croker King), and serving different courts, were conditions requiring an administration seen to be close to the problems and with which workers could identify.[34]

For a solution the Committee had only to refer to its own conclusions about the value of administration by local magistrates. The stipendiary magistrates in the Metropolitan area could form the basis of a London probation committee on which there should also be representatives of the higher courts using the probation service, the Chairman of London Sessions, and one or two judges of the Central Criminal Court. The Committee could be the local probation authority for London, and the Home Office could take up an unambiguous position as central authority. Such an arrangement, it was suggested, would 'not only command the loyalty of London officers, but, by interesting the magistrates in the work of the London service as a whole, would encourage the sense of unity in the service which we have noted to be lacking.'[35]

In estimating future manpower needs the Committee faced the problems common to exercises of this kind. Some factors, such as the loss of officers by retirement, were not difficult to calculate, but others such as future crime rates, the use of probation by the courts, and the amount of extra work likely to arise as a result of new responsibilities, were less predictable. It was also necessary to allow for an increase in supervisory posts and for more staff to reduce existing case-loads. Altogether, the Committee tentatively estimated, an increase from 1,749 to 2,000 officers would be needed 'in the near future', and a further increase to 2,750 might, it thought, be necessary in the next few years.[36]

Although a quarter of a century had passed since the 1936 Committee recommended that there should be no appointment of probation officers without prior training, 45 per cent of new probation officers appointed between January 1958 and October

215

1961 were 'direct entrants'. In spite of good intentions on the part of the Home Office, 'the aim of achieving a trained service must be regarded as only partially accomplished', the Committee reported. The National Association of Probation Officers, which had for some time been pressing for entry to be restricted to persons qualified by training, had asked the Morison Commitee to recommend that the Home Secretary should appoint a day, not later than two years from the publication of the Committee's report, after which entry to the service should be barred to those without the minimum specified qualification.[37] Entry to medical and psychiatric social work was already restricted in this way. The probation officers were not yet demanding direct control over entry by the profession which had been achieved in these other two spheres of social work.

Sympathising with the objects behind the proposal, the Committee considered it unrealistic to fix a date in view of the need for further expansion, and before the effect of its own recommendations for improving recruitment had been seen. It was not prepared to say that a minimum educational qualification for entry to training should be rigidly applied, though it thought the normal standard should be no lower than the ordinary level of the general certificate of education. Whilst the service needed a 'leavening of good graduates', there was, in its view, room for a range of intellectual and educational attainment.[38]

Since it was not in their opinion necessary for all probation officers to be graduates, Morison and his colleagues recognised that starting salaries for the basic grade could not be fixed with the object of attracting persons with a university education. Instead they hoped to make prospects appear good for the well qualified by providing attractive salaries for the higher grade posts.[39]

The Committee chose to base its estimate of salary levels not on the change in the range of duties, or other factors known to be used for these purposes, but on the amount thought necessary to accelerate recruitment considerably (thus enabling direct entry to be terminated and case-loads to be reduced); and to raise the proportion of people with above average qualifications, including graduates, entering the service.[40] A recent small salary increase did not appear in the short run to have made a sufficiently appreciable difference, and the Committee thought it worthwhile trying 'bold increases in salaries which will put the service on a different plane of attraction, and encourage, as can no other measures, interest in the opportunities which the modern service offers for a professional career'.[41] It accordingly proposed new scales representing considerable increases, recommending also that, in order not to inhibit older people from taking up the work, credit should in future be given in assessing starting salaries to previous relevant experience.[42]

In spite of alleged dissatisfaction with salaries, there had been no considerable movement out of the service.[43] The fields of work likely to be open to probation officers were probably not much more remunerative, nor was experience in one branch of social work recognised as being relevant in another as it is today. Some part of the explanation must also have lain in the attraction of the work, and, in the case of some officers, a sense of vocation.

There had been considerable dissatisfaction in the service—and not entirely on the employees' side—with the Minister's right to prescribe salary scales, and the Committee recommended that in future the salaries of the probation service should be freely determined by negotiation. The need had now passed for central control to ensure that reasonable salaries were paid, and ministerial control had had the disadvantage of nurturing ill-feeling between the service and the central authority, making more difficult the latter's task of leadership.[44]

The members of the Morison Committee clearly considered the adjustment of salary scales the most necessary step to be taken to deal with the recruitment problem. Urged to recommend the appointment of a Director of Recruiting and the organisation of recruitment on a regional basis, they found the former unjustified and the latter unnecessary. And, although they were in favour of improved publicity along various lines, they found no reason to think there was any general unawareness of the work of the service among the public. The problem was 'not so much to interest people ... as to interest the right people'. The major need was to make the service more attractive and this they hoped could be achieved by improving salary scales and career prospects.[45]

The National Association of Probation Officers was disappointed[46] with the Committee's failure to recommend a radical change in the training authority. With the arrangements for training in child care no doubt in mind, the Association had proposed that responsibility for it should be transferred from the Home Office to an independent Training Council with which the Home Office would be associated only through representation as a paying authority. It would be composed of representatives of the various interests in the service, including six probation officers, and would employ a Director and staff. The advice of the Advisory and Training Board on training would no longer be required, a necessary change in the Association's view, since the degree of skill required for professional

217

casework was now such that 'the policy and organisation of the training to provide those skills is no longer within the competence of the layman'.[47]

Having heard evidence from the Home Office and the Association on the difficulties arising from the central authority's training functions, the Committee concluded that these were outweighed by 'the advantages of using the knowledge and ability of inspectors in an educational role'.[48] The service was not of a size to warrant a separate training authority, and it was open to the Home Office to increase its use of suitable courses in universities and other institutions as an alternative to providing training direct.[49]

More flexibility in the choice of training was an important feature of the Committee's recommendations on the future pattern of training. This had become more feasible as a result of the proliferation over the previous few years of generic professional courses in universities and later of the establishment of courses of training in social work in colleges of further education. The duration of the latter and similar courses for non-graduates was, the Committee noted, two years, compared with the twelve months course run by the Home Office. In its opinion one year was insufficient time for training for work of the range and complexity of the probation officer's, and it recommended that 'from the earliest possible date' every officer should receive at least two years' training before appointment. All who were able should take a university training, including those over thirty, and the admission of older as well as young entrants to two-year courses should be arranged.[50]

Agreeing with the National Association of Probation Officers[51] that there was much to be said for the decentralisation of training provision, the Committee recommended that the Home Office should seek the co-operation of colleges of further education and university extra-mural departments in developing courses of probation training at provincial centres.[52]

Rainer House, the London training centre provided since 1946 by the London Police Court Mission, with support from public funds, had by now become too small to serve both as residential accommodation and as an educational centre. Furthermore the Committee had received evidence suggesting that it was inappropriate that the responsibility for providing the training centre for a public service should be left with a voluntary body or a body mainly associated with a religious denomination. The Mission had expressed willingness either to continue with the provision or to accept a decision to the contrary. The Committee now suggested yet another form for the expression of Mission interest in the service: it should be asked to maintain Rainer House as a hostel for probation students, the provision of training accommodation then becoming the direct responsibility of the Home Office.[53]

In a separate report on the approved probation hostel system the Committee expressed the view that 'for certain people residence in approved hostels ... has been an essential ingredient of successful supervision', and that the provision of hostels specifically for probationers should be continued.[54]

In 1962 there were 32 hostels providing 548 places. Finding demand difficult to estimate, the Committee suggested expansion initially to the extent of one or two hostels for each age group, and then a further review of the position.[55] The absence of a specific Home Office duty to see that sufficient hostels were provided, and the fact that the actual establishment of new hostels was dependent on voluntary initiative, had rendered it 'difficult for the hostel system to keep pace with demand'. Accordingly, it was recommended that in future hostels should, where necessary, be provided by probation committees. The committee had indeed found that one existing hostel was managed by members of a probation committee turned voluntary body for the purpose.[56]

One of the main difficulties within the system had been to obtain suitable wardens. The salaries, living arrangements, and career prospects were not attractive and it had been possible to procure only a very few wardens with any relevant training. Lack of training, the Committee pointed out, sometimes resulted in the failure of wardens to appreciate the objectives of probation officers as caseworkers. It urged a review of the salary levels of hostel staff and of their relationship with salaries in competing fields, and an improvement in accommodation provided for these workers.[57]

The Committee was not prepared to recommend, as some witnesses urged, amendment of the legislation to enable requirements of residence to specify periods of more than twelve months, since this would be 'contrary to the spirit of probation as treatment "in the open"'. It did suggest that probation committees should be able to support probationers staying for a short time on a voluntary basis after their twelve months period. Appreciating the argument that the statutory review of the requirement of residence after six months had an unsettling effect on probationers, it recommended that this should be abandoned and each case kept under constant review by the probation officer in consultation with the warden, with a view to applying to the court for a deletion of the requirement as soon as it appeared appropriate.[58]

In spite of the generally approving tenor of its Report, the

Morison Committee was not so complacent as to suggest that all was well. It successfully communicated the widely felt sense of urgency about the need to take action in regard to salaries and recruitment before increasing work responsibilities, and before frustration at seeming government inaction overwhelmed the service and caused deterioration in efficiency. Its contribution was to bring to notice points of irritation in the administrative system which might have gone unheeded without close independent examination; to confirm the professional nature and publicise the breadth of probation work; to raise morale and assist expansion by confirming the need to increase salaries; to give a last impetus to the implementation of the 1936 recommendations (for example in relation to combination), and to exert a broadening and modernising influence on training.

The Report attracted general approval. It contained nothing likely to offend any interest group. The probation officers felt it had justified their agitation, and for the Probation Division of the Home Office it represented a useful lever in effecting further combination, a guide to planning recruitment and training, and lent support in the struggle for resources within the government machine.

The speed with which the recommendations were implemented by the government—almost all had been dealt with by the end of 1965[59]—was perhaps influenced by the decision made in December 1963 to act on the recommendation made by the Advisory Council on the Treatment of Offenders in its report on the organisation of after-care, that 'after-care in the community, both compulsory and voluntary, should be undertaken by an expanded and reorganised probation and after-care service'.[60]

The Council had found the existing arrangements for after-care confusing and administratively inefficient, and the quality of work varied because of uneven financial resources and the difficulty of providing supervision.[61] It saw a strong case for a single, unified organisation to provide all forms of after-care. It discussed but rejected a proposal that an *ad hoc* organisation should be set up for the purpose, one argument against this being that it would be in (possibly unequal) competition for staff with the probation service. There was also the perennial after-care problem of low demand in less-populated parts of the country, rendering specialised national coverage inefficient. And the Council also saw the setting up of a specialised service as liable 'to perpetuate the fragmentary approach to problems of delinquency' and therefore contrary to prevailing policy.

Not all witnesses to the Council had been in favour of giving this

220

responsibility to the probation service. Some suggested that offenders would resent being supervised by one who was formerly their probation officer, or who may have reported unfavourably to the court and thus contributed to their custodial sentence. It was also pointed out that after-care had been 'the "Cinderella" of the probation service', and that probation committees and 'to a degree probation officers themselves' tended to regard the work as extraneous to their normal functions.[62] Three of its members, anxious that after-care, 'next to the local prisons . . . the weakest link in our system for dealing with offenders', should receive undivided attention and imaginative development, felt strongly enough to record their dissent and their doubts about the ability of the proposed reorganisation to 'match this natural and inbred pull towards probation by an equally powerful impetus towards after-care'.[63]

The government saw fit, however, to agree with the Council and to extend the activity of the probation service 'beyond its hitherto accepted role of a social service of the courts'.[64] This accorded with the inclination of the probation officers as expressed by their Association, which in its memorandum of evidence to the Advisory Council suggested 'that the only apparently practical alternative to the creation of a new service, would be the extension of the duties of the probation service to include responsibility for all prison, borstal and detention centre after-care in the field'.

Considerable adjustment was consequently necessary at all levels of the service. In particular it was important to see that probation officers had as much support as possible in undertaking new and difficult work, and to ensure that after-care received the necessary amount of attention from both officers and committees.

At the central level the Probation Division of the Home Office was expanded to become the Probation and After-Care Department.[65] In view of the Advisory Council's assertion that an *ad hoc* body, such as the Central After-Care Association, was not necessary to act as a channel of communication between caseworkers within and without the prisons ('the greater the expertise and professionalism of the case-workers employed, the smaller . . . the need for any third party to act as go between'), and of its recommendation that the few essential functions of a central body should be in the hands of the Home Secretary,[66] the new Department was given full responsibility for the overall development of the system. Between 1965 and 1967 the existing centralised arrangements for the allocation of after-care were gradually wound up[67] until the probation service became entirely responsible[68] for all except approved school after-care (which, following the concurrence of the Advisory Council and the government with the Ingleby Committee's recommendation that the Approved School Welfare Service should be completely run down,[69] continued to be provided by either the probation or the children's service, at the discretion of the school managers).

In keeping with the new responsibilities, the Probation Advisory and Training Board (since 1962 under independent chairmanship as suggested by the Morison Committee), was expanded in 1965 to become the Advisory Council for Probation and After-Care.[70] At the local level, where magistrates had for over fifty years become accustomed to administering a service to deal with persons they had placed on probation or with matrimonial problems arising from their work, the problem of integrating after-care was less simple. There was no guarantee that the magistrates would be interested in after-care. In the knowledge that probation committees had made little use of their powers of co-option under the 1948 Act, the Advisory Council considered it necessary to recommend that justices should be obliged to appoint to committees a certain number of non-justices with knowledge or experience of after-care.[71] Relying initially on persuasion, the Home Office recommended in a circular that probation committees should 'consider afresh the exercise of their existing powers of co-option, in the light of their new responsibilities for after-care and in the consequent closer involvement of the probation service with other community agencies and interests';[72] and when the opportunity to legislate arose in 1966, probation and after-care committees (so renamed) were required to co-opt a suitable number (not more than two-thirds of the total membership) of lay persons with knowledge or experience of work with discharged prisoners.[73] Thus, the extension of the functions of the probation service to include work not directly arising from the decisions of the magistrates resulted in some erosion of the principle that the magistracy alone should administer and supervise the work of the local probation officers.

The Advisory Council's comprehensive consideration of the organisation of after-care necessarily covered arrangements within the prisons in preparation for release and after-care. In their joint evidence to the Council the National Association of Probation Officers and the Principal Probation Officers' Conference put forward two proposals for consideration: that this should be the responsibility of the prison service, or alternatively of the probation and after-care service, either of which arrangements would be 'in keeping with modern ideas about the unity of the correctional

222

services'.[74] The Council, agreeing that the envisaged extension of after-care would put the work beyond the scope of a voluntary agency, recommended that social workers in prisons, possessing 'essentially the same qualities and skills as a probation officer' and similarly remunerated, should be appointed by the Home Secretary. An over-riding consideration against the extension of the functions of the probation service to include work within prisons seems to have been the fear that such an arrangement might weaken the essential cohesion of the effort required from the staff of the institution.[75]

Nevertheless, when the time came two years later for attention to be given to this arm of the new after-care arrangements the Home Secretary, Sir Frank Soskice, having decided that it would be impossible to provide a competitive career structure in a separate prison welfare service, told the Commons that he had reached the conclusion that the quality of the welfare service, and the interchange and collaboration between it and the probation and after-care service which are essential to an effective system of after-care, would be best ensured by filling prison welfare posts by the secondment for limited periods of probation officers, rather than by perpetuating a separate prison welfare service.[76] Following full discussion with the probation officers, and after natural anxieties about arrangements for secondment had been allayed, the scheme was introduced in January 1966. Posts in the prisons were to be filled by the probation committees for the locality of the prison, in consultation with the governor of the prison. The latter was to be responsible for the service provided by the prison welfare officer, and the principal probation officer for the 'professional content' of his work. The Home Office was to have control of establishments and to reimburse to the local committee the salary of seconded officers. The provision of advice and the inspection of prison welfare officers' work was added to the duties of the probation and after-care inspectorate, which, along with the rest of the service, had to begin to familiarise itself with the new field of work and its particular problems, and to foster the growth of understanding and communication between the two branches of the service. Training had also to be arranged for prison welfare officers already in post and for probation officers being seconded.[77]

At the suggestion of the Conference of Principal Probation Officers and the National Association of Probation Officers a similar arrangement for carrying out social work in detention centres and girls' borstals was introduced at the beginning of 1969.[78]

In the space of three years major changes had taken place in the

223

responsibilities of the probation service. It had become a probation and after-care service, and responsible for social work within penal institutions. These developments gave rise not only to administrative adjustments, but to examination on the part of probation officers of the relevance of traditional ways of working to these spheres of work, where the needs and expectations of those under supervision or requiring help, and of their families, might differ from those of probationers.[79]

Another development, concurrent with and closely related to the assumption of responsibility for after-care, was the examination of and experiment with the use of volunteers. There can be no doubt that this was a policy intended in part to relieve the very great pressure on the manpower in the service. In making the recommendation that after-care should be the responsibility of the probation service, the Advisory Council had noted that it would be 'impossible for the probation and after-care service to undertake this formidable task unaided'.[80] It would also have had in mind that the implementation of its recommendations would relieve the voluntary organisations of some of their existing responsibilities, and that the opportunity for continued involvement with offenders would probably be welcomed on their part.

In 1965 the Home Office devoted a circular to the subject of volunteers in after-care, encouraging and giving advice on their use and drawing attention to the Home Secretary's view that 'since the main object of after-care is the integration, or re-integration, of the offender into the community, the participation of ordinary members of the community is a necessary part of the process'.[81] Other social services with expanding demand were also examining the possibility of drawing upon the help of the public in this way, the setting up in 1966, by the National Council of Social Service and the National Institute for Social Work Training, of an independent Committee to study the role of voluntary workers in the social services and their relationship with professional social workers[82] being indicative of the interest and concern engendered by these developments. To look in detail at the contribution which might be made by voluntary effort to the provision of after-care, the Home Secretary set up a Working Party under the Chairmanship of Lady Reading, which reported in 1967 on the variety of forms which this might take. It stressed the advantages which could acrue from the use of properly selected and prepared volunteers and the importance of breaking new ground by involving working-class people in the work. Attention was also drawn to the need to include the management of volunteers in the training of probation officers.[83]

224

By the end of 1970 just over two thousand volunteers were employed in the service.[84] The House of Commons Expenditure Committee, which examined probation and after-care in 1971, noted however, that this development had taken place mainly in connection with after-care, and recommended that consideration should be given to using volunteers to a greater extent in the probation field,[85] a proposal with which the Home Secretary was reported to concur, with the reservation that less scope existed for their use in that sphere than in after-care.[86]

Harnessing the energies of volunteers, and working with prisoners' families, involved the service in new and more complicated relationships,[87] as did the new work in prison welfare which also required probation officers to adjust to a very different environment. The assumption of after-care and prison welfare duties had the effect of drawing the service closer to the penal institutions and of extending a much greater proportion of its work beyond the courts. It also increased the possibility that the service would become associated in the public mind with custodial institutions and discharged adult offenders.

The connection established between the probation and after-care service and the rest of the penal system was further emphasised by its subsequent involvement in a system of parole. In a White Paper, *The Adult Offender*, published in 1965, the government proposed that long-term prisoners whose character and record rendered them suitable should be released on licence, one of the conditions of which would normally be supervision by a probation officer. A considerable number of such prisoners, it was argued, reach a peak in their training at which they 'may respond to generous treatment, but after which, if kept in prison ... they may go downhill'.[88] This proposal reflected contemporary views about both the purpose of imprisonment and its effectiveness. In the background there was also the fact that the prison population was increasing.

The probation officers, accepting that parole supervision was an appropriate function for the service 'experienced in the use of social work methods in dealing with offenders',[89] were anxious that the supervisory role should be seen as a treatment rather than a custodial one,[90] and that the need for an expansion in the service to enable it to perform the additional work should be recognised.[91]

Proposals for a parole scheme were included in a wide-ranging Criminal Justice Bill in 1966. Introducing the second reading, the Home Secretary, Roy Jenkins, acknowledged that the scheme would depend very largely on the 'devoted work' of the probation service.[92]

In the Upper House, Lord Hamilton of Dalzell, who had

225

accepted the presidency of the National Association of Probation Officers on the death of Lord Feversham in 1963, reported that whilst the probation officers saw the proposed new work as a proper part of their duties as 'a casework service for all offenders', they were anxious about whether or not they would be capable of doing it.[93] Reference was indeed made throughout the debates to the need to expand the service,[94] and for the government Lord Stonham assured their Lordships that they were aware that the scheme involved expansion of the service both in the prisons and in the community.[95]

Parliamentary discussion about the introduction of parole ranged largely around the machinery for licensing and recall. The Bill as introduced allowed for the revocation of a licence at the discretion of the Home Secretary on the basis of reports from the supervising probation officer. Quintin Hogg, for the opposition, said they were against the responsibility for recall being so obviously in the hands of a political figure. The probation officers, for their part, were known to fear that the role envisaged for them, involving action without reference to a court, might endanger their relationships with parolees.[96]

At the close of the debate on the Second Reading, the Attorney General assured the House that the Home Secretary had an open mind about the machinery,[97] and after the matter had been discussed at length in Committee the government proposed an alternative scheme featuring an independent Parole Board to consider reports and to advise the Home Secretary in relation to licensing and recall. These proposals were well received by the House[98] and remained substantially as put. Conscious of the continued concern of some probation officers about the effect of their part in recall arrangements even with an independent Board, Lord Hamilton of Dalzell tried to get accepted an amendment to allow a recalled parolee to appear in person before the Board (as would a probationer before a court in the case of an alleged breach). Lord Stonham, however, refused to accept this. 'Supervising officers', he said, 'must accept the responsibility of their office'.[99]

With the provision for parole on the statute book it remained for the Home Secretary to decide when to make an order bringing it into force. The National Association of Probation Officers, desperately concerned that this new responsibility should not be undertaken until the service was in a better position to cope with it, asked the Home Secretary to postpone its implementation. Either this was seen as unnecessary by the Home Office, or there were more pressing factors on the other side (such as the need to give some relief to the prisons), and the scheme was brought into operation from the 1st

226

April 1968.

A Parole Unit, responsible for the overall administration of the system, was set up in the Probation and After-Care Department, since the probation service was to undertake the supervision of parolees and also because 'it was important for the prisoner to see that parole belonged to the period of his rehabilitation rather than his imprisonment',[100] and the service began its involvement with yet another aspect of the penal system. In practical terms this meant extra duties for prison welfare officers and more work for probation officers outside through the provision of reports in connection with each case and the mandatory participation of a probation officer on each local review committee, as well as the actual supervision of those on parole. The work was likely to be different and in some ways more demanding and less rewarding than the supervision of probationers. On the other hand, like probationers and unlike other ex-prisoners receiving compulsory after-care, parolees would be a group selected as likely to respond to supervision.

The opportunity was taken to include in the new legislation provisions enabling a probation officer to apply to the court to have a probation order replaced by conditional discharge;[101] a supervising court to discharge a probation order except where a superior court had specifically reserved the power to itself;[102] and a court to make a probation order at the same time as disqualifying or endorsing a licence for a driving offence;[103] the existing provision compelling the review of a requirement of residence after six months was removed[104] and in accord with the wishes of the National Association of Probation Officers the measure repealed the provision in the 1948 Act that a probation officer for a girl or woman must be a female.[105]

A proposal was made by Sir John Hobson during the passage of the Bill that courts should be prohibited from passing a custodial sentence on persons who had not previously served a sentence of imprisonment or borstal training, unless the court had considered a probation officer's report. The Home Secretary promised to have consultations with the National Association of Probation Officers, and at the Report Stage the Minister of State at the Home Office successfully introduced a clause giving power to the Home Secretary to make rules requiring courts to consider a social enquiry report in cases prescribed by him. She told the House that whilst present arrangements worked well in general, 'in a small number of cases it happens that a court passes a custodial sentence without obtaining the reports necessary to enable it to form a proper judgment'. It was possible, she went on, that with the proposed

227

power in the hands of the Home Secretary, the desired effect might be achieved through the issue of circulars to the courts.[106]

Following his decision to implement the recommendations of the Streatfeild Committee relating to social enquiries for the superior courts the Home Secretary in 1963 asked all courts to co-operate with him in carrying out the recommendations.[107] Further requests that courts should extend the practice of always considering a report for further categories of accused have since been made,[108] the Home Secretary obviously hoping thus to avoid the use of his powers under the 1967 Act.

The number of enquiries for adult courts have continued to rise.[109] On the other hand, in the sphere of matrimonial work, demands on the service declined during the period,[110] due perhaps in part to the introduction in 1961 of legal aid for summary matrimonial proceedings. The Morison Committee had made out a justification for the retention by the service of all its existing matrimonial work, but in 1971 the Expenditure Committee of the House of Commons, looking at the probation and after-care service in the context of its contribution to the penal system as a whole, saw this as one function which could be abandoned. It considered matrimonial duties 'out of place beside offender supervision'. Probation officers seemed to the Committee eager to keep these in order to maintain a broad human image[111] (by that time threatened not only by their increased involvement with the rest of the penal system but also by the loss of duties connected with the juvenile courts),[112] and argued that work which takes place in a court is best dealt with by the social worker of the court. The government subsequently observed that the Home Secretary was not clear that the balance of advantage was in favour of restricting the matrimonial conciliation functions of the service but that the opinions of relevant bodies would be sought.[113]

The Expenditure Committee was no doubt influenced by the knowledge that the probation and after-care service was finding difficulty in effectively carrying out all its responsibilities because its officers were over-burdened with work.[114] The Morison Committee had recommended in 1962 considerable expansion of the service to deal with existing inadequacies and to meet new demands. With the assumption of further responsibilities for prison welfare and parole the need had become even greater. The fact that the Home Secretary had only to a very limited extent used his powers to bring in after-care supervision for additional categories of offenders under the 1961 Act indicates official awareness of the great pressure on personnel throughout the decade. The Home Office reported that after 1962 the main task had been to secure essential expansion[115] and the service certainly increased in size (from 1,898 officers in 1962 to 3,774 in 1972); but the expansion, judging by the (very rough) indication provided by average case-loads, was insufficient in the face of rising crime rates and added duties, to improve very much on the 1962 position. The disengagement of the service from work with children following the Children and Young Persons Act, 1969, appeared in 1971 however, to be having an effect on the size of case-loads.[116]

The problem has had three dimensions: additional and not always foreseen demands on the service; failure, in spite of increased efforts, to procure a sufficient number of entrants to training; and wastage, some of it to other expanding services, particularly the integrated social services departments of local authorities which were established by the Local Authority Social Services Act, 1970.[117]

Other fields of social work, such as the local authority children's, and subsequently social services, departments, offered attractive career prospects and salary levels, and scope for preventive work. Also, more opportunities for training in social work had opened up for people without university entrance qualifications, for whom the probation service would have previously been one of the few entrées. The Home Office was particularly disappointed, however, with the recruitment of graduates who were also amongst those most likely to move to other services, in which there were a greater proportion of senior posts.[118] Changes and proposed changes in the functions of the service and anxiety about its future as opinion grew that a more integrated approach should be taken to the provision of social services, may also have influenced levels of recruitment and wastage. An official inquiry by Mr. J. B. Butterworth set on foot as a result of an agreement forming part of a pay settlement in 1971, suggested that the manpower policies of the Home Office, 'more conservative than those of local authorities' might also have had an effect on recruitment.[119]

The further extension of social work training facilities in universities and other establishments enabled the Home Office to use more places on such courses, and therefore to add the variety to its training scheme recommended by the Morison Committee. In addition it expanded its own course and arranged for a number of educational establishments to provide courses of professional training for entrants without the usual entrance qualification, thus establishing an alternative to its own course in other parts of the country. It did not, however, implement the Morison recommendation that two-year training should become the rule, fearing, at a time of great shortage of workers, the loss of older recruits.

As in other fields of social work, the demand for in-service training increased. The new responsibilities in after-care, parole and prison welfare, the importance accorded to the development of casework supervision, and a new interest common to other social services in the application of management techniques, all contributed to training demands. Provision also had to be made for the training of direct entrants, still a feature of the service. To meet increased training requirements the Home Office arranged for the appointment of regional training officers to plan further training at all levels in co-operation with various other interests in the area.[120]

The inspectorate was, with some difficulty, considerably expanded, and later began to operate through three regional teams, a development akin to that in the training field. It became possible in the course of this period to resume full inspection of probation and after-care areas.[121] The load of the inspectorate was somewhat lightened by the decision to transfer from the Home Office to the local probation and after-care committees the duties of confirming professionally trained officers in their appointments, and of approving the appointments of senior probation officers.[122] In response to the new appreciation of the importance of management, the inspectors 'shifted the emphasis from detailed inspection of different aspects of probation and after-care work', and gave more attention to the management of the service.[123]

Efforts to effect the combination of small areas continued, the number of areas being reduced from 104 in 1962 to 79 in 1969.[124] In London the service was reorganised along the lines recommended in the Morison Report and minor controls of the service were abandoned by the Home Office as the opportunity arose.[125] The Home Secretary made no move, however, to relinquish the right to prescribe the salaries of the service.

Nor was the considerable increase in salaries recommended by the Morison Committee immediately forthcoming, since the incomes policy of the government did not permit changes of that dimension. Increases were given over a period, an arrangement giving rise to feelings of dissatisfaction no doubt coloured by past experience. However, the first of the biennial reviews agreed upon in 1963 produced in 1966 fairly substantial increases and a reconstructed basic scale taking into account the Morison Committee's recommendation relating to the recognition of training and previous experience. Again, however, the negotiations on the salaries for senior officers were caught up in a policy of standstill on incomes followed by a period of severe restraint; increases were eventually awarded six months after those for the basic grade.[126] Both this and a subsequent settlement in 1968 increased the differentials between the basic and higher grades, further emphasising the commitment to a hierarchical structure promoted by the policy of combination, and increases in the size of the service and the complexity of the work.

Although the recommendations of the Advisory Council on the Treatment of Offenders on the organisation of after-care, and of the Morison and Streatfeild Committees, together with the government's decision to use the service for prison welfare, after-care, and parole supervision, were such as to confirm the value and status of the probation service, for probation officers the following years were nevertheless fraught with an anxiety, shared to some extent by other social workers, about the effect on their work of possible changes in the organisation of the personal social services. Proposals for a local authority 'family service' had been aired whilst the Ingleby Committee[127] was sitting in the late 1950s; and although the Committee did not go so far as to recommend this, its report did lead to an expansion of the size and scope of children's departments through the duty laid upon local authorities by the Children and Young Persons Act, 1963, to take preventive action with families where there was a risk of children being taken into care or brought before the courts.[128]

Soon after assuming office in 1964 the Labour government published 'for the purposes of discussion' a White Paper, *The Child, The Family and The Young Offender*,[129] which owed much to the report of a Labour Party study group under the chairmanship of Lord Longford. The proposals in the Longford Report were based on the contemporary belief that delinquency is only one manifestation of problems resulting from family malfunctioning and other environmental influences, 'causes for which the child has no personal responsibility'. For the purpose of forestalling delinquency it suggested the setting up of a Family Service with responsibility for 'helping every family to provide for its children the careful nurture and attention to individual and social needs that the fortunate majority already enjoy'. The same philosophy underlay the complementary proposal for the removal of children under school leaving age from criminal jurisdiction so that they would be able to 'receive the kind of treatment they need, without any stigma or any association with the penal system'.[130]

The government's White Paper contained the closely related proposal that the cases of all children under 16 where the facts were undisputed should be dealt with by reference to family councils

231

outside the judicial system. The local authority children's departments, already engaged in preventive work with families, would be responsible for the making of social enquiries and any supervision of children for the councils.[131] The choice of the child care rather than the probation and after-care service for these tasks was consistent with the views about the significance of delinquent acts and the approach to treatment expressed in the Longford Report. The child care service was free from the stigma of the criminal courts with which the probation service was inevitably tinged.

The assumed connection between family and other environmental influences and juvenile delinquency also influenced the action of the government in setting up an independent committee under the chairmanship of Mr. Frederic Seebohm, to review the organisation and responsibilities of the local authority personal social services, and to consider what changes were desirable to ensure an effective family service.[132]

The comment on its proposals revealed, according to the government, considerable agreement with the objectives of the proposed policy, but less with the machinery.[133] The proposal to abolish juvenile courts was opposed by, amongst others, the Magistrates' Association and the National Association of Probation Officers. Whilst of the opinion that the juvenile court system could be improved, the latter body wished to see its retention on the grounds that there should be no interference with liberty without judicial assessment of the fact or allegations said to justify such action. On the related matter of social work support for the councils the Association reported that probation officers saw it as logical for the children's service to deal with the children whose difficulties might manifest themselves in different ways but whose needs were basically similar, though there existed among them a 'substantial minority' who considered that service not necessarily the most suitable to deal with 'difficult or inadequate young offenders who lack consistent or adequate control at home and who need the authority . . . supplied by a probation officer who carries in his work the authority of the court'. It also considered it necessary that the proposed family councils should be able to avail themselves of the probation service for the provision of social enquiry reports in cases where the local authority could be regarded as an interested party; and deprecated the suggestion in the White Paper that some of the extra staff which would be required under these proposals by children's departments might be recruited from the probation service.[134]

232

Whilst the government was re-considering its proposals and whilst the Seebohm Committee was making its review of the local authority social services, the insecurity felt in the probation and after-care service was intensified as a result of the government's proposal to integrate Scottish local authority social services and the Scottish probation service to form new social work departments of local authorities.[135]

In April 1968, when the government set out in a further White Paper, *Children in Trouble*, firm proposals to amend the law relating to children and young persons, it was clear that some of the protest had been heeded. Juvenile courts were to be retained, though it was intended to reduce the number of children appearing before them by narrowing down the circumstances in which court proceedings would be possible. The proposal that supervision of all persons under 17 should be by the children's departments was modified to allow the courts to decide in the case of young persons between 14 and 17 whether to ask the probation or the children's service to do this. 'This means', it was observed in the White Paper, 'that the association of the probation service, with young persons ... will be preserved'.[136] It was a proposal with which the Seebohm Committee reporting three months later did not agree, on the grounds that it ran counter to the general principle that there must be a clear allocation of responsibility for the social care of children and young people.[137]

The main recommendation of the Seebohm Committee was that unified local authority social service departments should be established by the amalgamation of the existing personal services provided by various departments of the local authority.[138] Since the Committee's terms of reference limited it to local authority social services, it did not concern itself with the probation and after-care service, though the instruction to it 'to consider what changes are desirable to secure an effective family service' might well have led it to consider recommending the integration of the probation service and other agencies in such a service.

The government, having by that time had the benefit of planning for amalgamation in Scotland, acted quickly to implement the Seebohm proposals.[139] The probation and after-care service retained its identity, though dwarfed by monolithic social service departments.

The movement favouring integration of social work services and stressing the generic aspects of social casework stimulated discussion among social workers and their various professional organisations about the desirability of forming a single organisation of social workers. As a result a Standing Conference of

Organisations of Social Workers was brought into being in 1963 with the National Association of Probation Officers as one of the founder members.[140]

Whilst, however, some of the better entrenched, though small, organisations such as the Association of Medical Social Workers were consistently prepared to move towards total integration, the National Association of Probation Officers exhibited considerable doubt and internal division on the matter. As was pointed out in its Journal, whilst recognising their firm place in the world of social work, probation officers were conscious of the value of a clear public image enabling people to appreciate their particular function as social workers in the penal system. They also had a longer history and a better developed association than most social workers. They could have felt they had more to lose than some other groups.[141] In favour at one stage of some form of federal organisation[142] the Association found itself in a difficult position when the Standing Conference decided in 1967 to plan for a unified body. At the Association's annual general meeting in 1969 a motion was passed to the effect that the meeting did not believe that the interests of members of the Association, or of those for whom the probation service cared, could be protected in a unified association of social workers.[143] So when the Standing Conference disbanded in 1969 on the establishment of the British Association of Social Workers, the probation officers' association remained independent, small in comparison with the new organisation.

A further effect on the probation and after-care service of the trend towards unification was the transfer of responsibility for the training of probation officers to the Central Council for Education and Training in Social Work. Set up in 1971[144] in accordance with the recommendations of the Seebohm Committee, the Council assumed responsibility for training previously in the hands of the Council for Training in Social Work, the Central Training Council in Child Care, and the Recruitment and Training Committee of the Advisory Council for Probation and After-Care. Probation and after-care interests were represented on the new Council and three inspectors were seconded by the Home Office to the Council.[145] There was, however, some understandable concern in the service that this development might result in less attention being paid to its needs in the context of general social work courses.[146]

The proposals announced in *Children in Trouble*, among them the replacement of probation orders for children and young persons under 17 by supervision orders,[147] were embodied in the Children and Young Persons Bill, 1969. Following a period of transition, all supervision of children under 14, and the making of social enquiries concerning all persons under the age of 17, would normally be the responsibility of the local authority children's service.[148]

The Home Secretary, James Callaghan, introducing the second reading, said it had been urged upon him that logic indicated that the children's departments should be responsible for all persons under 17 (as the Seebohm Committee had advocated).[149] Nevertheless, whilst it was generally agreed that the overall responsibility for preventive work was an essential part of the work of local authority children's departments, the probation service made a great contribution to work with children and young persons and had valuable experience which he would regret losing. The Bill therefore preserved an overlap where the functions of the two services met.[150] Courts were to have discretion to allocate the supervision of a person over 14 and under 17 to either the local authority or the probation officer.[151]

The probation officers, in sympathy with the general objectives of the Bill, were naturally alarmed at their potential exclusion from all work with children under 14 and the reduction of their involvement with young persons. As the President of their Association later told the Lords, many of them found the greatest satisfaction in this part of their work; children were 'likely to be more rewarding clients for probation officers than many of the inadequate adults whom they have to try to prop up on probation or in after-care'.[152] Like their employers, many of the probation officers considered they had a particular contribution to make in the supervision of some types of case and in the making of social enquiries for the courts.

Members of Parliament were pressed by the National Association of Probation Officers,[153] the Magistrates Association and the Central Council of Probation and After-Care Committees[154] to amend the Bill to permit the probation service to make a greater contribution than was contemplated by the government. At the Report Stage Mr. Mark Carlisle, an opposition spokesman put, but did not press to a division, an amendment to the effect that probation orders should be available for persons aged 12 and upwards. Although the Bill allowed for the supervision of children over 14 by probation officers under the proposed supervision orders, he foresaw their eventual exclusion from work with even that age group, since 'the whole aim of this measure is to bring children and young persons under the care of the local authority'. Parliament was 'committing a grave error in removing the knowledge and the expertise gained by probation officers from this whole sphere'. In his

235

view children's officers were not as suitable as probation officers to deal with young people over 12 convicted of offences.[155] Those in favour of the amendment pointed out that the sanctions available under a probation order in the event of a failure to observe conditions were greater than under the proposed supervision order, an assertion refuted by the Home Secretary so far as young persons of 14 and over were concerned. He considered that the supervision order, and the power to make conditions for 'intermediate treatment',[156] provided more flexibility and wider possibilities in connection with supervision than did the system of probation. It was, he thought, 'not very sensible to have two almost identical systems running side by side'.[157]

Unsuccessful attempts were made in Committee and at the Report Stage to make it possible for probation officers to continue to participate, on the same basis as previously, in social enquiry work for the juvenile courts. Stress was laid on the impartiality which would be seen to be brought to proceedings in which the local authority was involved if the enquiries were carried out by the probation service. For the government, Mr. Elystan Morgan, Under-Secretary of State for the Home Department, at the Committee Stage, and Mr. Callaghan at the Report Stage, pointed out that much of the necessary information would already have been assembled in the course of the consultation required in the Bill before a case was brought to the court. It would be a duplication of effort for the probation service also to be involved in enquiries prior to the court appearance. 'We should not', said the Home Secretary, 'continue roles for a service if there are other agencies as well or better fitted to do the job.' Once a case was before the magistrates they still had power under the Criminal Justice Act 1948[158] to request a probation officer to make enquiries, and Mr. Morgan undertook that attention would be drawn to this in circulars.[159]

Throughout the debates doubt was expressed as to whether the children's service would be able to sustain the additional work if the Bill was enacted: the Home Secretary assured the House that the changes would not be introduced until they could be borne.[160] In the Lords members of the government emphasised that plenty of work remained for the probation service, both in the community and within the penal establishments.[161]

The Children and Young Persons Act 1969 foreshadowed the end of the direct concern of the probation and after-care service with children under 14, the group perhaps uppermost in the minds of many who had sought the introduction of the probation system.

A wider use of the probation and after-care service in connection

236

with the treatment of adult offenders was soon however envisaged. During the 1960s a number of factors had contributed to an increased interest in providing courts with further opportunities to avoid the use of imprisonment. The prisons were under great pressure as a result of the continued rise in crime rates[162] and in 1970 it was predicted that committals to prison were likely to increase further.[163] Sociological studies had brought about a greater awareness of the disadvantages of custodial provision, which was also seem as representing a heavy and unwelcome financial burden. Furthermore, there was no indication that imprisonment was any more successful in preventing crime than non-custodial sentences.

Indicative of this concern and of the interest in the provision of alternative ways of dealing with offenders was the Home Secretary's request in 1966 to his Advisory Council on the Treatment of Offenders to consider what changes and additions might be made in the existing range of non-custodial penalties (the terms of reference were subsequently extended at the Council's request to include semi-custodial penalties). A sub-committee under the Chairmanship of Baroness Wootton having studied the question, the Council reported in 1970 recommending the introduction of a number of new forms of treatment, some involving the participation of the probation service, and anticipating that probation by itself would continue to play an important part in the total system.[164]

The Advisory Council drew the attention of Mr. Reginald Maudling, the Home Secretary in the newly elected Conservative government, to its recognition of 'the central position of the probation and after-care service in relation to non-custodial methods of treatment'. It saw room for broadening the scope of the service to deal with a wider range of offenders and its proposals accorded with that philosophy.[165]

Perhaps the most imaginative of these proposals was that courts should be able to order offenders to carry out service to the community, a scheme which, after discussion with interested bodies, the Council recommended should be administered by the probation and after-care service. It had an extensive network of local offices, carried out duties connected with the treatment of offenders in the community, and had a tradition of working through the use of general community resources.

Having considered whether an order for community service should stand on its own or be a condition of a probation order, the Council concluded that courts should be empowered to take whichever course appeared most appropriate to the case.[166]

The use of probation orders in combination with other existing orders was the subject of study by the Council which recommended that courts should have the opportunity to combine, where appropriate, a suspended sentence (introduced by the Criminal Justice Act 1967) with compulsory supervision. Appreciative of the argument that this would not wholly accord with 'the British concept of probation as an alternative to, rather than a suspension of, punishment', it nevertheless considered it desirable that offenders subjected to a suspended sentence should not be deprived of any guidance of which they might stand in need. The witnesses from the probation service who had appeared before the sub-committee had concurred in this view.[167]

A proposal to combine a probation order with a fine was on the other hand opposed by the National Association of Probation Officers and the Conference of Principal Probation Officers, the Magistrates Association and the Central Council of Probation and After-Care Committees being in favour. It was argued that probation required consent, and was based upon the principle of withholding punishment subject to good behaviour. The proposed combination would mean a departure from the principle and in practice the voluntary element would have to be sacrificed, otherwise procedural difficulties could arise. There was also a fear that such an arrangement would seriously impair the relationship between the probation officer and the probationer. The Council concluded that there were cases in which the power would be of value, for example where the primary concern was to punish the offender, but where it was thought that he might respond to supervision; or where it was considered necessary to stiffen supervision by the imposition of a financial penalty.[168]

To make provision for certain people who were being put in prison 'because there is nowhere else suitable', the Council affirmed the need for experiment and development in hostel provision for adults, to be used either in connection with a condition of residence attached to a probation order or with a new order standing alone. The Home Office had in fact already begun to use four hostels no longer required for children for experiments with adults up to thirty years of age.[169]

The government lost no time in including in a Criminal Justice Bill proposals that courts should have power to make a community service order,[170] to combine compulsory supervision with a suspended sentence[171] and to order attendance at a day training centre as a requirement of a probation order[172] (a feature of this part of the Bill not emanating from the Wootton Report). At the centres, it was explained in the Explanatory and Financial Memorandum to

238

the Bill, 'social education will be provided in conjunction with intensive supervision'.

Probation and after-care committees were to have responsibility for administering the community service scheme and were also to be given power to provide and run day training centres, probation homes and hostels, bail hostels (to accommodate persons with no settled address who would otherwise not be given bail and would have to await trial in prison) and other establishments for use in connection with the rehabilitation of offenders.[173]

As the Advisory Council had suggested, the government proposed to establish pilot community service schemes in a limited number of areas initially. This principle was also to be applied to day training centres.

The government was concerned, the Home Secretary told the Commons, to deal with 'the growth of crime' and the concomitant 'enormous increase in the prison population'. The 'very grave overcrowding' in the prisons made for great difficulty in the work of the prison service. Welcoming the proposals on behalf of the Opposition, Mr. Callaghan also referred to their relevance to the 'period of great strain in prison policy and administration'.

Introducing the debate on the Second Reading, the Home Secretary referred to the fact that a very large proportion of the new provisions depended on the probation and after-care service, and he and his Parliamentary Under Secretary assured the House of the government's intention to expand the service accordingly, a requirement frequently stressed during the passage of the Bill. Reference was also made in this connection to the salaries of probation officers and their relationship with those of other social workers, then the subject of the inquiry by Mr. J. B. Butterworth.

As a result of doubts expressed by Members and also by the National Association of Probation Officers about the ability of the service to take on the work which might arise from a wide use of the suspended sentence supervision order, the government successfully introduced an amendment at the Report Stage which effectively limited its use to higher courts. The length of suspended sentence against which a supervision order could be made was to be more than six months for a single offence; the additional provision of an aggregate of two or more terms exceeding six months, which appeared in the original Bill, being dropped. Power was given to the Secretary of State to extend the provision when its value and its effect on the work of the probation and after-care service had been assessed and when the service was able to undertake the additional workload.[174]

The implications of the Bill's proposals for the probation service were welcomed by the National Association of Probation Officers provided that the necessary resources were made available to relieve the existing pressure of work and to enable the new responsibilities to be undertaken.[175] The Expenditure Committee of the House of Commons, whose review of Probation and After-Care took place in the knowledge of the government's legislative proposals, also emphasised the need for manpower requirements to be reviewed in view of the likelihood that the functions of the service would be further increased.[176] It also reported its belief that the probation and after-care service 'suffers from the provision of too little rather than too much money'.

The Criminal Justice Act 1972 further confirmed the role of the probation service as the principal agency for the treatment in the community of offenders of 17 and over. It was hoped that the development of more and effective alternatives to custodial sentences would lead to a reduction in committals to penal institutions. The Expenditure Committee of the House of Commons observed that 'an alteration of the emphasis of penal treatment in favour of probation could thus leave imprisonment mainly for those from whom society needs to be protected'.[177] The sentiment had a familiar ring. Sixty-five years earlier in the debates on the Probation of Offenders Bill, 1907,[178] the Earl of Meath had expressed faith in the potential of the probation system to bring about a considerable reduction in the population of the prisons.

BIBLIOGRAPHY

PUBLIC GENERAL ACTS

Youthful Offenders Act, 1847
Reformatory Schools (Youthful Offenders) Act, 1854
Criminal Law Consolidation Acts, 1861
Reformatory Schools Act, 1866
Industrial Schools Acts, 1866 and 1880
Prevention of Crime Acts, 1871 and 1879
Summary Jurisdiction Act, 1879
Probation of First Offenders Act, 1887
Probation of Offenders Act, 1907
Criminal Justice Administration Act, 1914
Criminal Justice Act, 1925
Children and Young Persons Act, 1932
Children and Young Persons Act, 1933
Money Payments (Justices' Procedure) Act, 1935
Summary Procedure (Domestic Proceedings) Act, 1937
Criminal Justice Act, 1948
Children and Young Persons (Amendment) Act, 1952
First Offenders Act, 1958
Matrimonial Proceedings (Children) Act, 1958
Matrimonial Proceedings (Magistrates' Courts) Act, 1960
Criminal Justice Act, 1961
Criminal Justice Act, 1967
Children and Young Persons Act, 1969
Local Authority Social Services Act, 1970
Criminal Justice Act, 1972

PUBLIC BILLS

Probation of First Offenders Bill, 1886
Probation of First Offenders Bill, 1887
Probation of First Offenders Bill (H.L.), 1887
Probation of First Offenders (No. 2) Bill (H.L.), 1887

First Offenders Bill, 1887
First Offenders Bill, 1887, as amended in Committee
Summary Jurisdiction (Children) (No. 2) Bill, 1905
Summary Jurisdiction (Children) Bill, 1905
Probation of First Offenders Bill, 1906
Probation of Offenders Bill, 1906
Probation of First Offenders Bill, 1907
Probation of Offenders (No. 2) Bill, 1907
Criminal Justice Administration Bill, 1914
Criminal Justice Bill (H.L.), 1923
Criminal Justice Bill (H.L.), 1924
Criminal Justice Bill, 1925
Children Bill, 1930
Children and Young Persons Bill, 1931/32
Summary Jurisdiction (Domestic Procedure) Bill, 1934
Criminal Justice Bill, 1938
Criminal Justice Bill, 1947/48
Criminal Justice Bill 1947 and Explanatory Memorandum
Criminal Justice Bill 1948 as amended by Standing Committee
Matrimonial Causes Bill, 1951
Criminal Justice Bill, 1960
Criminal Justice Bill, 1961
Criminal Justice Bill, 1966
Children and Young Persons Bill, 1969

OFFICIAL PAPERS

Hansard's Parliamentary Debates
Home Office Circulars
The Probation Officers' Superannuation Rules
The Probation Rules
Reports to the Secretary of State for the Home Department on the State of the Law Relating to the Treatment and Punishment of Juvenile Offenders, 1881, C. 2808.
Report of the Royal Commission on Reformatories and Industrial Schools, 1884, C. 3876, and Minutes of Evidence.
Reports of the Commissioners of Prisons, 1891–1961.
Report of the Departmental Committee on Prisons, 1895, C. 7702.
Memorandum on the Summary Jurisdiction (Children) (No. 2) Bill, 1905.
Memorandum on the Probation System as at present in force in the United States of America, 1907, Cd. 3401.
Memorandum issued by the Secretary of State for the Home Department with reference to the Probation of Offenders Act, 1907, 1908, Cd. 3981.
Report of the Departmental Committee on the Probation of Offenders Act, 1907, 1910, Cd. 5001, and *Minutes of Evidence*, 1910, Cd. 5002.
Report of the Departmental Committee on Local Taxation, 1914, Cd. 7315.

Report of the Departmental Committee on the Training, Appointment and Payment of Probation Officers, 1922, Cmd. 1601.

Home Office. *Reports on the Work of the Children's Branch*, 1923–38.

Report of the Committee on the Employment of London Probationers, 1924.

Criminal Justice Bill, 1925. Memorandum explaining financial resolution, 1924–25, Cmd. 2380.

Report of the Departmental Committee on Sexual Offences Against Young Persons, 1925, Cmd. 2561.

Report of the Committee on the Superannuation of Probation Officers, 1926.

Report of the Departmental Committee on the Treatment of Young Offenders, 1927, Cmd. 2831.

Report of the Departmental Committee on Persistent Offenders, 1932, Cmd. 4090.

Board of Education. *The Work of Juvenile Organisation Committees*, 1933.

Report of the Departmental Committee on Imprisonment by Courts of Summary Jurisdiction in Default of Payment of Fines and Other Sums of Money, 1934, Cmd. 4649.

Report of the Departmental Committee on the Social Services in Courts of Summary Jurisdiction, 1936, Cmd. 5122.

Report of the Departmental Committee on Courts of Summary Jurisdiction in the Metropolitan Area, 1937.

Final Report of the Committee on Procedure in Matrimonial Causes, 1947, Cmd. 7024.

Report of the Departmental Committee on Grants for the Development of Marriage Guidance, 1948, Cmd. 7566.

Home Office. *Reports on the Work of the Children's Department*, 1951–5.

Report of the Committee on Discharged Prisoners' Aid Societies, 1953, Cmd. 8879.

Report of the Royal Commission on Marriage and Divorce, 1956, Cmd. 9678.

Home Office. Report of the Advisory Council on the Treatment of Offenders. *Alternatives to Short Terms of Imprisonment*, 1957.

Home Office. Report of the Advisory Council on the Treatment of Offenders. *The After-Care and Supervision of Discharged Prisoners*, 1958.

Home Office. *Penal Practice in a Changing Society*, 1959, Cmnd. 645.

Home Office. Report of the Advisory Council on the Treatment of Offenders. *The Treatment of Young Offenders*, 1959.

Report of the Working Party on Social Work in Local Authorities' Health and Welfare Departments, 1959.

Report of the Committee on Children and Young Persons, 1960, Cmnd. 1191.

Report of the Inter-Departmental Committee on the Business of the Criminal Courts, 1961, Cmnd. 1289.

Report of the Departmental Committee on the Probation Service, 1962, Cmnd. 1650.

Second Report of the Departmental Committee on the Probation Service, 1962, Cmnd. 1800.

Home Office. *Reports on the Work of the Probation and After-Care Department*, 1962–71.

Home Office. Report of the Advisory Council on the Treatment of Offenders. *The Organisation of After-Care*, 1963.

Home Office. *The Child, The Family and The Young Offender*, 1965, Cmnd. 2742.

Home Office. *The Adult Offender*, 1965, Cmnd. 2952.

Scottish Education Department and Scottish Home and Health Department. *Social Work and the Community*, 1966, Cmnd. 3065.

Home Office. First Report of the Working Party on the Place of Voluntary Service in After-Care. *Residential Provision for the Homeless Discharged Prisoner*, 1966.

Home Office. Second Report of the Working Party on the Place of Voluntary Service in After-Care. *The Place of Voluntary Service in After-Care*, 1967.

Home Office. *Children in Trouble*, 1968, Cmnd. 3601.

Report of the Departmental Committee on Local Authority and Allied Personal Social Services, 1968, Cmnd. 3703.

Home Office. Report of the Advisory Council on the Penal System. *Non-Custodial and Semi-Custodial Penalties*, 1970.

First Report from the Expenditure Committee, Session 1971–2. *Probation and After-Care*, 1971, H.C. 47.

Department of Employment, *Report of the Butterworth Inquiry into the Work and Pay of Probation Officers and Social Workers*, 1972, Cmnd. 5076.

UNPUBLISHED PAPERS

Public Record Office: Home Office Files

Home Office Files

Home Office. Minutes of Evidence, Departmental Committee on the Social Services in Courts of Summary Jurisdiction, 1936.

Files and Minutes:

Church of England Temperance Society

London Police Court Mission

National Association of Probation Officers

National Police Court Mission

ANNUAL REPORTS OF THE FOLLOWING BODIES:

Church of England Temperance Society

Clarke Hall Fellowship

Howard Association

Howard League for Penal Reform

London Police Court Mission

Magistrates' Association

National Association of Probation Officers

BOOKS AND ARTICLES

ADLER, N. 'Probation in the Courts'. *Journal of Comparative Legislation and International Law*, No. 17, 1935.

AVES, G.M. *The Voluntary Worker in the Social Services*. 1969.

AYSCOUGH, H.H. *When Mercy Seasons Justice. A Short History of the Work of the Church of England in the Police Courts*. 1923.

BARRETT, Rosa M. *The Treatment of Juvenile Offenders*. 1900.

BELL, E.M. *The Story of Hospital Almoners*. 1961.

BOWLBY, J. *Maternal Care and Mental Health*. 1951.

CARR-SAUNDERS, A., RHODES, E.C. & MANNHEIM, H. *Young Offenders*. 1942.

CHAPMAN, CECIL. *The Poor Man's Court of Justice. c.* 1926.

CLARKE HALL, W. *The State and the Child*. 1915.
Children's Courts. 1926.

COUNCIL OF EUROPE. *Juvenile Delinquency in Post-War Europe*. 1960.
Probation and After-Care in Certain European Countries. 1964.

COX, Edward W. *The Principles of Punishment as Applied in the Administration of the Criminal Law by Judges and Magistrates*. 1877.

DAVIES, Martin. *Probationers in their Social Environment*. A Home Office Research Unit Report. 1969.

DAVIES, Martin and KNOPF, Andrea. *Social Enquiry Reports and the Probation Service*. Home Office Research Studies, No. 18. 1973.

DAWTRY, F. 'Fifty Years of Probation'. *The Friends' Quarterly*, January 1958.
'Whither Probation?' *The British Journal of Delinquency*, Vol. VIII, No, 3, January 1958.

DRESSLER, David. *Practice and Theory of Probation and Parole*. 2nd edition, 1969.

ELKIN, W.A. *English Juvenile Courts*. 1938.

ELLISON, Mary. *Sparks Beneath the Ashes. Experiences of a London Probation Officer*. 1934.

FINER, H. *English Local Government*. 1946.

FLEXNER, B. and BALDWIN, R.N. *Juvenile Courts and Probation*. 1915.

FOLKARD, S., LYON, K., CARVER, M.M. and O'LEARY, E. *Probation Research. A Preliminary Report*. Home Office Research and Statistics Department, Studies in the Causes of Delinquency and the Treatment of Offenders, No. 7.

FORDER, R.A.D. 'Lay Committees and Professional Workers in the English Probation Service'. *Social and Economic Administration*, Vol. 3, No. 4, October 1969.

GAMON, H.R.P. *The London Police Court To-day and To-morrow*. 1907.
'The Probation of Offenders Act, 1907: An Appreciation and a Criticism'. *The Law Magazine and Law Review*, Vol. 33, No. CCCXLIX, 1908.

GLUECK, S. (Ed.) *Probation and Criminal Justice*. 1933.

GRUBB, E. *Methods of Penal Administration in the United States*. 1904.

GRÜNHUT, Max. *Penal Reform. A Comparative Study*. 1948.
'Probation as a Research Field, A Pilot Survey'. *The British Journal of Delinquency*, Vol. II, No. 4, April 1952.
Juvenile Offenders Before the Courts. 1956.
Probation and Mental Treatment. 1963.

HALMOS, P. (Ed.) *Sociological Studies in the British Penal Services*. The Sociological Review: Monograph No. 9, 1965.

HARRIS, J. *Probation. Thirty-Four Years' Work in the Local Police Courts*. 1937.

HARRIS, S.W. *Probation and Other Social Work of the Courts*. 1937.

HENRIQUES, B.L.Q. *The Indiscretions of a Magistrate*. 1950.

HERBERT, W.L. and JARVIS, F.V. *A Modern Approach to Marriage Counselling*. 1959.

HEYWOOD, J. *Children in Care*. 2nd edition, 1965.

HILL, M.D. *Suggestions for the Repression of Crime Contained in Charges Delivered to Grand Juries, Supported by Additional Facts and Arguments*. 1857.

HILL, R.D. and F.D. *The Recorder of Birmingham: A Memoir of Matthew Davenport Hill*. 1878.

HOLMES, R. *Them That Fall*. 1923.

HOME OFFICE. *Probation Work in England and Wales*. 1937.

　The Probation Service: Its Objects and Its Organisation. 1938 (1st ed.), 1952 (2nd ed.).

　Probation as a Career. 1952.

HOOD, R. *Borstal Re-Assessed*. 1965.

HOWARD ASSOCIATION. *Juvenile Offenders*. 1881.

　The Probation of First Offenders Act, 1887. 1892.

　Juvenile Offenders. 1898.

　Probation Officers and the Gift of Guidance. 1901.

　Children's Courts and the Probation System. 1904.

　Imprisonment of Youthful Offenders. 1913.

HOWARD LEAGUE FOR PENAL REFORM. *The Treatment of Young Offenders*. 1927.

HUGHES, E.P. *The Probation System of America*. 1903.

HUGHES, E.W. 'An analysis of the records of some 750 probationers'. *British Journal of Educational Psychology*, Vol. 35, 1945.

JARVIS, F.V. *Probation Officer's Manual*. 1969.

JARVIS, F.V. and UTTING, W.B. Aspects of Training. *Probation Papers*, No. 2, 1965.

JEYES, S.H. and HOW, F.D. *The Life of Sir Howard Vincent*. 1912.

KING, J.F.S. (Ed.) *The Probation Service*. 1st edition, 1958. 2nd edition, 1964.

LABOUR PARTY, THE. *Crime—A Challenge to Us All*. 1964.

LE MESURIER, L. (Ed.) *A Handbook of Probation and the Social Work of the Courts*. 1935.

LEESON, Cecil. *The Probation System*. 1914.

　The Child and the War. 1917.

LOVAT FRASER, J.A. *Child Offenders*. 1926.

MACADAM, E. *The New Philanthropy*. 1934.

MACE, D.R. *Marriage Counselling*. 1948.

MACRAE, F.J. 'The English Probation Training System'. *The British Journal of Delinquency*, Vol. VIII, No. 3, January 1958.

MAGISTRATE, A. *Metropolitan Police Court Jottings*. 1882.

MAXWELL, A. The Home Office: Its Function in Relation to the Treatment of Offenders. Second Annual Lecture In Criminal Science, Faculty of Law, University of Cambridge, 1947.

MILL, J. *Probation: An Instrument of Imaginative Justice.* 1946.

MINN, W.G. 'Training for the Work of a Probation Officer in England and Wales'. *The Journal of Criminal Science,* Vol. 1, 1948.

MONGER, M. *Casework in Probation.* 1964.

    Casework in After-Care. 1967.

MORRIS, C. (Ed.) *Social Casework in Britain.* 1950.

MORRISON, R.L. *Stresses of Change in Probation and After-Care.* Second Dennis Carroll Memorial Lecture, 1969.

MORRISON, W.D. *Juvenile Offenders.* 1896.

    The Treatment of Prisoners. 1897.

NATIONAL ASSOCIATION OF PROBATION OFFICERS. *H.E. Norman: An Appreciation.* 1944.

NATIONAL PROBATION ASSOCIATION, NEW YORK. *John Augustus, First Probation Officer.* 1939.

ORCHARD, H.C. *The Police Court Missionary's Story.* 1931.

PAGE, Leo. *The Probation System. A Memorandum for Justices.* N.d.

PARSLOE, P. *The Work of the Probation and After-Care Officer.* 1967.

PENAL REFORM LEAGUE. *A National Minimum for Youth.* 1917.

PEPLER, D. *Justice and the Child.* 1915.

POTTER, J.H. *Inasmuch: The Story of the Police Court Mission 1876–1926.* 1927.

PRINCIPAL PROBATION OFFICERS CONFERENCE. *The Place of Probation and After-Care in Judicial Administration.* 1968.

PRINS, H. 'Social Enquiries and the Adult Courts'. *The British Journal of Delinquency,* Vol. VIII, No. 3, January 1958.

RADZINOWICZ, L. *Ideology and Crime.* 1966.

RADZINOWICZ, L. and TURNER, J.W.C. (Eds.) *Penal Reform in England.* 1946.

ROSE, G. *The Struggle for Penal Reform.* 1961.

    Schools for Young Offenders. 1967.

RUGGLES-BRISE, E. *Some Observations on the Treatment of Crime in America.* 1897.

RUSSELL, C.E.B. and RIGBY, L.M. *The Making of the Criminal.* 1906.

SAMUEL, Herbert. *Memoirs.* 1945.

SANCTUARY, G. *Marriage Under Stress.* 1968.

SILBERMAN, M. and CHAPMAN, B.; SINCLAIR, I. and SNOW, D.; LEISSNER, A. *Explorations in After-Care.* Home Office Research Studies, No. 9, 1971.

SLATER, G. *Poverty and the State.* 1930.

SMITH, M.J. *Professional Education for Social Work in Britain.* 1965.

TALLACK, W. *Humanity and Humanitarianism.* 1871.

    Defects in the Criminal Administration and Penal Legislation of Great Britain and Ireland, with Remedial Suggestions. 1872.

    European and American Progress in Penal Reform. 1895.

    Penological and Preventive Principles. 1896.

THOMAS, J.E. *The English Prison Officer Since 1850.* 1972.

TIMASHEFF, N.S. *One Hundred Years of Probation.* 1941.

TIMMS, N. *Psychiatric Social Work in Great Britain (1939–1962).* 1964.

TOBIAS, J.J. *Crime and Industrial Society in the 19th Century.* 1967.

TROUGHT, T.W. *Probation in Europe.* 1927.

UNITED NATIONS. *Probation and Related Measures.* 1951.

   Practical Results and Financial Aspects of Adult Probation in Selected Countries. 1954.

   Training for Social Work. 1958.

UNIVERSITY OF CAMBRIDGE, FACULTY OF LAW, DEPARTMENT OF CRIMINAL SCIENCE. *The Results of Probation.* 1958.

WALKER, N. *Crime and Punishment in Britain.* 1945.

   Crime and Insanity in England. Vol. 1: The Historical Perspective. 1968.

WAUGH, B. *The Gaol Cradle, Who Rocks It?* 1873.

WILKINS, L.T. 'A Small Comparative Study of the Results of Probation'. *The British Journal of Delinquency,* Vol. VIII. No. 3, January 1958.

NEWSPAPERS AND PERIODICALS

British Journal of Delinquency
British Journal of Educational Psychology
The Church Temperance Times
The Friends' Quarterly
The Howard Journal
The Journal of Criminal Science
The Journal of the National Association of Probation Officers
The Law Magazine and Law Review
The Magistrate
The Penal Reform League Monthly Record
The Penal Reform League Quarterly Record
Probation
The Times

REFERENCES

CHAPTER 1

1. William Tallack, *European and American Progress in Penal Reform*, 1895, page 3.
2. Page 89.
3. Gordon Rose, *Schools for Young Offenders*, 1967, page 7.
4. *Annual Report of the Howard Association*, September 1875, page 3.
5. Edward W. Cox, *The Principles of Punishment as Applied in the Administration of the Criminal Law by Judges and Magistrates*, 1877, page 5.
6. Ibid., page 29.
7. Ibid., page 31.
8. Ibid., pages 37 and 39.
9. H. O. Circular, 15th October 1880.
10. S. 7, 10, and 16.
11. E.g. The Youthful Offenders Act, 1847; the Criminal Law Consolidation Acts, 1861.
12. The evidence is reviewed in United Nations, *Probation and Related Measures*, 1951, pages 16 to 26.
13. M. D. Hill, *Suggestions for the Repression of Crime Contained in Charges Delivered to Grand Juries, Supported by Additional Facts and Arguments*, 1857, page 350.
14. *Report of the Departmental Committee on the Treatment of Young Offenders*, 1927, Cmd. 2831, page 10.
15. M. D. Hill, op. cit., 1857, page 347.
16. Ibid., page 350.
17. Ibid., page 117.
18. William Tallack, *Defects in the Criminal Administration and Penal Legislation of Great Britain and Ireland, with Remedial Suggestions*, 1872, page 36.
19. Page 46.
20. M. D. Hill, op. cit., 1857, page 118.
21. Ibid., page 601.
22. R. D. and F. D. Hill, *The Recorder of Birmingham: A Memoir of Matthew Davenport Hill*, 1878, page 156.
23. M. D. Hill, op. cit., 1857, page 602.
24. Ibid., pages 118 and 350.
25. Ibid., page 350.
26. Ibid., page 350.
27. R. D. and F. D. Hill, op. cit., 1878, page 156.
28. *Dictionary of National Biography*, Vol. IV, 1908, page 1334.
29. Edward W. Cox, op. cit., 1877, page 39.
30. N. S. Timasheff, *One Hundred Years of Probation*, 1941, part I, page 13.
31. United Nations, op. cit., 1951, page 47.
32. H.O. 123.946/57, and *Minutes of Evidence, Departmental Committee on the Probation of Offenders Act, 1907*, 1910, Cd. 5002, pages 1, 54 and 77.
33. United Nations, op. cit., 1951, page 19.
34. Augustus's own account of his work appears in *John Augustus, First Probation Officer*, National Probation

Association, New York, 1939.

35. Quoted in the United Nations, *Probation and Related Measures* from Charles L. Chute, 'The Development of Probation in the United States', in Sheldon Glueck (ed.), *Probation and Criminal Justice*, 1933, page 228.

36. P.R.O. H.O. 45/9594/93897H.

37. H.O. Circular, 22nd October, 1880.

38. P.R.O. H.O. 45/9594/93897H.

39. *Reports to the Secretary of State for the Home Department on The State of the Law Relating to the Treatment and Punishment of Juvenile Offenders*, 1881, C. 2808.

40. *Annual Report of the Howard Association*, 1881, page 3.

41. Howard Association, *Juvenile Offenders*, 1881, page 1.

42. *Annual Report of the Howard Association*, 1881, page 3.

43. Howard Association, op. cit., 1881, pages 1–4.

44. *Reports to the Secretary of State for the Home Department on The State of the Law Relating to the Treatment and Punishment of Juvenile Offenders*, 1881, C. 2808.

45. *Report of the Royal Commission on Reformatories and Industrial Schools*, 1884, C. 3876.

46. Gordon Rose, *The Struggle for Penal Reform*, 1961, pages 46–8.

47. *Minutes of Evidence, Royal Commission on Reformatories and Industrial Schools*, 1884, page 158.

48. *Annual Report of the Howard Association*, 1885, page 4.

49. S. H. Jeyes and F. D. How, *The Life of Sir Howard Vincent*, 1912, page 153.

50. *Concise Dictionary of National Biography*, 1920, Supplement page 119.

51. S. H. Jeyes and F. D. How, op. cit., 1912, page 198.

52. P.R.O. H.O. 45/9593/93897A.

53. Probation of First Offenders Bill, 1886, Cl. 1.

54. Hansard, 5th May 1886.

55. See page 11.

56. Hansard, 5th May 1886.

57. Ibid.

58. Ibid.

59. Ibid., 18th February 1887.

60. P.R.O. H.O. 45/9662/A43317.

61. *The Times*, 26th July 1886.

62. Hansard, 18th February 1887.

63. Lords' Debates, 22nd June 1886.

64. *The Times*, 26th July 1886.

65. P.R.O. H.O. 45/9662/A43317. Letter from Monro to Vincent.

66. Ibid.

67. Ibid.

68. Probation of First Offenders Bill (H.L.), 1887.

69. Lords' Debates, 28th January 1887.

70. Probation of First Offenders (No. 2) Bill (H.L.), 1887.

71. Probation of First Offenders Bill, 1887.

72. Lords' Debates, 25th March 1887.

73. First Offenders Bill, 1887, Cl. 2.

74. Hansard, 16th February 1887.

75. Ibid., 7th March and 5th May 1887; and Probation of First Offenders Bill, 1887, as amended in Committee.

76. Lords' Debates, 5th, 21st and 26th July 1887.

77. Howard Association. *The Probation of First Offenders Act, 1887*, 1892, page 3.

78. *Annual Report of the Howard Association*, 1892, page 2.

79. Hansard, 28th March 1892.

80. H.O. Circular, 25th April 1892.

81. *Report of the Commissioners of Prisoners* (Part 1), 1891, C. 6470, page 4.

82. W. D. Morrison, *Juvenile Offenders*, 1896, page 189.

83. *Annual Report of the Howard Association*, October 1892, page 4.

84. Hansard, 25th February 1901.

85. *Annual Report of the Howard Association*, 1897, page 5.

86. W. D. Morrison, *The Treatment of Prisoners*, 1897, page 93.
87. *Annual Reports of the Howard Association*, 1896 and 1897.
88. Howard Association, op. cit., 1898, page 3.
89. Ibid., pages 3–16.
90. *Annual Report of the Howard Association*, 1899, page 3.
91. Howard Association, *Probation Officers and the Gift of Guidance*, 1901, page 4.
92. *Annual Report of the Howard Association*, 1903, pages 6–7.
93. E. P. Hughes, *The Probation System of America*, 1903, page 10.
94. Ibid., page 12.
95. E. Ruggles-Brise, *Some Observations on the Treatment of Crime in America*, 1897, H.M.S.O., page 1.
96. P.R.O. H.O. 45/9751/A59137.
97. E. Ruggles-Brise, op. cit., 1897, H.M.S.O., page 23.
98. Rosa M. Barrett, *The Treatment of Juvenile Offenders*, 1900, page 8.
99. E. Ruggles-Brise, op. cit., 1897, H.M.S.O., page 23.
100. See pages 20–22.
101. H.O. 112.648/5.
102. H.O. 112.648/5/9.
103. H.O. 123.946/21 to 28, /30, /34, /35, /40, /41.
104. Howard Association, *Children's Courts and the Probation System*, 1904, page 4.
105. H.O. 123.946/24.
106. H.O. 123.946/4.
107. H.O. 123.946/6–18.
108. H.O. 123.946/19 and 20.
109. *Annual Reports of the C.E.T.S.*, 1900 to 1904.
110. Ibid., 1875.
111. Ibid., 1883.
112. H. H. Ayscough, *When Mercy Seasons Justice*, 1923, page 17. To mark the fiftieth anniversary of its work in the police courts, the C.E.T.S. erected plaques in Rainer's memory in All Soul's Church, Hertford, where he worshipped, and the Guildhall, Windsor, of which he was a native.
113. *Annual Report of the C.E.T.S.*, 1878.
114. Ibid.
115. Ibid., 1883.
116. Ibid., 1898 and 1900.
117. Ibid., 1888.
118. J. Hasloch Potter, *Inasmuch: The Story of the Police Court Mission, 1876–1926*, 1927, page 8.
119. H.O. 125.632/1.
120. Howard Association, op. cit. ref. 104, 1904.
121. *The Times*, 5th October 1904, 28th September 1904.
122. Ibid., 1st December 1904.
123. Summary Jurisdiction (Children) Bill, 1905.
124. H.O. 123.946/56.
125. Summary Jurisdiction (Children) (No. 2) Bill, 1905.
126. Memorandum on the Summary Jurisdiction (Children) (No. 2) Bill, 1905.
127. H.O. 123.946/56.
128. H.O. 123.946/74.
129. Probation of First Offenders Bill, 1906.
130. Ibid., Cl. 1.
131. Ibid., Cl. 3.
132. Herbert Samuel, *Memoirs*, 1945, page 51.
133. *Report of the Departmental Committee on Prisons*, 1895, C. 7702.
134. *Probation*, Vol. 8, No. 6, June 1957, page 81. (Viscount Samuel's address to N.A.P.O. Conference, 1957).
135. H.O. 123.946/69.
136. *Probation*, Vol. 8, No. 6, June 1957, page 81 (Viscount Samuel's address to N.A.P.O. Conference 1957).
137. Herbert Samuel, op. cit., 1945, page 53.
138. H.O. 123.946/76.

139. Ibid. Paper by Fenwick, March 1906.
140. See page 20.
141. H.O. 123.946/72.
142. H.O. 123.946/69.
143. H.O. 123.946/76.
144. Ibid.
145. Ibid.
146. Ibid.
147. Ibid.
148. See pages 110 and 147.
149. Probation of Offenders Bill, 1906, Cl. 1.
150. See page 13.
151. H.O. 140.503/7.
152. H.O. 123.946/76.
153. H.O. 140.503/1.
154. See page 15.
155. H.O. 123.946/76.
156. Probation of Offenders Bill, 1906, Cl. 1.
157. H.O. 140.503/1.
158. Probation of Offenders Bill, 1906, Cl. 3.
159. Ibid., Cl. 2(1).
160. Ibid., Cl. 2(2) (b).
161. Ibid., Cl. 2(1).
162. Ibid., Cl. 2(2).
163. Ibid., Cl. 2(3).
164. Local Government Act, 1888, S. 30.
165. Ibid., S. 30(1).
166. See page 46.
167. Probation of Offenders Bill, 1906, Cl. 2(3).
168. Ibid., Cl. 3(2).
169. H.O. 140.503/12 and /21 and /7.
170. H.O. 140.503/18.
171. Hansard, 13th December 1906.
172. Ibid., 19th March 1907.
173. Probation of First Offenders Bill, 1907.
174. Ibid., Cl. 2(3).
175. H.O. 140.503/21.
176. Ibid.
177. Hansard, 19th March 1907.
178. Ibid.
179. Ibid., 8th May 1907.
180. Ibid.
181. Herbert Samuel, op. cit., 1945, page 5.
182. Hansard, 8th May 1907.
183. *Report of Standing Committee B on the Probation of Offenders (No. 2) Bill*, 1907.
184. H.O. 140.503/45.
185. *Report of Standing Committee B on the Probation of Offenders (No. 2) Bill*, 1907.
186. Ibid.
187. Frank Dawtry suggests in 'Fifty Years of Probation', *The Friends Quarterly*, January 1958, that the phrase 'advise, assist and befriend' was substituted for 'admonish, assist and befriend' (a term used by Samuel during the second reading), at the committee stage. However neither appeared in the original bill, which contained no description of duties; and when this omission was remedied at the Committee stage, the word 'admonish' was not used.
188. *Report of Standing Committee B on the Probation of Offenders (No. 2) Bill*, 1907.
189. Ibid.
190. Ibid.
191. Hansard, 26th July 1907.
192. H. R. P. Gamon, 'The Probation of Offenders Act, 1907: An Appreciation and a Criticism', *The Law Magazine and Law Review*, Vol. 33, No. CCCXLIX, 1908, page 449.
193. Lords Debates, 5th August 1907.
194. Hansard, 21st August 1907.
195. *Probation*, Vol. 8, No. 6, June 1957, page 82.

CHAPTER 2

1. Probation of Offenders Act, 1907, S. 10(3).
2. H.O. 140 503/52.
3. Probation of Offenders Act, 1907, S. 3(4).
4. H.O. 156.623/1.
5. H.O. 140 503/7.
6. H.O. 123.946/76; 123.946/72 and 140.503/8.
7. H.O. 123.946/100 and 140.503/12.
8. H.O. 140.503/20.
9. H.O. 140.503/13 and /21.
10. C. E. B. Russell and L. M. Rigby, *The Making of the Criminal*, 1906, page 146.
11. H.O. 140.503/20.
12. Hugh R. P. Gamon, *The London Police Court To-day and To-morrow*, 1907, page 189.
13. *Minutes of the Annual Meeting of the Council of the C.E.T.S.*, 29th April 1895.
14. *Annual Report of the London Diocesan Branch of the C.E.T.S.*, 1893.
15. Ibid., 1894.
16. *Annual Reports and Minutes of Council and Committees of the C.E.T.S.*, 1875–1905.
17. *Minutes of the Executive Committee of the C.E.T.S.*, April 1906.
18. H.O. 123.946/91.
19. Hugh R. P. Gamon, op. cit., 1907, pages 162–3.
20. Ibid., page 181.
21. Ibid., pages 177 and 182.
22. Ibid., page 177.
23. H.O. 140.503/3.
24. H.O. 125.632/5.
25. C. E. B. Russell and L. M. Rigby, op. cit., 1906, page 146.
26. H.O. 156.623/27.
27. Probation of Offenders Act, 1907, S. 3(2).
28. Ibid.
29. H.O. 156.623/27.
30. H.O. 159.319/31.
31. H.O. 159.319/6 and /1.
32. H.O. 156.623/27.
33. See pages 70, 75 and 84.
34. H.O. 156.623/27.
35. H.O. 159.319/1.
36. H.O. 159.319/29.
37. H.O. 159.319/2.
38. Ibid.
39. Probation of Offenders Act, 1907, S. 7.
40. *The Probation Rules*, 1908, Nos. 2 and 3.
41. Ibid., Nos. 8 to 14.
42. Ibid., Nos. 15 to 18.
43. *Memorandum with reference to the Probation of Offenders Act, 1907,* 1908, Cd. 3981.
44. Alexander Maxwell, *The Home Office: Its Function in Relation to the Treatment of Offenders.* 2nd Annual Lecture in Criminal Science. Faculty of Law, University of Cambridge, 1947.
45. H.O. 156.623/29.
46. *Memorandum with reference to the Probation of Offenders Act, 1907,* 1908, Cd. 3981.
47. *Report of Departmental Committee on the Probation of Offenders Act, 1907,* 1910, Cd. 5001, page 5.
48. H.O. 156.623/36.
49. *Annual Report of the C.E.T.S.*, 1907, pages 22 to 24.
50. *Minutes of Evidence to the Departmental Committee on the Probation of Offenders Act, 1907,* 1910, Cd. 5002.
51. H.O. 156.623/70.
52. H.O. 156.623/72.
53. H.O. 156.623/91 and 159.319/3.
54. H.O. 156.623/94.
55. H.O. 175.294/20.
56. H.O. 163.781/2.
57. *Memorandum with reference to the*

Probation of Offenders Act, 1907, 1908, Cd. 3981.

58. H.O. 163.781/6a.

59. H.O. 163.781/37.

60. *The Penal Reform League Monthly Record*, Vol. 1, No. 1, January 1909.

61. H.O. 163.781/37 and H.O. 163.781/43.

62. H.O. 163.781/37.

63. H.O. 163.781/30.

64. *Penal Reform League Monthly Record*, Vol. 1, No. 7, July 1909, page 2.

65. H.O. 163.781/25.

66. *Annual Report of the Howard Association*, 1908, page 73.

67. H.O. 163.781/40.

68. H.O. 163.781/30.

69. H.O. 163.781/37.

70. H.O. 163.781/30.

71. H.O. 163.781/30, /37 and /40.

72. H.O. 163.781/25, /30, /37 and /40.

73. H.O. 159.319/44.

74. H.O. 159.319/50.

75. *Report of the Departmental Committee on the Probation of Offenders Act, 1907*, 1910, Cd. 5001.

76. H.O. 159.319/50 and *Report of the Departmental Committee on the Probation of Offenders Act, 1907*, 1910, Cd. 5001.

77. *Report of the Departmental Committee on the Probation of Offenders Act, 1907*, 1910, Cd. 5001, page 3.

78. Ibid., pages 3 and 4.

79. Ibid., page 4.

80. Ibid., page 5.

81. Ibid., page 5.

82. *Report of the Departmental Committee on the Training, Appointment and Payment of Probation Officers*, 1922, Cmd. 1601, page 6; *Report of the Departmental Committee on the Social Services in Courts of Summary Jurisdiction*, 1936, Cmd. 5122, page 91.

83. Ibid., pages 90–1.

84. *Minutes of Evidence, Departmental Committee on the Probation of Offenders Act, 1907*, 1910, Cd. 5002, page 5.

85. Ibid., page 63.

86. Ibid., pages 3, 5 and 6.

87. Ibid., pages 14 and 15.

88. *Report of the Departmental Committee on the Probation of Offenders Act, 1907*, 1910, Cd. 5001, pages 5 and 6.

89. *Minutes of Evidence, Departmental Committee on the Probation of Offenders Act, 1907*, 1910, Cd. 5002, pages 54 to 61.

90. *Report of the Departmental Committee on the Probation of Offenders Act, 1907*, 1910, Cd. 5001, page 6.

91. Ibid., pages 5 and 6.

92. Ibid., page 2.

93. Ibid., page 8.

94. Ibid.

95. It was limited to London by its terms of reference.

96. *Report of the Departmental Committee on the Probation of Offenders Act, 1907*, 1910, Cd. 5001, pages 7 and 10.

97. Ibid., page 9.

98. Ibid., page 10.

99. *Minutes of Evidence, Departmental Committee on the Probation of Offenders Act, 1907*, 1910, Cd. 5002, page 89.

100. *Penal Reform League Monthly Record*, Vol. 1, No. 7, July 1909, pages 2 and 3.

101. Gordon Rose, *The Struggle for Penal Reform*, 1961, page 85.

102. *Report of the Departmental Committee on the Probation of Offenders Act, 1907*, 1910, Cd. 5001, page 10.

103. Ibid., page 13.

104. Ibid., page 9.

105. Ibid., page 10.

106. H.O. 159.319/50.

107. H.O. 163.781/37.

254

CHAPTER 3

1. Hansard, 27th May 1908.
2. H.O. Circular, 21st April 1910.
3. Ibid.
4. H.O. 176.696/3.
5. Ibid.
6. H.O. 176.696/4.
7. Home Office, *Register of Probation Officers*, 1911.
8. H.O. 186,854/19a and /28.
9. H.O. 186.854/3 and /19a.
10. H.O. 196,854/28.
11. *Minutes of Evidence, Departmental Committee on the Probation of Offenders Act, 1907*, 1910, Cd. 5002, page 14.
12. H.O. 186.854/28.
13. H.O. 186.854/3.
14. H.O. 186.854/48.
15. H.O. 186.854/28.
16. H.O. 186.854/3.
17. H.O. 186.854/48.
18. H.O. 186.854/11.
19. H.O. 186.854/28.
20. H.O. 186.854/19a.
21. *Probation*, Vol. 1, No. 19, April 1934, page 292.
22. *Minute Book, N.A.P.O.*, 1912.
23. *Journal of the N.A.P.O.*, No. 1, April 1913, page 1.
24. Minutes of Inaugural Meeting of N.A.P.O., 22nd May 1912.
25. *Minute Book, N.A.P.O.*, 1912.
26. Minutes of First Annual Meeting of N.A.P.O., 11th December 1912, and *Journal of the N.A.P.O.*, No. 1, April 1913, page 7.
27. *Journal of the N.A.P.O.*, No. 3, February 1914, page 25, No. 6, June 1915, page 115.
28. *Penal Reform League Monthly Record*, Vol. 4, No. 3, March 1912, pages 2–4.
29. Ibid., No. 5, May 1912, page 2.
30. Gordon Rose, *The Struggle for Penal Reform*, 1961, pages 87 and 90.
31. *Penal Reform League Monthly Record*, Vol. 4, No. 5, May 1912, page 2.
32. H.O. 176.696/13.
33. H.O. Circular, 3rd October 1912.
34. H.O. 176.696/13.
35. H.O. 203.154/21.
36. Ibid.
37. H.O. Circular 22nd August 1917.
38. Cecil Leeson, *The Probation System*, 1914, pages 30–1 and 128.
39. *Penal Reform League Quarterly Record*, July 1919, page 64.
40. Cecil Leeson, op. cit., 1914, pages vii, to ix.
41. Ibid., pages 125–6 and 182–4.
42. Ibid., pages 86–7.
43. Ibid., page vi.
44. Ibid., page 89.
45. See page 50.
46. Criminal Justice Administration Bill, 1914, Cl. 8.
47. Ibid., Cl. 9.
48. Ibid., Cl. 7(1) and (4).
49. Hansard, 15th April 1914.
50. H.O. 452.608.
51. Minutes of Meeting of Executive Committee of the C.E.T.S., 9th June 1914.
52. Hansard, 20th July 1914.
53. Lords' Debates, 29th July 1914.
54. Hansard, 10th August 1914.
55. H.O. Circular, 22nd August 1917.
56. Gordon Rose, op. cit., 1961, page 89.
57. See page 63.
58. Penal Reform League, *A National Minimum for Youth*, 1917, pages 7–10.
59. W. Clarke Hall, *The State and the Child*, 1915, pages 54 and 102.
60. B. Flexner and R. N. Baldwin, *Juvenile Courts and Probation*, 1915.
61. Ibid., pages 84–6 and 96–8.
62. W. Clarke Hall, op. cit., 1915, page 107.
63. H.O. 203.154/84.

64. Ibid.
65. Ibid.
66. H.O. Circular, 22nd August 1917.
67. Ibid.
68. H.O. 203.154/84.
69. Ibid., and 203.154/82.
70. Minutes of Meeting of the Council of the C.E.T.S., 12th May 1915.
71. Ibid.
72. *Report of the Departmental Committee on the Training, Appointment and Payment of Probation Officers*, 1922, Cmd. 1601, page 9.
73. See page 70.
74. Hansard, 25th November and 20th December 1920.
75. Minutes of the Executive Committee of the C.E.T.S., 20th November, 1919.
76. *Annual Report of C.E.T.S.*, 1919, page 11.
77. Minutes of Meeting of the Executive Committee of the C.E.T.S., 1st June 1920.
78. Ibid., 4th June 1919.
79. Ibid., 23rd November 1920.
80. H.O. 361.385/19.
81. Minutes of Meetings of the Executive Committee of the C.E.T.S., 23rd March 1920, to 20th July 1920.
82. Ibid., 23rd November 1920.
83. *Journal of the N.A.P.O.*, Vol. 1, No. 3, February 1914, page 33 and No. 7, July 1916, page 114.
84. Ibid., No. 7, July 1916, page 114, and No. 10, February 1919, page 179.
85. Ibid., No. 9, July 1918, page 156.
86. Ibid., page 166.
87. Ibid., No. 7, July 1916, page 117.
88. Ibid., No. 6, June 1915, pages 95 and 102.
89. Ibid., No. 4, June 1914, page 52.
90. Ibid., No. 3, February 1914, page 31.
91. Ibid., No. 9, July 1918, pages 164–5.
92. H.O. 175.294/74.
93. H.O. Circular, 11th January 1919.
94. H.O. 175.294/91A.
95. Ibid.
96. Ibid.
97. H.O. 175.294/78.
98. *Journal of the N.A.P.O.*, Vol. 1, No. 9, July 1918, pages 176 and 177.
99. Ibid.
100. Finer, H. *English Local Government*, 1946.
101. H.O. 175.294/91A.

CHAPTER 4

1. *Report of the Departmental Committee on the Training Appointment and Payment of Probation Officers, 1922, Cmd. 1601.*
2. *Annual Report of the Howard League for Penal Reform*, 1921–2.
3. *Report of the Departmental Committee on the Training, Appointment and Payment of Probation Officers*, 1922, Cmd. 1601, pages 25 and 26.
4. H.O. 395.473/1.
5. *Report of the Departmental Committee on the Training, Appointment and Payment of Probation Officers*, 1922, Cmd. 1601, Pages 4 to 6.
6. Ibid., page 7.
7. *Penal Reform League Quarterly Record*, May 1920, pages 18 and 43–8.
8. The Howard League for Penal Reform subsequently claimed that the Committee misrepresented their proposals, which had not included the appoint-

ment and payment of officers by the state, but only some regulation by the central authority of local appointments. (Annual Report of the League, 1921–2, page 11.)

9. *Report of the Departmental Committee on the Training, Appointment and Payment of Probation Officers*, 1922, Cmd. 1601, page 7.

10. Ibid., page 7.

11. Ibid., page 20.

12. See pages 98 and 102.

13. *Report of the Departmental Committee on the Training, Appointment and Payment of Probation Officers*, 1922, Cmd. 1601, page 9.

14. Ibid., page 10.

15. Ibid., page 9.

16. Ibid., page 19.

17. Ibid., page 9.

18. Ibid.

19. Ibid., page 10.

20. Ibid., pages 8 and 10.

21. Ibid., pages 10 and 19.

22. Ibid., page 19.

23. Ibid.

24. Ibid., page 9.

25. Ibid., pages 14, 15 and 16.

26. Ibid., page 15.

27. *Journal of the N.A.P.O.*, No. 17, July 1922, page 337.

28. Ibid., No. 14, page 260.

29. *Report of the Departmental Committee on the Training, Appointment, and Payment of Probation Officers*, 1922, Cmd. 1601, pages 16 and 17.

30. United Nations, *Training for Social Work*, 1958, pages 107–15.

31. Marjorie J. Smith, *Professional Education for Social Work in Britain*, 1965, page 58.

32. Ibid., page 54.

33. *Minutes of Evidence, Departmental Committee on the Probation of Offenders Act, 1907*, 1910, Cd. 5002, page 12.

34. *Journal of the N.A.P.O.*, No. 10, February 1919, page 179.

35. H.O. 361.385/53.

36. *Journal of the N.A.P.O.*, No. 16, September 1919, page 195.

37. *Report of the Departmental Committee on the Training, Appointment and Payment of Probation Officers*, 1922, Cmd. 1601, page 14.

38. Ibid.

39. Ibid., page 18.

40. Ibid., page 21.

41. *Journal of the N.A.P.O.*, No. 18, December 1922, page 368.

42. *The Magistrate*, No. 1, page 3.

43. *Journal of the N.A.P.O.*, No. 13, July 1920, page 241.

44. Ibid., No. 12, March 1920, page 219.

45. Ibid., No. 17, July 1912, page 342.

46. *Annual Report of the Howard League for Penal Reform*, 1921–2, page 12.

47. Home Office Circular, 27th July 1922.

48. *Journal of the N.A.P.O.*, No. 18, December 1922, page 363.

49. Home Office, *Report on the Work of the Children's Branch*, 1923, Page 63.

50. *Journal of the N.A.P.O.*, No. 18, December 1922, page 370.

51. *Probation Rules*, 1923.

52. Home Office *Report on the Work of the Children's Branch*, 1923, page 57.

53. *Annual Report of the Howard League for Penal Reform*, 1922–3, page 14.

54. Home Office *Report on the Work of the Children's Branch*, 1923, page 63.

55. *Minutes of Meeting of the Council of the C.E.T.S.*, 18th July 1922.

56. *Church Temperance Times*, August 1922, page 16.

57. *Annual Report of the C.E.T.S.*, 1922, page 10.

58. *Report of the Departmental Committee on the Training, Appointment and*

Payment of Probation Officers, 1922, Cmd. 1601, page 9.

59. This became the Rainer Foundation in 1962.

60. *Report of the Departmental Committee on the Social Services in the Courts of Summary Jurisdiction*, 1936, Cmd. 5122, page 104.

61. Ibid., pages 105 and 120.

62. *Annual Report of the C.E.T.S.*, 1923, page 21.

63. *Minutes of Meeting of the Council of the C.E.T.S.*, 20th November 1923.

64. *Minutes of Inaugural Meeting of the C.E.T.S. Police Court Missionaries' Guild*, 4th October 1923.

65. *The Magistrate*, No. 2, May 1923, page 7.

66. *Journal of the N.A.P.O.*, No. 20, December 1923, page 436.

67. *Howard League Pamphlet*, No. 1. (new series), 1923.

68. *Annual Report of the Howard League for Penal Reform*, 1922–3, page 3.

69. Hansard, 19th July 1923.

70. H.O. 452.608.

71. Ibid.

72. Cmd. 1589, 1922.

73. H.O. 452.608/2 and 3.

74. Criminal Justice Bill (H.L.), 1924.

75. Ibid., 1923.

76. *Journal of the N.A.P.O.*, No. 21, July 1924, page 460.

77. Lords' Debates, 14th and 26th February 1924.

78. Ibid., 26th February 1924.

79. Ibid., 18th March 1924.

80. *Minutes of Meeting of the Council of the C.E.T.S.*, 15th May 1924.

81. *Minutes of Meeting of Committee of the London Police Court Mission*, 13th February 1924.

82. Ibid.

83. Lords' Debates, 18th March 1924.

84. *Minutes of Meeting of Committee of the London Police Court Mission*, 8th May 1924.

85. Hansard, 1st May 1924.

86. Ibid., 7th May 1924.

87. Criminal Justice Bill, 1925. *Memorandum explaining financial resolution*, 1924–5. Cmd. 2380.

88. Home Office Circular, 13th February, 1925.

89. Criminal Justice Bill, 1925, Cl. 4(3).

90. Ibid., Cl. 1(1).

91. Ibid., Cl. 2(1).

92. Ibid., Cl. 2(4).

93. Ibid., Cl. 2(3) and (5).

94. Ibid., Cl. 1(2).

95. Hansard, 16th November 1925.

96. Criminal Justice Bill, 1925, Cl. 7.

97. Ibid., Cl. 1(3).

98. *Report of the Departmental Committee on the Training, Appointment and Payment of Probation Officers*, 1922, Cmd. 1601, pages 10 and 11.

99. Criminal Justice Bill, 1925, Cl. 1(3).

100. Ibid., Cl. 3(2).

101. *Minutes of Meeting of Committee of the London Police Court Mission*, 12th March 1925.

102. Hansard, 11th May 1925.

103. Ibid., 16th November 1925.

CHAPTER 5

1. *The Probation Rules*, 1926, Nos. 22–4.

2. Ibid., No. 33.

3. H.O. Circular, 31st July 1930.

4. *The Probation Rules*, 1926, Nos. 31

and 32.

5. Ibid., No. 60.

6. Ibid., Nos. 59 to 64.

7. Ibid., No. 66.

8. H.O. Circular, 6th November 1924.

9. *The Probation Rules*, 1926, No. 48.

10. Ibid., Nos. 1–20.

11. *Report of the Departmental Committee on the Training, Appointment and Payment of Probation Officers*, 1922, Cmd. 1601, pages 5 and 6.

12. *The Probation Rules*, 1926, No. 38.

13. Ibid., No. 39.

14. H.O. 479.566/1.

15. *Report of the Probation Officers' Superannuation Committee*, 1926.

16. *The Probation Officers' Superannuation Rules*, 1926.

17. H.O. Circular, 8th November 1926.

18. *The Probation Officers' Superannuation Rules*, 1926.

19. Missionary Members of N.A.P.O., *Petition to Home Secretary*, 1927. *Minutes of Executive Committee of N.A.P.O.*, 2nd March 1928 and 22nd July 1929.

20. Home Office, *Fourth Report on the Work of the Children's Branch*, 1928, page 15.

21. Ibid., page 16.

22. Ibid., page 27.

23. Ibid.

24. H.O. 452.608.

25. *Report of the Departmental Committee on the Treatment of Young Offenders*, 1927, Cmd. 2831, page 5.

26. Ibid., page 51.

27. Ibid., page 62.

28. Ibid., pages 111 and 112.

29. See page 64.

30. Home Office, *Third Report on the Work of the Children's Branch*, 1925, page 9.

31. *Report of the Departmental Committee on the Treatment of Young Offenders*, 1927, Cmd. 2831, pages 34 and 35.

32. See pages 116 and 172.

33. *Report of the Departmental Committee on the Treatment of Young Offenders*, 1927, Cmd. 2831, page 35.

34. Ibid., pages 54 and 55.

35. Ibid., page 55.

36. Ibid, pages 54 to 57.

37. Ibid., page 6.

38. Ibid., page 120.

39. Ibid., page 111.

40. Ibid., page 112.

41. Under the Criminal Justice Administration Act, 1914, S. 1(3).

42. *Report of the Departmental Committee on the Treatment of Young Offenders*, 1927, Cmd. 2831, pages 82–4.

43. Ibid., page 61.

44. *The Probation Rules*, 1926, No. 60.

45. *Report of the Departmental Committee on the Treatment of Young Offenders*, 1927, Cmd. 2831, page 60.

46. *The Probation Rules*, 1926, No. 60.

47. *Report of the Departmental Committee on the Treatment of Young Offenders*, 1927, Cmd. 2831, pages 59 and 60.

48. Ibid., page 60.

49. See page 92.

50. See page 137.

51. William Clarke Hall, *Children's Courts*, 1926, page 130.

52. *Report of the Departmental Committee on the Treatment of Young Offenders*, 1927, Cmd. 2831, page 61.

53. Ibid., pages 51 and 52.

54. Ibid., page 57.

55. Children and Young Persons Act, 1933.

56. H.O. Circular, 20th July 1928.

57. H.O. Circular, 30th September 1927.

58. H.O. Circular, 20th July 1928.

59. *Report of the Departmental Committee on the Treatment of Young Offenders*, 1927, Cmd. 2831, page 61.

60. Criminal Justice Act, 1925, S. 3(2).

61. H.O. Circular, 31st July 1930.

62. H.O. Circular, 30th September 1927.

63. H.O. Circular, 21st October 1932.
64. H.O. Circular, 30th September 1927.
65. H.O. Circular, 20th July 1928.
66. Criminal Justice Act, 1925, S. 5(3).
67. H.O. Circular, 20th September 1928.
68. *Report of the Departmental Committee on the Treatment of Young Offenders*, 1927, Cmd. 2831, pages 54–6.
69. H.O. Circular, 20th July 1928.
70. *Minutes of Evidence, Departmental Committee on the Social Services in Courts of Summary Jurisdiction*, 1936, No. 82(f).
71. *Report of the Departmental Committee on the Social Services in Courts of Summary Jurisdiction*, 1936, Cmd. 5122, page 118.
72. Ibid., page 134, and W. G. Minn, 'Training for the Work of a Probation Officer in England and Wales', *Journal of Criminal Science*, Vol. 1, 1948, page 167.
73. *Minutes of Meeting of the Council of the C.E.T.S.*, 12th October 1926, and 8th July 1930.
74. *Report of the Departmental Committee on the Social Services in Courts of Summary Jurisdiction*, 1936, Cmd. 5122, page 134.
75. E. Moberley Bell, *The Story of Hospital Almoners*, 1961, pages 110 and 114.
76. N. Timms, *Psychiatric Social Work in Great Britain (1939–1962)*, 1964, page 21.
77. Hansard, 15th February 1928; 7th July 1931.
78. *Annual Report of the Howard League for Penal Reform*, 1929–30, page 5.
79. Children Bill, 1930. Hansard, 22nd July 1930.
80. *Annual Report of the Howard League for Penal Reform*, 1929–30, page 5; *The Magistrate*, No. 29, 1930, page 420.
81. *Minutes of Meeting of the Council of the C.E.T.S.*, 17th October 1930, and of *Meetings of the London Police Court Mission*, 6th November and 4th December 1930.
82. *Annual Report of the London Police Court Mission*, 1930, page 6.
83. Children and Young Persons Bill, 1931/32. Cl. 8(1) (d).
84. *Report of Standing Committee on the Children and Young Persons Bill*, 1931/32.
85. Children and Young Persons Bill, 1931/32, Cl. 8(1) (d).
86. Ibid., Cl. 12(1).
87. Ibid., Cl. 73(4).
88. Ibid., Cl. 20(1) and (2).
89. Lords' Debates, 9th June 1932.
90. *Minutes of Special Meeting of Executive Committee*, N.A.P.O., 22nd February 1932 and 22nd June 1932.
91. *Annual Report of the Magistrates' Association*, 1931/32.
92. *Minutes of Meeting of Executive Committee of N.A.P.O.*, 23rd March 1932.
93. *Report of Standing Committee B on the Children and Young Persons Bill*, 1931–32.
94. Hansard, 15th May 1932.
95. Lords' Debates, 9th June 1932.
96. *The Probation Rules*, 1926, No. 37.
97. National Association of Probation Officers, *Secretary's Report* for June, July and August 1932.
98. See pages 118–119.
99. Lords' Debates, 26th May 1932.
100. Ibid., 9th June 1932.
101. *Minutes of Meeting of Executive Committee of N.A.P.O.*, 30th July 1928.
102. *Journal of the N.A.P.O.*, No. 27, July 1927, page 633.
103. *Probation*, Vol. 1, No. 2, December 1929, page 20.
104. *The Times*, 6th August 1951.
105. *Minutes of Meeting of Executive Committee of N.A.P.O.*, 20th April 1927.

106. *Probation*, Vol. 10, No. 2, June 1962, pages 17–18.

107. *Minutes of Meeting of Executive Committee of N.A.P.O.*, 24th September 1928.

108. *Probation*, Vol. 1, No. 4, July 1930, page 50.

109. Ibid., No. 16, July 1933, page 245.

110. *Journal of the National Association of Probation Officers*, No. 21, July 1924, page 474.

111. *Probation*, Vol. 1, No. 1, July 1929, pages 3–4.

112. Ibid., Vol. 10, No. 2, June 1962, page 17.

113. Ibid., Vol. 1, No. 3, April 1930, page 37.

114. *Minutes of Meeting of Executive Committee of N.A.P.O.*, 10th April 1930.

115. Ibid., page 34.

116. *An Appreciation*, N.A.P.O., 1944.

117. *Probation*, Vol. 1, No. 4, July 1930, page 55.

118. Ibid., page 54.

119. Ibid.

120. *Secretary's Report, N.A.P.O.*, 23rd January 1933.

121. *Minutes of Meeting of Executive Committee of N.A.P.O*, 28th September 1932.

122. *Who Was Who*, 1929–40, page 580.

123. *Minutes of Meeting of Executive Committee of the National Association of Probation Officers*, 28th September 1932.

124. *Letter from the Secretary to the Executive Committee of N.A.P.O.*, 4th November 1932.

125. *Probation*, Vol. 1, No. 14, January 1933, page 210.

126. *The Times*, 22nd December 1932.

127. *Minutes of Meetings of Executive Committee of N.A.P.O.*, 1933–45.

128. *Probation*, Vol. 1, No. 6, January 1931, page 81; *Annual Report of the N.A.P.O.*, 1935, page 2.

129. *Minutes of Meetings of Executive Committee of N.A.P.O.*, 25th September 1930, and 14th January 1932.

130. Ibid., 23rd March 1932 and 28th September 1932.

131. Ibid., 10th October 1929.

132. See page 64.

133. *Probation*, Vol. 1, No. 6, January 1931, page 95.

134. *Annual Reports of the Magistrates' Association*, 1926–35.

135. *Probation*, Vol. 1, No. 11, April 1932, page 162.

136. Ibid., No. 3, April 1930, page 45.

137. Ibid., No. 1, July 1929, page 16; No. 3, April 1930, page 42; No. 10, January 1932, page 148; No. 11, April 1932, page 168.

138. N. Timms, op. cit., 1964, pages 19–21.

139. *Probation*, Vol. 1, No. 3, April 1930, page 38.

140. Ibid., No. 1, July 1929, pages 10 and 12.

141. Ibid., No. 4, July 1930, pages 56 to 59.

142. *Report of the Departmental Committee on the Social Services in Courts of Summary Jurisdiction*, 1936, Cmd. 5122, page 92.

143. *Report of the Departmental Committee on the Treatment of Young Offenders*, 1927, Cmd. 2831, page 49.

144. G. Rose, *Schools for Young Offenders*, 1967, page 11.

145. *Probation*, Vol. 1, No. 1, July 1929, page 8; No. 2, December 1929, page 20.

CHAPTER 6

1. *Annual Report of the N.A.P.O.*, 1934, page 3.
2. Summary Jurisdiction (Domestic Procedure) Bill, 1934.
3. *Minutes of Meeting of Executive Committee of N.A.P.O.*, 23rd April 1934.
4. Lords' Debates, 15th May 1934.
5. Ibid., 25th July 1934.
6. Hereafter referred to as the 'Social Services Committee'.
7. *Report of the Departmental Committee on the Social Services in Courts of Summary Jurisdiction*, 1936, Cmd. 5122.
8. Ibid., page vi.
9. Ibid., page 106.
10. Ibid., page 90.
11. Ibid.
12. Ibid., page 95.
13. *Minutes of Evidence, Departmental Committee on the Social Services in Courts of Summary Jurisdiction*, 1936, No. 23.
14. Ibid., No. 82.
15. *Report of the Departmental Committee on the Social Services in Courts of Summary Jurisdiction*, 1936, Cmd. 5122, pages 91 to 94.
16. Ibid., page 93.
17. *Minutes of Evidence, Departmental Committee on the Social Services in Courts of Summary Jurisdiction*, 1936, No. 70.
18. Ibid., Nos. 31, 29 and 52.
19. *Report of the Departmental Committee on the Social Services in Courts of Summary Jurisdiction*, 1936, Cmd. 5122, page 93.
20. Ibid.
21. Ibid.
22. Ibid., page 92.
23. Ibid., page 90.
24. See pages 55, 59, 87, 105.
25. *Report of the Departmental Committee on the Social Services in Courts of Summary Jurisdiction*, 1936, Cmd. 5122, pages 116 and 117.
26. Ibid., page 117.
27. *Minutes of Evidence, Departmental Committee on the Social Services in Courts of Summary Jurisdiction*, 1936, No. 55.
28. *Report of the Departmental Committee on the Social Services in Courts of Summary Jurisdiction*, 1936, Cmd. 5122, page 117.
29. *Minutes of Evidence, Departmental Committee on the Social Services in Courts of Summary Jurisdiction*, 1936, No. 55.
30. *Report of the Departmental Committee on the Social Services in Courts of Summary Jurisdiction*, 1936, Cmd. 5122, page 117.
31. Ibid., page 116.
32. Ibid., Appendix VII.
33. Ibid., page 118.
34. Ibid., page 119.
35. *Annual Report of the N.A.P.O.*, 1934, page 6.
36. *Report of the Departmental Committee on the Social Services in Courts of Summary Jurisdiction*, 1936, Cmd. 5122, pages 96–8.
37. Ibid., page 99.
38. See page 98.
39. *Report of the Departmental Committee on the Social Services in Courts of Summary Jurisdiction*, 1936, Cmd. 5122, pages 99–101.
40. See page 126.
41. *Report of the Departmental Committee on the Social Services in Courts of Summary Jurisdiction*, 1936, Cmd. 5122, page 101.
42. See page 98.
43. *Report of the Departmental Committee on the Social Services in Courts of Summary Jurisdiction*, 1936, Cmd. 5122, page 96.

44. *Minutes of Council Meetings of the C.E.T.S.*, 9th October 1934 to 9th July 1935.

45. *Minutes of Meeting of Committee of the London Police Court Mission*, 4th October 1934.

46. *Minutes of Evidence, Departmental Committee on the Social Services in Courts of Summary Jurisdiction*, 1936, Nos. 53, 61 and 65.

47. *Report of the Departmental Committee on the Social Services in Courts of Summary Jurisdiction*, 1936, Cmd. 5122, page 104.

48. *Minutes of Evidence, Departmental Committee on the Social Services in Courts of Summary Jurisdiction*, 1936, Nos. 39, 48, 55, 70 and *Report of the Committee*, 1936, Cmd. 5122, page 103.

49. *Report of the Departmental Committee on the Social Services in Courts of Summary Jurisdiction*, 1936, Cmd. 5122, pages 103–4.

50. Ibid., page 105.

51. *Minutes of Meeting of the Council of the Church of England Temperance Society*, 10th June 1936.

52. *Report of the Departmental Committee on the Social Services in Courts of Summary Jurisdiction*, 1936, Cmd. 5122, page 104.

53. Ibid., page 105.

54. *Minutes of Evidence, Departmental Committee on the Social Services in Courts of Summary Jurisdiction*, 1936, No. 82B.

55. *Report of the Departmental Committee on the Social Services in Courts of Summary Jurisdiction*, 1936, Cmd. 5122, pages 105–6.

56. *Minutes of Evidence, Departmental Committee on the Social Services in Courts of Summary Jurisdiction*, 1936, No. 41.

57. *Report of the Departmental Committee on the Social Services in Courts of Summary Jurisdiction*, 1936, Cmd. 5122, page 106.

58. Ibid., page 108.

59. Ibid., page 110.

60. See page 109.

61. *Minutes of Evidence, Departmental Committee on the Social Services in Courts of Summary Jurisdiction*, 1936, Nos. 48 and 70.

62. *Report of the Departmental Committee on the Social Services in Courts of Summary Jurisdiction*, 1936, Cmd. 5122, pages 109–10.

63. Ibid., pages 58 to 61.

64. *The Probation Rules*, 1926, No. 37.

65. See page 115.

66. H.O. Circular, 9th August 1933.

67. *Report of the Departmental Committee on the Social Services in Courts of Summary Jurisdiction*, 1936, Cmd. 5122, pages 49–50.

68. *Minutes of Evidence, Departmental Committee on the Social Services in Courts of Summary Jurisdiction*, 1936, No. 72.

69. *Report of the Departmental Committee on Imprisonment by Courts of Summary Jurisdiction in Default of Payment of Fines and Other Sums of Money*, 1934, Cmd. 4649, page 83.

70. S. 5(1).

71. *Report of the Departmental Committee on the Social Services in Courts of Summary Jurisdiction*, 1936, Cmd. 5122, pages 79–82.

72. *Minutes of Evidence, Departmental Committee on the Social Services in Courts of Summary Jurisdiction*, 1936, No. 82(0).

73. *Report of the Departmental Committee on the Social Services in Courts of Summary Jurisdiction*, 1936, Cmd. 5122, page 8.

74. *Minutes of Evidence, Departmental Committee on the Social Services in Courts of Summary Jurisdiction*, 1936,

263

No. 70.

75. Ibid., No. 10.

76. *Report of the Departmental Committee on the Social Services in Courts of Summary Jurisdiction*, 1936, Cmd. 5122, page 12.

77. Ibid., pages 12–16.

78. *Minutes of Evidence, Departmental Committee on the Social Services in Courts of Summary Jurisdiction*, 1936, Nos. 1, 7, 8, 11 and 12.

79. Ibid., Nos. 28, 40 and 41.

80. *Report of the Departmental Committee on the Social Services in Courts of Summary Jurisdiction*, 1936, Cmd. 5122, pages 77 and 78.

81. Ibid., page 132.

82. *Minutes of Evidence, Departmental Committee on the Social Services in Courts of Summary Jurisdiction*, 1936, No. 73.

83. Ibid., No. 64.

84. *Report of the Departmental Committee on the Social Services in Courts of Summary Jurisdiction*, 1936, Cmd. 5122, pages 134–5.

85. Ibid., pages 133 to 137.

86. Ibid., pages 135 to 138.

87. Ibid., pages 125 and 127.

88. Ibid., pages 124 to 128.

89. Ibid., pages 129 to 130.

90. Ibid., page 113.

91. Ibid., page 126.

92. Ibid., pages 41 to 42.

93. Ibid., pages 41 and 69–70.

94. Ibid., page 43.

95. Ibid., page 42.

96. Ibid., pages 43 and 72.

97. 2 K.B., 278(1919).

98. *Report of the Departmental Committee on the Social Services in Courts of Summary Jurisdiction*, 1936, Cmd. 5122, pages 73–4.

99. Ibid., pages 146–7.

100. Ibid., pages 50–1.

101. Ibid., pages 67 and 68.

102. See page 109.

103. *Report of the Departmental Committee on the Social Services in Courts of Summary Jurisdiction*, 1936, Cmd. 5122, pages 146 and 147.

CHAPTER 7

1. *Minutes of Evidence, Departmental Committee on the Social Services in Courts of Summary Jurisdiction*, 1936, Nos. 48 and 70.

2. Ibid., No. 55.

3. *Probation*, Vol. 2, No. 7, January 1937, page 100.

4. Ibid., No. 9, July 1937, page 133.

5. Ibid., No. 7, January 1937, page 104.

6. Ibid., No. 10, October 1937, page 160.

7. *The Magistrate*, Vol. 4, No. 72, February/March 1937.

8. *Report of the Departmental Committee on the Social Services in Courts of Summary Jurisdiction*, 1936, Cmd. 5122, page 136.

9. *The Magistrate*, Vol. 4, No. 73, April/May 1937.

10. Hansard, 1st December 1938.

11. *Probation*, Vol. 2, No. 9, July 1937, page 140.

12. W. G. Minn, 'Training for the Work of a Probation Officer in England and Wales', in *The Journal of Criminal Science*, Vol. 1, 1948, page 169.

13. Home Office, *Probation Work in England and Wales*, May 1937.

14. W. G. Minn, op. cit.

15. Ibid., page 168.

16. *Probation*, Vol. 2, No. 9, July 1937, page 136.

17. Ibid., Vol. 3, No. 7, September 1939, page 111.

18. *The Probation Rules*, 1937, No. 4.

19. Home Office, *Probation Work in England and Wales*, May 1937.

20. *The Probation Rules*, 1937, No. 3.

21. Ibid., No. 4.

22. H.O. Circular, 26th June 1937.

23. *Probation*, Vol. 2, No. 7, January 1937, page 104.

24. *The Magistrate*, Vol. 4, No. 74, June/July 1937, page 1178.

25. *Probation*, Vol. 2, No. 7, January 1937, page 99.

26. Home Office, *The Probation Service: Its Objects and Its Organisation*, 1938.

27. H.O. Circular, 16th January 1939.

28. H.O. Circular, 30th July 1936.

29. Summary Procedure (Domestic Proceedings) Act, 1937, S. 1, 2 and 3.

30. Ibid., S. 7.

31. Ibid., S. 8.

32. *Minutes of Meeting of Committee of the London Police Court Mission*, 3rd December 1936 and 16th November 1937, and of the *Committee of the Central Police Court Mission*, 12th January 1937.

33. *Minutes of Meeting of the Committee of the Central Police Court Mission*, 7th October 1936.

34. *Annual Report of the London Police Court Mission*, 1937, pages 4–6, and *Minutes of Meeting of Council of the C.E.T.S.*, 8th February 1938.

35. *Annual Report of the London Police Court Mission*, 1938, page 4.

36. Ibid., 1940, page 5.

37. *Minutes of Meeting of Council of the C.E.T.S.*, 10th June 1936.

38. *Minutes of Meeting of Committee of the London Police Court Mission*, 14th December 1937 and *Report of Discussion between representatives of the Home Office and the Central Police Court Mission in Minutes of the Mission*, 1937.

39. *Minutes of Council of the C.E.T.S.*, 13th July 1937.

40. *Annual Report of the London Police Court Mission*, 1939, page 12.

41. *Minutes of Meeting of Council of the C.E.T.S.*, 8th February 1938, and *Annual Report of the London Police Court Mission*, 1938, page 5.

42. *Probation*, Vol. 3, No. 2, August 1938, page 22.

43. *Report of the Departmental Committee on the Social Services in Courts of Summary Jurisdiction*, 1936, Cmd. 5122, page 66.

44. H.O. Circular, 16th December 1937.

45. Gordon Rose, *The Struggle For Penal Reform*, 1961, page 224.

46. *Probation*, Vol. 3, No. 1, June 1938, page 2.

47. Hansard, 10th November 1938.

48. Criminal Justice Bill, 1938, Cl. 17 and 18.

49. See pages 110 and 147.

50. Criminal Justice Bill, 1938, Cl. 18(1).

51. Ibid.

52. Ibid., Cl. 18(3).

53. Ibid., Cl. 66(2).

54. Ibid., Cl. 7.

55. Ibid., Cl. 19(1).

56. Ibid., Cl. 1.

57. Ibid., Cl. 2(2).

58. Ibid., Cl. 1(4).

59. Ibid., Cl. 2(1)(a).

60. *Probation*, Vol. 2, No. 7, January 1937, page 99.

61. Criminal Justice Bill, 1938, Cl. 4(2).

62. Ibid., Cl. 75(3)(d).

63. Ibid., Cl. 2(2).

64. *Probation*, Vol. 3, No. 4, January 1939, page 52.

65. *Report of the Departmental Committee on the Social Services in Courts of Summary Jurisdiction*, 1936, Cmd. 5122, page 75.

66. Home Office, *Fifth Report on the Work of the Children's Branch*, 1938, page 32.

67. *Probation*, Vol. 3, No. 4, January 1939, page 52.

68. Minutes of Meeting of Executive Committee of N.A.P.O., 9th December 1938, and *Secretary's Report for the period December, 1938–February 1939*, N.A.P.O.

69. *Probation*, Vol. 3, No. 5, April 1939, page 69.

70. *Secretary's Report for the period December 1938–February 1939*, N.A.P.O.

71. *Probation*, Vol. 3, No. 7, September 1939, page 107.

72. Ibid., No. 5, April 1939, Pages 69 to 70.

73. Criminal Justice Bill, 1938, Cl. 18(1).

74. Hansard, 29th November and 1st December 1938.

75. Criminal Justice Bill, 1938, Cl. 20(1).

76. *Secretary's Report for the period December 1938–February 1939*, N.A.P.O.

77. Hansard, 22nd June, 6th July and 24th October 1939.

78. Ibid., 9th November 1939.

79. H.O.Circular, 17th July 1939; *Probation*, Vol. 3, No. 13, March 1941, page 177.

80. *Probation*, Vol. 3, No. 8, December 1939, page 114; and No. 10, July 1940, page 146.

81. Ibid., No. 15, August 1941, page 200.

82. Ibid., No. 14, May 1941, page 195.

83. Ibid., No. 15, August 1941, page 200.

84. Ibid., No. 14, May 1941, page 196.

85. Ibid., No. 15, August 1941, page 217.

86. *Minutes of Meeting of Executive Committee of the N.A.P.O.*, 10th September 1940.

87. H.O. Circular, 19th May 1942.

88. Information provided by the Home Office.

89. *Probation*, Vol. 3, No. 11, September 1940, page 155.

90. Ibid., Vol. 4, No. 12, July 1945, page 131.

91. Ibid., Vol. 3, No. 15, August 1941, page 200.

92. Ibid., Vol. 4, No. 5, July 1943, page 54.

93. H.O. Circular, 31st August 1939.

94. Letter from Home Office, dated 5th February 1943, in N.A.P.O. Minute Book.

95. *Annual Reports of the London Police Court Mission*, 1939–45.

96. W.G. Minn, 'Training for the Work of a Probation Officer in England and Wales', in *The Journal of Criminal Science*, Vol. 1, 1948, page 168.

97. Information provided by the Home Office.

98. *Probation*, Vol. 4, No. 12, July 1945, page 132.

99. *Annual Report of the National Association of Probation Officers*, 1942.

100. *Minutes of Meeting of Executive Committee of the N.A.P.O.*, 11th December 1942.

101. *Probation*, Vol. 4, No. 3(2), January 1943, page 32.

102. Ibid., No. 5, July 1943, pages 55–6.

103. Ibid. and No. 4, April 1943, page 45; and No. 8, July 1944, page 91.

104. Ibid., Vol. 4, No. 4, April 1943, page 43.

105. *The Times*, 4th August 1944.

106. Information in files of N.A.P.O.

107. *The Magistrate*, September/October 1944, page 55.

108. Ibid., November 1945, page 134.
109. Report of Meeting with Advisory Council, in files of N.A.P.O.
110. *Annual Report of the National Association of Probation Officers*, 1945.
111. Ibid.
112. *Report of Secretary of the Clarke Hall Fellowship*, February 1943.

113. *Probation*, Vol. 3, No. 14, May 1941, page 191.
114. *Annual Report of the National Association of Probation Officers*, 1945.
115. *Minutes of Meetings of Executive Committee of the N.A.P.O.*, 6th December 1946, and 7th March 1947.

CHAPTER 8

1. The age was 16 in the 1938 Bill.
2. Lords' Debates, 1st and 29th June 1948.
3. Gordon Rose, *The Struggle for Penal Reform*, 1961, pages 231 and 232.
4. N. Walker, *Crime and Punishment in Britain*, 1945, page 137.
5. *Explanatory Memorandum, Criminal Justice Bill*, 1947.
6. Criminal Justice Bill, 1947, Cl. 3 and 7. Dismissal and binding over were replaced by absolute and conditional discharge.
7. Ibid., Cl. 3(1) and (5).
8. Ibid., Cl. 11.
9. Ibid., Cl. 3(1).
10. Ibid., Cl. 3(4).
11. Ibid., Cl. 4.
12. *Report of the Departmental Committee on the Social Services in Courts of Summary Jurisdiction*, 1936, Cmd. 5122, pages 52–3.
13. Criminal Justice Bill, 1947, Cl. 3(2).
14. Ibid., Fifth Schedule, Para 1–3.
15. Ibid., Para 2(3).
16. Ibid., Para 3(1)(a).
17. Ibid., Para 4(2).
18. Ibid., Para 3(5).
19. See pages 158–159.
20. Criminal Justice Bill, Fifth Schedule, Para 3(5).
21. Ibid., Para 6.
22. Criminal Justice Act, 1925, S. 8.
23. Hansard, 27th and 28th November 1947.
24. *Report and Proceedings of Standing Committee C on the Criminal Justice Bill*, 1947/8.
25. Lords' Debates, 27th April 1948.
26. Ibid., 3rd June 1948.
27. *Minutes of Meeting of Executive Committee of the N.A.P.O.*, 14th November 1947.
28. Criminal Justice Bill, 1948, as amended by Standing Committee.
29. Lords' Debates, 3rd June 1948.
30. Joan F. S. King (Ed.), *The Probation Service*, 2nd ed., 1964, page 33.
31. Lords' Debates, 3rd June 1948.
32. See, for example, J. Heywood, *Children in Care*, 2nd edition, 1965, pages 133–40 and 175–82.
33. J. Bowlby, *Maternal Care and Mental Health*, 1951.
34. H.O. 99/1953, 20th July 1953.
35. P. Parsloe, *The Work of the Probation and After-Care Officer*, 1967.
36. *Minutes of the General Purposes Sub-Committee of N.A.P.O.*, 7.3.52, 16.5.52, 12.9.52, and of the *Executive*

Committee, 13.6.52.

37. See pages 116–117.

38. Lords' Debates, 15th July 1952.

39. National Association of Probation Officers, *Evidence to the Committee on Children and Young Persons.*

40. *Minutes of the General Purposes Sub-Committee of N.A.P.O.*, 22.2.55.

41. *Report of the Committee on Children and Young Persons*, 1960, Cmnd. 1191, page 71.

42. Rule 49.

43. Rule 50.

44. Rule 51.

45. Rule 54.

46. Rule 48.

47. Parts II to V.

48. Rule 28.

49. *Report of the Departmental Committee on the Probation Service*, 1962, Cmnd. 1650, page 69.

50. Ibid.

51. *Probation*, Vol. 9, No. 2, June 1959, page 14.

52. Ibid.

53. Home Office, *Report on the Work of the Probation and After-Care Department, 1962 to 1965*, 1966, Cmnd. 3107, page 5.

54. *Report of the Departmental Committee on the Probation Service*, 1962, Cmnd. 1650, page 84.

55. Ibid., pages 73 and 74.

56. Ibid., page 28.

57. Ibid., page 29.

58. M. Grünhut, *Juvenile Offenders Before the Courts*, 1956, page 83.

59. *Report of the Departmental Committee on the Probation Service*, 1962, Cmnd. 1650, page 29.

60. *The Magistrate*, Vol. VIII, No. 18, Nov. 1949, pages 163 to 1966.

61. M. Grünhut, op. cit., 1956, Chapter III.

62. *Report of the Departmental Committee on the Probation Service*, 1962, Cmnd. 1950, page 101.

63. Home Office, *The Probation Service: Its Objects and Its Organisation*, 1952, page 20.

64. *Report of the Departmental Committee on the Probation Service*, 1962, Cmnd. 1650, page 101.

65. *Probation*, Vol. 5, No. 21, May/June 1949, page 269.

66. Ibid., Vol. 6, No. 2, March/April 1950, page 13.

67. *Report of the Departmental Committee on the Probation Service*, 1962, Cmnd. 1650, page 106.

68. *The Magistrate*, Vol. VIII, No. 16, July/August 1949, page 240.

69. *Report of the Departmental Committee on the Probation Service*, 1962, Cmnd. 1650, page 101.

70. *Probation*, Vol. 6, No. 1, Jan/Feb. 1950, page 11; *Report of the Departmental Committee on the Probation Service*, 1962, Cmnd. 1650, page 113.

71. *Probation*, Vol. 6, No. 1, Jan./Feb. 1950, page 11.

72. Home Office, *Probation as a Career*, 1952.

73. *Report of the Departmental Committee on the Probation Service*, 1962, Cmnd. 1650, page 113.

74. *Probation*, Vol. 9, No. 2, June 1959, pages 15 and 16.

75. Home Office, *Sixth Report on the Work of the Children's Department*, 1951, Appendix X.

76. Ibid., page 53.

77. A. Carr-Saunders, E. C. Rhodes, and H. Mannheim, *Young Offenders*, 1942, pages 158 and 159.

78. Home Office, *Sixth Report on the Work of the Children's Department*, 1951, pages 53 to 55.

79. Ibid., page 44.

80. Ibid., page 55.

81. S. 77.

82. Home Office, *Sixth Report on the Work of the Children's Department*, 1951, pages 55 and 56.

83. Home Office, *Seventh Report on the Work of the Children's Department*, 1955, page 461.

84. M. Grünhut, 'Probation as a Research Field, A Pilot Survey', in *The British Journal of Delinquency*, Vol. II, No. 4, April 1952, page 287.

85. Ibid.

86. University of Cambridge Faculty of Law, Department of Criminal Science, *The Results of Probation*, 1958, page 61.

87. Ibid., pages 2 to 4.

88. United Nations, *Practical Results and Financial Aspects of Adult Probation in Selected Countries*, 1954, page 16.

89. E. W. Hughes, 'An analysis of the records of some 750 probationers', *British Journal of Educational Psychology*, Vol. 35, 1945, pages 113 to 125.

90. M. Grünhut, 'Probation as a Research Field, A Pilot Survey', *British Journal of Delinquency*, Vol. II, No. 4, April 1952, page 300.

91. Leslie T. Wilkins, 'A Small Comparative Study of the Results of Probation', *The British Journal of Delinquency*, Vol. VIII, No. 3, January 1958, page 201.

92. *Probation*, Vol. 5, No. 21, May/June 1949, page 271.

93. Hansard, 19th February 1954.

94. Max Grünhut, *Probation and Mental Treatment*, 1963, pages 46 to 50.

95. Ibid., pages 37 and 40.

96. Cherry Morris (Ed.), *Social Casework in Britain*, 1950.

97. Ibid., pages 193 and 194.

98. *Probation*, Vol. 8, No. 5, March 1958, page 135.

99. Joan F. S. King (Ed.), *The Probation Service*, 1958.

100. Ibid., page 72.

101. Ibid., pages 71 and 72.

102. Ibid., page 74.

103. Ibid., page 73.

104. F. J. Macrae, 'The English Probation Training System' in *The British Journal of Delinquency*, Vol. VIII, No. 3, January 1958, page 212.

105. Ibid.

106. Ibid., page 213.

107. *Probation*, Vol. 8, No. 2, June 1956, page 22.

108. Ibid., Vol. 7, No. 9, May/June 1955, pages 99 and 100; Vol. 8, No. 2, June 1956, page 23.

109. Joan F. S. King (Ed.), op. cit., 1958.

110. *Probation*, Vol. 7, No. 6, Nov./Dec. 1954, page 65.

111. Ibid.

112. Ibid., No. 3, May/June 1954, page 27.

113. Ibid., Vol. 6, No. 21, May/June 1953, page 242; No. 14, March/April 1952, page 166.

114. Ibid., No. 10, July/Aug. 1951, page 117; No. 14, March/April 1952, page 166; No. 15, May/June 1952, page 173; No. 19, Jan./Feb. 1953, page 222; No. 21, May/June 1953, page 241.

115. Ibid., Vol. 8, No. 10, June 1958, page 146.

116. Ibid., Vol. 6, No. 13, Jan/Feb. 1952, page 148; No. 16, July/Aug. 1952, page 187.

117. National Association of Probation Officers, *Evidence to the Committee on Discharged Prisoners' Aid Societies*, 1951; and Home Office, Report of the Advisory Council on the Treatment of Offenders, *The After-Care and Supervision of Discharged Prisoners*, 1958, page 12.

118. S. 56(2), S. 21(3) and S. 57(1).

119. *Report of the Commissioners of Prisons and Directors of Convict Prisons for 1948*, Cmd. 7777, page 45.

120. *Report of the Commissioners of Prisons for the Year 1955*, Cmnd. 10,

269

page 28.

121. *Report of the Departmental Committee on the Social Services in Courts of Summary Jurisdiction*, 1936, Cmd. 5122, page 88.

122. A suggestion made in *The Howard Journal*, Vol. IX, No. 4, 1957, page 282.

123. Gordon Rose, *Schools for Young Offenders*, 1967, page 75.

124. Home Office, *Sixth Report of the Work of the Children's Department*, 1951, page 67. The Children and Young Persons (Amendment) Act, 1952, gave power to Children's Committees to do this work, thus giving legal sanction to what had been unofficial practice since 1948.

125. Home Office, *Seventh Report on the Work of the Children's Department*, 1955, pages 63 and 64.

126. *The Magistrate*, Vol. VIII, No. 17, Sept./Oct. 1949, pages 245 and 246; Vol. VIII, No. 18, Nov./Dec. 1949, pages 273 and 274; Vol. IX, No. 14, March/April 1952, pages 186 and 187.

127. B. L. Q. Henriques, *The Indiscretions of a Magistrate*, 1950, page 156, and *The Magistrate*, Vol. IX, No. 14, March/April 1952, pages 186 and 187.

128. *The Magistrate*, Vol. VIII, No. 18, Nov./Dec. 1949, pages 273 and 274 and Vol. IX, No. 14, March/April 1952, pages 186 and 187.

129. Home Office, *Seventh Report on the Work of the Children's Department*, 1955, pages 63 and 64.

130. *Report of the Committee on Children and Young Persons*, 1960, Cmnd. 1191, pages 137 and 138.

131. *Report of the Committee on Discharged Prisoners' Aid Societies*, 1953, Cmd. 8879, Chapter 1.

132. Ibid., Warrant of Appointment.

133. Report of Howard League Conference, *British Journal of Delinquency*, Vol. II, No. 1, July 1951, pages 64 and 65.

134. *Report of the Committee on Discharged Prisoners' Aid Societies*, 1953, Cmnd. 8879, page 19.

135. Ibid., page 18.

136. Ibid., page 19.

137. Ibid.

138. Ibid., page 23.

139. Ibid., page 25.

140. *Report of the Commissioners of Prisons for the Year, 1953*, Cmnd. 9259, page 63.

141. *Report of the Commissioners of Prisons for the Year, 1956*, Cmnd. 322, page 80.

142. *Report of the Commissioners of Prisons for the Year, 1960*, Cmnd. 1467, page 25.

143. *Report of the Commissioners of Prisons for the Year, 1961*, Cmnd. 1798, page 27.

144. *Report of the Committee on Discharged Prisoners' Aid Societies*, 1953, Cmnd. 8879, page 25.

145. *The Howard Journal*, Vol. IX, No. 4, 1957, page 280.

146. Home Office, Report of the Advisory Council on the Treatment of Offenders, *The After-Care and Supervision of Discharged Prisoners*, 1958, page 2.

147. Hansard, 17th March 1958.

148. Home Office, Report of the Advisory Council on the Treatment of Offenders, *The After-Care and Supervision of Discharged Prisoners*, 1958, pages 9 to 11.

149. Ibid., page 21.

150. Ibid., page 12.

151. Home Office, *Penal Practice in a Changing Society*, 1959, Cmnd. 645.

152. Ibid.

153. Home Office, Report of the Advisory Council on the Treatment of Offenders, *The Treatment of Young Offenders*, 1959, page 22.

154. Ibid.
155. Criminal Justice Bill, 1960, Cl. 20.
156. Criminal Justice Act, 1961, S. 20 and 3rd Schedule.
157. Ibid., S. 13 and 1st Schedule.
158. Criminal Justice Act, 1967, 7th Schedule.
159. *The British Journal of Delinquency*, Vol. II, No. 1, July 1951, page 67.
160. Criminal Justice Act, 1948, S. 17.
161. First Offenders Act, 1958, S. 1.
162. Probation Division of the Home Office, 'Probation Today and To-morrow', *The Howard Journal*, Vol. IX, No. 3, page 249.
163. Home Office, Report of the Advisory Council on the Treatment of Offenders, *Alternatives to Short Terms of Imprisonment*, 1957, page 18.
164. Ibid.
165. *Report of the Committee on Children and Young Persons*, 1960, Cmnd. 1191, page 70.
166. H. Prins, 'Social Enquiries and the Adult Courts', *The British Journal of Delinquency*, Vol. VIII, No. 3, January 1958, pages 228 to 229.
167. H.O. Circular, 83/1963.
168. *Report of the Inter-Departmental Committee on the Business of the Criminal Courts*, 1961, Cmnd. 1289, pages 76 and 77.
169. Ibid., pages 77 to 85.
170. *Probation*, Vol. 9, No. 10, June 1961, pages 144 to 147.
171. Ibid., pages 92 to 97.
172. Ibid., pages 99 to 102.
173. Ibid., page 101.
174. *Final Report of the Committee on Procedure in Matrimonial Causes*, 1947, Cmd. 7024, page 5.
175. Ibid., page 7.
176. Ibid., pages 8 and 9.
177. *Report of the Departmental Committee on Grants for the Development of Marriage Guidance*, 1948, Cmd. 7566.

178. Ibid., page 6.
179. Ibid.
180. *Final Report of the Committee on Procedure in Matrimonial Causes*, 1947, Cmd. 7024, page 14.
181. Gerald Sanctuary, *Marriage Under Stress*, 1968, Chapter 1.
182. Ibid., pages 14 and 27; W. L. Herbert and F. V. Jarvis, *A Modern Approach to Marriage Counselling*, 1959, cover; and D. R. Mace, *Marriage Counselling*, 1948, page 16.
183. *Probation*, Vol. 8, No. 4, December 1956, page 57; and Vol. 8, No. 1, March 1956, page 4.
185. *Final Report of the Committee on Procedure in Matrimonial Causes*, 1947, Cmd. 7024, pages 14 and 15.
186. Ibid., page 19.
187. *Probation*, Vol. 6, No. 8, March/April 1951, page 91.
188. Home Office, *The Probation Service: Its Objects and Its Organisation*, 1952, page 17.
189. *Report of the Royal Commission on Marriage and Divorce*, 1956, Cmd. 9678, page 109.
190. Matrimonial Causes Bill, 1951.
191. *Royal Commission on Marriage and Divorce*, 1956, Cmd. 9678, pages 99 and 100.
192. Ibid., pages 104 to 109.
193. *Final Report of the Committee on Procedure in Matrimonial Causes*, 1947, Cmd. 7024, page 20.
194. Ibid., pages 109 and 110.
195. Ibid., page 111.
196. S. 6(1) and (2).
197. S. 2(1)(f).
198. Cl. 5(2).
199. Lords' Debates, 24th October, 1956.
200. *Probation, (No. 2) Rules*, 1959.
201. See page 197.
202. Minutes of Meetings of Salaries and Services Sub-Committee, N.A.P.O., 30.6.54 and 2.9.55.

271

203. *Probation*, Vol. 5, No. 20. March/ April 1949, page 257.

204. Ibid., Vol. 6, No. 2, March/April 1950, page 21.

205. Minutes of Meeting of National Executive Committee of the National Association of Probation Officers, 27th February 1959.

206. Minutes of Meeting of General Purposes Sub-Committee of the National Association of Probation Officers, 16th May 1952.

207. Minutes of Meeting of National Executive Committee of the National Association of Probation Officers, 7th March 1958.

208. Ibid., 1st June 1956.

209. Ibid., 11th February 1955 and 13th December 1957.

210. Ibid., 4th March 1949.

211. Replaced in 1961 by representatives of the newly constituted Central Council of Probation Committees.

212. *Report of the Departmental Committee on the Probation Service*, 1962, Cmnd. 1650, pages 133 and 134.

213. Minutes of Meetings of Salaries and Services Sub-Committee of the National Association of Probation Officers, 7th July 1950 and 30th August 1950.

214. Ibid., 20.7.50 to 12.12.50.

215. N.A.P.O., Press Release immediately preceding the publication of the report of the Departmental Committee on the Probation Service, 12th March 1962.

216. Minutes of Meeting of Salaries and Services Sub-Committee of N.A.P.O., 9.8.56.

217. Minutes of Meeting of Executive Committee of N.A.P.O., 12.2.54.

218. *Annual Report of the N.A.P.O.*, 1956.

219. *Probation*, Vol. 7, No. 9, May/June 1955, page 98; Vol. 8, No. 2, June 1956, page 22; Vol. 8, No. 10. June 1958, page 147.

220. Hansard, 2nd July 1956.

221. Ibid., 19th July 1956.

222. *N.A.P.O. Notes*, No. 6, June 1957.

223. Hansard, 6th February 1958.

224. Ibid.

225. Ibid., pages 133 and 134.

226. *Report of the Departmental Committee on the Probation Service*, 1962, Cmnd. 1650, page 102.

227. *Annual Report of the N.A.P.O.*, 1958.

228. Minutes of Meeting of National Executive Committee of N.A.P.O., 7.3.58 and 13.3.58.

229. Hansard, 6th and 13th February, 13th and 17th March, 15th May, 17th and 29th July, and 3rd, 9th, 10th and 11th December 1958.

230. Ibid., 13th March 1958.

231. F. Dawtry, 'Whither Probation?', *The British Journal of Delinquency*, Vol. VIII, No. 3, January 1958, pages 180–187.

232. *Probation*, Vol. 8, No. 10, June 1958, page 152.

233. Ibid., page 147.

234. Hansard, 31st October 1958.

235. Ibid., 11th December 1968.

236. Ibid.

237. Ibid., 2nd February 1959.

CHAPTER 9

1. *Report of the Departmental Committee on the Probation Service*, 1962, Cmnd. 1650, page 1.

2. National Association of Probation

Officers, *Annual Report, 1959.*

3. *Report of the Departmental Committee on the Probation Service*, 1962, Cmnd. 1650, pages 23 to 26.
4. Ibid., page 44.
5. Ibid., page 10.
6. Ibid., page 63.
7. Ibid., pages 11 to 13.
8. Ibid., pages 13 and 14.
9. National Association of Probation Officers, *Memorandum of Evidence to the Departmental Committee on the Probation Service*, Part 1.
10. *Report of the Departmental Committee on the Probation Service*, 1962, Cmnd. 1650, pages 14 to 15.
11. Ibid., page 14.
12. Ibid., pages 17 and 18.
13. Ibid., pages 28 to 29.
14. Ibid., pages 31 to 33.
15. Ibid., pages 39 to 44.
16. Ibid., pages 41 to 44.
17. Ibid., page 42.
18. Ibid., page 51.
19. Ibid.
20. Ibid., pages 55 to 57.
21. Ibid., page 62.
22. Ibid., pages 63 and 64.
23. Ibid., pages 66 to 68.
24. Ibid., pages 66 and 67.
25. Ibid., pages 69 and 70.
26. Ibid., pages 75 to 79.
27. Ibid., page 77.
28. Ibid., pages 71 and 72.
29. Ibid., pages 73 and 74.
30. Ibid., pages 81 and 82.
31. Ibid., page 84.
32. Ibid., page 85.
33. Ibid., pages 88 and 89.
34. Ibid., pages 88 to 91.
35. Ibid., page 91.
36. Ibid., pages 107 and 110.
37. N.A.P.O., *Memorandum of Evidence to the Departmental Committee on the Probation Service*, 1959/60, Part 3.
38. *Report of the Departmental Committee on the Probation Service*, 1962, Cmnd. 1650, pages 106 and 107.
39. Ibid., page 107.
40. Ibid., pages 138 to 139.
41. Ibid., page 141.
42. Ibid., page 143.
43. Ibid., page 110.
44. Ibid., pages 134 and 136.
45. Ibid., pages 112 and 113.
46. Minutes of Meeting National Executive Committee of N.A.P.O., 29th March 1962.
47. N.A.P.O., *Memorandum of Evidence to the Departmental Committee on the Probation Service*, 1959/60, Part 3.
48. *Report of the Departmental Committee on the Probation Service*, 1962, Cmnd. 1650, page 116.
49. Ibid., page 115.
50. Ibid., pages 119 and 120.
51. N.A.P.O., *Memorandum of Evidence to the Departmental Committee on the Probation Service*, 1959/60, Part 3.
52. *Report of the Departmental Committee on the Probation Service*, 1962, Cmnd. 1650, pages 120 and 121.
53. Ibid., pages 121 to 122.
54. *Second Report of the Departmental Committee on the Probation Service*, 1962, Cmnd. 1800, page 7.
55. Ibid., page 9.
56. Ibid., pages 12 and 13.
57. Ibid., pages 14 to 16.
58. Ibid., page 17.
59. Home Office, *Report on the Work of the Probation and After-Care Department, 1962 to 1965*, 1966, Cmnd. 3107, page 1.
60. Home Office, Report of the Advisory Council on the Treatment of Offenders, *The Organisation of After-Care*, 1963, pages 30 and 31.
61. Ibid., pages 16 to 20.
62. Ibid., pages 21, and 29 to 31.
63. Ibid., page 83.
64. Ibid., page 31.

273

65. Home Office, *Report on the Work of the Probation and After-Care Department 1962 to 1965*, 1966, Cmnd. 3107, page 3.

66. Home Office, *Report of the Advisory Council on the Treatment of Offenders, The Organisation of After-Care*, 1963, pages 21 and 43 to 46.

67. Home Office, *Report on the Work of the Probation and After-Care Department, 1966 to 1968*, 1969, Cmnd. 4233, page 42.

68. Under *The Probation Rules*, 1965, Rule 30.

69. Home Office, *Report on the Work of the Probation and After-Care Department, 1962 to 1965*, 1966, Cmnd. 3107, page 45.

70. Ibid., page 4.

71. Home Office, Report of the Advisory Council on the Treatment of Offenders, *The Organisation of After-Care*, 1963, pages 41 and 42.

72. H.O. Circular 144/1965, June 1965.

73. Criminal Justice Act, 1967, S. 95.

74. N.A.P.O. and Conference of Principal Probation Officers, *Memorandum of Evidence*, 1961.

75. Home Office, Report of the Advisory Council on the Treatment of Offenders, *The Organisation of After-Care*, 1963, pages 23 and 24.

76. Hansard, 14th July 1965.

77. Home Office, *Report on the Work of the Probation and After-Care Department, 1962 to 1965*, 1966, Cmnd. 3107, pages 37 and 38, and *Report on the Work of the Probation and After-Care Department, 1966 to 1968*, 1969, Cmnd. 4233, pages 22, 43 and 46.

78. Home Office, *Report on the Work of the Probation and After-Care Department, 1966 to 1968*, 1969, Cmnd. 4233, pages 45 and 46.

79. R. L. Morrison, *Stresses of Change in Probation and After-Care*, Second Dennis Carroll Memorial Lecture, 1969, pages 45 to 46; Home Office, *Explorations in After-Care*, 1971, pages 6 to 11.

80. Home Office, Report of the Advisory Council on the Treatment of Offenders, *The Organisation of After-Care*, 1963, page 35.

81. H.O. Circular, 238/1965, 2nd November 1965.

82. G. M. Aves, *The Voluntary Worker in the Social Services*, 1969, page 15.

83. Home Office, *The Place of Voluntary Service in After-Care*, 1967, pages 1 to 9.

84. Home Office, *Report on the Work of the Probation and After-Care Department, 1969 to 1971*, 1972, Cmnd. 5158, page 45.

85. House of Commons, *First Report from the Expenditure Committee, Session 1971–72, Probation and After-Care*, H.C. 47, page xi.

86. *Observations by the Government on the First Report from the Expenditure Committee, Session 1971–72*, 1972, Cmnd. 4968, page 5.

87. R. L. Morrison, *Stresses of Change in Probation and After-Care*, Second Dennis Carroll Memorial Lecture, 1969.

88. Cmnd. 2952, pages 3 and 4.

89. National Association of Probation Officers, *Second Memorandum of Evidence to the Royal Commission on the Penal System*, 1955, page 5.

90. National Association of Probation Officers, *Observations on the White Paper, 'The Adult Offender'*, 1966.

91. Minutes of Meeting of the Executive Committee of the National Association of Probation Officers, 6th January 1967.

92. Hansard, 12th December 1966.

93. Lords' Debates, 12th June 1967.

94. Hansard, 12th December 1966; Lords' Debates, 10th May and 12th

June 1967.

95. Lords' Debates, 10th May 1967.

96. Hansard, 12th December 1966.

97. Ibid.

98. Ibid., 26th April 1967.

99. Lords' Debates, 12th June 1967.

100. Home Office, *Report on the Work of the Probation and After-Care Department, 1966 to 1968*, 1969, Cmnd. 4233, page 54.

101. Criminal Justice Act, 1967, S. 53.

102. Ibid., S. 54.

103. Ibid., S. 51.

104. Ibid., S. 54(3).

105. Ibid., S. 55.

106. Hansard, 26th April 1967.

107. H.O. Circular, 138/1963.

108. H.O. Circulars 188/1968, 189/1968, 59/1971.

109. Home Office, *Report on the Work of the Probation and After-Care Department, 1962 to 1965*, 1966, Cmnd. 3107, page 83; and *Report on the Work of the Probation and After-Care Department, 1966 to 1968*, 1969, Cmnd. 4233, page 79; *Report on the Work of the Probation and After-Care Department, 1969 to 1971*, 1972, Cmnd. 5158, Appendix D.

110. Home Office, *Report on the Work of the Probation and After-Care Department, 1962 to 1965*, 1966, Cmnd. 3107, pages 26 and 84: and *Report on the Work of the Probation and After-Care Department, 1966 to 1968*, 1969, Cmnd. 4233, pages 31 and 80.

111. House of Commons, *First Report from the Expenditure Committee, Session 1971–72, Probation and After-Care*, H.C. 47, pages v, ix and x.

112. See pages 234–236.

113. *Observations by the Government on the First Report from the Expenditure Committee, Session 1971–72*, 1972, Cmnd. 4968, page 4.

114. House of Commons, *First Report from the Expenditure Committee, Session 1971–72, Probation and After-Care*, H.C. 47, page vii.

115. Home Office, *Report on the Work of the Probation and After-Care Department, 1962 to 1965*, 1966, Cmnd. 3107, page 12.

116. Home Office, *Report on the Work of the Probation and After-Care Department, 1966 to 1968*, 1969, Cmnd. 4233, page 13; and *Report of the Departmental Committee on the Probation Service*, 1962, Cmnd. 1650, page 102; *Report on the Work of the Probation and After-Care Department, 1969 to 1971*, 1972, Cmnd. 5158, pages 14 to 15.

117. Home Office, *Report on the Work of the Probation and After-Care Department, 1966 to 1968*, 1969, Cmnd. 4233, page 12; *Report on the Work of the Probation and After-Care Department, 1962 to 1965*, 1966, Cmnd. 3107, pages 13 to 15; *Report on the Work of the Probation and After-Care Department, 1969 to 1971*, 1972, Cmnd. 5158, pages 14 to 17.

118. Department of Employment, *Report of the Butterworth Inquiry into the Work and Pay of Probation Officers and Social Workers*, 1972, Cmnd. 5076, page 7.

119. Ibid., page 41.

120. Home Office, *Reports on the Work of the Probation and After-Care Department, 1962 to 1965*, 1966, Cmnd. 3107, pages 49 to 58; *1966 to 1968*, 1969, Cmnd. 4233, pages 16 to 25, and *1969 to 1971*, 1972, Cmnd. 5158, pages 21 to 23.

121. Home Office, *Report on the Work of the Probation and After-Care Department, 1962 to 1965*, 1966, Cmnd. 3107, page 3; and *Report on the Work of the Probation and After-Care Department, 1966 to 1968*, 1969, Cmnd. 4233, pages 1 and 2.

122. Probation Rules, 1965; Probation

275

Rules, 1972.

123. Home Office, *Report on the Work of the Probation and After-Care Department, 1966 to 1968*, 1969, Cmnd. 4233, page 2.

124. Home Office, *Report on the Work of the Probation and After-Care Department, 1962 to 1965*, 1966, Cmnd. 3107, pages 5 and 6; and *Report of the Work of the Probation and After-Care Department, 1966 to 1968*, 1969, Cmnd. 4233, pages 3 and 4.

125. Home Office, *Report on the Work of the Probation and After-Care Service, 1962 to 1965*, 1966, Cmnd. 3107, pages 7 and 8.

126. Ibid., pages 61 and 62; and *Report on the Work of the Probation and After-Care Department, 1966 to 1968*, 1969, Cmnd. 4233, pages 8 and 10.

127. *Report of the Committee on Children and Young Persons*, 1960, Cmnd. 1191, page 19.

128. S. 1(1).

129. Home Office, *The Child, The Family and The Young Offender*, 1965, Cmnd. 2742.

130. The Labour Party, *Crime—A Challenge to Us All*, 1964, pages 1 and 21.

131. Home Office, *The Child, The Family and The Young Offender*, 1965, Cmnd. 2742, pages 5 to 9.

132. Ibid., page 4.

133. Home Office, *Children in Trouble*, 1968, Cmnd. 3601, page 3.

134. Observations by N.A.P.O. on *The Child, The Family and The Young Offender*, 6th October 1965.

135. Scottish Education Department and Scottish Home and Health Department, *Social Work and the Community*, 1966, Cmnd. 3065.

136. Home Office, *Children in Trouble*, 1968, Cmnd. 3601, pages 6 and 7.

137. *Report of the Committee on Local Authority and Allied Personal Social Services*, 1968, Cmnd. 3703, page 78.

138. Ibid., pages 44 to 51.

139. Local Authority Social Services Act, 1970.

140. N.A.P.O., *Annual Report for 1963*.

141. *Probation*, Vol. 13, No. 1, March 1967, page 4.

142. N.A.P.O., *Annual Report for 1967*.

143. N.A.P.O., *Newsletter*, No. 50, May 1969.

144. Under the Health Visiting and Social Work (Training) Act, 1962, as amended by Statutory Instruments 1221 and 1224, 1971.

145. Home Office, *Report on the Work of the Probation and After-Care Department, 1969 to 1971*, 1972, Cmnd. 5158, page 7.

146. *Probation*, Vol. 19, No. 1, March 1973, page 4.

147. Children and Young Persons Bill, 1969, Cl. 13.

148. Ibid., Cl. 13(2) and Cl. 9(1).

149. *Report of the Committee on Local Authority and Allied Personal Social Services*, 1968, Cmnd. 3703, page 78.

150. Hansard, 11th March 1969.

151. Children and Young Persons Bill, 1969, Cl. 13(2).

152. Lords' Debates, 19th June 1969.

153. Minutes of Annual General Meeting of the National Association of Probation Officers, 29th March 1969.

154. Hansard, 9th June 1969.

155. Ibid.

156. Children and Young Persons Bill, 1969, Cl. 12 and 19.

157. Hansard, 9th June 1969.

158. Schedule 5.

159. Hansard, 9th June 1969; and Parliamentary Debates, House of Commons Official Report, Standing Committee G, Children and Young Persons Bill, Sixth Sitting, 17th April 1969 and Seventh Sitting, 22nd April 1969.

160. Hansard, 9th June 1969.

161. Lords' Debates, 19th June 1969.

162. Home Office, *People in Prison,* 1969, Cmnd. 4214, pages 10–19.
163. Home Office, *Report on the Work of the Probation and After-Care Department, 1969 to 1971,* 1972, Cmnd. 5158, page 2.
164. Home Office, Report of the Advisory Council on the Penal System, *Non-Custodial and Semi-Custodial Penalties,* 1970.
165. Ibid., pages vi, 63, 64 and 70.
166. Ibid., pages 12 to 21.
167. Ibid., pages 62 to 63.
168. Ibid., page 63.
169. Hansard, 22nd November 1971.
170. Criminal Justice Bill, 1971, Cl. 14.
171. Ibid., Cl. 11.
172. Ibid., Cl. 19.
173. Ibid., Cl. 38.
174. Hansard, 25th May and 15th June 1972; and House of Commons Official Report, Standing Committee G, 10th February 1972.
175. *Probation,* Vol. 16, No. 3, November 1970; Vol. 18, No. 1, March 1972.
176. House of Commons, *First Report from the Expenditure Committee, Session 1971–1972, Probation and After-Care,* H.C. 47, page 3.
177. Ibid., page xxv.
178. See page 31.

SUBJECT INDEX

Adult courts, 58, 191–2, 228
Adult offenders, 17, 24, 34–5, 40, 45, 194, 225, 237
Advise, assist and befriend, 30, 169, 181, 252
Advisory Committee on Probation, 88, 90–92, 106, 112, 146
  on Probation and After-Care, 112–13, 121, 130, 131, 150, 151, 153, 162
Advisory Council: for Probation and After-Care, 222, 234
  on the Treatment of Offenders, 164, 187, 189, 190–2, 209, 220–2, 224, 237, 239
After-care, 106, 108, 112, 142, 150, 168, 173, 182, 184–91, 196, 209, 220–5, 228, 230, 231, 234
Age, of offender, 7, 26, 28, 34, 147, 156, 166
Almoners, 86, 114, 143, 183
Alternatives to imprisonment, 1, 2, 3, 6, 7, 15–16, 34, 43, 112, 176, 193
Alternatives to Short Terms of Imprisonment, 192
America, 3, 18, 121, 122
  see also United States
Approved School after-care, 142, 173, 185–6, 209, 222
Approved Schools, 115, 138, 142, 185, 186
Assistant Probation Officers, 113, 144
Assize Courts, 27, 102, 111, 152, 174
Association of Municipal Corporations, 79, 201, 211
Attendance centres, 176
Aylesbury Association, 184

Bail, 3, 4, 6, 7
  hostels, 239
Binding over, 110, 147, 156, 159, 166
Birmingham, 4, 5, 11, 28, 48, 86, 113, 122
Borough council, 27, 88
Boroughs, 104, 174
Borstal, 58, 66, 142, 147, 184, 190, 223, 227
  after-care, 142, 173, 184–5, 209, 221
  Association, 108, 142, 184
Boston, Massachusetts, 6, 7
British Association of Social Workers, 234

Cambridge University, Department of Criminal Science, 179
Care Committee Organisers, 143
Case committees, 54, 132, 133, 157, 167, 174, 209, 214
Case-loads, 121, 163, 183, 215, 229
Casework, 53, 121, 122, 143, 173, 180–5, 187, 200, 206–7, 209, 213, 214–18, 226, 233
  supervision, 182, 183, 214, 230
Catholic Aid Society, 45
Catholic Marriage Advisory Council, 197
Central After-Care Association, 173, 185, 188–9, 221
Central Association for the Aid of Discharged Convicts, 184
Central authority, 43, 87, 90, 128, 133, 152, 162, 175, 201, 212, 215, 217, 218
Central control, 30, 78, 88, 95, 101, 105, 128, 164, 173, 211–13, 217

Central Council for Education and Training in Social Work, 234
Central Council of Probation and After-Care Committees, 235, 238
Central Council of Probation Committees, 206
Central Police Court Mission, 71–2, 93, 96, 154
Character, of offender, 13, 18, 26, 28, 115, 140, 156, 192, 225
Charitable organisations, 19, 139
Charity Organisation Society, 25, 36, 85, 86, 114, 125, 143
Chief Constable, 11, 45, 46, 53, 73, 113, 124
Chief Metropolitan Magistrate, 11, 24, 33, 38, 42, 49, 50
Chief probation officers, 49, 54, 65, 109
    see also Superintendent and Principal Probation Officers
Child care service, 171–2, 185–6, 199, 200, 217, 222, 232–6
Children Act, 1908, 47, 58
Children and Young Persons Acts:
    1932, 140
    1933, 140, 172
    1963, 231
    1969, 229
Children and Young Persons (Amendment) Bill, 1952, 172
Children and Young Persons Bills:
    1931, 114–17
    1969, 234
Children Bill, 1930, 114
Children in Trouble, 233–4
Children's Courts, 110
Children's courts, 17, 20, 22, 58, 110
    Departments, see Child care service
Church Army, 35, 40, 46, 87
Church of England, 70, 82
Church of England Temperance Society: 20, 37, 60, 79, 89–91, 93, 96–7, 103, 113, 137
    and police court missionaries, 6, 19, 36
    and provision of probation officers, 24, 36, 37, 39, 41, 45, 52, 60, 66, 67, 71–4, 81–3, 91–4, 110, 114, 135–7
Church of England Total Abstinence Society, 20
Clarke Hall Fellowship, 120, 130, 165
Clerks of the Peace, 124, 153, 177
Clerks to the justices, see Justices' Clerks
Colleges of Further Education, 218
Combination, 81, 96, 103, 128, 131–2, 138, 152, 161, 174–5, 212, 213, 214, 220, 230–1
Combined areas, 98, 104, 128, 132, 133, 138, 157
Commissioner of the Metropolitan Police, 11, 24, 25, 34
Committee on National Expenditure (Geddes), 85, 95
Committee on Wage-Earning Children, 20, 35, 41, 47–8, 62
Community, 3, 4, 5, 10, 19, 51, 58, 184, 197, 220, 222, 224, 226, 236, 237, 240
Community service orders, 237, 238
Conciliation, see Matrimonial conciliation
Condition of residence, 50, 106–7, 112, 115, 133, 155, 156, 238
    see also Residence with probation
Conditions of licence, 191, 225
    of probation, 13, 18, 27, 29, 30, 43, 50, 61, 65, 66, 106, 148, 156, 236
Confirmation of appointments, 99, 175, 213, 230
Conservative government, 97, 105, 237
Contamination, 2, 16, 142, 185
Contribution towards maintenance, 99, 108, 112, 149
Conviction, 7, 15, 23, 26–7, 107, 111, 114, 148, 149, 159, 167, 169
Counties, 131, 175
County boroughs, 131, 174, 175, 178
    borough councils, 201
    councils, 27, 47, 88, 178, 201
    Councils Association, 79, 201
    districts, 104
Court welfare officers, 197–9
Courts, relationship with probation service, 211

Crime, 1, 2, 9, 10, 11, 12, 31, 68, 171, 175, 178, 189, 190, 191, 215, 231, 237, 239
Criminal courts, 193, 232
Criminal Justice Acts:
  1925, 103, 105, 108, 111, 122, 125, 126, 127, 128, 149, 154, 157, 212
  1948, 170, 173, 176, 178, 184, 191, 236
  1961, 271
  1967, 191, 238
  1972, 240
Criminal Justice Administration Act, 1914, 67, 96, 106, 115
Criminal Justice Administration Bill, 1914, 61, 65–7
Criminal Justice Bills:
  1925, 97–9, 103
  1938, 156, 158–60, 165
  1947/8, 166–7, 201
  1960, 190–1
  1966, 225, 238
Criminal Justice Bills (H.L.):
  1923, 96
  1924, 96
Criminology, 178, 180, 182, 190
Croydon, 61, 62

Day training centres, 238–9
Denominational test, 110
Departmental Committees:
  on Prisons, 23, 58
  on the Probation of Offenders Act, 1907, 49–59, 61, 62, 65, 79, 85, 87, 134
  on the Probation Service (Morison Committee), 207–20, 222, 228–31
  on the Social Services in Courts of Summary Jurisdiction, 124–58, 166, 168, 174, 175, 185, 211, 213
  on the Training, Appointment and Payment of Probation Officers, 79–99, 102, 104, 105, 106, 124, 126, 133, 134, 137, 148
  on the Treatment of Young Offenders, 105–12, 114, 115, 122, 124, 130, 138, 147
Detention centre after-care, 173, 191, 221
Detention centres, 166, 176, 190, 191, 193, 223
Direct entrants, 177, 213, 216, 230
Directory of probation officers, 55, 61, 72, 153
Discharge, 6, 12, 208, 227
Discharged Prisoners' Aid Societies: 13, 79, 185, 187–8, 201
Dismissal, 10, 15, 26, 110, 147, 156, 159, 166
Divorce, 195, 198, 199
  courts, 197, 198, 199, 200
Domestic proceedings, 153
Dual control, 39, 68, 72–3, 109–10, 128, 135–6, 148, 150

Education, Authorities, 112, 115, 116, 117, 141, 158, 172
  Minister of, 171, 178
Enquiries, 18, 36, 54, 63–4, 93, 105–7, 116–17, 140–1, 159, 161, 168, 172, 192–5, 198
  see alo Social enquiries; and Investigations
Entrants, 104, 144, 145, 146, 152, 218, 229
  see also Direct entrants
Escort, of children, 109, 112, 114, 122
Exchequer, 47, 56, 78, 88, 94, 196, 197, 198, 212

Families, 5, 139, 171, 187, 210, 224, 225, 232
Family, service, 231, 233
  Welfare Association, 197
Federation of Local Free Church Councils, 40
Fines, 3, 8, 19, 41, 46, 53, 108, 141, 156, 209, 238
Fining, 176
First Offenders, 2, 7, 10–13, 26, 28, 51, 192

First Offenders Act, 1958, 271

Geddes Axe, 84–5
Graduates, 216, 229
Grants, government, 47, 56, 66, 78, 88–9, 94–7, 101, 104, 105, 113, 129, 145, 154, 155, 157, 161, 168, 196, 197, 198, 206
Guardian, 4, 5
  ad litem, 143

Handbook of Probation, 131, 181
Health, of offender, 26, 115, 140, 166
Hierarchical structure, 173, 214, 231
Higher courts, 26, 102, 113, 114, 148, 152, 174, 176, 193, 195, 215, 239
Home Office, 62, 63, 64, 69, 73, 74, 75, 78, 79, 88–90, 91–7, 104, 112, 119, 124, 127–30, 135, 148, 149, 150, 152–8, 161–5, 174, 178–9, 192, 198, 201, 205, 212, 220–4, 227
  and a grant for probation, 47, 78, 95–6
  and the remuneration of probation officers, 76–7, 80, 84, 96, 101, 127, 201
  and reports on the work of the probation service, 87, 91, 130, 213
  and training, 113, 151, 162, 177, 182, 217–19, 230
  circulars, 14–15, 59, 62–4, 70–2, 77, 111, 127, 128, 140, 141, 159, 222, 228, 239
  contact with the probation service in the provinces, 45–7, 87–8, 128–9, 175, 213
  see also Home Secretary
Home Office, schools, *see* Approved schools
Home Secretary, 2, 7, 9, 35, 37, 44, 48, 66, 70–1, 93, 98–9, 103, 130, 179, 203–4, 228
  as authority for the Metropolitan Police Court District, 33, 39–41, 44–5, 49, 59, 72, 76, 201, 214
  as central authority, 30, 42–4, 46, 87, 95, 98–9, 101, 104, 152, 202, 204, 217, 230
  see also Home Office
Home surroundings reports, *see* Social enquiries
Home visiting, 139, 160, 173
Homes, 105, 107–8, 112, 148, 167
  see also Probation homes
Hostel for probation trainees, 154–5, 218–9
Hostels, 105, 108, 112, 148, 167, 238
  see also Probation hostels
House of Commons Expenditure Committee, 225, 228, 240
Howard Association, 2, 7–9, 14–17, 22, 30, 47–8, 62, 65, 72, 80, 85
Howard League for Penal Reform, 79–80, 89, 91, 94, 114, 116, 124, 135, 206

Imprisonment, 1–4, 10–12, 15, 18, 28, 141, 143, 156, 166, 176, 189, 191, 192, 195, 225, 227, 240
  of children, 2, 3, 7, 16, 34
Industrial Schools, 3, 9, 66, 107
  officers, 6, 40, 114
Ingleby Committee (Children and Young Persons), 172, 186, 207, 222, 231
Inspection, 104, 105, 107, 108, 129–30, 162, 213, 223, 234
  of institutions, 112, 115, 156
Inspectorate, 88, 129, 164, 175, 213, 223, 230
Inspectors, 42, 129, 130, 135, 150, 163, 175, 218, 230
Institutional treatment, 15, 95, 107–8
Institutions, 16, 19, 105, 107, 113, 115, 122, 145, 156, 168, 224, 240
Integration, 211, 212, 224, 233, 234
Inter-Departmental Committee on the Business of the Criminal Courts, 193–5, 207, 228, 231
Intermediate treatment, 236
Investigations, 8, 121, 124, 128, 153, 199
  see also Enquiries *and* Social Enquiries

Joint Negotiating Committee for the Probation Service, 201–3
Joint University Council for Social Studies, 125, 143, 144, 206
Judges, 3, 14, 151, 153, 197, 198, 199, 211, 215
Judiciary, 130, 134, 205
Justice and the child, 68
Justices, 43, 48, 51, 59, 73, 74, 77, 79, 80, 81, 82, 89, 91, 103, 118, 132, 150, 222
  and appointment of probation officers, 42, 45–7, 80, 81
  and payment of probation officers, 27, 77, 80, 90, 95
  see also Magistrates
Justices' Clerks, 14, 43, 47, 51, 52, 53, 77, 90, 118, 121, 124, 126, 129, 133, 150, 177
  Incorporated Society of, 94, 124, 130, 135, 206
Juvenile courts, 47, 48, 62–3, 68, 99, 106, 107, 111, 115, 116, 120, 122, 140, 158, 172, 192, 193, 228, 232, 233, 236
  see also Children's courts
  delinquency, 67, 171, 176, 232
  offenders: *see* Young offenders
  Organisations Committees, 67
Juvenile Courts and Probation, 69

Labour government, 96, 97, 166, 231
Lancashire, 11, 174
Liberal government, 3, 7, 23–7, 31, 37, 58
Liverpool, 11, 22, 39, 45, 53, 73, 86, 113, 191
  Ladies Temperance Association, 45, 73
Local Authorities, 20, 44, 47, 66, 79, 83, 85, 88, 89, 90, 95, 98, 99, 103, 104, 108, 112, 115, 117, 129, 134, 140, 155, 156, 168, 172, 175, 186, 193, 205, 206, 211, 212, 214, 229, 231, 232, 233, 235, 236
Lodgings, 149, 155
London, 5, 20, 25, 33, 35, 39, 40, 44–5, 49, 56, 57, 59, 79, 84, 85, 88, 91, 92, 143, 160, 169, 179, 198, 199, 214–15, 230
London Police Court Mission, 92, 93, 135, 154–5, 162, 206, 218
London School of Economics, 68, 85, 86, 114, 178
Longford Report, 231–2

Magistrates, 6–8, 14–16, 19, 22, 25, 30, 31, 36–9, 42–4, 46–8, 50–1, 53, 54, 63, 68–70, 81, 86, 87, 89, 90, 91, 95, 109, 116, 122, 124, 133, 177, 211, 212, 214, 222, 236
  see also Justices
Magistrates' Association, 31, 65, 80, 89, 91, 94, 96, 116, 121, 127, 135, 138, 150, 164, 186, 192, 201, 202, 206, 232, 235, 238
Manchester, 11, 35, 73, 113
Marriage guidance, 196, 197
  Welfare Service, 196
Massachusetts, 6–9, 14, 22, 27, 31
Matrimonial conciliation, 123–5, 128, 142–3, 153, 161, 182, 184, 195–7, 209–10, 228
Medical social work, 181, 216
  see also Almoners
Mental condition, 26, 29, 148, 166, 167, 168, 192
  treatment, 157, 167, 179, 180
Metropolitan magistrates, 11, 20, 31, 39, 52, 58, 60, 69, 86, 90, 92, 142, 214
  magistrates' courts area, 175, 214, 215
  Police Court District, 20, 33, 39, 41, 49, 59, 79, 88, 91, 102, 109, 124, 152
  Police Courts, 21, 22, 24, 30, 31, 33, 36, 50, 60, 78, 92, 154, 160
Minor offences, 11, 12
  offenders, 2, 15
Misconceptions about probation, 110–11, 130, 147, 156
Missionary work', 74, 82, 143, 153, 154
Morison Committee, *see* Departmental Committee on the Probation Service

282

National Association of Probation Officers, 61–2, 74–5, 89, 90, 91, 94, 117–24, 127, 130, 131, 138, 150, 155, 158, 163, 164, 169, 183, 184, 201–5, 217, 223, 226, 232, 234, 235, 238, 240
and dual control, 72, 135–6
and enquiries and reports for the courts, 116–17, 158–9, 172, 193, 227
and probation officers' remuneration, 75, 85, 127, 200–4
and probation officers' superannuation, 85, 89, 103
evidence to committees of enquiry, 79, 124, 126, 130, 135, 137, 193, 205–6, 216, 222
relations with the Home Office, 74–5, 121, 162, 165, 201
National British Women's Temperance Association, 40
National government, 123
National Police Court Mission, 113, 134, 137, 151
National Society for the Prevention of Cruelty to Children, 25, 46, 83
Neglected children, 8, 9, 58, 105, 108
Negotiation of salaries, 201–4, 217, 230
New York, 24, 25, 55
New Zealand, 12, 19
Non-custodial and semi-custodial penalties, 237

Organisation of after-care, 220, 222
of probation service, 124, 125, 128, 152, 173, 205, 206, 211
of probation work, 55, 59, 63, 75, 81, 88, 90, 103, 109, 132, 139

Parole, 225–7, 228, 230, 231
Penal policies, 31, 184, 191
Penal Practice in a Changing Society, 190, 204
Penal Reform Group, 94, 114, 116

Penal Reform League, 47, 48, 52, 55, 62, 63, 64, 67, 80
Petty sessional division, 27, 42, 45, 54, 81, 98, 111, 116, 127, 128, 131, 157, 167, 169, 174
Penal system, 1, 18, 155, 170, 185, 190, 205, 227, 228, 231, 234
Pilgrim Trust, 120
Police, 5, 6, 8, 10, 11, 12, 13, 14, 18, 19, 23, 25, 27, 29, 30, 33, 34, 35, 38, 44, 46, 53, 72, 73, 83, 84, 91, 116, 139, 185, 193, 194, 211
Police court missionaries, 6, 20, 22, 37–8, 60, 61, 76, 86, 87, 93, 103, 110, 129, 137, 150
appointment of, 71, 82, 83, 110
as probation officers, 24–5, 29, 33–5, 38–41, 45, 48–50, 52–3, 56, 63, 68, 69, 70–4, 81–3, 93, 103, 110, 134–7, 150
Guild of, 93–4
Police court missions, 71–3, 81–3, 87, 90–3, 99, 103, 110, 125, 129, 134–7, 144, 150, 151, 154–5
Prevention of Crime Acts, 10, 11, 12, 13, 58
Principal posts, 139, 146, 161, 175
Principal Probation Officers, 102, 109, 138–9, 152, 173, 175, 182, 198, 214
see also Chief and Superintendent Probation Officers
Principal Probation Officers' Conference, 222, 223, 238
Prison after-care, 142, 168, 173, 184–5, 187–91, 209, 221–2
Commissioners, 14, 18, 19, 31, 34, 90, 113, 151, 185, 187, 188, 190, 193
governors, 14, 193, 223
population, 10, 26, 34, 225, 237–40
service, 222, 239
welfare, 187–8, 223–8, 230, 231, 236
Prisons, 1, 10, 15, 16, 17, 23, 34, 47, 58, 147, 168, 170, 201
Private Member, 9, 80, 123, 200
Probation Advisory and Training Board, 177, 201, 203, 204, 205, 217, 222
Probation and after-care areas, 230

Probation and After-Care Committees, 222, 239

Probation and after-care service, change to, 220

Probation areas, 98, 104, 116, 131, 157, 174, 175, 213

Probation Commission, 55

Probation Committees, 54, 81, 98, 101, 102, 110, 113, 124, 125–7, 132, 138, 144, 145, 151, 153, 157, 162, 163, 164, 167, 168, 173–4, 201, 205, 209, 210, 212–13, 219, 222, 223

Probation homes, 113, 138, 148–9, 154–5, 157, 168, 239

Probation hostels, 113, 138, 148–9, 154–5, 157, 168, 205, 219, 239

Probation, Institute of, 183

Probation, length of, 66, 167, 208

   reservation of the term for release under the supervision of a probation officer, 111

   result of, 43, 179

   use of, 50–1, 56, 58, 59, 62–4, 80, 102, 111, 147, 152, 166, 174, 175–6, 215

Probation of First Offenders Act, 1887, 14–16, 18, 23, 26, 27, 28, 43, 51

Probation of First Offenders Bills:

   1886–7, 10–13

   1906–7, 23, 28

Probation of Offenders Act, 1907, 15, 30, 33, 41–50, 58, 59, 73, 76, 99, 110, 148

Probation of Offenders Bills, 1906–7, 26–30, 35, 37, 240

Probation officers, 44, 48, 49, 63, 157, 184

   age of, 101, 103, 126, 133, 146, 152

   and Probation Committees, 126, 133, 138, 209

   appointment of, 17–19, 23, 25, 27, 28, 29, 33, 39, 41, 42, 45, 49, 79, 80, 88, 90, 91, 94–6, 98, 109, 133–4, 149, 152, 157, 164, 167

   conditions of employment and service, 122, 125, 126, 146, 163, 168, 191, 201, 202, 205

   duties and work of, 18, 19, 29, 42–3, 46, 53–4, 108–9, 112, 122, 125, 133, 139, 142–3, 152–4, 157–8, 167–8, 173, 184, 195, 200, 205–11, 216, 229

   full-time, 60, 64, 72, 74, 81, 84, 102, 103, 126, 127, 132, 138, 152, 161, 162, 176

   independent, 103, 110, 137

   number of, 75, 122, 175, 176, 215, 229

   on advisory bodies, 90, 113, 131, 177

   overburdened, 109, 127, 228

   part-time, 41, 42, 56, 84, 102, 113, 121, 126, 127, 176

   qualifications, 44, 61, 68–9, 77, 101–2, 122, 126, 133, 146, 151, 168, 201, 202, 205, 216

   recruitment of, 18, 57, 65, 77, 146, 177, 204, 213, 216, 217, 220, 229

   relationships with probationers, 81, 109, 149, 169, 170, 206, 238

   remuneration, 17, 25, 27–8, 41–2, 44, 46, 49, 54, 57, 59–60, 63, 64, 66, 68, 69, 75–7, 80, 83, 84–5, 89, 90, 94, 95–6, 98, 101, 109, 118, 122, 126–7, 129, 144, 146, 161, 163, 168, 191, 201–4, 213, 216–17, 220, 229, 230, 239

   selection of, 101, 111, 134, 145, 152

   society of, 55

   see also National Association of Probation Officers

   special children's, 29–30, 40, 41, 42, 60, 61, 69, 79, 84, 99

   superannuation, 94, 99, 101, 103, 109, 122, 129

   women, 22, 44, 99, 111, 113, 126, 127, 128, 129, 153, 157, 161, 167, 183, 198, 212

Probation order, 26, 27, 30, 43, 45, 50, 75, 102, 107, 111, 114, 116, 133, 140–1, 148, 149, 152, 156, 158, 159, 160, 166–7, 169, 170, 175, 179, 191, 207, 208, 227, 234–8

Probation rules, 30, 41, 42–3, 46, 49, 90–1, 101–2, 109, 116, 126, 128, 140, 152, 172–3, 175, 183, 200, 201

Probation service, functions of, 122, 125, 207, 208, 222, 223, 225, 228–9, 240
Probation Training Board, 145, 150, 151, 162, 177
  see also Probation Advisory and Training Board
Probationary year, 129
Profession, 84, 122, 164, 183, 206, 216
Professional approach and skill, 189, 206, 217–18, 221
  image and status, 181, 183, 202
Psychiatric social work, 114, 180, 181, 216
Psychiatric social workers, 121, 143
Psychology, 68, 121, 177, 178, 180
Punishment, 1, 2, 3, 4, 6, 10, 147, 225, 238

Quarter Sessions, 7, 11, 16, 27, 50, 98, 102, 152, 174, 192

Rainer House, 218–19
  see also hostel for trainees
Receiver for the Metropolitan Police Court District, 41, 60, 102
Recognizances, 3–6, 10, 12, 26, 27, 30, 43, 148, 156, 166
Records, of work, 48, 102, 201
Reformation, 2, 7, 21, 23
Reformatory schools, 2, 3, 9, 15–16, 66, 107, 114
  and Refuge Union, 40
Rehabilitation, 1, 31, 184, 185, 189, 191, 227, 239
Release on licence, 168, 225
  see also Parole
Religious conviction, 135
  motives, 81, 82
  test, 91, 110, 114
Reports, for courts: see Enquiries and Social enquiries
Research, 171, 178–80, 189, 190, 201, 208
Residence, length of, 112, 219, 227
  requirement of, 219, 229

with probation, 68
  see also Condition of residence
Roman Catholic Westminster Education Fund, 40
Royal Commission on Reformatories and Industrial Schools, 9
Royal Society for the Assistance of Discharged Prisoners, 40
Ruskin College, 113

Salvation Army, 35, 46
School Attendance Officers, 35, 83, 91, 106, 140
  Board Officers, 20, 24
  records, 115, 140
Scotland, 205–6
Scottish probation service, 233
Seebohm Committee, 233–5
Senior grades, 203
  posts, 146, 161, 162, 163, 164, 175, 229
  probation officers, 139, 152, 173, 182, 214, 230
Sentences, 8, 10, 192, 193, 194, 208, 221, 227, 237, 240
Social Enquiries, 58, 115–17, 122, 158, 167, 174, 184, 191–4, 200, 207, 227–8, 232, 235, 236
  see also Enquiries; and Investigations
Social Science, 85, 86, 87, 113, 144, 151
  Association, 9
Social services, 134, 139, 162, 170, 171, 224, 229, 230, 231, 232, 233,
  of the courts, 123–4, 130, 131, 150, 211
Social Work, 25, 33, 35, 85–6, 87, 112, 114, 121, 126, 139, 143, 161, 170, 171, 177, 180, 181, 183, 188, 197, 205, 214, 216, 217, 218, 224, 225, 229, 230, 232, 233
Social work of the courts, 83, 110, 121, 123, 125, 137, 143, 149, 153
Social Workers, 48, 83, 85, 87, 121, 133, 141, 143, 170, 171, 181, 189, 199, 202, 223, 224, 228, 231, 233, 234, 239

Standing Conference of Organisations of Social Workers, 232
Standing Joint Committee, 27, 46, 76, 77, 89
State Children's Association, 23, 35, 47–50, 62, 70
Stigma, 2, 3, 10, 196, 231, 232
Stockholm Prison Congress, 8
Streatfeild Committee, see Inter-Departmental Committee on the Business of the Criminal Courts
Summary Jurisdiction Act, 1879, 3, 6, 10, 13, 14, 15, 22, 26, 50
Summary Jurisdiction (Children) Bills, 1905, 22
Summary Procedure (Domestic Proceedings) Act, 1937, 153–4, 195
Superintendent Probation Officers, 42, 49, 54
    see also Chief and Principal Probation Officers
Supervision, early use of, 4–7
    of adults, 35, 40, 45, 70, 73, 162
    of children in divorce cases, 200
    of neglected children, 108
    of persons allowed time to pay fines, 108, 112, 113, 124, 141–2
    of persons released on licence, 225–7
    orders, 114, 122, 234–6, 238
Supervision of probation work, 42, 49, 54, 65, 98, 102, 109, 126, 132, 138, 214, 222
Supervisory grades, 149, 214
    posts, 138, 152, 213, 214, 215
Suspended sentence, 238
    supervision order, 239
Suspension of sentence, 4, 6, 7

Techniques, of probation, 122, 143, 144
Temperance, 21, 36, 38, 45, 71, 73, 83, 91–3, 137
The Child and the War, 68
The Child, the Family and the Young Offender, 231
The Probation Service, 181, 183
The Probation System, 64

The State and the Child, 68
The Young Delinquent, 121
Ticket-of-leave, 10–12, 185
Town Council, 46, 47
Toynbee Hall, 42
Toynbee Trustees, 35
Trainees, 113, 144, 151, 154
Training, 17–18, 48, 55, 65, 79–80, 85–7, 89, 101, 113–14, 122, 133, 138, 141, 143–6, 151–2, 154–5, 157, 162, 164, 177, 182–3, 190, 193, 201–2, 203, 204, 205, 209, 213, 217–19, 220, 223, 224, 229–30
Treasury, 47, 89, 95–6, 99, 103
Treatment, 10, 15, 47, 51, 59, 89, 105, 106, 108, 111, 140, 147, 167, 176, 178, 179, 180, 189, 190, 193–5, 208, 219, 225, 232, 237, 240
Tutor officers, 182–3

Unemployment, problem of, 121, 170
Uniform, for probation officers 43, 46, 173
United States, 7, 12, 18, 22, 178
    see also America
Universities, 68, 86, 87, 113, 178, 205, 218, 229
University courses of training, 65, 87, 114, 144, 146, 152, 218
    qualifications, 109, 113, 122, 144, 151, 183, 202, 216
    settlements, 41, 85

Vacancies, advertisement of, 109, 111, 114
    filling of, 145
Vocation, sense of, 137, 143, 163, 217
Voluntary agencies, see voluntary societies
    cases, 210–11
    organisations, see voluntary societies
    societies, 18, 24–5, 39, 44, 47, 56, 62, 67, 68, 74, 79, 83, 99–100, 102, 110, 114, 133, 134–7, 149, 154, 168, 173, 187, 198, 218, 223,

Voluntary (*cont.*)
societies, agents of, 27, 30, 41, 46, 56, 60, 64, 72–3, 80–2, 97, 102, 110, 114, 134, 157
workers, 7, 8, 37, 48, 49, 64, 69, 121, 138, 224–5

War, 9, 80, 160, 162, 165, 171, 190, 195
Warwickshire magistrates, 4–5

Wesleyan Mission, 45

Young offenders, 3–5, 7–8, 15–16, 26, 32, 34, 35, 48, 51, 105, 107, 111, 156, 176, 190, 232
Young Offenders Committee: *see* Departmental Committee on the Treatment of Young Offenders
Youth, of offender, 13, 26

INDEX OF NAMES

Acland, R.D.B., 50
Adler, Miss, 41, 44
Augustus, J., 6–7, 249
Aves, Geraldine M., 274
Ayscough, H.H., 251
Baird, Sir J., 79, 90–1
Baldwin, R.N., 69, 255
Balfour, Lord, 23
Barnett, Canon S., 42
Barrett, Rosa M., 18, 251
Bartlett, Lucy, 48, 55
Bell, E. Moberley, 260
Belmore, Earl of, 12
Bentinck, Lord H., 64, 69, 94
Birkett, Sir N., 164
Bowlby, J., 171, 267
Bridgeman, W.C., 94, 95
Burt, C., 121
Butler, R.A., 190
Butterworth, J.B., 229, 239
Callaghan, J., 235–6, 239
Carlisle, M., 235
Carr-Saunders, A., 178, 268
Carrington, Mrs. W., 119
Cave, G. (Lord), 28, 69, 92, 94
Cecil, Sir E., 105
Chalmers, Sir McK. D., 24

Chapman, C., 86
Childers, E., 11
Chinn, W.H., 122
Chorley, Lord, 169
Churchill, W.S., 58
Chute, C.L., 7, 250
Clarke Hall, W., 68–9, 90, 110, 118, 120–1, 131, 255
Cochrane, T.H., 29
Corner, E. Phyllis, 183
Cox, E.W., 3, 5, 6, 249
Croker-King, Miss, 42, 60, 215
Cunningham, Sir C., 177
Curtis Bennett, H., 20, 22, 24, 52
Darling, Lord, 148
Dawtry, F., 201, 204, 252, 272
Denning, Mr. Justice (Lord), 195
Dickenson, J., 50, 52
Digby, W., 4
Ede, C., 166
Edridge, S., 61–2, 72, 74–5, 79, 89, 117–8
Erne, Earl of, 13
Fenwick, E.N.F., 24, 33, 38, 50, 252
Feversham, Lord, 23, 116–21, 123–4, 140, 165, 226
Field, H.C., 52

Finer, H., 256
Flexner, B., 69, 255
Fry, Margery, 79, 163–4
Gamon, H.R.P., 30, 31, 35, 38, 252–3
Gladstone, H., 23, 28, 39, 43–4, 58
Gladstone, W.E., 7, 9, 11, 23
Glueck, S., 250
Goldstone, Mr., 73–4
Goode, Miss W.M., vii, 205
Gordon Walker, P.C., 191
Greenwood, A., 203–4
Grubb, E., 22
Grünhut, M., 176, 179, 180, 268–9
Guest, J., 98
Haldane, Lord, 96–7
Halsbury, Lord, 12
Hamilton of Dalzell, Lord, 225–6
Harcourt, Sir W.V., 3, 7
Harris, S., 84–5, 90, 92, 104, 119, 121,
    124, 126, 137, 150, 158, 197
Hayward, E.J., 124
Helmsley, Lord, 23
Henderson, J.F., 59
Henriques, B.L.Q., 186, 270
Henry, E.R., 24, 25
Herbert, W.L., 271
Herschell, Lord, 12
Heywood, J.F., 267
Hill, F.D., 249
Hill, M.D., 4, 6, 249
Hill, Octavia, 85
Hill, R.D., 249
Hoare, Sir S. (Lord Templewood), 155,
    158, 168
Hobson, Sir J., 227
Hogg, Q., 226
Holden, Lord, 169
Holmes, T., 39
Houston, H., 90
How, F.D., 250
Hughes, Miss E.P., 17–18, 251
Hughes, E.W., 179, 269
Ivimy, Miss, 42, 60–61, 215
Jarvis, F.V., 271
Jenkins, R., 225
Jeyes, S.H., 250
Jones, L., 30

Joynson-Hicks, Sir W. (Lord Brentford),
    67, 97, 105, 114
King, Joan F.S., 267, 269
Lance, Miss, 61
Lane, R.O.B., 36
Le Mesurier, Mrs. L., 131
Leeson, C., 64–5, 68, 86, 89, 121, 255
Listowel, Lord, 123
Longford, Lord, 231
Lord, C., 35, 48
Lushingham, G., 12
Lytton, Earl of, 50, 62, 69
Mace, D.R., 271
Macrae, F.J., 182, 269
Mannheim, H., 178, 268
Matthews, H., 12–13
Maudling, R., 237
Maxwell, Sir A., 43, 74–5, 176, 187, 253
Meath, Earl of, viii, 31
Merthyr, Lord, 172
Minn, W.G., 260, 264–6
Molony, Sir T., 105
Monro, J., 11–12
Morgan, E., 236
Morison, R.P., 205, 216, 229
Morris, Cherry, 269
Morrison, R.L., 274
Morrison, Rev. W.D., 15–16, 250–1
Moyle, A., 200
Mullins, C., 142
Nelson, Mr., 21
Nicholson, G., 158–9
Noble, T.A.F. (Sir), 205
Norman, H.E., 119, 123
Osborn, S., 124
Parsloe, Phyllida, 267
Pearson, Rev. H., 92–3
Pepler, D., 68
Potter, J.H., 251
Prins, H., 271
Raglan, Lord, 169
Rainer, F., 21
Reading, Lady, 224
Reynolds, B.J., 150, 161, 163
Rhodes, E.C., 178, 268
Rigby, L.M., 35, 39, 253
Rose, G., 55, 63, 249, 250, 254–5, 261,

265, 267, 270
Rose, J., 52
Rosling, Miss D.M., 150
Ruggles-Brise, Sir E., 18–19, 26, 33–4, 48, 251
Russell, C.E.B., 35, 39, 63–4, 253
Salisbury, Marquis of, 67
Samuel, H. (Lord), 23–5, 28, 37, 40, 50, 120, 147, 251–2
Sankey, Lord, 123
Seebohm, F., 232–3
Sewell, Margaret, 85
Shortt, E., 79
Skipworth, Sir. G., 4
Smith, Marjorie J., 257
Smith, S., 14
Snowden, Lord Philip, 117
Soskice, Sir F., 223
Stewart, W.J., 39
Stonham, Lord, 226
Streatfeild, Mr. Justice (Lord), 193
Sturge, J., 9
Sudeley, Lord, 12
Symons, Madeleine, 124, 148

Tallack, W., 2, 4, 249
Templewood, Lord (Sir Samuel Hoare), 170
Tennant, H.J., 22
Timasheff, N.S., 249
Timms, N., 260, 261
Trought, T.W., 86
Troup, Sir C.E., 20, 23–4, 26, 33, 56, 92
Tuckwell, Gertrude, 118–21, 164–5
Vickers, Joan, 200
Vincent, C.E.H., 9–15, 22–3, 26, 28, 37, 43
Wall, Miss J.I., 124, 148
Walsh, N.C., 20, 22
Ward, Mrs. H., 40
Warren, G., 62
Waugh, B., 2, 64
Westwood, J., 99
White, Mrs. Eirene, 198
Wilkins, Alderman, 89
Wilkins, L.T., 179, 269
Wilmot, Sir E., 4
Wootton, Baroness, 237
Younghusband, Eileen, 180, 205